P9-AFF-177

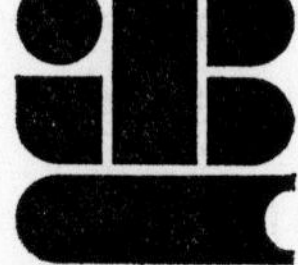

BY ANY MEANS NECESSARY

The Revolutionary Struggle at San Francisco State

Robert Smith
Richard Axen
DeVere Pentony

by any means necessary

Jossey-Bass Inc., Publishers
615 Montgomery Street • San Francisco • 1970

BY ANY MEANS NECESSARY
The Revolutionary Struggle at San Francisco State
by Robert Smith, Richard Axen, DeVere Pentony

Address all inquiries to:

Jossey-Bass, Inc., Publishers
615 Montgomery Street
San Francisco, California 94111

Library of Congress Catalog Card Number 75-128701

International Standard Book Number ISBN 0-87589-075-X

Manufactured in the United States of America
Composed and printed by York Composition Company, Inc.
Bound by Chas. H. Bohn & Co., Inc.

JACKET DESIGN BY WILLI BAUM, SAN FRANCISCO

FIRST EDITION

Code 7024

THE JOSSEY-BASS SERIES IN HIGHER EDUCATION

General Editors

JOSEPH AXELROD
San Francisco State College
and University of California, Berkeley

MERVIN B. FREEDMAN
San Francisco State College
and Wright Institute, Berkeley

Preface

The decade between 1964 and 1974 in American higher education will undoubtedly be characterized as the decade of student unrest. Issues of institutional purposes, educational quality, and teaching styles are either dwarfed by this dominant concern or interpreted within its context. Despite the flood of commentaries and analyses appearing in both the professional literature and the popular press on this phenomenon, in-depth studies of colleges engulfed in turmoil have been scarce. The primary intent of this study of the year of the strike (1968–69) at San Francisco State College—and its two-year prelude of growing tensions and confrontations—is to aid in filling this gap in the literature. The study incorporates a dual approach: a case study of the tumultuous operation of the college over a three-year period, and some analytical probing of some fundamental problems in higher education that surfaced at the college during this time.

We have studied and written with three key premises in mind: (1) the practice of higher educational governance at present has no adequate theoretical base appropriate to our time, hence detailed case studies from a variety of contemporary situations are needed for the development of functional theory; (2) more immediately, there is little understanding of the dynamics of this last half-decade of campus tumult in which so many actors cast in novel situations have been forced back on trial-and-error behavior in explosive situations; and (3) there is much evidence that concerned people outside the colleges have been almost at a loss to understand what is really going on and how best to respond to deeply disturbing threats to the educational futures of their sons and daughters. We have sought not to reassure, but to inform—even if this means attention to the obscured seamy side as well as to the constructive achievements. We believe the crisis in higher education is a grave one, critical to the future of the nation and its citizens. We doubt that it is being resolved.

The intense conflict and disorder on the campus at San Francisco State College grew through the academic year 1967–68 to a crescendo during the four-month period, November 1968 to early March 1969. The struggle continues in less dramatic forms within the college and within the California State College System. In its turn, San Francisco State was caught in the forefront of regional and national news and public attention, as were the University of California, Berkeley, Columbia University, the University of Paris, Cornell University, the University of Wisconsin, the University of Tokyo, Harvard University, the National University at Mexico City, and a long and rapid succession of other leading institutions of higher education in both the Eastern and Western worlds.

Campus disruptions continue to grow in number and intensity as this is written. We see little evidence that an end to disorder in the colleges is in sight or that the circumstances that feed campus disruptions have been changed substantially either within colleges and universities or in the societies that sustain them. In California, the seedbeds of campus rebellion have, if anything, been aggravated. Dissidents turn more easily to violence and the opinion in the state has increasingly moved toward support of suppressive measures and the reduction of financial support for public higher education. Governor Ronald Reagan campaigned for re-election, as he did for his first term, by leaning heavily on these disruptions in higher education and the need for a "no-nonsense" approach to campus dissent. Having given up campaigning on campuses because of student hostility, he enhanced his political stature in April 1970 with the remark that a "bloodbath" may come on some campus and that we may as well get it over with.

Embittered white radical students appear to welcome this swing toward repression. They reason that it justifies more violent countermeasures on their part and that it will radicalize the disenchanted liberals, thus enlarging their base of power. In the spring 1970 the University of California, Berkeley, endured three days of chaos that moved Chancellor Roger Heyns to comment, "The Berkeley campus today was the victim of wanton destruction unprecedented in the history of the university. Any attempt to link today's grim events with moral issues is a travesty on morality and a pallid attempt to pass off criminal acts as political acts." The day his statement was published a student was killed by a bullet at the University of California, Santa Barbara. Escalations of dissent breed escalations of repression and the spiral continues.

The public rhetoric of the past two decades has been shot through with the term *revolution*. The term is perhaps most optimistically used in the areas of scientific and technological advances: revolutions in travel, including space travel, in weaponry and military tactics, in communications and the development of communications technology, and in medical and health care. In these respects the nation applauds itself as a "revolutionary society." Revolutionary themes in the performing and fine arts and styles of expression cause more anxiety. They press on the traditional customs and moral codes and world views of our citizens.

Some are exhilarated and others are frightened by the symptoms of revolution within our social institutions: in our family structures, in the churches, in race and ethnic relationships, in politics and education, and in the prospect of revolutionary patterns and premises applied to our economic life. Many more appear to want revolution in some dimensions of our life, stability in others, as though different sectors of the culture were independent of one another. The young, and growing numbers of faculty, increasingly reject this compartmentalized view. They appear to believe that inventiveness and freedom of revolutionary proportions in the scientific and technological areas, if coupled with too deep commitments to traditional institutions and styles, will kill us through uncontrolled war, pollution, starvation, or domestic conflict born of interracial tensions. These thinkers are in the schools and colleges. Many are in quiet rebellion. Some are demanding and generating revolutionary approaches across the board in our social and economic institutions. Those who expect social change to come through evolution and reform are caught between the stridency and aggressiveness of those demanding radical change or revolution in all dimensions of the society, on the one hand, and those who are determined to support traditional institutional patterns while containing or stamping out demands for massive change.

San Francisco State College is a prime example of a college caught between two such conflicting movements. Most of the basic ingredients that are central to institutional instability have been represented in its recent experience: a high proportion of intelligent, aggressive, alienated white students; a burgeoning block of disenchanted, rebellious black students, reinforced by other ethnic groups; a faculty caught between new powers that have not been successfully integrated, and an absence of influence in vital areas; an unstable central administration that is forced to spend a disproportionate amount of energy coping with omnipresent, misdirected systemwide control and internal stresses; a financial squeeze that inhibits the capacity to maintain prior quality performance, let alone respond to the new urgencies; and a hostile public climate exacerbated by political figures using student unrest as an issue for political advancement and growing domination of college operations. The fact that these factors, which are increasingly common to urban colleges, coalesced in the brief span of one year to totally disrupt the college operation justifies, in our view and in the view of those who have supported this venture, this intensive analysis.

By Any Means Necessary must be viewed as the product of our efforts as observer-participants in the events described and interpreted here. We are all tenured professors who have, at various times, engaged in teaching, research, and administrative and faculty leadership roles within the college for more than a decade. We differ among ourselves in our views of society, social change, and higher education, yet we see ourselves as part of the liberal establishment within higher education. Our primary academic specialties are: Axen, higher education; Pentony, international relations; and Smith, sociology of education. Smith has been Dean of the School of Education, Acting Dean of Instruction, and President. Pentony has served as chairman of the department of international relations, Dean of the School of Behavioral and Social Sciences, and Deputy President. Axen has functioned as Dean of Admissions and Records, chairman of the department of higher education, and Chairman of the Academic Senate. All three of us were deeply involved in the institutional operation during the period depicted in this case study, with attendant advantages and disadvantages for the purposes of this study. The sources of strength deriving from these on-the-scene roles are obvious. We also recognize that these perspectives undoubtedly skew our interpretation despite an effort to obtain balance through widespread interviews and use of primary documents. Much of the literature of higher education is written with efforts to maintain a scholarly, detached, dispassionate point of view. We have chosen to achieve balance without neglecting the personal elements basic to understanding these complex contemporary issues. We make no apologies for what biases appear. We understand the radical student and the striking faculty perspectives will be depicted in other books emerging from our year of travail, and the media leverage of Governor Ronald Reagan and others has ensured more than adequate coverage of particular political interpretations.

The materials from which the report has been developed have included written documents, generated on campus and off, audio and visual recordings of events, interviews with participants, a sample survey of students and faculty, and newspaper files, including campus newspapers, the metropolitan dailies, and the Bay Area underground press. We have made limited use of the growing literature on the crisis in higher education and in social ideology but have drawn extensively on our own direct experiences as we lived and worked in the context of the struggle, often in conflict roles. These experiences and fugitive sources of data do not lend themselves to elaborate documentation, and we have not attempted extensive, specific documentation.

We are aware that our approach includes considerable detail beyond the needs or interests of some readers. However, we believe that the issues are sufficiently complex—and have been so distorted by simplistic media and "official" treatment—that it is better to err in the direction of elaboration than to present a constricted account. Such an intensive narrative is also in the nature of the case-study technique of investigation, especially of such a complex phenomenon as student and faculty unrest. Crisis issues trenchant enough to arouse an entire state have a history and a broad context, and profit from detailed analysis. Hopefully other traumatized colleges will receive similar in-depth study and thus add to the basis for fuller understanding and improved theory.

The second major purpose of our study is to examine in greater detail a variety of major problems and issues revealed within the campus crises described in this study and to make recommendations in these areas. This portion of the study will be published in spring 1971 in a volume which, though it draws upon these events, is self-sufficient.

Eventually higher education must develop a new faculty ethic and professional practice consonant with our times, it must solve the complex problems of student justice in a period of student alienation and confrontational stress, it must develop viable black and ethnic studies programs, it must readjust its governance process to take into account a range of political realities, and it must renovate its educational programs so as to better serve modern students and society and thus reduce the sense of student hostility upon which revolutionary approaches feed. The year of the strike at San Francisco State also witnessed the introduction in a pervasive fashion of an ethical principle relatively new in academic life though ancient in our civilization: the end justifies the means. Most parties to the conflict—students, faculty, administrators, trustees, politicians, the police, the media—began to believe that their purposes were so deeply moral that they justified support "by any means necessary." We believe the explicit and implicit acceptance of this principle negates the essence of higher education and poses a powerful threat to our colleges and to our society.

We acknowledge with deep respect and gratitude the unremitting efforts and responsibilities assumed by Sandra Standifird and Diane Crosetti who shared in the administration of the project and prepared the manuscript; the assistance of Kris McClusky and Joe Burlas in collecting and summarizing data; and the patient cooperation of many students, faculty, staff members, and administrators who provided materials, agreed to extensive interviews, and read portions of the manuscript. Diane Winokur and William Schulyer were particularly helpful in the revision of several sections. Bishop Mark Hurley, George Johns, and Mayor Joseph Alioto assisted us with long interviews.

We are especially indebted to three agencies whose concern for young people and for the improvement of higher education prompted them to extend partial support to this project, thereby making it possible. The Statewide Academic Senate of the California State Colleges paid a major portion of Robert Smith's salary during the spring semester 1968, leaving him free to proceed as he saw fit with the study. Grants from the Danforth and Rosenberg Foundations provided substantial support for us and our research assistants through the summer 1968 and provided secretarial help. The San Francisco Consortium also lent its support as a repository of funds.

None of the collaborating organizations and individuals bear responsibility for the content of this report. We pursued the study and reported the results as we saw fit. Communication among the three of us in the final stages of writing was compounded by DeVere Pentony's absence from the campus during the academic year 1969–70, when he accepted an appointment as Professor in International Relations at the University of Istanbul.

The three years spanned in this project have been hard years at San Francisco State for many working on that campus and for their families. We especially appreciate the stresses endured by our own wives and children during the cycle of events preceding the completion of the study.

San Francisco
August 1970

Robert Smith
Richard Axen
DeVere Pentony

Contents

PART TWO: ROBERT SMITH

PART THREE: S. I. HAYAKAWA

BY ANY MEANS NECESSARY

The Revolutionary Struggle at San Francisco State

PART ONE

JOHN SUMMERSKILL

Chapter 1

Intimations

On the surface, San Francisco State College had many sources of strength and good reasons for optimism as it began instruction in the fall semester of 1966 under the leadership of its new president, John Summerskill. Yet beneath this attractive façade, time bombs ticked.

In the decade from 1956 to 1966 the college completed its transformation from a good teachers college educating 10,900 students to a large, liberal urban state college with a student population of 18,100. When President Glenn S. Dumke replaced the architect of the teachers college reputation, Paul Leonard, in 1957, the liberal arts faculty members were chafing at their service role and were pressing for the legitimate professional aspirations of chemists, sociologists, historians, and English professors. By 1966 this battle had been won and departments were sufficiently large to encourage the specialized ambitions of all those faculty who identified first with their discipline, secondly with teaching it. No longer did the imagined stigma of the teacher education function disturb many of the liberal arts faculty as it had for the past fifteen years.

But this period of unfettered hopes had been nourished by the soaring growth of the college and the concomitant need to enlarge departments, hire many new faculty every year, and expand course offerings. Under these circumstances there was little need for the internecine strife for scarce resources that is the traditional state of life in most institutions of higher education. What most faculty took as the natural order of things—almost a God-given right—was to prove to be only a transient phenomenon during a brief period of expansion.

Growth projections for the future indicated a period of almost flat stability and then very slow increases. Any department's gains now would need to be sliced from another department's allocation. Since many more students were now applying than could be accommodated, a master plan for controlled admissions according to departmental quotas loomed ahead. Would past drawing power be the major criterion for these allocations or would some abstract concept of a "balanced" college prevail? And who would make such decisions?

The Free Speech Movement at the University of California, Berkeley, in 1964, has become the benchmark in the history of American higher education for a beginning awareness of widespread student discontent with many of society's institutions, including our colleges. Given the proximity of San Francisco State College to Berkeley, and certain similar student life styles and commitments, it seemed natural to expect a flare-up sooner or later at the burgeoning state college. But between 1964 and 1966 all remained relatively peaceful. Student noncurricular energies focused upon urban problems in the ghettos and educational reform through a student-initiated Experimental College. Speech was so free that the centrally located Speakers Platform once supported a fascist, a communist, and a capitalist all within one week. Student discipline was not an issue; no radical student group required legal rules, effective administration of justice, or elaborate judicial procedures.

Faculty, administrators, and students together basked in the comforting thought that this harmony was a tribute to the unique, liberal, hang-loose atmosphere at the college. It also seemed a direct consequence of the interaction of a student body that increasingly reflected creative, nonconformist tendencies and a faculty that was rated as probably one of the most liberal and productive in the state college system. But the chapters to come all document the hidden frustrations of many of these New Generation students with the bureaucratization of this large, urban college, with its basically traditional, discipline-centered curriculum, and with its benevolent paternalism toward the student demands to govern their own lives.

Faculty at San Francisco State College not only prided themselves on the general climate of the college and the quality of its educational offering, they also cherished the reputation of a faculty that had successfully asserted the legitimate faculty right to legislate all major college policy. But the policies that had emerged from this delegation of authority from president to faculty had not been notable for their foresight in meeting the accumulated problems of a college increasingly troubled with restive students, restricted resources, and an explosive urban environment. And what had once been harmonious administrative cooperation in this arrangement for governance now took on overtones of the customary faculty-administrative struggles for power.

The college's faculty was well-known both for its assertion of power through its Academic Senate and for its image as a consistent, tough, vocal challenger of the emerging authority of the recently created Board of Trustees for the California State Colleges and its chancellor's staff. When Buell Gallagher, the system's first chancellor, unexpectedly resigned after a brief six months in office—his reasons still unclear but his wisdom enhanced by time—the State faculty led a statewide movement to resist the trustee intention to replace Gallagher with San Francisco's former president, Glenn S. Dumke. This battle was lost, but it left bitter memories and strained relationships.

Henceforth, the San Francisco State faculty was in the forefront of all drives to preserve institutional autonomy against the encroachments of the centralized authority. The battle reached a crescendo in the spring of 1964 when a respected dean, Robert Smith, resigned and saw fit to publish his letter of resignation. The letter catalogued the deficiencies of the chancellor and the trustees with such barbs as:

> Major efforts of this college's administrative officers to assist in shaping the policies under which we work have come to nought, and

> many of the plans we have developed in good faith have been ignored or summarily rejected by the chancellor or the trustees. . . . The drive for centralized control over the individual colleges poses a major threat to their uniqueness and their capacity to respond to the needs of the state and the nation. . . . It appears that strong college presidents with a penchant for independent thinking are under increasing pressures to conform to an imposed orthodoxy lest they be picked off quietly behind the scenes. . . . The system does not need a chancellor running scared before an aggressive and misguided Board of Trustees.

Within a matter of days the faculty gathered over 400 signatures on a petition to the Legislature requesting a "thorough public investigation of the administration of the state colleges before irreparable harm is done to the students that we, and you, are charged to serve." (Paradoxically, Smith succeeded Summerskill as president and in turn was replaced by S. I. Hayakawa, one of the sponsors of the petition.) The issue was now publicly joined. To circumvent legislative investigation, the trustees agreed to a faculty-administration-trustee blue-ribbon probe. Before it was concluded, a year and one-half passed, each college thoroughly aired its multiple grievances against the chancellor and the trustees, and San Francisco State College was firmly entrenched in the position of chief critic and troublemaker for the California State College System. To many faculty this belligerence and independence seemed a source of strength and pride. But with power rapidly shifting in California to conservative forces, and with a general public climate of hostility developing toward colleges, faculty, and students, this assertive faculty proved to be a blessing John Summerskill did not need.

In its dealings with its minority students San Francisco State College imagined itself as enlightened. After all, it was a "liberal" college, and liberal institutions were certainly not racist. Had it not encouraged the development of the Black Students Union? But here, once again, hidden within the recesses of the structure, ticked a bomb soon to explode.

San Francisco State ventured into the two-year Summerskill interregnum confident, though, in its emerging image as a swinging college where students, faculty, and administrators were not up tight but could work together creatively to meet the educational aspirations of youth of the New Generation, of self-conscious and assertive black students, and of a society needing new social forms and values. Stagnation, disillusionment, and conflict could thus be avoided at the burgeoning college. In John Summerskill it believed it had an ideal leader for this creative surge. He was youthful, personable, liberal, and apparently endowed with skills that could facilitate change yet make it palatable to the power structure of San Francisco and the state.

Not much that transpired in the fall semester of 1966 disabused the college constituency of this belief. Admittedly, the new president was not chained to his office and did not involve himself too deeply in internal problems. But then there had been a general consensus communicated to him prior to employment that one of his major tasks was to elicit community acceptance so that college programs would receive financial and political support, the image of a leftist, red-tainted teachers college could be dissolved, and the general public could distinguish at last between the Jesuit University of San Francisco and San Francisco State College. Besides, there were those within the college who believed that its exceptional students and faculty could handle their affairs quite well without paternalistic administrative interference.

Relative harmony prevailed. The faculty liked the relaxed, irreverent image projected by President Summerskill at his first faculty meeting—although some traditionalists might have wondered where the substance was. His anecdote that Governor Rockefeller, at a party, on hearing of Summerskill's leaving Cornell to go to California, commented, "Don't resign until you see how that gubernatorial election comes out; you'd do better to take a leave of absence," tickled the liberal, anti-Reagan political tendencies of most of the faculty. It also proved to be prophetic.

The theme at the beginning of the year was "faculty-student cooperation to achieve a more viable college." Students sat as voting members on all of the college's major committees except those dealing with personnel decisions. The student body president, Jim Nixon, was a member of the Academic Senate—and the liberal, articulate, highly intelligent, nonhostile tone of his comments and recommendations convinced even the skeptics that sharing power—in a forty-two-to-one ratio—was risk free and even salutary. As long as student representatives projected the rationale image of professors-to-be, what was to be feared?

Vastly more important than student representation in this era of goodwill were the successes of the student-initiated programs aimed at educational and institutional reform and student involvement in urban problem solving. Activist students were proud that they were able to weld traditional student government forms to the urgent tasks of educational reform and social change. Faculty were content that the student movement had not taken radical, destructive directions at State as it had during the Free Speech Movement at Berkeley, but rather was moving consistently with the college's liberal ethos.

Although much hard, grubby work was undertaken in the Associated Students' Tutorial Program in the ghettos and in its efforts to assist depressed communities to find the means for solving their most urgent problems, the activity that caught the imagination of students and educators across the nation was the Experimental College. Begun tentatively the previous year, the "other college," as the student newspaper named it, focused upon student-initiated courses and activities that introduced content not normally encompassed in the traditional curriculum and teaching styles that broke down teacher-student barriers, shifted educational responsibility to the students, and included emphasis on affective as well as cognitive learning. Although enrollment figures are difficult to come by in an institution that was the very antithesis of registrar-oriented education, it is estimated that the Experimental College had approximately fifteen courses in the fall, enrolling 300 students, and sixty courses with 800 students in the spring, 1967. By any standards this was a startling success for a voluntary program. Students normally did not receive credit for their work, although independent study arrangements and other devices did lead to some formal credit in certain cases. Not only did this venture allow for a sampling of exotic subject matter and nonconventional teaching, but it also met individual needs to have personal, intimate associations—needs glaringly overlooked by the massive, impersonal commuter college burgeoning on the campus at 1600 Holloway.

Not as clear to the casual observer but a dominant motive in the minds of the chief student theorists was the view of the Experimental College as a new model for institutional change. The successes of the student college would contrast with the failings of the faculty college. Pragmatic proof would substitute for carping rhetoric. Hopefully, students experiencing fulfillment in the Experimental College activities would press in various ways for changes in the formal college. Hopefully, faculty who ventured into the student-initiated education would risk new approaches in their conventional roles after experiencing the satisfaction of the self-propelled learning.

San Francisco State's Experimental College has been probably the most highly publicized project of its kind in the modern history of higher education. Magazine reporters, radio and television agents, foundation representatives, and guests from other colleges saturated the skimpy premises to such a high degree that success began to spoil day-to-day activities. Rarely was a major conference on higher education planned that Jim Nixon or one of his associates was not invited to give the word. The program directors took advantage of this notoriety and soon began to develop proposals for project grants so that their beachhead could be expanded and their personal efforts to reform the college rewarded.

Within the institution there were two major reactions to the Experimental College. For the most part, faculty and administrators accepted its success as testimony to the unique genius of the college's life style and believed it offered a constructive alternative to the surges for student power and institutional reform that led to damaging consequences at other colleges. Within the Academic Senate and its committees a few timid suggestions that "we ought to look into this" were engulfed with plaudits and self-congratulations.

However, another segment of the college, small and inconsequential to this point, began to feel betrayed and bypassed by these numerous Associated Student liberal reforms. This was the radical student element, concentrated in such organizations as Students for a Democratic Society (SDS), the Progressive Labor Party (PLP), and the Young Socialist Alliance (YSA). There was considerable overlapping among the membership of these organizations but all accepted the point of view that radical—not liberal—restructuring of the American society and all of its institutions was demanded. Consequently, the reformist thrust of the Associated Students and their apparent success in cooperating with the power structure in modifying the college were a distinct threat. The "inherently repressive and coercive nature of the Establishment" was not exposed, and potential recruits to the radical cause were mollified into believing they did not need to risk destructive behavior. Strategy and tactics for radicalizing these alienated young people—a group San Francisco State attracted in large number—were urgently needed. But the Students for a Democratic Society and allies were a mere thimbleful of thirty or so zealots, and their previous focus on the Vietnam War, the draft, and ROTC had produced neither a serious confrontation nor a mass base. Somehow they must take the initiative away from their enemy—those pressing for social and institutional change in political, not revolutionary, ways.

From the most pedestrian of sources came their stroke of genius: why not stage a cafeteria boycott? Though not an issue of cosmic importance, it did have the potential for mass support. Who could side with the Establishment when the quality or price of campus food was concerned? Over the years this has been a rallying cry for angry students the world over. The revolutionary beauty of the idea was that it could provoke a confrontation at no risk to the mass participants. There certainly was no campus rule that said students must eat cafeteria food or that they could not picket. So reduced prices and increased student control of the enterprise that was designed to serve them became the slogan; picketing and a boycott became the technique.

For two weeks in December 1966 the boycott ran its successful course only to run afoul eventually of Christmas holidays. In terms of producing a confrontation with the administration and an intemperate power response, the boycott was a failure. President Summerskill and his aides played it cool even to the point of allowing the strikers to bring in a private entrepreneur to sell sandwiches, doughnuts, and coffee in the struck facility. Tweaking the nose did not produce the hoped-for retaliatory action; the radicals were not pleased, but from the perspective of the college's revolutionary history in the next two years, this SDS-initiated stab at confrontation politics was a signal success. First, it actively involved a large number of students in their first campus attempt to seize control militantly of some aspect of their lives—a minor aspect to be sure, but still one of symbolic importance. In doing so, they defied authority—and found the act pleasurable, relatively successful, and risk-free. As the tactics of the boycott shifted from peaceful picketing to shoulder-to-shoulder obstruction of the entrance to the serving lines, the participants also had their first taste of the "steel" of campus warfare, physical intimidation.

Second, the cafeteria boycott represented a critical shift in student leadership and style, a shift away from liberal reform toward radical action, a shift away from the Associated Student leaders toward the political revolutionaries, and a shift away from cooperation with the administration toward confrontation. The style of having a small group of militants unilaterally take action against the Establishment became the political style in future encounters. In essence it left the reformers, liberal and militant alike, only one place to go no matter what their feelings about the radicals. For in the student culture of the Vietnam period—particularly at San Francisco State—you certainly could not side with the power structure, the administration. This tactic presented a crisis for Jim Nixon and his entourage in the Associated Students. Are you for us or against us? Will you stand with the students or with the administration? Almost to a man the Experimental College leaders, the tutors, the community service workers joined the picket line. From then on, with just a brief period of remission the following summer and fall, the cutting edge of student leadership on the campus became radical. The boycott also gave premonitions of the nature of future black student cooperation in white radical ventures. When it served their purposes, the blacks briefly joined the picket line, but they did it on their own terms. After all, this was not their "thing," and it could hardly be construed as an attack on racism.

Beyond beginning the radicalization process of a large segment of students and of the student leadership cadre, the Students for a Democratic Society boycott also was to achieve its major overt goal of student control of the cafeteria management, and at no price to its leadership. Thus, the formula that was to dominate radical black and white activities in the days ahead was forged: confrontation, success, no risk. The radicals believed this stemmed from the justice of their cause and the corruption of the administration. The public and the politicians began to murmur about appeasement.

Another traditional instrument of reformist tendencies in the student body to buckle beneath the radical surge was the student newspaper, *The Daily Gater*. Like the Associated Students, it had moved rapidly in the past several years in the direction of criticism of the status quo and pressure for institutional change. Neither moved quickly enough. Tied as it was to the journalism department, the *Gater* could not divest itself of some trappings of the journalistic profession, namely a pretense of objectivity and a penchant for wide-ranging criticism. In pursuit of these canons it editorialized against the excesses of the boycott and then compounded its sins by engaging in a muckraking campaign against what it considered the financial nepotism and corruptions of the Jim Nixon Associated Student administration. The wrath of radical and reformist was quick to vent itself.

In the lexicon of the radicals "you are either for us or against us"—there is no comfortable role of ambivalence or independence. With students being the oppressed and the administration being the oppressor, the role of the student body's newspaper was obvious: serve the cause of student power. The student body leaders were equally incensed. Criticized as they were by the radicals for having been coopted by the administration, they now found their liberal, coopted activities being challenged by the paper. Both groups moved on the *Gater.* The efforts of the disgruntled student body leadership resulted in the creation of a new weekly publication called *Open Process.* It was not long before *Open Process* took on the format and substance of an underground newspaper, defying authority and social conventions as an act of basic policy.

The *Gater,* however, played an important role in the conservative backlash to radical and liberal student leadership in the spring 1967 student body elections. A crusading columnist, Phil Garlington, used the newspaper as his vehicle for notoriety, a notoriety that resulted in his conservative candidacy for the student body presidency. In both his column and his campaign he took dead aim at the Jim Nixon administration for placing social and institutional reform ahead of the needs of his larger constituency, the "silent majority," and for doing it in a self-righteous manner that tolerated no scrutiny or criticism. To the surprise of many, Garlington and his conservative slate defeated the choice of both the incumbent student administration and the Black Students Union, Peter Pursley. Here we have the irony that the conception of the role of student government that made San Francisco State nationally famous led to the defeat of its supporters on the home campus.

Within student and faculty circles San Francisco State has had more than its share of articulate critics of the Vietnam War. The entire Bay Area is one of the major United States foci for draft resistance and antiwar activists. Parades, picketing, and demonstrations are commonplace. An account of one such spring parade in 1967 featured a picture of President Summerskill marching with his two-year-old son perched on his shoulders. Although this visible commitment of their leader pleased many students, there were those in the power structure, particularly among trustees, who had second thoughts about their presidential choice.

For over a year General Lewis Hershey's decision to use rank in class as a basis for draft deferment had evoked almost unanimous resistance from the nation's academic community. In May 1966, the Academic Senate at San Francisco State had raised the issue by advising its acting president, Stanley Paulson, not to cooperate with the directive and to order the Registrar's Office not to compute a student's rank in class. When President Paulson declined to accept this advice, the Senate did not press its point. After a year's hibernation the issue emerged to present Paulson's successor with his first major confrontation.

In the spring semester, 1967, the Academic Senate was again pressed by its antiwar members to take a stance on this matter. This time it confirmed its prior position as college policy, not as advice to the president. This joined both the constitutional issue of whether the Senate or the president had final authority for educational policy (an issue both the Senate and Summerskill had been tiptoeing around despite specific delegation of power in the Senate's constitution by former President Paul Dodd) and the issue of local autonomy. When Chancellor Dumke informed the college that all institutions in the system had an obligation to cooperate with the Selective Service, it appeared that Summerskill's reluctant acceptance of Dumke's directive and the faculty's infinite capacity to substitute rhetoric and resolutions for action would avoid any confrontation.

Had it been left purely to the faculty they undoubtedly would have found a way to compromise liberal rhetoric and pragmatic self-interest. However, the radical students, spoiling for an issue since the cafeteria boycott, were not in a mood to allow such an excellent chance to slip by. It is somewhat difficult to radicalize students over the price of a hamburger, but the peace issue was deeply serious, touched many of the students' strongest convictions, and had been rather well preempted by the revolutionaries. A referendum on the issue during the student body election presented the radicals with their mandate; soon President Summerskill was to receive his ultimatum. When Summerskill attempted to "dialogue" it, the students quickly moved from the conference room to his office. State had its official sit-in. When their president did not choose to engage them in battle but rather went home to polish up his inaugural address for the ceremonies on the following day, the thirty or forty militants retreated after extensive debate and pictures for the media. President Summerskill was not to be so fortunate on the morrow.

If any event vividly marks the emergence of active student dissent and the decline of the college's yet-to-be-inaugurated president, it was the inaugural ceremony itself. Neither the college's intelligence apparatus nor its security forces were to operate effectively on that eventful day, with the result that the administration neither divined the tactics of the militants nor was able to contain them. Thus, as the notables sat in solemn splendor awaiting the academic procession to wind about the campus, thirty sign-waving activists chanted and shouted in their ears. When the procession did arrive, the students audaciously attached themselves to the front and became its herald as it marched into the stadium. No security officer was in sight.

Although the audience no doubt soon forgot the inaugural speeches, the vision of the militant pickets and their disruptive efforts at the ceremony was more memorable. Placing themselves on the running track directly between the platform and the audience in the stadium, the pickets were a visible and at times vocal accompaniment to the entire ceremony. Then, as the platform party—including two trustees and other academic celebrities—prepared to depart, the militants surrounded them, jostling and berating them in turn. At least two of the system's governing board went away with an indelible impression of the administration's incapacity to control its most militant students. The activists also learned an important lesson: such administrative humiliation could be accomplished with impunity, for no student encountered any campus discipline for his disruptive activities.

Two other incidents in May added to the college's mounting problems. For several months the brilliant black writer, Leroi Jones, had been on campus as a funded guest of the Associated Students. Among his activities was work with the newly organized Black Students Union in filming black theater. This was expensive, and the BSU was forced to request additional funds from the student legislature. When the legislature at first refused the request, despite student personnel support of the budget, a brawl was narrowly averted.

Open Process, the non-Establishment, semi-underground competitor to the student newspaper, was the focal point of the next brush with authority. Being in the tradition of underground newspapers and competing for student readers with such publications as the *Berkeley Barb, Open Process* was destined to outrage conventional mores. In its early history the paper nibbled away at these conventions, but never quite stepped over the line. Even Jefferson Poland, leader of the Sexual Freedom League and a careerist at such tweaking of authority, wrote under wraps. But then one edition calmly carried a quarter-page frontal view of a young lady completely naked. Immediately Summerskill suspended both the paper and the Board of Publications. Outraged cries of "freedom of the press" from some students and chuckles from some of the freer souls among the faculty followed.

Both the "nude in the news" and the BSU-student legislature altercation might have blown over had it not been for a conservative whiplash that began to strike. Behind the effort were two conservative student politicians, Bill Burnett and Ron Kinder, who had been running for office for a number of years on a platform aimed at shifting student government away from community action programs and back to more traditional modes. Both were instrumental in the conservative swing that spring in the student body elections. Political allies that they helped elect in the student legislature issued a report on the BSU incident that was distributed widely to the state Legislature, college trustees, political figures such as Governor Reagan and Max Rafferty, and newspapers. "We specifically charge the college administration of encouraging racism and countenancing intimidation and threats of violence," the letter stated. Accompanying the letter was a position paper, "Black Power at San Francisco State College." The message of the paper was that the BSU had taken on a militant slant and that the "administration policy seems to be one of appeasement at every point." The materials attempted to document alleged black intimidation of student legislators.

The charges were repudiated by the conservative coalition's new student body president, Garlington, but they fell upon eager ears. Burnett and Kinder introduced a relatively new phenomenon in college politics by reinforcing their message with frequent visits to the state Legislature. Since the legislators had only recently had their sacred precincts invaded in startling fashion by gun-bearing Black Panthers from the Bay Area, the question of black intimidation caught their attention and political instincts. Eventually the trustees cooled the conflagration by requesting a chancellor investigation of the charges, and the chancellor's report hushed the issue even further with its relative exoneration of the BSU and the college.

The attack on the BSU and the administration's complicity were only the first salvo in the conservative campaign to appeal to the public and the politicians for a full-scale investigation of the "mess at San Francisco State." At considerable expense some of the same forces distributed widely throughout the state a statement that expanded upon the *Open Process* predilection for frank, earthy statements, and it also included a reprint of Jefferson Poland's vivid column and the "nude in the news." Since pornography as well as student unrest had become major issues in the state's elections, there was a ready audience for these allegations of pornographic license, racist intimidation, and administrative appeasement. The letter openly asked for a legislative investigation. From this point on San Francisco State College, the administration of John Summerskill, and the California State Colleges became major political issues in legislative elections. Even liberal supporters of higher education risked political defeat by not being circumspect in their utterances. Bill Burnett worked his strategy so successfully that he parlayed it into a position on the staff of one of the new conservative senators from Southern California, John Harmer, as an expert on "the radical mess in California colleges."

In one of the ironies that has plagued California higher education and contributed in no small measure to its unhealthy condition, the faculties became increasingly distrustful and hostile toward their lay governing boards and the Legislature at almost the same moment that these groups became suspicious and apprehensive about the colleges and their faculties. Within the state colleges the faculties had pinned their economic and political hopes on official faculty governance institutions such as individual academic senates and a Statewide Academic Senate and on unofficial membership organizations of the nature of the Association of California State College Professors and the California Federation of Teachers. Even under Governor Brown's administration the aspirations of the faculty had been blunted and coopted. The early months of Governor Ronald Reagan's administration made cooption appear to be a great victory. Within weeks Reagan launched a drive for severe budget cuts in both the state colleges and the university and for the imposition of student tuition in both systems.

The focus of the faculty surge to alleviate their economic and governmental impotency became a collective bargaining campaign in fall 1966 by the two faculty organizations, ACSCP and AFT, a campaign that again basically originated at the chancellor-trustee *bete noire,* San Francisco State. Following a petition campaign, a "poll/election" was conducted on the campus in which 69.1 per cent of the faculty surprisingly indicated a preference for power rather than indulgence by favoring the vague term *collective bargaining*. Later they were to choose ACSCP over AFT as their "bargaining agent." The Statewide Academic Senate then hassled with the problem for a year and concluded its efforts in the spring of 1967 with an official statewide election. Although the systemwide faculty barely turned down collective bargaining, 3,016 to 2,741, in several large colleges a significant majority supported it. The results amazed many who had held the traditional belief that college faculty, inclined toward individual rather than collective action and white-collar professional status rather than a blue-collar labor image, were seriously considering united activity involving the ultimate sanction of withdrawal of services. But those who were amazed had not been in tune with the accumulated sense of frustration, lack of confidence in the powers in the state and the system, and impotency among state college faculty. Tragically, emerging events on the campuses were to create a similar lack of confidence and frustration among the public and the legislators toward the academicians. At center stage in the tragic development stood California's new governor, Ronald Reagan. By his views on budget and tuition, by his antiintellectual and antifaculty stance, and, covertly, by his anti-mass higher education attacks, he had become a symbol to the college community of the conservative political threat to their profession and values. Yet, by the same token and for the same reasons, he had become a symbol to a large segment of the public of their defense against leftist professors and colleges, militant, unregenerate students, and a burgeoning tax bill.

These issues loomed large over San Francisco State as the first year of John Summerskill's stewardship ended and obscured the healthy progress in such basic areas as general education reform, long-range planning for the disadvantaged ethnic students, and innovative educational ventures. Summerskill encouraged high hopes in the latter two areas by encouraging in summer 1967 a grant request for a Center for Innovative Studies that was to be sent to a supposedly receptive Carnegie foundation. Almost lost in the million-dollar dream were more tangible and realizable goals toward which the black students and the administration had been working cooperatively. Also casting a pall over these ambitions and the college was President Summerskill's marital estrangement and his obvious fall from grace in the Chancellor's Office. The latter was attested to by a rare, peremptory five-minute dressing down—with witness—after he made a special trip for the occasion to the Chancellor's Office in Los Angeles.

Thus, San Francisco State was to enter the 1967–68 academic year challenged by student radicals and black students both of whom had successfully tested their muscles in the past period, taxed by problems in the areas of student journalism, student government, ethnic studies, the draft and military recruitment, led by an increasingly insecure administration, manned by a bitter, frustrated faculty, and operating in a context of great political concern, legislative and executive hostility, and the omnipresent eye of the mass media.

Chapter 2

The Bubble Bursts

In contrast to the blithe, witty, confident stance of the year before, President Summerskill struck a worried, conservative, "innovation but order" pose as he welcomed the faculty to their second year under his leadership. Obviously his critics in and about the trustees, Legislature, public, and faculty had gotten to him and he knew his job was on the line. The events of the first months of 1967–68 were troublesome but mere mild portents of the future. The war upon the sensibilities of the uptight Establishment centered upon the reconstruction of the Board of Publications and the editorial staff of *Open Process,* although a spontaneous "nude-in" by a couple from the streets gave the local media and their thirsty public a more vivid image of continuing life at State. In the battle for the mind-blowing *Open Process* the students displayed resourcefulness, tenacity, and dedication to their cause. A new tactic of packing committee meetings with tough, vocal, abusive partisans of the liberal line came into first flower.

Both bitterness and optimism pervaded the Associated Students: bitterness because the conservative student legislature slashed the black, ghetto-oriented programs budget, optimism because of the continued progress of educational ventures such as the Experimental College and the faculty evaluation program, MAX. Intimations of the painful travail of the next few months occurred on the more critical fronts of the BSU and the white radical students. A special admissions program of minuscule proportions was initiated in order to compensate for the inequities in pre-college education of black students. When the Senate became aware of the development, it raised the question of who has the authority to choose which underprivileged student is admitted—the faculty and the administration or the black community? This issue as well as the dimension of the program—since it could well mean excluding eligible white students in order to make room for ineligible black students—was to plague the college during the hectic days of the next two years.

To this point the anti-war movement, in the broad Bay Area and on the campuses, had been primarily confined to blunt rhetoric and nonviolent harassment of ROTC programs and military and Dow recruiters. The events that were to surround the Stop the Draft Week Committee's attempt to close down the Oakland Armed Forces Examining Station radically enlarged the involvement and introduced the tactics of violent protest confrontation and police repression. For the entire week of October 16–20 the Oakland Induction Center was to be the scene of alternating nonviolent sit-ins and peaceful arrests and wide-ranging street fighting and guerrilla warfare that pitted rock-throwing youths against club-wielding, gas-spraying police. Since many of the participants were Berkeley students with a sprinkling of San Francisco State students and even some faculty and since a portion of the planning and coordination occurred illegally on the UC campus, the issue of college complicity with the movement was squarely before the body politic. This became a major issue at the regents meetings as political figures such as Reagan and Rafferty on the Board of Regents questioned the colleges' role.

At San Francisco State the issue became totally reversed, and the events of Oakland became the occasion for the college's first serious soul-searching on the crucial topic of the institution's complicity with the war effort—or, in the emerging antiwar shorthand, complicity with the military-industrial complex. In the aftermath of Bloody Tuesday at Oakland, scarred students from San Francisco State returned to their favorite forum, the Speakers Platform, to berate the institution in unusually harsh terms. The violence of Oakland and the bitter recriminations against the Establishment penetrated the consciousness of the large crowd far beyond incidents and rhetoric of the past.

Among the audience were several committed antiwar, anti-Establishment members of the college's still-influential Academic Senate. The Senate happened to be meeting that afternoon, October 17. In a flood of passionate oratory which admittedly took an almost apocalyptic view of the crisis of the college, the Senate pushed aside its pedestrian agenda and for the first time faced up to the issue of the role of the institution in the United States' war effort. Critical at this juncture was the brilliant, persuasive analysis of one of the college's distinguished, liberal scholars in the field of international relations, Marshall Windmiller. For years Windmiller had been an articulate voice in liberal journals and over Pacifica Foundation's noncommercial radio stations, warning of the nation's peril as it increasingly bent to the domination of this same military-industrial complex to which Eisenhower had alerted the country in his famous farewell address. So deep had been Windmiller's commitment of energy and talent to this crusade that friends had only recently been able to persuade him to participate in the college's fairly pallid politics. Rising above random comments and parliamentary entanglements, he boldly suggested that the college commit itself to a week-long convocation of faculty, students, and administration on the topic of the appropriate role of the college in the country's war effort. By an overwhelming vote the Academic Senate committed the college to this extremely serious, unusual undertaking. Five weeks later, in November, the War Crisis Convocation was held.

In questioning a variety of its activities that touched upon the war effort, the college implicitly validated the radical thesis that our country's institutions interlocked to support a basic value system, an economic enterprise, and a foreign policy. Although no specific college policy changed directly as a result of the convocation or the full academic community vote on twenty-six specific issues that emerged from the week-long soul-searching, in the future the college could no longer push aside the complicity issue as not worthy of serious consideration. During the course of the convocation debate the student war critics, although suspicious of the entire process as liberal Establishment cooption of a radical cause, monopolized the microphones and had full campus exposure as they reiterated day after day their basic litany. Whereas before they had to depend upon radical action to obtain an audience for their beliefs, in the convocation the institution itself sanctioned their dialogue. Many heard, some reinforced, others became open to new interpretations. The task of the radicals now became one of building upon their intellectual converts with an action and confrontation campaign that would force the institution to admit by its behavior what it had only tentatively questioned in the dialogue.

Within the faculty the event was portentous. Ever since the Academic Senate began to become involved in questioning the college's complicity with the nation's draft rule, significant numbers within the faculty began to openly criticize both the politicizing of faculty governance and the Senate's arrogant disregard of its obligation to solicit total faculty wishes before committing the college to such radical departures as the War Crisis Convocation. The use of class time and college facilities to seriously discuss the war and the military-industrial complex confirmed the opinion within these ranks that "leftist, anti-war, AFTers" had control of the Senate and that nothing short of establishing an indigenous faculty political party could counteract their hegemony and put the college properly back on its traditional intellectual track. To this end a new group sprang into being, the Faculty Renaissance. Although drawing from the more conservative sectors of the campus, such as the faculties in business, physical education, and industrial arts, it had a wide sprinkling from other areas as well, including the man of the future, semanticist S. I. Hayakawa.

With the willing arrest of three San Francisco State faculty members at the Oakland Induction Center bust—Kay Boyle, Ted Keller, and Ken Bartelme—faculty dissent began to shift away from marching in peace parades, contributing to draft resistance funds, and signing a variety of liberal statements to some active, physical involvement. A number earned their "oak leaf clusters" by being cited by the House Committee on Un-American Activities in the spring of 1966; still others became deeply involved in Happening House, an attempt to bridge the generation gap in a flexible, constructive, educational fashion in the Haight-Ashbury district. One of their number, Leonard Wolf, poet, author, and nationally respected member of the English department, was actually arrested, though later acquitted, for alleged involvement in a Happening House conference on juvenile delinquency that concluded with a performing group's nude dance before 500 "juveniles." The growing estrangement between some in the academic community and conventional mores is indicated by Wolf's comment when arrested: "I thought the dance was beautiful. Young people are trying to say things in modes we are not used to. People my age don't seem to understand what is going on." The number of faculty actively challenging society's conventions and priorities grew rapidly during this period, and this cadre was to prove critical in the "bodies-on-the-line" commitment during the faculty strike of the next year just as the Renaissance group was to be central in the "law-and-order" reaction.

Radical students failed to obtain their anti-ROTC, antiwar recruiters mandate in the vote that followed the War Crisis Convocation. The results were equivocal, and the radical students felt bitter that their commitment of energies and priorities to planning and participating in the convocation should spread out over five weeks and conclude in a watered-down ballot covering twenty-six disparate issues. As important as the War Crisis Convocation was in enlarging the base and impact of the white radical students, it was overshadowed by a development in one other sector of student unrest, the black student community. On November 6, 1967, a week before the initiation of the Convocation, a dozen black students marched into the offices of the student newspaper, the *Gater,* and engaged in a mass physical attack on the student editor, staff members, and a faculty adviser. Five minutes later they raced down the corridors leaving a badly beaten editor, Jim Vaszko, an office in shambles, and a staff in shock. Even more astonished were the academic community and the general public. Judged by conventional standards, the attack seemed brutal and unprovoked. The blacks later asserted that the newspaper and its editor had for a long time published articles and editorials with a racist slant; specifically, that Vaszko had printed an editorial critical of Cassius Clay's avoidance of the draft. Some said the BSU was enraged over the disputed tallying of the vote for Homecoming Queen that led to their candidate's loss by a small margin. A student, E. Eulau, who claimed to be virtually the only white student in the mass BSU meeting the day following the attack, commented in a letter to the editor that it became apparent in the meeting that the battle was merely a tactic in the radical-moderate struggle for power within the BSU: "If they wanted to get just you, they would have gotten you alone. But they wanted publicity. And they thought an incident such as this would turn whitey against all Negroes, and that the moderates in the BSU would be polarized to the extremist fringe simply from white pressure on all Negroes on campus" (November 30, 1967).

The day of the *Gater* attack marked a significant shift in the struggle for black identity and black recognition at San Francisco State. From that moment on "by any means necessary" ceased being empty rhetoric and instead became an aggressive battle strategy for a black college community now fully organized and dedicated to the elimination of institutional racism. Total resources were committed to defending the brothers who had been seriously implicated in the *Gater* incident by an alert student photographer who "stopped the action" in a remarkable series of clear photographs. Several lawyers led by local Assemblyman Willie Brown rose to the defense of the nine accused of the assault by the police and the college. Immediately the issue loosely called "double jeopardy" arose: how could the accused defend themselves in the campus hearings when their statements might be used in the subsequent, and more serious, criminal action? In consequence of this dilemma they remained mute during the college trials. President Summerskill suspended the accused nine pending college action, citing a section of the systemwide rules that allowed such suspensions if serious trouble were envisioned by the continued enrollment of the students. For this action Summerskill was blasted by both white and black activists as yielding to political pressures. To be sure, the accused were yet to be convicted, and several were as omnipresent in their suspended status as they would have been as continuing students.

The apparent disparity between black justice and white justice became a student issue in the wake of yet another *cause celebre* on the campus. Week by week the "underground" paper, *Open Process,* had been edging closer to the vague boundaries of propriety despite an agreement with the president when the paper was reinstated that the staff, and Jefferson Poland in particular, would eschew the type of utterance that caused trouble the previous spring. Then there appeared the following in the November 22, 1967, issue, an edition heralded by a large snapshot of a defiant cat with the inscription, "Beauty is a defiance of authority," and concluded on the back page with a full view picture of the ubiquitous—but, on this occasion, completely naked —Poland, with only a bunch of grapes frustrating the pruriently inclined:

> DOWN THE SELF HOLE. Alone I lift my supplicating cat in heat asshole to white hot poker of imagined spankers. Each motion is

line scribed in the air, Grand monumental shifting of profound mass. I am leader spring dinosaur fawn, Crawling along the floor to the long stairway down, My ass up to God. Each step grabs at my pants as I slide belly down, Teasingly strips them off inch by inch. Now my cock/my balls/are seen/are seen/are touched/are hurt/are seen. Now I am long and nude and beautiful, Pink eel slippering long gray stairs/bumped and whipped/shamed and overcome/ wanted/raped/wanted/By fantasied Others. Cold concrete at the bottom; I'm afraid I'll lose control and go out the door to the street, But merely yank off my diaper pants from my girl ankles, And sit very asshole sucking the floor.

My legs aside, my core hole from mouth to ass is straight radial trunk. I am moist erotic emptiness around which/Symmetrical organs flower/Mandragera mandala. Legs in front of me now, tilting back on conventions bumbs That shield the asshole from developing its own world view, My find deep into that hole

now into my mouth
hole
mouthole
jag
jag
holemouth
jag
jag

COME

In a preface Poland dedicated the poem to the director of the division of health, physical education, and recreation, "one of the leading intellectuals of our faculty."

Criticized by faculty and trustees for agreeing to the War Crisis Convocation, frustrated, almost bitter, that his deep commitment to the black cause—recently a sixteen-hour-a-week mediation after the *Gater* attack—had only produced a racist label, Summerskill reacted with uncharacteristic lack of cool to the reoccurrence of the pornography baiting. In quick succession he jabbed the faculty-student Board of Publications, then suspended the publication, then temporarily suspended both Jefferson Poland and the *Open Process* editor, Blair Paltridge, from the college pending a disciplinary hearing. His patience was obviously wearing thin.

Liberal and radical students immediately reacted with cries of "Censorship!" Many faculty joined them, especially faculty from the humanities area. "Violation of due process," "lack of consultation," "freedom of the press" were the ringing phrases of the moment. When it became a matter of public record that a peninsula assemblyman, Leo Ryan, had excoriated Summerskill with a scorching letter, asking him "when the leadership of San Francisco State is going to suspend the faculty and students involved in this incident," one more banner was raised: "political interference." The American Civil Liberties Union lit still another faggot under the beleaguered president: they stated that "to suspend the editor without giving him a hearing is a violation of basic rights" and indicated they would seek a federal injunction to force the president to reinstate Paltridge and Poland pending their trial.

Both Summerskill's impulses and his advice from the chancellor's legal staff had obviously been faulty. Confronted by an angry crowd of 500 demonstrators outside his office he swallowed his pride and apologized: "I acted precipitously in suspending *Open Process*. I am personally sorry I did so. I was mad and impatient and I acted improperly." Within hours his office announced that Paltridge and Poland and *Open Process* had been reinstated.

Although one of the San Francisco newspapers was impressed with President Summerskill's frank, boyish capacity to cool the mob and headlined its story "President Meets, Charms Students," the general reaction of the public, trustees, and important legislators—many of whom witnessed the apology on the six o'clock news that evening—was a revulsion against appeasement when coerced by an ugly mob. Summerskill's tolerance while being reviled by expert militant hecklers—listening to BSU leader Jimmy Garrett promise a black rally in two days that "They might even move to close down the campus"; giving serious consideration to radical Professor John Gerassi's thundering challenge, "If you feel that the Vietnam War is wrong morally, then why are you not willing to risk your job now and go down with us on a moral issue?"—conjured up the image of the "spineless" college administrator that political hopefuls such as Max Rafferty had been telling the public were the cause of most of the campus unrest. The *San Francisco Examiner* reflected the growing disenchantment of a large segment of the public with this approach to militant students with an editorial two days later:

> This is an apology. On Friday, the Examiner gave Dr. John Summerskill, President of San Francisco State, an editorial salute for

> finally having the courage to take a stand on some vital campus issues. We were wrong. Before the ink was dry on the salute, Dr. Summerskill was proving he is a high priest of the cult of permissiveness. He was proving he is faster in reverse than he is in moving ahead. The president won our nod when he suspended *Open Process*, a weekly campus publication, its editor and Jefferson Poland, a perennial campus trouble-maker. These actions by Summerskill followed the publication in *Open Process* of a sick and disgusting verse by Poland. The verse was a series of poorly constructed sentences describing in the most repulsive gutter language a perverted sex act. This garbage reflected the warped mentality of its author. . . . The suspensions brought a prompt protest by a small percent of the student body. The protestors were noisy and threatening. They ranted and raved. And Summerskill caved. He won the applause of the protestors when he took the microphone and—in effect—said he had been naughty and impulsive and petulant. . . . It is our guess that his backdown will open the campus to more permissiveness, more insolence and more upheaval. . . . So far as Dr. Summerskill is concerned he has proved to be the campus chameleon of all time.

President Summerskill was to discover that a conciliating, middle-ground approach endears the administration to neither side. For two weeks the campus black community had been blasting him for temporarily suspending the alleged *Gator* attackers prior to a trial, and for permitting the campus trial prior to the scheduled criminal action. Its judgment was blunt: Summerskill was castigated for bowing to political pressures in order to keep his job. A leader of the BSU, which until recent events acted as though it appreciated Summerskill's sympathy with its cause, stated the disenchantment coldly: "We'll take a hard stand against whatever Summerskill stands for in the future." When the cumbersome, antiquated college student discipline process recommended a year's suspension for two of the accused, a semester's suspension for two others, and probation or letters of warning for the other five—and Summerskill supported the recommendation—the hostility became magnified.

Then his reinstating the two white students involved in *Open Process* provided the final energizing force for the ensuing college conflagration. Racism! Two standards of justice! White students reinstated; black students suspended! This set the stage for the black initiative to step up the tempo of its aggressive attack on the institution.

It also provided a rallying cry for the white radicals who had not been able to obtain a very large piece of the action since being blunted in the War Crisis Convocation. Later they were deprived of a target when the administration decided to cut down on its battlefronts by delaying the military and Dow recruiters.

The first ominous though vague hint of a new strategy by the BSU in their escalating defense of their convicted black brothers came at the Friday, December 1, demonstration at which President Summerskill apologized. It was then that the BSU leader, Jimmy Garrett, accused Summerskill of liberal rhetoric, smiles, and stabs in the back in his dealings with black students on campus. He concluded by announcing a black community rally for the following Wednesday of "one thousand to five thousand black students and members of the black community." The purpose of the rally was to protest the suspension of the black students. "We are going to move for student power. We're gonna act. We might even move to close down the campus."

One of the distinctive features of many of the confrontations at State as contrasted with those of other campuses has been the loose coordination of attack, goals, timing, and strategy between the black militants and the SDS-PLP white radicals. Both feed off each other, thus gaining added power although at some expense of coherent leadership and modified objectives. Now the SDS-PLP students decided the time was ripe. They planned the demonstration that led to Summerskill's apology, followed this with some fiery speeches, enlisted some of their new recruits by a token sit-in in the Administration Building (carefully designed and timed to produce no busts), and then adjourned for a mass, participatory democracy meeting to launch their campaign. About one hundred showed up—forty or fifty being new faces. Elaborate, convoluted debate and procedures produced the preordained results: a new organization to be called the Movement Against Political Suspensions (MAPS)—in tribute to their MAPS colleagues at Berkeley who were now at an advanced stage of sit-ins and arrests centering around some of the same issues. Demands were drawn up and the administration was to be given until noon on the following Wednesday, December 6 (the day of the planned BSU demonstration), to respond. The demands were quite straightforward and spoke to the issues at hand: (1) all suspensions of students be dropped and trials be by elected peers, not administrators; (2) reinstatement of *Open Process;* (3) no political harassment of faculty, staff, students, or administrators; (4) no outside police on campus; and (5) student control of student affairs, particularly student publications. Jimmy Garrett appeared at the meeting briefly to give his blessings to their efforts without disclosing any specifics on the BSU strategy. A steering committee was elected (same old faces), tasks assigned, and the Movement launched.

As San Francisco State headed for a showdown, it did so in a context of events all of which had some impact on the action and the resolution. On October 27, Huey Newton, Black Panther Minister of Defense, gave a ringing, militant message on the campus; the following day he was arrested in a shoot-out between police and Black Panthers. Early in November student body president Phil Garlington attempted to ensure black representation in the college decision-making process by appointing predominantly black students as the student representatives on the official faculty committees, including Jimmy Garrett to the Academic Senate. His conservative student legislature initially turned down most of these appointments. The radical students lost, for the most part, in the referendum that followed the War Crisis Convocation. The Board of Trustees met on November 30 and made freedom of recruitment, including military recruitment, official systemwide policy. It also took a tough law-and-order position on student demonstrations, advocating use of police if necessary and student suspensions. By now the Reagan influence was beginning to be felt on the board through three direct appointments, the significant ex-officio representation of himself, Finch, and Rafferty, and his obvious political and financial power.

A "silent majority" group attempted to become organized on the campus under the title "Students to Keep the Campus Open" and elicited approximately 3,000 signatures on a petition to do just this. On November 20, war protests had become violent when police were called to neighboring San Jose State's campus to quell a riot centering on a protest against Dow recruiters. A month before, the same bloody scene had been played at the University of Wisconsin. Across the nation Dow and military recruiters were being challenged at such disparate colleges as the University of Iowa, UCLA, the University of Chicago, Stanford, and Oberlin. At San Jose State, a black community threat to disrupt a football game unless the institution moved immediately to eliminate racist practices led to the cancellation of the game and support of many of the black demands by President Clark. High schools in the Bay Area were plagued with riots, some leading to the closing of the schools temporarily, and most hinging on the race issue.

And neighboring UC, Berkeley, was still suffering from the aftermath of student discipline administered in connection with the Oakland Induction battle, with new tactics such as troublesome "mill-ins" in the administration buildings being employed.

As Wednesday, December 6, approached, the campus took on an apprehensive tone. The administration declined to give credence to the MAPS ultimatum. The AFT met around a keg of beer at the neighboring Ecumenical House and faced the issue raised by some of its younger members and by representatives from MAPS and the BSU, of whether it should endorse the MAPS demands. By 11 P.M. they had almost cast their destiny with the radical students against racism and political suppression and for student power. By midnight the arrival of some seasoned veterans put them back in their historical track: economic issues, collective bargaining, local autonomy. Summerskill moved about in the San Francisco black community attempting to obtain responsible black intercession. Administrators made final arrangements for police coordination, including the establishment of a command post in the president's office. Faculty, for the most part, went about their teaching chores with a vague awareness something was in the wind. Jimmy Garrett suggested, "A Vietnam might happen on this campus. . . . we're calling for full support from the black community because that's the only people we can count on." As to the possibility of violence, an SDS leader pronounced the line that was to become increasingly popular in the future: "There's not going to be any violence on campus Wednesday unless the administration brings it on." The student newspaper had other thoughts. In a Wednesday edition under the bold streamer "NOON SHOWDOWN" the editor gave his opinion that the planning group had even considered the possibility of snipers. George Murray, the part-time instructor in the English Department who was soon to be the focus of much acrimonious dissent in the system, commented: "We will not tolerate racism on this campus any more and we'll move to destroy the institution before we will tolerate it."

The events of that momentous Wednesday, December 6, more than measured up to the expressed anxieties and fears of violence. Since apparent student strategy seemed to center around a mill-in or takeover of the Administration Building along the lines of recent Berkeley tactics, President Summerskill and his aides decided to block this line of attack by locking the building around ten o'clock and sending all employees home. Around eleven-thirty the scheduled MAPS rally began at the Speakers Platform. The enactment of a scenario that was to be a basic position piece all during the strike of the following year began: fiery speeches decrying the ineptitude and resistance of the Establishment, a clarion call to march on the Administration Building, the mass march across the central campus greensward to the building, a large congregation of curious, sometimes sympathetic students, more incitements to action. An added fillip in this scene was the leadership of a fill-in faculty appointee in the international relations department, admitted-radical-if-not-revolutionary, John Gerassi. Challenging the assembled multitude in front of the Administration Building that the building was rightfully the students' and that they had been "violently" locked out, he placed the issue squarely on the line: "Either we have got to keep it closed permanently, or we still have to go in."

Student compatriots and Professor Gerassi chose the latter course: glass was broken and the core leadership of two hundred or so invaded the building. After about an hour of declaiming and cavorting somewhat good-naturedly around the halls, with some slight damage here and there, the group—initially almost all white, but integrated later on—left peacefully when challenged by the administration. In the meantime BSU direct activity had centered around sending raiding parties into the various buildings to close as many classes as they could. There were several hairy incidents and quite a number of outraged faculty.

The third act of this day's drama took place in the center of the campus. BSU leader Jimmy Garrett had promised 1,000 to 5,000 from the black community. Reporters guessed that about 100 high school age students showed up from the ghettos. What they lacked in numbers they balanced with violence. In short order they ransacked the cafeteria, raided the bookstore, broke several windows, started a bookstore fire, destroyed a number of news photographer's cameras, and engaged in several fistfights—at times against black college students. Rumor had it that a few knives and guns were flashed. The entire tableau was a frightening mob scene, for with the advent of classroom disruptions the administration had told faculty to dismiss their classes and these students, too, poured onto the campus. The consensus of plainclothes police in the midst of the swirling mob was that it would not have taken much to have provoked a full-scale race riot.

Within about one hour the ghetto blacks withdrew, other students left campus, and the college attempted to pick up the pieces.

The greatest hue and cry arose from the media, trustees, and politicians. On such an obvious law-and-order issue, each politician tried to outdo the other. Governor Reagan called on officials at the college to take "whatever action is necessary" to maintain law and order on the campus. As for disrupters, he reiterated his standard invitation: "Either they obey the rules or they get their education elsewhere." Powerful Speaker of the Assembly Jesse Unruh immediately moved in and ordered an Assembly investigation within the week. "I'm inclined to believe the state college president, Summerskill, ought to be fired but I will await until the facts are gathered by the committee," he commented. Max Rafferty proposed a policy of firing faculty members and suspending students who either advocate or participate in campus violence.

Underneath the current of editorial, trustee, and political criticism, was a basic feeling that the riot was not an incidental act but rather that it reflected a growing softness and permissiveness and a dispersed and sentimental college authority that permeated higher education in general, and the rogue college, San Francisco State, in particular. Two specific criticisms led all the rest: the administration should have called the police to protect property and the moderate students and to punish the rioters; and under no circumstances should the college have been closed. To assert trustee authority on these issues, to punish inadequate administrators, to assure the public that ultimate lay authority would not tolerate this revolutionary misuse of taxpayers' facilities, and—in the minds of many faculty and students—to garner a few votes on a can't-miss political issue, several trustees and political figures prevailed on trustee chairman Donald Hart to call an emergency trustee meeting for the following Saturday to discuss the case of San Francisco State. Hart did not deny the possibility that Summerskill's dismissal might be a topic of the deliberations.

On the night before the emergency trustee meeting the Assembly Education Committee got into the act out on the campus. The college was fortunate that their investigation was done without fanfare or publicity. As a result they dined with students and discovered that almost to a man they praised Summerskill for not creating a riot by calling the police. In their private session they were able to hear the respected chief of police in San Francisco, Thomas Cahill, indicate that agents in the crowd totally concurred with the decision not to bring uniformed police on campus. They later announced the committee belief that the "calculated policy of restraint prevented serious damage and personal injury." By reason of the absence of reporters and TV cameras there was a frank exchange between the administrators and the legislators with a high degree of mutual understanding.

Summerskill went down to the emergency trustee meeting with still one other new source of support: his faculty turned out in record numbers Friday afternoon and the group of 800 virtually unanimously endorsed his handling of the riot and expressed unity in desiring his continued leadership. He needed all the support he could muster, for it became obvious at the police-ringed meeting that the political stakes were high, that the long history of San Francisco State as a rebellious, troublesome college was ever in the background, and that an accumulation of doubts about Summerskill's style of leadership lingered in many trustee minds. Few doubted that he would be asked to resign. But majority opinion overlooked three unexpected variables: Summerskill's boyish charm and ingenuousness in testifying, the ugliness of politicians moving in for the kill, and the capacity of TV to communicate both of these qualities to the public. For in order to make political capital out of the "inquisition," the chairman and chancellor had agreed to allow the proceedings to be televised, a "first" in trustee history. This was a great mistake by those in power.

A newspaper column by Robert Maynard Hutchins, former chancellor at the University of Chicago and currently at the Center for the Study of Democratic Institutions in Santa Barbara, entitled "Dreadful Show by the Trustees," caught the mood of the meeting and reflected considerable public opinion:

> When I saw on television a meeting of the trustees of the California state colleges, I trembled for my country. . . . The first question that crossed this viewer's mind was how could these successful businessmen have become successful? Did they conduct their private affairs the way they managed this meeting? If so, how did they stay out of bankruptcy? They could not decide at times what they were voting on. . . . Their remarks were distinguished only by their banality. They displayed no knowledge of and no feeling for the institutions in their charge. . . . Their primary interest appeared to be not the welfare of the colleges but their own posture before the public. They had evidently come to the meeting convinced that the people demanded drastic action to repress disturbance in the colleges. Each member of the board tried to appear more dedicated to "law and order" than the others. A fundamental defect of higher education in California is the presence of politicians in its governing

> bodies. These men use their position in these bodies to advance their political fortunes. So Governor Ronald Reagan and Max Rafferty, superintendent of public instruction, both of whom could be persuaded to accept higher office, presented themselves in this meeting as the toughest sheriffs in the West. . . . The board of trustees of the California colleges, instead of joining in the outcry against San Francisco State and its president, should have used its prestige to educate the people about the difference between a penitentiary and an academic community, between a warden and a college president.

Flustered by the unexpected opposition, the trustees took three emergency actions: they decreed that henceforth all presidents would need to suspend or expel any student or faculty member found guilty of disrupting a campus through violence or threat of violence; they confirmed that local police, not college presidents, had ultimate responsibility for the decision of whether to call in police; and they created a task force to investigate the stewardship of President John Summerskill.

The conduct of the meeting, the specific actions of the trustees, and, in particular, the undercutting of Summerskill shocked many in the academic community and most of those at San Francisco State. Faculty-funded reruns of the TV film added to the widespread disgruntlement. This provided a setting for the by now almost automatic San Francisco State faculty reaction: unite in aggressive defiance and opposition to the charlatans causing all the problems—the trustees, the chancellor, and the politicians. Thus, the greater proportion of faculty energy and ingenuity went into protecting the college and its president from this attack, rather than into internal problem solving.

After the Senate proved inadequate for leadership at this crucial moment, the arena shifted to a full faculty meeting. Here there were three leadership initiatives: a pallid resolution from the Senate, the takeover strategy of the AFT, and a comprehensive, tough line from the School of Humanities. The AFT was now in a precarious position since it had persuaded the national labor leadership that the situation in California was so ripe for the nation's first major collective bargaining campaign among college professors that a battle fund of $250,000 and a cadre of organizers had just recently been employed to stage such a major campaign. The riot and trustee action now threatened this entire effort. The question before the AFT was how to turn the dilemma into a victory. In a meeting that went on into the night the grey eminence behind the AFT's college success in California, Arthur Bierman of the San Francisco State philosophy department, and the organizers decided on a bold stroke. They would persuade a large number of their members on the Senate to resign publicly in repudiation of its leadership, and then the AFT would jump into the leadership vacuum with a four-part resolution that concluded with a tough, three-day strike proclamation. It was a desperate try; events proved that the timing and judgment of faculty sentiment were grossly miscalculated. Of thirteen Senators that had agreed to importunings in the wee hours of the morning to publicly resign, only one carried out his pledge; he later retracted it. The strike resolution was overwhelmingly rejected by more than a four-to-one ratio. The AFT had to wait for a year to obtain their next opportunity of this magnitude. When they seized it they revealed they had learned several important lessons from this debacle. The national organizers packed their tents and stole away not quietly but in a huff.

But although they rejected the AFT-suggested immediate strike, the faculty did indicate in an unexpectedly powerful resolution that they might well move to withdraw their services if Summerskill were dismissed or if the trustees did not quickly modify their precipitous disciplinary ruling: "We affirm our confidence in President Summerskill . . . and declare that if he is dismissed, as a consequence of the resolutions passed by the trustees December 9, we will call on our fellow faculty members to initiate immediate collective action, including a strike if necessary." A similar warning was given should the trustees not suspend their hastily passed resolution "pending open and full discussion between the trustees and the colleges." To ensure a full-scale defense of the college, and an adequate hearing on the new regulations, the faculty taxed themselves heavily to create a Fund for the Defense of San Francisco State College. The intellectual and moral initiative for these actions came from the School of Humanities, which met extensively while most other units went their disorganized ways. Much of the strike initiative the following year also came from the School of Humanities, the articulate, passionate moral preceptors for the college. Acceptance of the sanction "collective action, including a strike if necessary" by a large majority of the faculty represented a new level of hostility and rebellion on the State campus. Since the sanction was only projected for the future, it was made more palatable.

Probably more constructive and influential in determining future college posture *vis-à-vis* the issue of black self-determination that precipitated the crisis was the decision of the Senate to hear out the militant blacks for the first time. Out of this came a genuine appreciation for the frustrations and goals of the blacks, and the Senate immediately moved with the Council of Academic Deans to meet the educational needs of the black community. The Senate did resist, however, a movement within its ranks to grant a Christmas spirit amnesty for the black students convicted in the *Gater* attack, but only by an eighteen-to-fourteen margin. This decision was made in an open meeting well attended by the black population, with the result that only three of the eighteen majority verbally supported their sympathies while almost all of the fourteen who desired to forgive and forget spoke passionately of their convictions. This was a precursor to future open debate on issues affecting the black community.

White radicals did not fare so well. In joining the BSU demonstration they had had little knowledge and no control over the tactics employed by the outside black community. But since they had become dominant in the publicity and in formulating the five demands, they bore much of the hostility that accompanied the violence. They never did quite regroup. The alliance with the blacks proved to be unreliable. Moderate white students and faculty began to assume leadership at rallies. The issues shifted from student demands and moved to Summerskill and the trustee action. So confused did they become that they ended up supporting their former enemy, Summerskill. They did attempt a couple of poorly attended rallies, made a few threats, and participated in a token sit-in at the Administration Building. Even the press paid them slight heed. Events had passed them by. In the spirit of spontaneous humor that incongruously could exist in juxtaposition to their most passionate, angry rhetoric, they concluded their venture with a coffin-carrying parade through both the student and faculty legislatures, chanting their poignant ditty, *The Liberal Song* (to the tune of *Maryann*).

Frederick Douglass broke the color bar
when he rode on a train in the white folks' car
they said get up but he would not go
what they told him we all know

Chorus:
You're only hurting your cause this way
that's what all of us liberals say
nobody likes things the way they are
but you're going too fast and you're going too far.

In the overworked cliche of the liberals among the students and faculty, this translated to "we support your goals but not your tactics." Viewed from the immediate perspective of the black community and its goals, however, one could hardly fault the tactics. Working through channels in a haphazard, disorganized fashion for several years they had achieved at best an initial sympathy for their plight and piecemeal gains. But then, beginning with the *Gater* incident, they changed tactics. As explained by one of their leaders, Benny Stewart, in a statement after the December melee:

> We are trying to communicate to bring about change, but no one wants to talk to us. If someone is stepping on your foot, you say "get off." If he cannot understand the rational, logical way of communicating—and he's causing you pain—then you must communicate in a fundamental way. If you push him off, then he understands not to step on your feet any more. That's what was happening last Wednesday.

The pragmatic tests proved the message got across: (1) after the *Gater* incident, Summerskill created a blue-ribbon committee to investigate the grievances of the black community; (2) the entire academic community began to address itself to the charges of institutional racism; (3) state regulations were changed allowing formerly ineligible ethnic students to be admitted to special programs in the state colleges; (4) black and other ethnic studies majors were created, to be administered by a semiautonomous School of Ethnic Studies; (5) black students and the black community obtained a degree of influence over curriculum, personnel, and administration never before granted to students or the lay community; (6) the college began to hire black administrators for the first time; (7) the fall disruption of the academic community had been achieved at virtually no cost (there was no disciplinary or criminal action stemming from the December demonstration; the nine students involved in the *Gater* attack received fines and probation in the courts; four were suspended at the college, two of these suspensions were commuted to one semester by President Summerskill; there was no faculty action taken against one of those convicted who taught part-time); (8) three of those suspended became leaders among the black students that the college officials had to deal with on almost an equal basis in future black studies developments; (9) community support began to rally around the black brothers and sisters; (10) the BSU posture definitely shifted from moderate to militant; (11) a range of intimidating or attention-getting tactics became increasingly acceptable to the academic community, including classroom "educational" visitations; and (12) a cohesion developed among the black students that gave power to their future efforts.

Chapter 3

Showdown

San Francisco State resumed operation after the Christmas holidays with a demoralized and discredited administration, an increasingly polarized faculty, an aggressive ethnic student movement—soon to be labeled the Third World Liberation Front—and a radicalized student government. The interplay of these elements between January and May made a showdown inevitable. It came with disastrous consequences in May.

Although Summerskill had superficial college support, it was more because of his enemies than his actions. After two perfunctory "investigatory" meetings the trustee task force curtly vindicated him, but their resolution indirectly accomplished its purpose. Realizing that the handwriting was on the wall, that a president of an incendiary campus could not survive without full support, John Summerskill offered his resignation on February 22. Nothing short of a hard-liner could elicit the backing of the forces building up within the state or the increasingly Reaganized trustees. Summerskill's style was far short of this philosophy. In addition, his internal administration of the college created as many problems as it solved. Events were to prove that a "lame-duck" caretaker administration was a certain calamity for the college.

The faculty of the college attempted to operate under the illusion of faculty power and "business as usual," but in actual fact the rifts of the past year became wider. The conservative Faculty Renaissance group enlarged the scope of its activities and eventually dominated the election of a five-man faculty committee to seek Summerskill's successor. Disillusioned liberals quit the Senate to seek jobs elsewhere, to immerse themselves in their more satisfying disciplines, or to seek a more radical alliance. The analysis of two Senate leaders from the department of philosophy on the occasion of their Senate resignations describe the gloom of the dedicated liberals. Said Arthur Bierman, joint-author of the Senate's constitution:

> I must say that I feel clean for the first time in a long while. . . . We must recognize the fact that the Senate is really capable of dealing only with policy matters internal to the college; it is incapable of handling external matters . . . [but] external matters affecting the very survival of the college as we have known it are our overriding concern now. . . . I cannot completely discount a refrain that invades my reflections on the declining morale and status of the college, a refrain that goes like this: Can this be Berlin in 1933 again? We saw a governor, a leading legislator, and many trustees not only bow to but join the lowest common denominator in California. . . . They not only failed to defend the college, they attacked it. Our troubles on this campus were relatively small; I can only shudder to think what will happen if our social fabric frays more dangerously, as it well may, and soon.

Bierman's colleague, Rudolph Weingartner, was equally critical:

> In the course of the past six weeks or so, the Academic Senate has shown itself unwilling to exercise effective leadership of the faculty of this college, although it clearly had the obligation to assume this function. . . . I found the Senate's response to the tension between certain student groups on the one hand and the faculty and admin-

> istration on the other to be almost criminally irresponsible and cynical in its evasiveness and in its unwillingness to confront the problems of this campus.

In a subsequent, more lengthy critique of the college and the California state colleges in general, Weingartner described another equally serious schism developing within the college, this one between Summerskill's new administrative crew and the faculty Weingartner labeled the "creative minority":

> With few exceptions, the present group of administrators is not at all concerned with exercising such educational leadership. They tend to be amateurs as faculty but are well on the way to becoming professionals as administrators. As has never been the case before, the administration is rapidly becoming a "team" with an interest of its own. It is shaping itself into a technocracy that is rapidly losing touch with the best creative impulses in the faculty and the student body. The administration now is coming to serve the "silent majority" of the faculty for the sake of quiet and order; it thinks its greatest task to be the saving of the faculty from itself: the creative minority has lost out. . . . When a vice-president of this college declares he will protect the sanctity of the classroom with the aid of tanks, if necessary, the affairs which are in his charge can be academic in name only. . . . Throughout this, the faculty has remained supine.

The central administration was equally bitter and disillusioned. With its president involved as much with his own problematic future as with the pressing problems of the college, caught between the commands of the trustees and the chancellor on one hand, and the militantly insistent actions of the black students and the white radicals on the other, challenged by what they considered the quixotic wishes of faculty not attuned to economic, administrative, and political realities, the college's administrative leadership clung more closely together for self-protection and mutual sympathy and to keep the college functioning. In particular, the schism that had been widening between the Senate and the Council of Academic Deans became so pronounced that the college was practically functioning with a bicameral legislature, one house being composed of members of the executive body.

Meanwhile the BSU was attempting to consolidate its gains under the leadership of recently hired Nathan Hare, a University of

Chicago sociologist of both academic and militant repute. Hare was hired by Summerskill despite vigorous protests from several in leadership posts in the School of Behavioral and Social Sciences. The SDS-led white radicals jabbed away occasionally at the Marine recruiters or ROTC and attempted to learn their lessons from the December alliance with the blacks. Initiative for student activism thus shifted to the formal student government organization. Resignations of conservative or middle-ground students had led to reelections and a radical white–Third World takeover of the legislature. Events had rolled over the student body president, Phil Garlington, to such a degree that he was seldom to be seen and the legislature became dominant. Students from this same political background also dominated the San Francisco Foundation that governed the bookstore and the cafeteria.

A quick succession of actions followed, all guaranteed to antagonize the administration or the trustees or the governor or the public or segments of the faculty, or all of these parties. First, the *Gater* and the journalism department parted ways and the *Gater* became a proud organ of student power. After all faculty but one resigned from the Board of Publications, it was reconstituted with a large, militant student majority, and this majority promptly seated Blair Paltridge as its chairman—the same individual who had been suspended, then reinstated by the president a few brief weeks before for his role in the Poland poem. The student-controlled foundation decided to use some of its cafeteria-bookstore profits to create a bail fund for San Francisco State students who might be arrested.

Using the power of the purse, the militant Associated Students recalled all organization budgets and reallocated the funds to their own action programs—Community Service, BSU, Draft Help Center. Feeling that their liaison man with the college finance office more often represented the administrative will than the student will, they fired him and sought their own replacement. Moving outside of the usual sphere of the student legislature, the new body gave support to faculty not rehired, to a threatened library strike, and to the pending International Student Strike Day. As seems customary among San Francisco State's activist white students after a major involvement, many of their spring activities were random and disorganized. At different times they invested in the recruitment issue, off-campus, antidraft, peace activities, and the attempt to form a union of student library employees through a strike. Successes were not numerous.

It remained for the energetic, determined, willing-to-risk black and brown students to move the campus closer to its next confrontation. Not satisfied with the promises of the Senate, they first pressed to take control of their own academic destinies by challenging the competency of a white history professor to teach their Afro-American history, and challenging him in the classroom with ghetto language and tactics. They eventually secured their own instructor—and the unending opposition of the large history department.

On the fringes of the black movement emerged a vague, fumbling organization that chose to call itself the Third World Liberation Front (TWLF). Composed primarily of a few Mexican-American and Latino students who believed the focus of discrimination was non-Caucasians, not just blacks, and later sprinkled with a handful of militants from Chinese, Filipino, native American, and Japanese ancestry, they began to make their demands. If their strategy was to provoke the administration and conservative elements within the faculty, they chose the right leader: Juan Martinez. Martinez, teaching on a one-year contract in the history department, had not exactly ingratiated himself with his history colleagues or the administration, nor was his area specialty the top priority of the department at that time. His contract was not renewed. Martinez immediately labeled the reaction "de facto racism" since he said he was the only Mexican-American on the faculty. Renewal of his contract, along with that of another one-year history instructor, Richard Fitzgerald, who had befriended the BSU in its dispute over the Afro-American history course, became the initial rallying point of a new challenge to the college.

For three weeks the *Gater* headlined these demands of the TWLF. In the midst of the campaign a broader sense of grievance became articulated. As one Chicano put it at a rally:

> I am a frustrated Mexican woman, but sex isn't the only reason for my frustration, because I know when I climb out of that bed that my people are still oppressed. . . . To get an education I had to strip myself of my Latin heritage; I had to unlearn my own Spanish language. To get my B.A. I had to kiss the asses of the white professors; their crap slid down my throat and it made me sick. . . . Those of you who can forget this aren't living—you're dead. And we brothers and sisters of the Third World movement are going to kick your dead bodies aside, because we want to live.

Ben Stewart of the BSU indicated black support of these demands when he commented at the rally:

> This is supposed to be a liberal college that caters to the needs of minority students, but if that's true why are they firing the people who are most instrumental in dealing with these problems? They must think we're chumps. . . . If we don't get what we want, things don't function. It's as simple as that.

When neither the history department nor the central administration showed any inclination to bow to these pressures and rehire Martinez and Fitzgerald, the TWLF began to escalate its activities and demands. In an action certain to antagonize all traditionalists with a sense of fair play, the TWLF abruptly "liberated" the office space occupied by the college YMCA and took over. Before the furor from this had calmed down—and the action even became an issue before the Senate—the TWLF demands had been expanded from personnel to students and programs. At a time when the college was attempting to clarify with the Chancellor's office its authorization under the new special admissions policy, Martinez and company took the college's tentative projection, 350 students, and stated: "This is the lowest number we will accept." In addition, the TWLF's programmatic demand was that the college establish a curriculum for Third World students comparable to the one it had agreed to for the black studies program.

An incident between Martinez and his Third Worlders and the Admissions Office added to the mutual distrust. Under the guise of touring the college, Martinez and his companions used a group of Spanish-American and other Third World high school students to stage a wild demonstration that roamed the halls of the Administration Building and finally settled on the dean of admissions. The upshot of the incident was a claim by the high schoolers that they had been duped to serve Martinez's political purposes, accompanied by their apology and an exacerbation of the mutual distrust between the administration and the Third World organization.

The final sparks that led to the May conflagration were the reintroducttion of the ROTC issue in the Academic Senate and the election in the Associated Students of a new group of officers and legislature committed to student power. For a long while faculty had questioned the legitimacy of AFROTC studies, especially since the Air Force had a degree of control of personnel and curriculum granted to no other off-campus group. The War Crisis Convocation raised the further question of the institution's direct involvement with the war effort through this program of training officers, regardless of the academic merits or demerits of the program itself. Since the Senate had committed itself to addressing the major issues raised in the Convocation, several deeply antiwar Senators pressed the issue. A committee was created, hearings held, and a split vote recommendation made to the Senate that the college discontinue the program. The committee arguments rested largely on academic, not ideological, grounds. After extensive debate the Senate surprisingly supported the committee recommendation by an overwhelming twenty-five-to-four vote. The voting transcended liberal-conservative lines. In deference to the increasing faculty concern that the ultimate policy decisions on crucial matters, particularly those with political tinges, be taken by the total faculty, the Senate agreed to a full-scale referendum.

The Associated Students elections in late April saw a swing back to the liberal, activist, Third World-oriented, community involvement party as Russell Bass and his entire slate swept into office by more than two-to-one majorities. In addition to committing the student government to the evolving programs of the past five years, Bass and his allies promised to support student organizing within the departments, "where the real power of the college rests," a School of Ethnic Studies, special admissions and financial aids for ethnic minority students, "fuller student participation in college decision-making processes," the work-study program's proposed B.A. and M.A. degrees in community work, "establishment of links with other colleges, so we can help and get help from other students in doing this work," "a student bill of rights to guide a revitalized Student Court," and a variety of programs of celebration and creativity.

One final platform statement both caught the temper of the antiwar student body and indicated that Bass and his government would attempt to compete with the radical students in their confrontation style and issues: "Any assistance the college gives to the military and the war-related industries—Placement Center services, use of classroom or other space, or a contract with the Air Force ROTC—is complicity with the war. The Associated Students must oppose these activities." True to this commitment, Bass and the legislature began to press for the removal of AFROTC. They were backed in this effort by a student referendum that accompanied the election ballot. The poll reversed the convocation student decision and asked for the removal of AFROTC. They also had competition for this leadership: several days earlier the local SDS chapter issued an ultimatum to President

Summerskill that unless the AFROTC contract was canceled by May 13, SDS would plan "any necessary action to make certain that the AFROTC program does not continue after this semester."

On Friday, May 10, five days before the Senate was due to take its action on AFROTC, SDS held a fateful meeting. Their task was to come to grips with their commitment to force the college to eliminate AFROTC. They held their meetings in the open, as usual, in what pitifully passes as a student union type room, the Gallery Lounge. Fifty or so activists—many the same cadre that a year ago had disrupted Summerskill's inaugural—lounged around on the floor and draped over sofas arguing the merits of various tactics. By fits and starts, accompanied by protracted speeches that elicited quiet attention, a strategy evolved. The following week was to be a low-key affair with the customary outdoor rallies, leaflets, attendance at the Senate meeting, and a peaceful teach-in in the AFROTC building—all with a watchful eye on Summerskill and his AFROTC decision. Then, rather casually, it was agreed to stage a sit-in at the Administration Building the following week, if necessary. There seemed some anxiety about "would they be there alone" and finally a pledge card arrangement was accepted to ensure unity and numbers. The significant decisions were made swiftly; superficial points were debated at length.

Up to this point it had been a typical SDS "participatory democracy" planning session. Five or six Third Worlders sat to one side, bored and laughing. Finally their position was sought. They remained equivocal on the sit-in—they were not sure it was their "thing"—but they did passionately argue for their demands: the renewal of Martinez' contract, 400 special admissions, and nine Third World faculty for the 400 students. Without debate SDS accepted these demands and added them to AFROTC. Still no commitment to sitting in was made. Suspicions between Third Worlders and honkies, dating back to the December riot, colored the discussion. In the end SDS agreed to fight the Third World battle; TWLF agreed to nothing.

The week of May 13 went according to schedule: rallies, polite attendance at the Senate meeting, a controlled teach-in at the "aerospace" building. But on Thursday a new militant note was added: the student legislature agreed to sit in with the SDS if demands were not met. Friday's final sit-in planning session in the Gallery Lounge was all business. The week's effort to "educate the campus to the issues and build a base" had proved partially successful: 200 were in attendance. The example of a three-day sit-in at Stanford University down the peninsula and the bloody disaster of Columbia undoubtedly added to the interest. The critical debate hinged around the issue of whether to begin the sit-in during the midst of the faculty meeting vote or wait to see how the vote concluded. The radical Progressive Labor Party group, wanting no compromise with the faculty and possibly hoping to swing a negative faculty vote to provoke a confrontation, prevailed. The vote went for a sit-in during the faculty meeting. At one point a liberal faculty member tried pointing out the realities to the group and he was sneered to silence.

The high drama point in the meeting occurred when a half-dozen Third World and black students stormed into the meeting and challenged SDS for advertising that the meeting was sponsored by both the SDS and the TWLF. The effort seemed more a power play than a substantive argument. After the TWLF had proved its militancy by urging an immediate sit-in, and had been voted down, the SDS shifted into its work groups. By then the hard core twenty-five or so were all that were left.

Although it was obvious the college was on the brink of a Columbia-type confrontation, neither the administrative nor the faculty leadership saw fit to do any planning over the weekend. Monday was another mild day.

On Tuesday, May 21, the SDS tested its battle plan, with the key question still unanswered: had the educational campaign and the pledge card commitments built a sufficient base to stage a successful confrontation? The rally speeches were true to form as the college's complicity with the military-industrial establishment was excoriated in typical radical rhetoric and the challenge to use the only resort left, bodies on the line, self-determination, was given. On signal an about-face was executed and the large crowd marched with enthusiasm and almost gaiety on the Administration Building. About 200—a considerable victory for the organizers—marched in and began their sit-in in the L-shaped hall outside President Summerskill's office. A crowd of the curious, the uncommitted, the apprehensive, numbering 500 or so, chatted on the outside and waited for the action.

In the meantime the faculty met in the auditorium, listened to passionate speeches pro and con on the critical ROTC issue, heard rumors of the Ad Building takeover, and then voted 282 to 250 to reverse the Senate twenty-five-to-four vote and retain the AFROTC program on the campus. When the news was communicated to the sit-ins they were shocked. Faculty antiwar leaders castigated the students for "having blown it" with their sit-in, being quite convinced that this tactic had shifted at least the fifteen to twenty votes that would have swung the issue the other way. The radical students' response was: If faculty are so juvenile as to vote on the tactic, not the issue, to hell with them! They are as corrupt as we have been saying.

With the faculty vote, the die was cast. The students were compelled to go ahead with their sit-in. This they did, with energy and skill. The first stage consisted of the attempts to plan strategy, delegitimize the authorities, radicalize the students sitting in (many of whom were non-SDS, new converts), and obtain commitment through the proven technique of mass "participatory democracy." The leaders came well equipped for this activity: a microphone in front of the president's office connected to two speakers, one down each side of the L-shaped hall. Any student or faculty member with the conviction and courage to wade through the sprawled-out bodies in the narrow corridors had the opportunity to say his piece, as Hari Dillon, a tough, committed old-time SDS, Third Worlder, presided with finesse and fairness. To obtain a greater input and a deeper sense of involvement, the group decided to break up into smaller groups to spread around and talk tactics.

For all of the group involvement, it was fairly obvious that there was a leadership pattern. When established SDS leaders left the group briefly to talk things over in private, the emergence of one of them at the microphone gave the signal of the next strategy. A hard line soon emerged: chain the doors and evict the administrators. At first the group went along with this, and Dillon headed a group that went to Dean of Students Ferd Reddell to inform him he had three minutes to leave the building or he would be evicted. Before they could act, a messenger told them the group had had second thoughts about this eviction and the chaining of the doors and was in the process of reconsidering. Dillon and his red-arm-banded security police went back to the group.

What prompted the reconsideration is not known, but it could be that the invaders' well-organized intelligence unit had learned that President Summerskill, worried about safety factors associated with the door-chaining, had telephoned the police asking for four or five plainclothes advisers in the building. But it was not four or five indistinguishable plainclothesmen who arrived; five police vans, a segment of the riot-controlling Tactical Squad, and forty motorcyclists came racing into the neighboring Park Merced apartment-house area with sirens screaming and crowds following. This was a critical moment. A police sweep in broad daylight could escalate the confrontation and give the SDS the radicalized converts they desperately desired. Or, if the police view prevailed, a mass bust could nip the takeover in the bud, before allies came sweeping in from Haight-Ashbury, Berkeley, and neighboring colleges, and thus teach the radicals a lesson the hard way.

This view was vigorously promoted by one of the police leaders. "Give us the word and we'll move in and do the job." At one point the troops began to move in, but several faculty persuaded them that was not the decision. Summerskill vacillated. He'd be damned if he did and damned if he didn't. In the casual surroundings of the dean of students office he wandered around seeking ad hoc advice as a vague coterie of administrators and faculty moved in and out of the office.

The arrival of the police also threw the students into a quandary. The converts seemed worried, the leaders seemed uncertain about tactics and the degree of mass commitment. The debate was hard, tough, and rational. Soon Summerskill got the signal he was waiting for—some unofficial observers fed in the word that the militant line had been defeated after the chains were cut and the police arrived, and that things were cooling down. Maybe the problem would solve itself. He took one last sounding of his administrative crew but, instead of advice, received disassociation or contempt. One key official told him directly that he "acted like a guy with his thumb up." Summerskill: "What does that mean?" Obviously these key aides sided with the police and believed if a showdown was inevitable, why not now? Nevertheless, Summerskill decided to send the police away after making an agreement, which later proved to be crucial, that if the students were not out of the building by ten o'clock the police would come back and move them out.

The administrative chaos continued for the next five hours as the students held their ground. Summerskill wandered in and out of offices, up and down the halls, available to anyone with an idea for the conflict resolution. At one point several advisers caught him with pen in hand in the halls ready to sign a basic admissions agreement being presented by Ron Quidachay, a Third World leader. After forty-five minutes of explanation and debate in the admissions office, Summerskill regretfully backed off. This was announced by Quidachay to the massed group and might well have been critical in their decision to stay on. Actually, the administration had announced through Mayor Alioto's office that very day that not only had the college agreed some while ago to admit 400 minority students not normally eligible for admission, but that the mayor himself would spearhead a community program to attempt to secure $750,000 support for these students. But certain details regarding freshman-transfer ratios and the precise number to be allotted from other state colleges had yet to be worked out. Most important, the Third World leaders did not trust, or did not believe it tactically wise to trust, the white man's Establishment.

By now the students were set in their plans to remain in the building since they had achieved no concessions from the administration and the faculty had voted to keep ROTC. The halls swarmed with all kinds of people, all kinds of advice. Even one of the system's trustees was found wandering around unrecognized. Command post decision-making still had no structure and key vice-presidents sat idly by awaiting the moment of action.

The moment came at ten o'clock. Whether by earlier agreement or in response to a final specific request from the president is not certain, but at this time four or five police leaders equipped for battle arrived at the command post and immediately began to organize the sweep with the president. But the president still agonized and turned to person after person for a ray of hope. Several key police advisers, openly critical of Summerskill's vacillation, still believed he would back out of the police sweep at the last minute. But finally Summerskill and his top administrators adjourned to a private room with the police leaders to make final plans.

At this juncture a last-minute effort to avert arrests, bloodshed, and escalation was made by a group of faculty and administrators who had high credibility with many of the student leaders and had worked closely with them in the past for liberal reforms. Five came into the compound, led by Jack Sheedy, the dean of undergraduate studies, to announce that in their judgment the moderates were winning out in the sit-in debate of the last hour, and that fifteen of their faculty colleagues had agreed to stay with the students in the building overnight if the administration would only agree to keep the building open. Although by now a general set had developed among those in the inner circles that a showdown was inevitable—demanded both by the radical students and the political forces—Sheedy was invited to make his plea to the president and his advisers. Five minutes later he came out a defeated man. The plans were too far in motion to be swayed by liberal thinking. It is interesting to note that the other four, Ted Kroeber, Eric Solomon, Henry McGuckin, and Jerry Podell, emerged as strike leaders a year later. Sheedy left the college for an administrative position in the East. If this option that was presented had been given full consideration in preplanning or earlier in the evening it might have prevailed, but this liberal wing of the faculty had little access to the administrative circles.

Out in the hall tension had been building up. A decision had been made to accept twenty-nine volunteers to be arrested, with the remainder leaving the building so as to provide leadership for the future. The mood of the group had changed from political debate to a singing, emotional, revivalist fervor. After hearing the official warning, the majority of the group left. The police then moved in in a quiet, businesslike fashion, booking each student as three official faculty observers looked on, then leading them out to the vans outside. (When some of these students violated the court's probationary penalties by participating in the student strike of the next year and being arrested, quick jail sentences made this token gesture expensive.)

By now a large crowd of over 500 had congregated just beyond the vans in the parking lot and the cordon of helmeted, batoned police. As each arrested student raised the victory "V" sign as he marched to the van, the crowd let out a mighty roar. The crowd was a mixture of the sit-in students, activist colleagues from within the college and the larger community, students of all kinds who had just concluded evening classes, and even local residents, including some people from the Park Merced apartment complex.

The obvious aim of the radicals now that they had forced the police to come on campus was to bait them into some club-swinging. "Pigs off campus!" thundered from the crowd; even the little old ladies joined in. One bulky girl, a veteran of radical causes since the City Hall riots, had her own bullhorn for taunting the police with obscenities, and she kept darting a few steps toward the police to give the impression they were going to be mobbed, then moving back. Some of the young police had frightened looks in their faces. Slowly but surely the crowd took on the characteristics of an ugly lynch mob. All might have gone off quietly if an *Examiner* truck had not dropped its regular pile of papers at the nearby corner. In a flash they were torn up, wadded, and hurled at the police line. One policeman could take it no longer: he charged the girl, she slipped, and the radical students' lawyer, Terrence Hallinan, intervened. In seconds he was clubbed and he staggered with blood pouring from his head wound. The crowd roared. Then the police moved out on them, primarily nudging and shoving with their clubs, occasionally swinging. Ten took their bruises to the hospital. Soon the last van left and the police moved out. The episode was over, but the radicals had their cause. Campus police brutality!

Unknown to any but the upper administrative circles, an unusual communication had been received during the day from the system's vice-chancellor, Raymond Rydell. Dictated word for word to the college's vice-president, and coming from Chancellor Dumke himself, the ultimatum stated that if the college did not move on the students that day, new administrators would come in the next day who would take police action. Such dictation of college policy had virtually no precedent in the system. It truly made the college president a branch manager. On the advice of the chancellor's observer on the campus, Dean Ernest Becker, the order was formally withdrawn.

Momentum picked up at the student rally the following day. Hallinan, bandaged, appeared on campus. The advent of club-swinging, helmeted police had had its effect: more students were being attracted to the lashing rhetoric of the radicals. Now they concentrated on the "police taking our campus away from us." Again they marched across the campus and began another sit-in.

The tenor of the faculty meeting that afternoon was set by the more passionate, articulate supporters of the students. This proved to be a pattern for the future, even when a majority of the faculty opposed the point of view. They opposed it in silence or by avoidance of the meetings. The ethos of any campus at this point, and particularly of San Francisco State, seems to support conciliation, amnesty, no police, minority students, antiwar sentiments, and student power even when the privacy of the voting booth indicates faculty believe otherwise. To openly oppose these sentiments puts one in the same category as Chancellor Dumke, Trustee Dudley Swim, Governor Ronald Reagan, Max Rafferty, Johnson, or Nixon, and few faculty preferred these associations. The next year the AFT was to formalize this line of associations by sending a message to all faculty seen crossing their picket lines that ended, "Reagan, Rafferty, Dumke, Hayakawa, and [scab's name]. Do you really feel comfortable on that team?"

President Summerskill, convinced that the college could not afford another police incident, worked hard to evoke a faculty response that would get him and the college off the hook. In private conversation, faculty member John Bunzel, a political liberal but labeled by students a campus conservative, agreed to lend his proven oratory and moderate reputation to a plea for a new approach, a teach-in, in which faculty would keep buildings open all night and attempt to engage in dialogue with the student militants. The idea received some support, no opposition. Summerskill said he interpreted that as the faculty will, the meeting ended, and the teach-in was on.

Back in the Administration Building the teach-in began. It did not seem very different from the conventional sit-in. Here and there a concerned faculty member or administrator tried dialogue with some of the new converts, but for the most part it was a repeat of the day before: harsh, tough, passionate, adamant, "no bullshit" speeches or harangues from one after another of the radical students.

As had happened the day before, the Third World and BSU representation was minimal: enough for appearances, since the majority of the demands were theirs, but they did not provide the shock troops. Apparently it was not their "thing." Word had gotten to their ranks that serious participation might jeopardize their gains, and they were fully aware that the demands of the Third World had already been achieved with the administration. In essence, this was an SDS, white confrontation for SDS, radical, antiwar purposes. If such confrontations could be used by the TWLF, fine, but they had their eyes on achievable, programmatic goals.

No administrative organization, structure, planning, or goals were apparent. What was to emerge as the dominant administrative group, Vice-President for Academic Affairs Donald Garrity, Vice-President for Administrative and Business Affairs Glenn Smith, and Dean of Students Ferd Reddell—later labeled by the media as the Troika—played it cool and distant; the teach-in was obviously a Summerskill-faculty piece, not theirs. They sat on the sidelines, pessimistic, cynical, detached, and critical, watching the unrealistic faculty, the despised radical students, and their vague leader wallow in self-created troubles.

In the evening a phenomenon developed within faculty ranks that was comparable in many ways—style, motives, background—to the ad hoc faculty group that emerged at the Columbia riot as a mediating, antiadministration, prostudent coalition of faculty. The thrust came from the students. As faculty stood on the outskirts of the student sit-in outside the president's office, wondering what their role in a teach-in under these circumstances might be, but hopeful and concerned, a student strike leader, Helen Meyers, turned to them and said, "Listen, if you are really serious, why don't you quit standing around and go down to Room 162 and come up with some plan to end this." Strangely enough, faculty did begin to wander down the halls to Room 162.

As the faculty assembled it was quite apparent that those who had chosen to leave their homes to see whether they could help through dialogue were almost totally sympathetic to the student cause, against ROTC, and inclined toward almost any compromise that would terminate the disturbance and get the police off the campus. In this atmosphere of almost group-therapy-for-accumulated-liberal-guilt-feelings, once again the few moderates or conservatives kept silent. The only organizational difficulty stemmed from the fact that few faculty knew the facts about the demands and no leadership was apparent. The latter problem was solved when Eric Solomon, one of the few radical faculty who had attempted to play a faculty Establishmentarian role by taking the vice-chairmanship of the Senate, moved into the chairman role. The group of approximately fifty was evenly divided between humanities and social science faculty with a few from education. Virtually no science, business, physical education, creative arts, or administrative representatives showed up. Again, this was to prove the core of strike leadership the following year—though by then it had expanded four- to sixfold.

As students, particularly Third World leaders, began to edge into the jam-packed room after an hour's desultory academic discussion, the group swung in the direction of firm commitment to the student cause and reconciliation. The range of viewpoints represented in the full faculty and in the body politic were not heard. Eventually Solomon seized the initiative and wrote out an ultimatum to the effect that if 400 minority students were not admitted by fall, the undersigned pledged not to meet classes that same semester. Circulation of the pledge obtained about thirty signatures. Since the college had already committed itself to this goal, the gesture was largely gratuitous. Possibly it impressed the suspicious Third Worlders of the faculty's sincerity.

The Martinez issue then came before the group, and Juan was sent for to make his own case. This he did with considerable plausibility. The group accepted him at face value and then addressed themselves to the question of how a slot could be provided for him. Some departmental faculty volunteered to give up a portion of one position from their allocation. The man to be president within a week, Bob Smith, who had just edged into the room after teaching a class, suggested that if the new dispensation was to be student hiring, then the answer was obvious: simply have the students fire a faculty member to make room. This was the first sharp note, but nobody challenged Smith. The Martinez hiring commitment was again pledged with the vow "We will not meet classes unless. . . ." (Martinez was later rehired under duress by Summerskill a few hours before his trip to Ethiopia, then fired by President Hayakawa a year afterwards. The faculty forgot their pledge.)

At this point people got tired and hot, and it was suggested that the group take a break and reassemble over in a humanities classroom. As happens late at night in such circumstances, the faculty group dwindled to a dozen or so concerned members. Students dominated the group. Discussion focused on the third TWLF demand of Third World faculty for the special admissions group of 400, these faculty to be chosen by Third World students. Although this represented a major departure in faculty hiring policy, the group basically acceded to the demand and closed shop well after midnight. As a last gesture they empowered Solomon to pick four faculty and present the group's demands to Summerskill in the morning. The evening had been controlled entirely by students and their faculty supporters; the administrative officers had isolated themselves in Vice-President Garrity's office and sadly discussed the decline of the college.

Although most of the militant students bedded down in the halls and tried to snatch some sleep, many of the fringe students accepted the faculty teach-in offer and engaged a number of faculty in some of the most provocative and rewarding discussions of the year, in or out of classrooms. Unfortunately this spirit could not be transferred to the remainder of the sit-in episodes.

Chapter 4

Capitulation

Thursday, May 23, was the day of Summerskill's capitulation. As students, eyes red-rimmed with fatigue, tried to clean up the residue of their sleep-in, President Summerskill was confronted at an early hour by Eric Solomon and his chosen negotiators: Henry McGuckin, Nancy McDermid, and Gary Hawkins from the speech department, Fred Thalheimer from sociology, and Leonard Wolf, a colleague in English. All were staunch AFT members. For the remainder of the day this group pressed Summerskill with their plan to settle the entire sit-in as the president listened, then moved to a Chicano community group, then went next door to talk with BSU leaders, then came back, and continued his round of negotiations endlessly. Not only did he desire to terminate the confrontation, and without bloodshed or additional police action, but he also had twice delayed a job-hunting trip to Ethiopia that could not be further postponed beyond the next day. At the first stage in these strange negotiations Summerskill called in his major administrative aides, the Troika. When these three saw the format for the decision-making—by now the room was also swarming with SDS and Third World leaders—they washed their hands of the entire affair. Thus, as Summerskill worked out his eventual capitulation, he did so without benefit of any of his major administrators or any representatives of the large group of faculty who were not sympathetic to the student cause.

The mood among SDS leaders such as John Levin, Alex Forman, and Hari Dillon was one of conquerors. At various stages of negotiations with Summerskill they would take to the microphone and brief their troops. By now the troops were playing a secondary role; power had passed to their leaders whom they reinforced by their generally passive presence. At a noon rally Hari Dillon, with the taste of victory on his lips, made a statement to the daily rally that ranks with Mario Savio's "We'll bring this institution to a grinding halt!" for inciting the general public. Said Dillon, "We have the administration on their knees. Now we're going to push them over on their backs." Earlier Levin had said, "The sit-in will go on until our demands are met!"

Communication with faculty had broken down since the faculty meeting on Wednesday and concerned professors knew only what they heard on television and read in the papers. Many were critical of Summerskill's permissiveness. On the other hand, Patrick Gleeson of the English department reported that eleven colleagues had agreed to stay and be arrested along with the students if the police came on campus again, provided fifty faculty would make a similar commitment. He was soon to be put to his test; when he looked around the following Friday evening he was to find not fifty but five.

By dinner time President Summerskill had his signature on a statement guaranteeing Juan Martinez a position in a new Center for Ethnic Studies, agreeing to the already accepted 400 minority admissions, and giving presidential approval to nine Third World faculty hirings for the special admissions program, with Third World students to have a voice and a vote in these hirings. He did state, however, that he supported the faculty referendum decision to keep AFROTC. By the time his administrative colleagues had returned from dinner he had been importuned to change his mind on AFROTC, and he agreed to a new vote of the entire academic community—students, faculty, and staff alike, one man, one vote—to decide the issue once and for all. In making this latter decision he announced that he made it with the full consultation of the chairman and vice-chairman of the Academic Senate, Walcott Beatty and Eric Solomon. Neither Beatty nor Solomon nor the Senate were to profit by this involvement. Summerskill left for the evening with commitments for several conferences the following morning. A cadre of students again took to their sleeping bags in the halls, jubilant in their victory.

The Council of Academic Deans was to register a powerful dissent to Summerskill's agreement, commenting in a formal statement:

> [The pact] is not in the best interests of the educational values to which we adhere. . . . To respond and act under duress, under threat of intimidation, is to set aside responsibility for orderly and effective academic process. It is to set aside the established policies of the academic community and, in effect, the life of the educational institution to which we are professionally committed.

Obviously their noninvolvement, the coercion, and some of the specifics of the agreement stung them. Their statement was sent to Dumke and the faculty.

The scene the next morning—Friday, May 24—was utter confusion. Faculty and administrators milled about trying to get the facts on Summerskill's agreements, incredulous and furious when they did. Student leaders tried to get to Summerskill to pin down the details of the referendum and to gain yet one more concession: college leadership before the district attorney's office to guarantee no prosecution of those arrested Tuesday night. But the youthful president was not to be found. Unbeknownst to any but his few close assistants, he was down at the airport ready to embark to Ethiopia. When reporters trapped him just before plane time he said he felt he had helped solve the college's problems and thus reduced tensions sufficiently to permit him to meet his personal obligations.

Soon the confusion over whether Summerskill had been fired, had resigned, or had only temporarily been replaced by an acting president hit the headlines. Chancellor Dumke's office announced that Summerskill's telephoned offer to resign had been accepted effective immediately, that Vice-President Garrity was temporarily in charge, and that a new president would be chosen shortly. At the San Francisco Airport, Summerskill smilingly jested with a reporter, "Well, should I resign or let them fire me?" Six hours later from Kennedy Airport in New York the embattled president was to phone reporters and deny that he had resigned, stating categorically that he had only agreed to a temporary replacement.

The fact of the matter was that his stewardship was terminated. The evening before, the Troika, after having seen another chaotic day on the campus, had placed a call to Dumke's personal residence and told him at length and in no uncertain terms that Summerskill needed to be replaced. After hearing them out, Dumke obtained key trustee approval and set the wheels in motion. He could hardly afford to continue any impression of concessions or a soft line. On the following day, the prestigious and relatively conservative statewide Academic Senate, representing all eighteen colleges in the system, was finally to act after six years of doubting Dumke's competence and a six-month investigation of his stewardship, and vote thirty-five to five no confidence in him and thirty to ten with two abstentions to ask for his resignation.

In the whirling confusion of Friday, as the ex-president slipped across the sky, the Troika and the Council of Academic Deans (CAD) moved into the leadership vacuum, supported powerfully by a group seldom used in the past, the fifty or more department heads. To legitimize their leadership, they presented for approval from the group their scorching statement of the day before criticizing the process of the concessions. It was approved by a vote of forty-two yes, five no, five abstentions. Vice-President Garrity then stated that in CAD's view the college would need to go along with Summerskill's hiring of Martinez, for all the irregularity of the procedure and doubts about the substance of the act, and that Summerskill's signed statement agreeing to 400 special admittees from the ethnic minorities and nine minority faculty to work with them merely confirmed previous college policy. The issue of support of Summerskill's AFROTC revote agreement went before the group and it almost unanimously stated that only the faculty could reverse its 282 to 250 decision to allow AFROTC to continue. In effect, the elders in solemn conclave supported the hierarchical structure. A liberal administrator at the meeting described the atmosphere as "frivolous."

As the new power structure moved into place, student leaders became disturbed. They knew they could handle Summerskill but the new crew looked like hard-liners. Events of the day and evening were to confirm this appearance. The basic issue that the new administration leadership had to face was, should the campus buildings, including the Administration Building, continue open in the fast-disappearing spirit of the teach-in, or should the buildings be closed that night? Within the administrative group there was agreement that no good purpose would be served by keeping the buildings open all night and all weekend with militant students bedded down all over. The Executive Committee of the Senate was consulted and gave varying opinions. Any unity in this group had been severely breached by the unilateral actions of Chairman Beatty and Vice-Chairman Solomon in apparently supporting Summerskill's AFROTC revote decision. The group formally renounced this act, three to two.

Late in the evening, just moments before the decision to call the police was scheduled, a final plea was made to the administration by the "pledged" faculty that one last attempt be made to persuade the sit-in leadership that the college would stick by the Third World agreements and that in return they should agree to pull out peacefully. It failed. Just before midnight Dean Reddell made the customary clearance announcement; all but the twenty-seven who had agreed to token arrest left; and the bust was made.

Five faculty members, feeling that the teach-in agreement was being breached and opposed to police on campus, also submitted themselves to voluntary arrest: the poet James Shevill, Anatole Anton of philosophy, Patrick Gleeson and Edward Van Aelstyn from English, and Sandra Schickele of the social sciences. For the most part the students arrested, like those of the first arrest, were either rank-and-file SDS members or new converts. But again a sprinkling of leaders joined them for morale's sake. Previously, it had been Gene Marchi, Margaret Leahy, and Hari Dillon; this time Bruce Hartford, Barry Biderman, Greg deGiere, Joy Magezis, Jan Solganick, and Dick Tewes were carted off.

The arrests were peaceful, as had been previously agreed to by the students' vote. As the police sought the student names for the booking the occasion almost took on the appearance of a social gathering: "My name is Captain O'Hara. What is yours?" All was polite and businesslike. Prior to the arrests the song "Oh, Freedom" echoed up the halls; outside, the chant "Pigs off campus!" again rang out. But there were no incidents. A furious John Levin was to announce an additional demand: "We have another demand, and that's the resignation of those pigs in drag who are passing for administrators."

There was to be no rest for the revolutionaries, the college leadership, or the concerned faculty. All met and planned over the weekend. Antagonized by what they felt to be administrative betrayal, a core group from the Wednesday faculty meeting stayed on until past four in the morning plotting policy and tactics and raising bail for their arrested colleagues. For the major share of Saturday and Sunday they also met, now augmented to about a group of forty by previously uncommitted but greatly concerned fellow faculty. Out of their deliberations came more pledges: (1) to stage their own teach-in in the Humanities Building (whether to be arrested or to retreat to another classroom if police came was left to the discretion of the individual faculty member); (2) to seek employment elsewhere if a system of shared student-faculty responsibility and authority for all phases of college governance were not effected by December 1, 1968, at the latest. Although a few departments began to consider such forms of governance, no significant action was achieved by that date. Like most such pledges "to seek employment elsewhere if . . . ," or "to strike unless . . . ," they were soon forgotten by their signators. Stating the previous votes on AFROTC were indecisive, the volunteer faculty committee resolved to support their former president's one-man–one-vote, student-faculty referendum idea.

From the statements made by the militant students in their open meetings over the weekend, the possibility of violence could not be discounted. Although they had realized their Third World goals (which, except for the Martinez case, had never been in question even before the sit-in), there were still the issues of ROTC, which had precipitated the entire confrontation, and the added demand for amnesty for their virtuous rebellion. Since the new administration would certainly bring the police on campus in the event of any more all-night sit-ins, and arrests were becoming painful, the strategy that emerged was patterned after Berkeley's recent mill-in technique. The intent of this tactic was to disrupt administrative operations by having groups of students moving in and out of offices under the guise of official business. It has the advantage of mobility, being in the nature of guerrilla warfare. The action could be mounted against any offices, and the history department of Fitzgerald and Martinez fame was targeted for special attention.

When the administrators met with the Executive Committee of the Senate on Sunday, attention focused on three priorities: the need to plan strategy for the Monday mill-in; the need to create some "constructive alternatives" to shift the attention away from the impassed demands toward more *fundamental* changes; and the need to communicate the college philosophy and position on the issues more clearly to students, faculty, and the total public.

The subgroup working on plans to combat the Monday mill-in came to the conclusion that the sit-in had been encouraged, and the need for outside police intervention had been mandated, by college inaction, during the entire school year, in detecting and punishing student violation of regulations. It therefore developed a plan for protecting offices against the mill-in and securing evidence that could lead to prosecution within the campus community should disturbances occur. When presented to the total group, the plan was not supported. Once again the college indicated no taste for internal disciplinary action.

Among the "constructive alternatives" agreed upon by the consortium were: a constitutional convention of students and faculty to realign the college power structure in a more democratic and effective manner; the creation of a division of innovative programs that would include a center for ethnic studies and the agreed upon department of black studies; commitment to the program of securing a million dollars to provide higher education for the disadvantaged; priority attention for the new Student Union Building; and an extension program that would eventually take the college resources to the center of the community's urban problems.

The philosophy piece accentuated such tried and true ideas as open negotiation, total consultation, respect for others, attention to minority points of view, and change through appropriate channels. It was not such as would encourage radicals.

From the militant student point of view the swirling, harassing mill-in on Monday was highly successful as a tactic but it produced a strategic impasse. Secretaries were insulted if not educated, offices were commandeered, administrative work came to a standstill, and a large phone bill developed as a result of calls to Columbia, Chicago, Cuba, and elsewhere. But where do you go from here? At their rally they were goaded on by a report that the Legislature was going to "come down on them" immediately with a new repressive bill. Rumors such as this, which were treated as fact if they had the possibility of encouraging converts, became a standard technique of the bullhorned exhorters. At one time it was stated as fact that the college was only going to admit ninety-two minority students, not the 400 that they "lied about."

At about the time that the humanities faculty were attempting to provide the conceptual leadership, the confrontation swept over all. In the Administration Building a new tactic had developed: the administrative leaders had been cornered in the dean of students office and for three hours the mob chanted, pounded on the walls, chinked a rat-a-tat-tat on the windows with coins, and finally voted to hold the administrators as hostages. A messenger was sent by the administrators to the concerned faculty in the Humanities Building that they had ten minutes to do "their thing" with the students or else the police would be called. Only three responded. Others stood outside with the students. One student sat at the door with his ear peeled for information, a dog at his feet and a flute at his lips.

An administrator suggested negotiation. In trouped six radical leaders. They laid it on the line, eliminate AFROTC and grant amnesty, or else! Since there was no inclination along these lines, a student said, "What is there to negotiate?" and all left. Little communication transpired between the parties. Within the administrative group, now augmented by deans and the Senate Executive Committee, leadership was a scarce quality. The pounding and chanting were taken up again. Three AFT members came in and suggested as a compromise that AFROTC be eliminated next year pending a study. There were no takers. Professor Bierman left disturbed, and then attempted to persuade Mayor Alioto to intervene with mediation. The mayor did, but he was too late.

Whenever they attempted to leave the room, the vice-presidents were surrounded by chanting students who made any departure impossible. The issue could no longer be avoided: should the police be called? In a decidedly haphazard fashion the police were called. Although it was assumed that they could be on the scene in fifteen minutes, an hour went by and still no police. By now the walls were shaking, a table was shoved against the door, a hole appeared in the outer wall, and a campus plainclothesman joined the group in case they needed protection. The group inside was getting tense and irritable, and to relieve the tension they were persuaded to break into a chorus of "We Shall Overcome." According to several students, this almost blew their minds: administrators singing!

Two intrusions also served to put the event in perspective. Poet Mark Linenthal, acting like the messenger from Garcia, said he had vital information and demanded to come in. His news: "The School of Humanities has just voted not to allow its majors to use

ROTC credits to graduate!" The proposed action was actually illegal. Later an expert in conflict resolution, Jerome Podell, shoved a note under the door: "Why don't you just leave and eliminate their target?"

The arrival of the police was anticlimactic. Students fled, finally to regroup on the library steps almost like a senior class posing for graduation pictures. For three hours they hassled, Where do we go from here? It was obvious a new escalation was needed, but examinations were coming up in a day, the administration seemed firm, busts were not pleasant. Yet converts swelled the movement to over 400; students had certainly been radicalized at least for the moment. After rejecting a move to throw ROTC out of their building the group vaguely agreed to surround the Administration Building in the morning and chain the doors so nobody could enter. A move to proclaim victory and quit was barely defeated.

While the college leadership consortium adjourned to a neighboring apartment to eat, drink, relax, and plan the morrow's tactics, the student leadership coalition went off to Ecumenical House across the street to assess their plight. The administrators agreed to take a tough internal stand and to issue an emergency proclamation:

> The administration, in consultation with the Executive Committee of the Academic Senate and the Council of Academic Deans, declares that a state of emergency exists on the campus of San Francisco State College. Students who disrupt the operation of the college are subject to immediate disciplinary action. This action is necessary to enable students to complete their academic programs for this semester and for the safety and dignity of students, faculty, and staff.

What it meant or how it might be enforced was never clarified. Nevertheless its mere promulgation was to be a critical act in the resolution of the conflict the following day.

The radical students had an equally tough decision: escalate with the risk of burning new converts, or preserve the movement for next year by proclaiming victory and leaving the field of battle? The next escalation step most of the group believed obvious was to move on the Registrar's Office and destroy college records. After fierce debate that almost was bathed by the rising sun, the group decided to avoid the escalation, plan for another sit-in, and see whether some last-minute negotiation could not be accomplished.

The following morning, Tuesday, May 28, the emergency proclamation was pasted all over and local security officers were prominent throughout the Administration Building. Three sit-in leaders, John Levin, Alex Forman, and Pat Salazar, sought out Vice-President Glenn Smith and said they wanted to talk. Their ingratiating, conciliatory stance was difficult to recognize. The Troika agreed to talk. Around the conference table it came out that the students realized the ROTC issue was down the drain, but their troops wanted blood. If the administration would agree to intercede with the D.A. in an amnesty plea, they could call their troops off. They were told the college would react to their proposal within an hour.

When the leadership consortium met, some of the Senate Executive Committee spoke passionately for not punishing, but otherwise there was agreement on no amnesty. The next issue to be faced was internal discipline for Monday's episodes. Here, it was felt, was the only bargaining point, and a split decision went in favor of taking no college action if the sit-in ended that day. (This was hardly a concession, given the fact that no enforcement machinery existed or had been used all year.)

Once again the college went through the routine of a rally, then a sit-in. Once in the halls the initial bitterness over no amnesty disappeared and again the moment of truth had to be faced. An additional factor intruded. Already the police were forming over in Park Merced. Did this and the emergency proclamation mean they could sweep in and bust the entire group without a warning? Many feared this was the intent. Since the 200-strong group was not in a mood to be trapped and arrested, they decided to adjourn to the outside steps to continue their debate. After all, they could always come back in. They never did.

On the steps a mood of weariness, reality, and celebration set in. After a spate of military rhetoric they sang songs and decided to call it quits. Next fall would be another story!—as it certainly was. A picnic was planned in Golden Gate Park. In one final defiant act a wall poster was pinned to the Administration Building to be signed by all members willing to disrupt graduation should the college take vindictive action against any student. About 150 members signed their names, then drifted off to celebrate and plan for the future. The eight day sit-in was over.

As the students were signing the wall poster, the Senate met to decide on its leadership for next year. For once the Senate was almost totally divided between liberals and conservatives, the Faculty Renaissance group having triumphed in internal elections. They also came prepared with a slate of officers to be elected and seventeen of the necessary twenty-one votes but in this they failed. Already the backlash was being felt in faculty circles.

That evening, at the Hilton Inn near San Francisco International Airport, the final curtain was rung down. There the trustees met to choose a replacement for John Summerskill. The faculty committee had recommended three names for acting president, including that of Professor Robert Smith. Smith, a former dean of the School of Education and dean of instruction and now professor in the School of Education, had been one of the faculty's candidates for two all-college administrative positions since leaving his deanship, and each time his candidacy had been opposed by Chancellor Glenn S. Dumke. Now he was being nominated a third time, under circumstances in which the chancellor and the trustees felt great pressure to develop some sense of order on the troubled campus and to act as quickly as their collective wisdom could fasten on a solution.

PART TWO

ROBERT SMITH

Chapter 5

An Unsolicited Telephone Call

Thursday, May 23, was a rough day on the campus as students and some faculty kept up the pressure while the ad hoc committee worked President Summerskill over. At my home, the kids were doing their homework and Gloria and I were having a five-thirty cocktail before dinner when Mansel Keene, Chancellor Dumke's assistant for personnel, called. "Bob, we're putting Summerskill out to pasture. We want you to come down to meet with the chancellor tomorrow morning."[1]

[1] This chapter is a first-person account of the events by Robert Smith.

"But why should I come down?" I asked, thinking perhaps they wanted my sage advice on how to shake the campus out of its crisis.

Keene made it clear that they wanted me to become acting president immediately so they could announce my appointment concurrently with the release of Summerskill on Friday. I assured him I had no interest in an acting presidency under the existing conditions—none whatever. He seemed dismayed and pressed me hard. My name had been submitted to the chancellor by the faculty committee consulting on the selection of a president as one of three possibilities for acting president. I had agreed to the committee's action earlier in the spring on four grounds: the committee needed three names; I was convinced there was little danger of my selection by Chancellor Dumke in the light of a history of interpersonal tension between us; it is good campus strategy to be represented in such "confidential" lists occasionally; and by the time the decision was made I might possibly have been interested in the position.

I agreed to call Keene back by eight o'clock to say whether I would come at all for a Friday interview. Gloria was clearly opposed even to considering the possibility. We had dinner and watched a television special we had planned to see. Just as we began talking seriously about the college situation, Keene called again—forty-five minutes early. It had occurred to me that no one—certainly not I—should enter that crisis as an acting president. Why should not the trustees appoint a president with full status and presidential powers—if only for a limited time?

I told Keene I was not at all receptive to an acting role, and should not waste the chancellor's time in a Friday conference, but he was adamant, saying that the chancellor and trustees had kept his phone ringing. He had to deliver a body on Friday. I proposed the alternate possibility of a term appointment as *president*. He doubted its feasibility but we agreed to meet in Los Angeles, Friday, May 24, to talk further with the clearly stated understanding that I would make no decision on the spot. Keene said he had talked Dumke into supporting me as the only alternative. This, too, sounded precarious. Gloria was voicing dismay in the background.

After the call, I promised Gloria I would make no decision without talking to her further on my return. She warned me that, given the disaffection between Dumke and me, I could walk into a lousy trap; that my research plans for 1968 and 1969 would go down the drain and extensive summer plans must be set aside. I argued that to talk with them was the least to be done; I reminded her that only two nights before she had said she felt ashamed for the first time in twenty years to be identified with San Francisco State College, and that for the first time in many years I had seriously considered an offer for another position. We were becoming convinced that if the college could not be stabilized without being destroyed, we would probably be forced to leave. She reminded me that we had agreed not to seek a college presidency five years before, when I had resigned as dean of the school of education to return to teaching.

Later, I called Dean Frank Sheehan, chairman of the San Francisco State College Presidential Consultation Committee, to inform him of the situation. He knew of Keene's move and supported it.

Friday was another day of campus disorder. President Summerskill flew off to an obligation in Ethiopia amidst a flurry of rumors. In Los Angeles, in a group interview with much of Dumke's key staff, I stuck with my refusal to consider an acting role. Ted Merriam, chairman of the Board of Trustees, telephoned, also pressing me to accept. All were insistent that I decide that day. I explained that I could not decide before Sunday, until after I had talked to my wife, the Consultation Committee, and the administrative staff that had taken over on Summerskill's departure.

Between discussions on Friday Dumke had met with the statewide Academic Senate and was in the process of being censured by them. By about two-thirty that afternoon it became clear to the chancellor and his staff that I would not agree to the acting role that day. A press release replacing Summerskill and appointing me had already been prepared, despite my insistence the evening before that, as a condition of the interview, no decision would be made that day. The press release therefore had to be revised, naming Vice-President Don Garrity as senior campus administrator in the interim.

Further, my insistence on a full appointment required a trustees' meeting in the event I decided to go that route by Sunday afternoon. I had insisted on a three-year term, if anything, explaining that the campus scene was well out of control, the faculty increasingly polarized, and several programs requiring development without delay were at stake. Three years would provide time to work things through, and to determine what kind of permanent appointment was appropriate. My intent to move out in any event at the end of that time was made clear, if such an appointment came to pass at all. Further, if such a term were not possible, either of the other two candidates on the list for acting president would have my support.

My seeming stubbornness grew out of my unwillingness to fill an interim role, thus encouraging the campus and trustees again to sweat out a period between presidents, as they had between Dumke and Dodd and again between Dodd and Summerskill; this would be the third such interim in some seven years. Further, after having chaired both faculty consultation committees that recommended first Dodd and then Summerskill, it was clear to me that San Francisco State was rapidly becoming a graveyard for presidents caught between the aggressive drives on campus and a centralized chancellor-trustee combination. Any edge one could get would be little enough. Both Presidents Dodd and Summerskill had been chewed up rather quickly by failure to receive steady support from the chancellor and the trustees, even though the trustees had made the final choice in both presidential selections.

Friday ended on campus with police clearing the Administration Building and arresting some twenty-seven additional people, including five faculty. Between Friday and Sunday, I met with the so-called Troika—Garrity, Smith, and Reddell—talked again with Sheehan, and talked to Gloria and our children, Heidi and Kevin.

Garrity and his colleagues informed me they had taken the initiative in urging my immediate appointment. They were clearly exhausted and shaken by the demonstrations and the disorder leading up to Summerskill's abrupt departure. They were distressed by my delaying the transition, knowing that administrative responsibility for the disorderly days ahead must fall to them. I made it clear that any appointment was far from certain, and that if appointed I would spend no time second-guessing their decisions, or Summerskill's, as long as the decisions were legal and reasonably ethical, and that they had to feel free to operate on their best judgment in the face of major campus disorders. The pledge was voluntarily given, though I suspected at the time that the legacy of decisions might well be heavy to carry.

The committee's charge from the Senate called for nominating persons for an acting role who were not candidates for president, which the committee had done in the spring, as stated earlier. The committee was in the process of searching for candidates for the permanent appointment. I explained to Committee Chairman Sheehan and to Leo McClatchy, chairman of the Academic Senate, my reasons for rejecting an acting role given the campus situation, and offered to take myself out of the picture, if the proposal was unacceptable to either the committee or the Senate. They decided to try to reconcile the procedural issues, given the crisis situation.

With the Sunday afternoon response to the chancellor giving me only a day and a half to come to a decision, I was in trouble with Gloria and my daughter. My son was in favor of my accepting the presidency, if offered; but he was only nine years old. Gloria still objected to my revamping so suddenly our extensive summer plans and my projected research (on student dissent and institutional response at San Francisco State). She also reiterated her concern that I was walking into a no-man's land of student-faculty-administrative struggle on campus and campus struggle with the trustees and chancellor.

I felt less pessimistic, increasingly of a mind to try the job, if offered essentially on my terms. We compromised by my agreeing to a physical exam, which was arranged immediately, and a joint discussion with a psychiatrist whom we both had known well for many years, and whom we both held in high regard. Both doctors knew something of the college situation and both knew our family. Neither found any major reason for my turning down the job, if offered on a satisfactory basis.

Gloria remained deeply skeptical, but did not wish to block my working the thing through. She was partially reconciled to what she viewed as a last desperate effort in my middle age to make the college my mistress for once and for all. On Sunday, telephone calls from the chancellor's personnel director, Mansel Keene, again came early. It was a counter-proposal that I accept an "interim" appointment rather than an "acting" role or a full appointment as president. This, the trustees had agreed, would clear the need for a personnel committee meeting and a full meeting of the board. The board's next scheduled meeting was four weeks away. An "interim" rather than an "acting" role was, however, merely a shift in terminology and I felt some irritation that a minor shift in labels was proposed as though such a shift would mollify me. I refused the offer, again making it clear that if they chose to appoint another of the recommended list of three acting candidates, he would have my support.

A special meeting of the trustees' personnel committee was called for the following Tuesday, May 28, at the Hilton Inn, located at the San Francisco airport. Sunday, the vice-president, deans, and the Senate Executive Committee had met at length and prepared a succinct recap of the events leading to President Summerskill's leaving, a review of college decisions related to the student demands, and proposals for future organization to accommodate some student-faculty concerns previously under contention. It became the basis for a campus report to the personnel committee on Tuesday.

During the lunch hour on Monday, May 27, Urban Whitaker urged me to meet with him and other members of the consultation committtee to discuss an emergency issue. Sheehan, the chairman, was off campus, I was told, but with the trustee meeting only one day away, time was pressing. Somewhat mystified, I agreed. The meeting turned out to be a short, clandestine one on the administrative parking lot—in a Volkswagen camper with the curtains drawn. Only two members of the committee were there: Whitaker and Hayakawa. At the time, Whitaker was one of the faculty members serving on the committee; he was later appointed dean of undergraduate studies by Hayakawa. They were visibly upset; so was I, but for different reasons. They were, in effect, charging me with overriding the Senate's charge to the committee to propose me as an acting president while the committee would be seeking a permanent president. My insistence on a three-year appointment with full presidental powers was the sour note. I insisted they make clear whether they were speaking for the full committee, since I had cleared every step with the chairman, and I had assumed that *he* was speaking for the committee; with the trustee meeting called for the next day, it was rather late for such serious objections. They stated that they were speaking for themselves. Their distress, they said, arose from the fact that a black candidate was under consideration for the permanent position. My response was that it was the committee that had approached me initially, and if a qualified black were available and accepted the appointment he could count on my full support. The tone of the session was disquieting.

My four to seven o'clock Monday class in higher education had been delayed by an impromptu visit from George Hart, San Francisco trustee, who "just wanted to talk to me" before the Tuesday meeting. It was my guess that he was sent by one faction of the board, perhaps that dominated by Reagan. We had not met previously. His questions were direct. I was frank, closed the discussion as quickly as possible, and joined my class a half-hour late.

Monday, May 27, ended for the staff with an evening meeting lasting until midnight at an apartment near the campus. It included the vice-president, the deans, the Executive Committee of the Academic Senate, and Ernest Becker of the chancellor's staff. It paralleled a continuing rally of demonstrators on the library steps, reports of which came intermittently to the meeting. I had been asked to attend the meeting and decided not to be coy. It concluded with the Emergency Proclamation described in the preceding chapter.

On Tuesday, the students again surged into the Administration Building, but vacated it after arguing in the halls about the meaning of the emergency notice. They feared an unannounced bust, which of course would ensnare their leaders rather than their patsies and their interns in radical action for whom an arrest was a necessary rite of passage. It was apparent that the zest was gone from those engaged in disorder.

It was clear that if we were to be sharp for the trustee meeting, we needed some rest and a change of shirts. We had worked until midnight the evening before and had arrived on campus at 7:30 A.M. to be more than busy without a break. We urged Don Garrity to take off for home about mid-afternoon to prepare his account of campus events, working from the detailed document prepared on Sunday; but he was called to the Administration Building to handle an emergency just as he was about to leave the campus. A few minutes later, a call came from the Chancellor's Office. Vice-Chancellor Ray Rydell was on the line to pass on instructions from Chancellor Dumke, who had left for the airport and the five o'clock meeting. Garrity was to stay on campus until four-thirty because of the disorder and then come directly to the meeting. We were astonished. Efforts to explain the impact of two sixteen-hour days in a row coupled with an upcoming long evening meeting of stress were to no avail. Assurances that we had other capable administrators to take charge for two hours had no impact. I was told Dumke could not be reached and Rydell, therefore, had to consider the instructions an order. The impression was left that as the man about to be appointed president I was to transmit the order. I told Rydell that I would give the message to Garrity accurately to respond to as he chose since he was in charge of the campus. The result was that both Garrity and I made the trustee meeting without a moment to spare and he was first on the agenda with an extended report on campus events.

Earlier in the week I had received telephone calls from an old friend and colleague then working in New York saying he was supporting me strongly and was in contact with one of Governor Reagan's advisers whom he knew well, assuring the governor I had the best chance of anyone to pull the college together. He admitted meeting some skepticism but was doing what he could. I cautioned him not to oversell me as a "hard-liner," which seemed to be one objective of the governor, and not to stick his neck out too far because of the precariousness of the tough scene facing us all even if I should be appointed. It was apparent that the governor intended to hold veto power over the appointment.

Given my own firm views about responsibility having to be balanced with the necessary independence for decision-making, the clues were all there that the job would be rough: students habituated by now to direct action; faculty groups willing to bypass their own government structure; a chancellor who felt free to order his chief campus officer by telephone from the other end of the state to stay on campus during a given hour; and a governor-trustee combine in which the governor apparently controlled the board in issues important to him. It did seem a challenge worth one's best efforts. A few friends told me gently that I was out of my mind to get involved.

The Hilton Inn was crowded with news media people, some students, a few faculty friends, and a dozen or so of the chancellor's key staff. Most trustees were present, though it was officially only a committee meeting. Those in attendance included then Lieutenant Governor Robert Finch and Alex Sherriffs, Governor Reagan's adviser for higher education. We were whisked into the dining room, introductions were made, and Don Garrity was on. More than an hour later, after all others had completed drinks, dinner, and dessert, Garrity was still answering questions effectively despite fatigue that made his face ashen. Ernie Becker, a member of the chancellor's staff, Glenn Smith, and I interrupted from time to time to give him a breather. (Returned prisoners of war and spacemen are also frequently interrogated without cease before they are permitted to rejoin their families.)

Despite the long hours of severe stress of the preceding five days, Garrity was factual, thorough, and coherent, if a bit tedious, about the progress of the disorders and the administration's efforts to cope with them. The trustees seemed disturbed, nettled, and embarrassed for the college but appreciative of the firm efforts of the administration to maintain control of the campus. They looked better than I expected. I could not blame them for the chancellor's panic, which pushed Garrity too close to his margin of endurance. After Garrity's report, I was excused while Sheehan reported to the trustees, who discussed my proposed appointment for almost two hours. The press and the public were excluded from attendance presumably because it was a "personnel" session, permitted under provisions of the Brown Act requiring open meetings of public policy-making bodies. In fact, however, the personnel portion of the meeting did not begin until approximately two hours after the meeting convened. Media representatives became increasingly restive in succeeding months as the trustees turned to more frequent and longer executive sessions.

In the meantime, I was in a room at the end of a long corridor away from the street, apparently unknown to the newsmen, kept company by several of the chancellor's staff not involved in the executive session. Two old friends from the faculty also sat in. I felt a bit like a bucking horse in the chute, being managed by handlers while waiting my turn in the arena. My attempts to review the dinner discussion and plan my own participation in the upcoming formal interview were futile. One after another, the chancellor's staff members slid up to me to reassure me and to give helpful advice. After the third such episode a pattern emerged that was repeated until, in frustration, I excused myself, curled up in a corner, and went to sleep. The pattern was about like this: "I want you to know, Bob, that if you are appointed you can depend on me for all possible help. It's a tough job and you can do it, if it can be done. You should know that not everyone on the chancellor's staff can be depended upon. But I am ready to go out of my way to help—so be sure to call on me." One man observed that his counterpart on our campus was a "nice guy" but did not seem too competent. In tight situations, he would be glad to come down to the campus and work directly with me during any future crisis. I suspected he had his evaluations reversed.

I thanked him, saying my first effort would be to work with the campus staff, assuring them of my support and assuming they were competent until they proved themselves otherwise. The exchanges seemed self-serving and showed a willingness to cut up their colleagues before an outsider—with the victim not present. In succeeding months, these symptoms of mistrust and lack of mutual support were etched more deeply with each subsequent exchange with the chancellor's staff members. Repeated examples of delayed and poorly coordinated responses at the system level raised serious questions of adequate staff work and staff isolation. Our own campus was perhaps no better. In crisis situations, communication and needed service became even more difficult to achieve and added to the testiness of the trustees.

The long discussion of my nomination suggested problems. Eventually, I was called again before the trustees. They were considerate and probed my approach to campus disruptions. It was clear that some yearned for a hard-liner. I made it clear that an administrative approach should be rooted in a social philosophy of education. Mine was not that of a mailed fist. Efforts would be made to control lawbreakers and those bent on disruption of campus activities and violence. We would depend on due process, live within the law, and, if forced to the wall, we would call off-campus police to protect life and property. Some trustees pressed for specific commitments on individual personnel issues, which I declined to make in that setting. I argued that we needed to mobilize support for stalled programs and to push ahead on educational reforms if we were to ease campus frustrations. We would also move to contain persistent disrupters and provocateurs dealing in coercion and violence. Although I was aware that they were worried about my disavowing a hard line, it seemed that the lengthy discussion had given them ample opportunity to probe my administrative approach and my notions about the directions the college should move in. I was satisfied with my part of the interview.

Back to the bullpen while the trustees deliberated further. As the hour passed at which I had told Gloria I should be home and there was no sign of a decision, it was clear things were not coming easy for the trustees. After midnight, I informed the chancellor's staff I was going home. If they still wanted me, they could call in the morning. A quick flurry of action brought word that a press release was all but completed and I was called in to review it. We argued over one final paragraph, a ringing denunciation of faculty and students for their behavior. In my view, it was inappropriate to such an announcement. We struck a compromise by dropping the paragraph. That was about my last victory with the chancellor and trustees. My last stand had to be a request for a meeting of the full board to act formally on my appointment. Fortunately, a friendly trustee raised the issue and it was decided quickly. Earlier in the week, the chancellor had proposed that formal action by the trustees could be deferred until the next regular meeting of the board the last week in June. I made it clear that with further potential for campus disorder and graduation less than two weeks away, I had no intention of assuming the president's responsibilities unless formally and legally appointed. One further campus conflict within the month might shift a nervous board to a negative vote, leaving all parties even worse off. A special meeting of the trustees was called for two days later, Memorial Day, in Los Angeles.

We were suddenly before some forty media people. I had been informed much earlier that the chairman of the board and the chancellor would handle the press conference. The brief statement was read by the chairman of the board noting that the personnel committee was recommending me for a three-year appointment as president. Chancellor Dumke introduced me and "gave me to the media people," who had sweated out the meeting from five o'clock until half past twelve. I tried to give them back to him after a brief comment. It did not work. Dumke said, "No. It's Smith's evening." What a spot in which to end a second eighteen-hour day! The media people worked me over for almost half an hour, but were good to me. The common tactic of some reporters of probing for possible areas of confusion or conflict showed through. For example, I was asked about the history of conflict between the chancellor and me, and whether trustees were closely in touch with today's students. I refused to bite on the first. On the second, I said, "No, they are not," intending to add that the same could be said of many campus administrators and faculty. A quick interruption cut the qualification off and the moment passed—with some uncomfortable stirring of trustees.

A half-hour later, I ended the news conference and began to work my way to the door. Two liberal trustees intercepted me and chose to inform me they had voted against me because they hoped a black candidate would be offered. Pete Lee, the only black trustee on the board, and William Norris were direct and aggressive about their feelings (nothing personal, I was to understand). I had merely accepted birth in the wrong race. I tried to remind them gently that I had not campaigned for the job, the problem of choice was with the college committee and the trustees, and there was still time to reconsider if a qualified black were available, and further that whoever was president would badly need full board support. (Both were absent at the September meeting when the Student Union was voted down and the trustees voted eight to five to "request" Murray's transfer to "duties other than instruction.") I felt a genuine tinge of regret if I had overrun a potential black president—but my feeling was moderated by the strong hunch that such a choice, regardless of his talents, would quickly bite the dust at San Francisco State at that time. The conversation with Norris and Lee was so much like my conversation the day before with Hayakawa and Whitaker that I wondered whether they had been in communication.

On Wednesday, the campus was marked with knots of student demonstrators and small groups of faculty speculating on the next developments. Student members of the Third World Liberation Front loitered outside the president's office trying to catch me on the move. They wanted badly to talk with me. We agreed to a short meeting at a later time in a vice-president's office with one staff member present. A SDS leader appeared to be eavesdropping. When we gathered, several SDS students were pressing to be included. The TWLF students seemed embarrassed and reluctant. I reminded them that it was their meeting and they should include or exclude SDS as they chose. They caved in and included John Levin, a prime strategist in radical activities on the campus, and an associate.

The issues were: Would I honor agreements made by John Summerskill and Don Garrity during the previous week? Would I agree to the proposed campus referendum on AFROTC? And a new demand for my help in securing amnesty from the courts. My responses: Previous agreements that were legal would be honored. The referendum would not be authorized in accordance with Garrity's earlier decision. I would not support any general stance for amnesty. Arrests and charges for disruptive action, I argued, are costs participants in radical action should learn to bear.

The SDS tried to convince the TWLF spokesman that disruption of graduation should be the consequence of my decision. I reminded them that there were 4,500 students to be graduated. We had little time to complete plans and we did not want to spend a lot of time and resources preparing for disruptions if they were not to be attempted. If the threat were an idle one, it would build a "reverse credibility gap." The brief meeting ended on a grumbling note.

The following day's trustee meeting named me president as expected. When I was called in to be informed of the action there was an edge of banter about cigars all around. I stated that I had one pack of black Italian Toscanellis and it would probably go around. As the trustees turned to a minor campus problem, I attempted to contribute to the discussion, but was cut off by the chairman. The curtain had fallen on the earlier pattern of give and take; I was now an employee. After the meeting, Dudley Swim, arch-conservative trustee, congratulated me and informed me that, although he voted against me on Tuesday, he had merely abstained on the final action. He said, with a touch of humor, that I had gained ground with him. The following day we accidentally met at the airport and sat together on the flight to San Francisco. Swim chided me for smoking and for having a drink, implying that both were signs of moral flaws. After some further discussion, he reported that he had long been successful in studying his opponent's weaknesses and using them to his advantage in the rough-and-tumble of a poor boy's rise to executive roles. It was clear, by then, that neither the most liberal nor the most conservative among the trustees supported my appointment.

I was appointed largely on my own terms, free of specific commitments, but the terms carried no guarantee of needed fiscal or administrative support from the chancellor or trustees. My own independence could be a hazard for lack of a hard-nosed constituency that had helped thrust me into office and therefore had a stake in making me a success as president. As congratulatory messages and comments rolled in, many included offers of help, but more assured me I was all that stood between chaos and a future for the college. They came from faculty, a few students, and professional associates across the state. It seemed clear that my colleagues were mostly supportive of the appointment. Most students appeared willing to wait and see. I suspected that there were few true believers willing to hit the barricades in my behalf. Administrators in the college seemed relieved that worse had not happened to the college and most seemed actively supportive. The bases existed for building active support if ways could be found to weld the scattered individuals into a working force. Through the summer, we developed a working list of individuals for roles in fall developments. Events outran me. After two weeks of the fall semester, we were up to our hips in crises.

Chapter 6

The Problems Smith Inherited

Robert Smith needed no analysis by management consultants to tell him he was taking over a very troubled college. Both he and San Francisco State were very much on the hot seat. For the past ten years the college had been the maverick college in the system, the rebel, the troublemaker. Now the disruptions of the past year, particularly in December and May, made some people in power wonder whether the college could ever shape up, and for the first time you could hear faint voices saying, half-jokingly, "Maybe we'd better just close the college up." Within six months this fate emerged as a distinct possibility.

What many in the state thought of as a "snakebit" college, many in the college itself, faculty and students, considered one of the best colleges in the system. Its reputation was a product of yesteryear; the troubles were rooted in today's anxious society. The administrative condition of the college was close to a shambles, the culmination of over a decade of discontinuity and ineffectiveness of leadership. New shifts of administrators spent most of their time trying to learn their jobs, fend off the restrictive and worried chancellor and trustees, and cope with the powerful, counterpunching Academic Senate. They seldom had time to plan ahead to anticipate troublesome issues. The events of the past year had merely compounded all of these difficulties. Problems seldom encountered previously even by mature, experienced administrative teams had to be met, and the process of coping with these confrontational issues took so much time and drained so much energy that the normal administrative tasks were sloughed aside, thus raising new problems.

Much had been expected of the Summerskill administration. The new president brought a new perspective, liberal values, administrative experience, and youth to the demanding task. He had had an opportunity to shape almost his entire first-line administrative organization. When his administration failed so completely, morale declined. Within liberal faculty circles a new note of pessimism developed in response to the relatively hard-line handling of the May sit-in. To this group it seemed that the reactionary forces represented by Governor Reagan and the trustees had actually been able to penetrate "their" college. Although this group had worked with President Smith when he had led some forays against the Establishment, and liked him personally, they withheld their total support until he indicated his own style in handling disorders and taking on the repressive external forces.

Smith inherited a top administration that was beginning to be discredited both in the Chancellor's Office and within certain faculty circles. Vice-President Garrity brought a tough, incisive mind to the academic affairs issues and had earned the support of his school deans, but within Senate, liberal faculty, and ethnic areas there were considerable suspicion and resistance. The new vice-president in the area of business affairs, Glenn Smith, had slight experience in the financial field at a time when it was becoming increasingly crucial. Advice came to President Smith from several campus factions that Dean of Students Ferd Reddell would cause numerous problems and should be replaced. Within this Troika itself the superficial unity that had developed in response to Summerskill's uncertain leadership and the student "enemy" was rapidly disappearing as disagreeable jobs had to be performed. In the eyes of radical students and the liberal faculty contingent, the Troika was also the symbol of the hard-line, police-on-campus approach to confrontations.

Faculty loyalties centered increasingly around their departmental identity with the result that a sense of academic community and a commitment to college policies and college problem solving was attenuated. Yet within the schools and departments the complaint was that they did not have enough freedom from college control. The Council of Academic Deans had evolved from a discussion group of a few years earlier to a potent competitor with the Senate for influence in college policy decisions. Leadership in this movement gave Vice-President Garrity a power base in the council and, by the same token, serious opposition in the Academic Senate. This feud had centered on the issue of whether the college should shift to the quarter system and begin year-round operation in the fall of 1969 as decreed by the chancellor and the trustees or delay this change until a more propitious time. The faculty and Senate had prevailed. Much departmental time had been wasted in the abortive planning for this largely undesired calendar change.

These were the administrative resources that had to contend with both a student government moving in a radical direction and a revolutionary SDS-led movement strengthened by the year's confrontations, and that had to create new programs to satisfy minority aspirations. The task, difficult under any circumstances, was made almost impossible by two fundamental realities: instead of having these new ventures funded, the college went into the 1968–1969 year with an anticipated $750,000 deficit, and for the past five years the college had come to almost a standstill in the growth of its student body and facilities. After a long history of college expansion and the concomitant curricula, personnel, and building growth, the faculty had a difficult time accepting the fact that not only would this growth be minimal in the future, but that the emergence of the ethnic programs might actually be at the expense of current departmental allocations. As the black students quite frankly stated it, this tested the faculty's "sense of priorities and commitment to eliminating institutional racism." Were the college to obtain relief for this financial dilemma it could be only at the request of the chancellor and the trustees. San Francisco State was hardly the college that either desired to favor. The relationship between the college and the chancellor and trustees, never anything but bad, was now at its nadir.

Given these circumstances, confrontations seemed inevitable. The college could hardly have been in worse shape for contending with such aggressive dissent. Although warned as early as 1964 by the Free Speech Movement that student conduct rules and disciplinary procedures needed to be shored up and clearly articulated, neither the faculty nor the students nor the presidents nor the dean of students had been moved by this early warning and by the events of the past several years to remedy this deficiency effectively. The Senate still acted as though student affairs were not in the mainstream of the academic operation. Student leaders were to gain no points in this area except by challenging the need for rules of conduct or, if a need did exist, by asking for student power in making the rules. Presidents came and went too fast; and to Dean of Students Reddell, any movement through this thicket was politically dangerous and, moreover, conflicted with the basic student personnel posture of facilitating and counseling students not disciplining or repressing them. Thus, the college had no clear-cut rules of conduct such as even the University of California had developed, no administrative unit that accepted responsibility for prosecuting justice, and no acceptable judicial process. It did have an almost unblemished record regarding student belligerence: despite two years of turmoil only the *Gater* attackers had been punished. The mess had been compounded by Summerskill's last-minute, unnoticed delegation of his disciplinary authority to a court consisting of five students and two faculty members. Since these powers were never used, the issue was never joined, but it is doubtful that either the trustees or the faculty would have agreed to this arrangement, especially since two of the student judges were SDS and BSU leaders.

The disorder in the administration was matched by the disintegration of faculty government. What had once been the college's pride, now became just another challenger for power—and a flabby, outmoded challenger at that. For far too long the faculty had encouraged a small group of leaders to use their experience and expertise in challenging the enemy from without and for ensuring that faculty had a dominant voice in college management. The particulars of the college decision were less important than the faculty voice. In areas requiring initiative and careful thought and planning, such as educational reform, response to the ethnic group challenges, and student affairs policy, the Senate had not produced. Faculty took the Senate for granted, membership in it was not a great tribute with few seeking the role, and the total membership turned to the same small group for leadership. Most faculty preferred to invest their time elsewhere.

The past year had witnessed considerable faculty polarization, the phenomenon that seems a certain accompaniment of institutional change and confrontations. Some apathetic faculty in the center moved to the right and sought their goals through a new organization, the Faculty Renaissance. They distrusted the representative democracy of the Senate, feeling that the total faculty should be involved in all important decisions now that the stakes had become higher. Many in the Renaissance group suspected that the total faculty reflected their thinking better than the current Senate membership did. "Order and tranquility on the campus" was a prominent goal of this group. Moving to the opposite extreme in this polarization process were many of the younger faculty. Often they represented a new breed, committed to social and institutional change, passionately antiwar, identifying with the student movement, and confident in their disciplinary skills and mobility. In the past neither the communications system within the college nor the power structure had encompassed these faculty. Whereas the older faculty militants had almost taken the conservatism and resistance of the higher education Establishment in California for granted after a decade of impotent challenging, the younger faculty were disgusted to the point of action as this power structure increasingly revealed itself. They resented the underfinancing, they resented the centralized control of the individual colleges, and they resented the move toward a hard-line against student rebels.

As these two conservative and liberal faculty groups sought power, the unity of the Senate and its casual operations were challenged to the point that decisions were difficult to achieve and action on decisions became haphazard. This divisiveness facilitated challenges to Senate power by students, by the administration, and by the chancellor and the trustees.

In the view of many of the younger faculty, the Academic Senate was an impotent, coopted structure that did not have the strength to achieve change now that the power interests of the state were deeply concerned with higher education. They therefore sought more effective machinery for reflecting their views. The American Federation of Teachers, with its promise of the technique of collective bargaining and the support of organized labor, offered such an organization.

The cutting edge in the AFT movement in general, but particularly at San Francisco State, was a coalition of old-time unionists who had held the faith for seven years and younger faculty, some part-time, some full-time, some liberal, some radical. Responding to the currents of the campus, this group enlarged the concerns of the union from economic issues and collective bargaining to encompass the "movement" and its quest for student power, elimination of racism and political repression, and the termination of the war. Always on the side of free speech and due process, the union supported the cause of *Open Process*. When the Movement Against Political Suspensions (MAPS) developed the previous December, the union had been on the verge of openly supporting the militant organization before it shifted to covert support. The BSU and its efforts had a friend in the AFT. The ad hoc group that developed in the May sit-in and pressed Summerskill for major concessions and not to bring the police on campus consisted almost entirely of AFT members. Although the Senate was not considered a major arena, the AFT was always careful to elect a significant number to the body, and this group provided much of the Senate's leadership, its issues, and its articulate debate. In short, the AFT leadership was paralleling the student movement in its concerns, its frustration with liberal reform and normal channels for change, and its tendency toward confrontation techniques. The issues of the Smith-Hayakawa year were made to order for the AFT. On the other hand, the emerging concern within the public, the Legislature and the trustees with the radical environment developing within higher education made the AFT a vulnerable target for these bodies. Legislation permitting collective bargaining for public employees became less and less a possibility.

With his administration and faculty in such disarray, President Smith also inherited deep problems with the Third World students. As a result of the confrontations in November, December, and May, these students had developed a sense of power. They also believed that power never remained static, that if you did not expand it, it diminished. Power could be achieved "at the barrel of a gun" and by pragmatic expansion. Their task was to keep a delicate balance between these two activities so that they reinforced each other. The threat of confrontations had influenced a commitment to 400 special Third World admittees and a black studies program. Enlargement of these programs and shaping them in the direction of a militant black ideology could satisfy black economic and identity goals while at the same time enlarging the confrontational capacity. Each depended on what students were admitted, who tutored and taught them, and what the ideology of the ethnic studies program was. With the advent of funds, hiring slots, and program possibilities, power had tangible rewards and therefore power battles developed within the TW ethnic groups.

While the past year had enhanced the power and the ambitions of the ethnic students, it had also contributed to a college environment that in many ways inhibited the realization of these ambitions. The expensive new programs had obtained no special state funds, and this meant their financing would have to be at the expense of other commitments at a moment when the college had its projected deficit of $750,000 for the normal operation. Planning for the program demanded a new range of collaborative skills, skills that would allow students and faculty, black and white and brown, to work together. Time was short for such complex program development. All had to be in place in three months, and these three months were summer months when administrators take vacations and faculty disappear. The program leadership expected of Nathan Hare when he was hired had produced slight gains and had antagonized many in power.

Many issues had developed when Dean of Students Reddell had given control of the special admissions program to a seven-man committee composed of four students and three faculty or administrators, six from Third World backgrounds, one Caucasian. Some of the issues were between the ethnic groups; at one time Diane Lewis, a distinguished black anthropologist, threatened to resign as chairman. In the back of some people's minds lurked the suspicion that a portion of these special admittees had been used by militant black groups deliberately to enlarge their cadres at the expense of black people more inclined toward integration. This became an issue at San Fernando Valley State College, the other state college to have deep conflict in this area in the future. There was also the question of which members of the BSU and TWLF would obtain teaching or tutorial jobs in this new program or in the black studies curriculum.

For the most part the other minority groups had capitalized on the successes of the black students. Although these groups felt they had achieved significant commitments, the college's sense of obligation to them had a lower level of priority.

A threat to the new administration from the white radicals

was also imminent. Although they had staged a confrontation the preceding May that had disrupted the college for over a week and had forced the administration to call in the police, they had not achieved their stated goal—the elimination of the Air Force ROTC. In fact, they had been closer to this objective before the sit-in. But if the SDS had failed in this respect, they had succeeded at more important levels. Their strategy and the use of police had enlarged their marching forces from about 200 to 500. Sympathy also developed in the student body at large. Tactics and strategy lessons had also been learned during the confrontation and the leadership core had expanded. Successful liaison and cooperation with the Third World students, which had been lacking during the MAPS December upheaval, had been developed.

This expansion of their movement and their strength at a time when radical student action had been legitimized by such other confrontations as that at Columbia raised only one major question: what would be the issue and the tactic and the timing for the fall semester? The sense of power and mission was great: a college had been stopped, administrators had literally quivered, no college penalty had been incurred, leaders had become the heroes of the new student generation, and the media flocked out at the issuance of a broadside or the clenching of a fist.

The task of Russell Bass and his new Associated Students governmental forces was to develop a program that would be sufficiently radical to take the initiative away from the radical students lest they overwhelm his administration as they had his two predecessors'. At the same time he had to continue and expand the reformist programs that had worked well in the past, such as the Experimental College, the students' faculty-evaluation system (MAX), and the tutorial and community service efforts.

While President Smith attempted to mobilize his administrative staff and elicit the cooperation of the polarized faculty in order both to solve the educational problems plaguing the college and to contain the radicals, he operated in a political environment that was hostile, restrictive, tight-fisted with funds, and unsympathetic. The Legislature had provided a minimal budget and had barely restrained itself by temporarily shelving a host of punitive bills aimed at pleasing the antagonistic public by punishing student and faculty campus subversives. Governor Reagan had ridden to victory on the wings of a tough line for campus agitators, a conservative social philosophy, and a vow to save taxpayers' money. Once in office he began a budgetary and tuition attack on higher education while at the same time he appointed governing board members of his persuasion. By now he had control of both the regents of the state university and the state college trustees. The trustees initiated a radical shift in policy in order to make administrators subservient to the trustees but powerful on their campuses, to strip faculty of the power and protection they had been accumulating, and to repress the incipient student rebellions. San Francisco State was a critical college in this effort: its administrators had been too independent and faculty-inclined, its faculty refused to recognize the authority of the chancellor and the trustees, and its student leaders were on the verge of a rebellion. On several occasions Chancellor Dumke had warned that we must avoid "Latinizing" the state colleges—that is, making them a center for revolution as in the Latin American countries.

Normally the placid summer months would have been an excellent time for a new administrator to do the planning and to obtain the perspective necessary to cope with a certain year of troubles. San Francisco State's new leader had no such respite. Enthusiastic, if vague, assurances had been given to him of administrative and financial assistance when he accepted the position; and so tired staff members put together job and budgetary justifications in order to obtain these essentials. After a long, drawn-out process, virtually nothing came of the effort.

The new student government presented the next major administrative problem during the summer when it flexed its muscles in support of its election platform by eliminating the intercollegiate athletic budget and several other traditional student activities and redistributing this saving to the ethnic programs. This action threatened a year's scheduling of athletic contests and some contractual relationships. From the perspective of student politics, the issue was a winner. In an era tending toward more student control of their own lives, who would be rash enough to challenge their control of funds developed by taxing themselves? As to the substantive issue, intercollegiate athletics was "out" on this swinging, urban problems-oriented campus and assisting blacks to achieve power was "in." The physical education department was a beautiful target for the activists and the black students: it was considered by them the center of reactionary values and they challenged its alleged racist tendencies. Late in the spring the black athletes had had a press conference to question their treatment; nor did a length-of-hair dictum for athletes endear the department to the long-haired, bearded students in control of student government.

Not only was the substance of the issue a natural but the timing could hardly have been better arranged. Coming at the beginning of a new student government that was committed to moving away from administrative cooption and toward radical confrontation, it could set the style of this student government and its relationships with President Smith and his colleagues. It hit at the administration when it was tired, looking for surcease, not friction, and when it was working through its own style of operation and interpersonal relationships. This battle-weariness and a disposition to avoid the pitfalls of the previous May tended toward a commitment to rational persuasion, and the entire summer was available for this dialogue.

As events were to prove, almost two months of administrative time would be chewed up with this relatively minor college issue and President Smith's prediction to student body president Russell Bass would come true: "If our energies are constantly absorbed by the intercollegiate athletic problem that your student government administration has created, I can assure you that several programs of far greater importance and widespread concern will be affected seriously."

The administrative perspective on this issue was stated by the president in one of his communications to the student government:

> This is the second year in a row that a change of Associated Students administration has brought drastic shifts in the pattern of support among the thirty-odd activities and functions which depend for financial support on student activity fees collected from all students. The results of "radical" redirection of Associated Students funds without necessary planning for a transition period leaves all programs, both traditional and new, subject to the political vagaries of student elections. . . . If the Associated Students government believes it can ignore the financial commitments of its predecessors, the entire system of student government in its present form is doomed.

This turned out to be a prescient observation. Although the problem was finally compromised at great expense of time and goodwill, alleged irregularities in student fund administration were to lead to the impounding of all of these funds by the state attorney general before the year was up and the virtual disappearance of formal student government.

Within trustee ranks a pattern of activity had been developing in 1967–68 that was to create the next crisis in the summer of 1968. Again it focused on the new directions of San Francisco State student government. Again it consumed far more administrative time and energy than it was worth. The pattern was simple: the new Reagan-appointed trustee, Dudley Swim, president of National Airlines, would recount an alleged atrocity at some one campus, consume a precious several hours of trustee time making offhand accusations about the nonagendized item, and then demand a full accounting by the next meeting. For President Smith's first trustee meeting since his appointment, attention was focused upon explaining and defending the concept of student Experimental Colleges and specifically one course at San Francisco State's student-developed college labeled guerrilla warfare. The basic philosophy of this highly successful experimental curriculum at State had been that if a person desired to organize a learning experience and there was a clientele, the "course" was offered. The end-product of this philosophy and administrative machinery was a series of courses in one semester that ranged from macrobiotic cooking, learning to sit still, and Zen basketball to essentials of Marxism, magic, Einstein and God, and meta-geology. Given the state of world affairs and radical inclinations of some State students, the topic of guerrilla warfare arose in the natural course of events. A knowledgeable individual by the name of Robert Kaffke was available and so the course took shape—but not for college credit. No academic credit was assigned in most Experimental College courses.

Events followed in quick succession. Seeking sensational topics to keep his talk show alive, a local radio and television announcer, Pat Michaels, zeroed in on guerrilla warfare and Robert Kaffke. Alleged activities in the course, ranging from bayonet practice to time bomb construction, were challenged by many irate citizens in the Bay Area. Then the newspapers picked up the controversial topic; then Dudley Swim did. Accusations, an investigation, a defense followed. Although experimental colleges, San Francisco State, and the course in guerrilla warfare came out of the meeting relatively unscathed, time was wasted, suspicions were planted, and a tradition of having attention at trustee meetings almost entirely focused on San Francisco State was established. This record was unblemished during Smith's brief tenure. At times, his chief function appeared to be preparing for the defense of the college at successive trustee meetings or else mopping up after the trustees took disastrous action.

While attention was focused on preparing budget justifications which produced nothing, mediating a battle between the student government and the athletic department, and protecting the student's innovative educational experimentation against trustee thrusts, three critical areas received far less attention than they should have. The cumbersome black-white-brown, student-faculty-administration planning for the unprecedented program for educationally disadvantaged minority students proceeded throughout the summer. A plausible but patchwork and underfunded operation emerged. Neither the black leadership nor the college administration made significant contributions to meeting the college's commitment to black and ethnic studies—a failure that was to plague the college all year. Rules for student conduct and procedures for student discipline were considered, but not developed. And the Academic Senate failed to meet its pledge during the summer to initiate planning for the fall constitutional convention that was to redistribute power. In August people took hard-earned vacations, leaving these problems unsolved.

Few institutional calamities are simple in origin. The tragedy that has overwhelmed American higher education in the late 1960s has been widely accepted as a concomitant of such diverse social problems as the Vietnam war, racial injustice, youth alienation, and widespread poverty. The tragedy that was to descend upon San Francisco State College in the 1968–69 academic year can be traced back to these broader causes as well as to some specific developments in the particular geographic context in which the college operates: the general San Francisco-Oakland Bay Area and the state of California.

In the month of August, alienated youth in Berkeley—the "street" people—did battle with the constituted authorities to such a violent degree that police sweeps, tear gas, bottles, rocks, guns, and a citywide curfew became a part of the daily scene. That this mood of violence and hostility toward the authorities should impinge on San Francisco State was understandable. The college's black student population identified with the Bay Area black community, drew strength from its successes and suffered when it suffered. Specifically, the college's Black Student Union had many connections with the Oakland-based, militant Black Panther Party, and this party, and these black people, were to suffer a grievous blow from the white Establishment during the months of August and September. This was the period of the trial of their magnetic leader, Huey Newton, for the alleged killing of a policeman in a Panther-police shootout. All summer the party put on its greatest show of strength. "Free Huey" buttons sprouted up all over State's campus. As the moment of decision approached, Panther leader Bobby Seale made his famous threat: "Huey P. Newton must go free or the sky's the limit around the world." Said Eldridge Cleaver, soon to be a headline education issue all by himself: "If Newton is sacrificed we will go down with Huey." Newton was "sacrificed" on the ninth of September; he was convicted and given a jail sentence. A day later the black community was outraged when the Panther headquarters was shot up by two off-duty policemen.

Not only were the colleges a target of black confrontations aimed to obtain redress of long-accumulated grievances and discrimination, but high schools, especially in the Bay Area, witnessed this same style of action. Within a week after the Newton verdict parents and teachers associated with Mission High School in San Francisco petitioned the Board of Education for police protection. The Oakland AFT requested that its board close school because it was not safe for students or faculty. Virtual anarchy developed at Ravenswood, a peninsula high school populated primarily by black students. After a sit-in, fires, beatings, and black demands, the principal quit, saying, "This place would have burned down if I had not resigned." In the short time span of two months similar scenes were enacted in over fifteen high schools in the Bay Area. San Francisco high schools were particularly hard hit by this black rebellion.

Black dissatisfaction manifested itself in other colleges as well. In October 1968, the University of California at Santa Barbara was shocked by the takeover of its million-dollar computer center by a band of black students who threatened to blow the center up unless their demands were met. In the same month a suburban junior college, the College of San Mateo, was racked with demands, sit-ins, and finally a full-scale, pipe-swinging riot that temporarily closed the college and brought a battalion of police on campus. Here the issues were similar to those to emerge at San Francisco State: underfunding of a special admission program, an insufficient black studies program, and alleged persecution of a black faculty leader. November witnessed serious black outbursts at two colleges within the state system, San Jose and San Fernando Valley. San Francisco State's black studies leader, Nathan Hare, enunciated the tactics of this black drive for college power when, in speaking in early September at the National Conference on Black Power, he commented, "We should develop tactics for physically taking over or disrupting racist learning whenever the situation demands."

These issues of racial injustice, black militancy in the schools, police brutality, law and order, and campus confrontations were to sway the voters in the elections that were coming up in November. With the nation's presidency at stake, with control of the state's two legislative houses hanging on the results, and with Rafferty magnifying and coloring these basic issues in his campaign for the U.S. Senate, they dominated the media and thinking and feeling in California. At the University at Berkeley and at San Francisco State two cases developed that united all these issues and precipitated California higher education totally into the political arena. At the university it was the Eldridge Cleaver course; at San Francisco State, it was the George Murray incident.

Chapter 7

George Murray

The public dispute over the hiring of George Murray at San Francisco State began to build on September 13, 1968.[1] There followed three months of struggle over Murray's role in the college and his public actions. Viewed from the administrative standpoint, a major public conflict over hiring a black graduate student as a part-time instructor promised an overload the college administration could hardly afford. We needed strong chancellor and trustee support for added faculty and administrative positions if we were to cope with the legacy of the previous spring's disorders and commitments. The issues surrounding black and ethnic

[1] This chapter is a first-person account by Robert Smith.

studies were not resolved. The efforts to gain support for some 400 special admissions minority students were disappointing (a major fund-raising project was bogged down). The college already faced a $750,000 deficit inherited from the previous year's budget planning. Three staff deans, the deputy president, and the director of the minority students' Educational Opportunity Program were new to the administrative staff. The college faced the first general accreditation visit in a decade in November. The trustees had demanded that a major study of instructional effectiveness begin fall semester (totally without funding). We were obligated to move aggressively to place in operation a basic revision of the entire general education program, the first major revision in twenty years. The Student Union building design had to gain approval if costs of construction were not to outrun fiscal resources. It was locked in a controversy among the three architects involved, the college, and the trustees. Major decisions were pending concerning the downtown center programs and the facilities to be sought to replace the condemned downtown building.

The pyramiding of administrative problems had accrued during several years marked by discontinuity in college administrative leadership. It was superimposed on the day-to-day administrative and instruction functions of a 20,000-member community already badly understaffed. Any three of the above tasks would have taxed the year's margin of energy of administrative-faculty-student leadership. There was also great need to project long-range plans for the college. We had borrowed from the future to achieve short-term gains ever since 1957—the entire decade following Paul Leonard's visionary administration. We really did not need the Murray issue to test the mettle of the college and its new administration. The School of Humanities and the English department, working with the vice-president of academic affairs, was the setting in which the Murray issue should have been settled rather than in the governor's office, or in executive sessions of the trustees held in Los Angeles and Fresno.

A decision had been made by the English department in May to rehire Murray for fall semester, 1968, to teach two sections of freshman English. He was one of ten graduate students selected from eighteen candidates to teach in the educational opportunity or special admission program in which 400 minority students were to be admitted in September. The students were to be admitted even though they did not meet the test score and grade criterion index used to select the upper 33 per cent of high school graduates eligible for state college admission. They were expected to show "compensating strength," however. Murray and his associates were to teach under the supervision of two experienced English professors in an adapted program planned to improve students' competence in English. He had a reputation of deep commitment to teaching students with difficulties in language arts. He reportedly separated his growing political militancy from classroom instruction. Several college faculty members judged him to be a gifted and serious young teacher. Murray had several semesters' experience in working with minority youth through the student-sponsored tutorial program. The English department had hired him part time for fall semester, 1967, to teach an experimental course enrolling half black students and half randomly selected white students. This gave Murray faculty status as a part-time instructor in addition to his status as a graduate student. This dual role complicated disciplinary and grievance procedures because charges of misconduct had to be reviewed through separate faculty and student avenues. He was rehired to continue through the spring semester, 1968, despite a turbulent fall, during which he had been arrested for participating in the *Gater* incident.

President Summerskill had asked the English department's Hiring, Retention, and Tenure Committee to consider suspending Murray from his faculty role. After unsuccessful efforts to get advice from the faculty Committee on Academic Privilege, the English HRT Committee recommended Murray's suspension. The president notified Murray of his suspension on November 13, 1967. The chairman of the English department reports that a few days later, the president and the chairman of the Academic Senate asked the HRT Committee to withdraw the suspension recommendation, which the committee did after further deliberation. They were informed that the case would be reviewed through other channels. The president lifted the student suspensions of those involved in the *Gater* incident because he believed serious questions of due process were involved.[2] Murray pleaded no contest before the court. He was sentenced to six months in jail. The sentence was suspended and he was placed on probation. No further action had been taken by the college against Murray by spring semester, 1968,

[2] The faculty Committee of Ten, appointed in November by President Summerskill to review race tensions on campus, recommended that he lift the suspensions because of questions of due process. The chairman of the Academic Senate was a member of that committee. On advice of Murray's counsel, State Assemblyman Willie Brown, Murray and his associates had refused to testify during the college hearings because of pending criminal court action.

and the English department renewed his employment for spring.

On April 26, Murray made a pugnacious speech on campus in which he said, "If you are really serious about doing away with racism, then you would take this racist president, Summerskill, out of this world. If you are really serious, you would take this racist Garrity out of this world" (referring to Vice-President for Academic Affairs Donald Garrity). No official notice was taken of this incident.

The problem of planning for the Educational Opportunities Program to begin in September 1968 with so little lead time was severe. Strong efforts were made to employ minority group members to provide both effective communication and strong role identification. It was apparent that the decision in late April to launch such a large program in September was a hazardous undertaking. The commitment was made under pressure and without assurance of needed support funds or personnel.

Earlier the president's Committee of Ten on Race Tensions had recommended a more limited program of 60 to 120 students for fall 1968. Caught in the May campus disorders, necessary planning was seriously disrupted. In the best of circumstances, it would have been a scramble all the way. It meant selecting students for admission, planning curriculum adaptations, recruiting, and organizing a staff with special competence, putting together an operating budget from odds and ends during a dismal budget year, and raising funds to assist students financially. Two committees worked hard through the early summer, one on admissions, and another on curriculum, while departments struggled with staffing problems without assured resources. Tired administrators also had to work in staggered vacation schedules, sometimes breaking the continuity of effort at unfortunate times. Those on hand worked well beyond the call of duty and the ability of the college to pay for extra services. The failure to gain approval of special funds stretched summer personnel beyond ordinary limits. The college's request in June for eight additional faculty positions had not been met. This clouded the decisions on hiring. Murray finally received his appointment letter during the first week in September. The San Francisco *Chronicle* carried a one-paragraph report on September 13. The San Francisco *Examiner's* Ed Montgomery broke a bylined story on Murray as a Black Panther minister of education and as one of those involved in the *Gater* beatings during the fall before. The story reported a trip by Murray to Cuba during the summer and quoted inflammatory statements attributed to him during an international Havana summer conference by *Granma,* a Cuban publication in English.

Three months in the president's office, I discovered the Murray case on reading Ed Montgomery's article. Its explosive potential was clear. With the Eldridge Cleaver blow-up across the bay, and with the senatorial and presidential campaigns of arch-conservative candidates Max Rafferty and George Wallace heating up in California, it was made to order for disruption of the fall semester. The Peace and Freedom Party on the far left, as well as the racial and ethnic militants, seemed sure to exploit the problem as they could. I agreed fully with my wife's diagnosis: "It couldn't mean anything but trouble!" Since the case was projected as a campaign issue along with the Cleaver controversy, the college could not win. The problem was to cut the losses without selling out. A Black Panther official convicted of violence on campus and still on probation, possessing a penchant for violent rhetoric, having attended a Third World conference dominated by neo-Marxists in a communist country, hired at faculty rank as an instructor with a legally binding letter of appointment! What a spot for establishing the president as a hard-liner in the backlash climate of California reaction. I could simply have focused the blame on any of those who had reviewed the appointment and have leveled a blast at them for irresponsible behavior while summarily firing Murray! The trustees' legal staff would have provided almost unlimited cover. The English department with its renowned reputation also had a reputation among more conservative faculty groups for erratic or left-wing lines of action anyway. More than one acquaintance asked if Murray was worth any trouble, and if it was not obvious that a president "could make it big" *off campus* by scuttling him in the political climate of California.

My colleagues and I found no reason during the first weeks of the controversy for taking action against Murray. A quick check showed that he had been hired through the established procedures of the college, his appointment having been reviewed beyond the English department by the dean of the School of Humanities and the vice-president for academic affairs, who had reluctantly decided not to intervene. Further, the English faculty, who had previously worked with him and supervised his teaching, supported him as an effective teacher, who took his role seriously. Throughout the controversy, Caroline Shrodes, the chairman of the English department, and her faculty associates took the blunt position that he was hired for the specific task of teaching minority students, which he did well. They could report no evidence from past performance that his political and organizational activities had infringed on his classroom work. He was a graduate student against whom no disciplinary action was pending at the college. The department's recommendation for suspension, made the previous year, had been withdrawn at the urging of the previous president and the chairman of the Academic Senate. Arbitrary action on Murray would be conclusive evidence to racial and ethnic minorities on campus that politics and racism controlled the campus.

The week following the *Examiner* story, I spoke to the San Francisco Junior Chamber of Commerce on the issues facing the college as viewed from my new role as president. The speech, prepared a week before, did not include reference to Murray. The question period brought a series of angry questions from a small knot of diners about the hiring of a Panther who had been involved in campus violence. It was clear the follow-up of the newspaper "expose" had begun.

The administrative staff was pinned down during that week by the registration of 18,000 students, some 7,500 of whom were new to the campus, while greeting the returning faculty and 150 faculty new to the college. Three threats to disrupt registration processes also demanded attention. First, the student body had arranged for agitprop groups to do their thing on campus in and around registration lines. I had been informed earlier in the summer that they would stay within some bounds "if asked to do so by student officers." The student body president was reminded that one pornographic episode at registration with the media present could tie up our energies for most of the fall. During the summer meetings of the State College Presidents the Chancellor had belabored the issues of campus control of radical social protest, and pornography in the arts. His immediate provocation was the extensive public and legislative outcry of the previous spring over a group of allegedly obscene sculptures displayed on the Long Beach State College Campus. Because of the long summer controversy over the student adopted activities' budget on our campus, rumors persisted of plans for provocative actions to disrupt registration, thus promising an early start in fall disorders. Some were predicting the college would not make it through registration.

A second issue arose among students who objected to action by the radical student body government to eliminate the athletic budget and funds for other traditional activities. They asserted they expected 3,000 students to refuse payment of the mandatory student activities fee as a protest movement. They were to request work assignments to substitute for the fee under an obscure provision of the State Education Code designed for those who could not afford the fee. The prospect of several thousand students demanding special last-minute exceptions in the fee payment line caused anxiety. The idea of contriving and accounting for an equivalent number of ten-dollar jobs helped administrators move with alacrity to resolve the problem with the help of legal counsel. The third threat took the form of reports that filtered in from some schools of plans to hijack registration cards, but restraint on the part of Associated Students leadership and hard work by the student personnel staff resulted in a reasonably smooth registration. Of course, those bent on challenging the Establishment through the year did need to complete registration.

The Murray problem gathered steam the following week. Angry mail began to trickle in. On September 18, a request came directly from the Governor's Office for information on Murray's qualifications for teaching, degrees, and credentials held. The information was provided. On September 20, the chancellor informed me that it was "imperative that you expedite the review [of Murray's entire case] prior to the meeting of the Board of Trustees" the following week. A five-page report was prepared and submitted on the twenty-fourth.

Chancellor Dumke, Lieutenant Governor Finch, and Vice-Chairman of the State College Board of Trustees Mrs. Philip Conley discussed possible action against Murray in a press conference in Los Angeles on September 20. The press called me for comment from Los Angeles, although I knew nothing of the press conference. The news story, carrying William Drummond's by-line, reported Dumke's view that the Murray issue was more serious than the Cleaver issue at Berkeley because he was teaching rather than performing as a lecturer. "We're looking to President Smith to come up with an appropriate answer." The news story included my statement pointing to Murray's legal appointment, his teaching effectiveness attested to by his supervisors, and the special minority program in which he worked. The story reported critical comments about Cleaver's appointment by Governor Reagan, Assembly Speaker Jesse Unruh, and Lieutenant Governor Finch. It also noted Cleaver's criminal record and lack of academic preparation. The story ended noting, "All of these objections cannot be raised about Murray. He has academic preparation. He is a graduate student in English. . . . [He] had served as a teaching assistant for two semesters. . . . He had no prison record." Chancellor and trustee action projected Murray's status statewide via the press conference before thorough inquiry could be completed. Clearly, Cleaver and Murray were to be tied together in the public mind for the duration.

Concurrently with the Murray buildup, the dean of students, the placement officer, and the deputy president, having weathered registration, were preparing for the threatened major disruption (by the radical left) of the October 8 military recruiting day. The students promised to throw recruiters' tables and their materials off campus by force. Meanwhile military officers were objecting strenuously to the arrangements designed by the placement officer to include all armed service recruiters in a one-day session along with pacifists and antiwar organizations. The placement officer and the deputy president had a mini-confrontation with representatives of several military services at a downtown meeting. One by one, representatives of the military withdrew rather than share the campus with antiwar groups and with each other.[3] The basic decision to continue Murray as a teacher was arrived at with concurrence of the college vice-presidents and deans and the Executive Committee of the Senate after review of available information. No major dissent came to my attention from the campus community. The decision of the college was stated by me in the introduction of the five-page report as follows:

> Mention of Mr. Murray's employment appeared in San Francisco newspapers without arousing public concern, until one reporter wrote a somewhat provocative article containing allegations no official agency has supported or denied. The public and political concern generated by one news article attacking Murray seems to center on matters not related to his teaching qualifications, but on his personal actions and political beliefs, neither of which are sufficient grounds to refuse employment or to revoke his contract. We have found no legal grounds to take action against George Murray. He has on file in the college the oath of loyalty to the Constitution required of all college employees.

[3] Erroneous reports persisted that the college administration canceled plans for the military information day to avoid a confrontation with SDS and allied groups. Such was not the case. We were committed to toughing it through in behalf of an open campus, with police assistance, if necessary.

That position remained basically unchanged until the last week of October.[4]

Preparation for the September trustees' executive meeting on Murray was compounded by scheduling it at the same meeting with the long-delayed reconsideration of the controversial Student Union building, a project under development on the campus for five years. The Student Union presentation was the result of an intensive summer effort coordinated with the student body officers and the student activities staff by Executive Dean Frank Sheehan. The preparation for the Student Union presentation ran into trouble as the state architect, a Reagan appointee, wrote a negative report on the design aspects of the building. It was received only a week before the crucial trustee meeting. The tension building around the Murray controversy further complicated the chance that the Student Union would get a friendly hearing before either the trustees' Finance Committee or the Campus Planning Committee. Advance information on the trustee meeting indicated that four of the ten members of the Finance Committee would not attend; among these four were all but one of the most likely supporters of the Student Union plan. It was too late to pull the Student Union off the agenda. Calls to the crucial trustees by a vice-president urging attendance netted a blank. All had urgent commitments they were unable to shift.

The Murray issue dominated the state college presidents' meeting, chaired by Chancellor Dumke, the day before the trustee meeting. Glenn Smith, vice-president, sat in for me, trying to convince the chancellor that we were doing a good job, that the Murray thing had grown out of proportion, that to beat it to death was to miss on three or four even more serious problems growing on campus. Facing a rough 7:30 P.M. trustee executive session, I decided that the principals should be there, vice-president, dean of the school, chairman of the English department, and chairman of the Academic Senate, in addition to my deputy and me. It seemed to promise good in-service training for administrators to have to appear before the trustees.

Late in arriving in Los Angeles from a flak-ridden day's work, we caucused over a drink and then drove to the scheduled 7:30 meeting around which we had managed a tough day's schedule. The trustees were not ready. They were at dinner. At 8:00 P.M. they were still

[4] However, faculty disciplinary procedures were initiated in Murray's case by Vice-President Garrity less than two weeks after the above statement.

at dinner. We had missed dinner. We sent for sandwiches. About 9:00 P.M. we were called.

The twenty-plus trustees and chancellor's staff members were crowded around a horseshoe-shaped dinner table. There were no extra places for our group. No one moved to find a place for us. We stood. Nine o'clock, a ten-hour work day already behind us, sandwiches in our stomachs, we surveyed the debris of a seven-dollar dinner with cocktails, wine, and the smell of good cigars and none but Caucasians in the room—an appropriate setting in which to assess character and instructional qualifications for a part-time black instructor teaching in a ghetto-oriented college program. Despite greetings which were friendly from several trustees, I made a mental note that hell would freeze over before our party made a move to solve the seating problem. Eventually the initiative was taken by one or two of the diners. We were seated at the foot of one leg of the horseshoe table.

The first phase of the next three hours was directed at cross-examination designed to test the facts about Murray and procedures in his hiring. A liberal trustee, Jim Thacher, a lawyer from San Francisco, played district attorney. We had some difficulty breaking up a sparring match between him and Leo McClatchy, chairman of our Senate, also a lawyer. Thacher appeared to be unusually gruff in his manner but we assumed he was playing a role to keep the inquiry out of the hands of the arch-conservatives on the board. His manner indicated he also suspected that the hiring of Murray despite his record of campus behavior was absurd. McClatchy, warmed by two martinis and no dinner, was on the "Aw, now listen, Jim!" level and Thacher, a bit flushed from anger, or *his* dinner, ordered McClatchy not to smile!

Through adroit efforts, Deputy President DeVere Pentony managed to shift the discussion to the basic reasons for supporting Murray in his teaching role, despite public clamor. For a moment, it had appeared that the scars of old battles between McClatchy and Dumke were to sink us. I thought, "Will Caroline Shrodes provide the coup when her turn comes?" She and the chancellor also bore scars of their campus battles when Dumke had been president of San Francisco State College. Shrodes participated in a straightforward, responsible way. Garrity, Pentony, and I had considered these factors in choosing the delegation and decided those legitimately concerned should be present, despite the hazards of old vendettas. In addition both McClatchy and Shrodes had knowledge and information we believed important and needed to be there in the interests of those for whom they spoke, including Murray.

We acknowledged that Murray's court probationary status as a result of the *Gater* incident raised a question of judgment in hiring him as a graduate student on faculty rank. The college had chosen to hire several of those involved in the same incident because of their teaching competency and the special nature of the program. Further, the Educational Opportunities Program, itself, was in real measure a result of militant actions on campuses expressing minority frustrations. We made it clear that we were deliberately sharing responsibility for the program with members of the same racial and ethnic groups capable of contributing to it. We hoped thereby to test new ways of working out rising urban campus conflict over minority group admission to college and over the relevance of instruction.

Murray had held his peace, despite the growing clamor in the state, and had gone about his activities without public fuss. The chairman of the English department had talked with Murray at my request on September 19 about the *Granma* article. He said he had attended the Cuban meeting but had been badly misquoted in *Granma.* My own judgment was that our decision to defend Murray's continuation as an instructor could well leave us exposed to further embarrassment by him or other militant black graduate assistants.

The rest of the meeting, adjourned at midnight, was a frank and serious discussion of basic issues facing the college and the trustees, arising from the growing statewide controversy over Murray. The trustees pressed us hard on the criteria for hiring. Willing to accept Murray's competence in teaching, they zeroed in on the political-ideological aspects of Murray the Panther and Murray the traveler to Cuba. Our group insisted that we hired Murray for demonstrated classroom performance. As far as we could determine there were no charges against him for illegal behavior. Although he was on probation, he had taught the previous semester under like circumstances. The trustee's legal counsel agreed that there was no legal basis for his dismissal.

The sensitivity of public opinion to political heresy and advocacy of violence was explored. We took the view that in a conflict-ridden time limits of faculty ethics outside the classroom must move very close to legally defensible behavior. To move on a minority faculty member in an extralegal way could only heighten racial tensions and be perceived to threaten the academic freedom of all minority faculty members, and others as well. We argued that trustee action against

Murray at this meeting would be inexplicable to minority groups and to the academic community. In effect, Murray would be judged in absentia in executive session by an all-white board of trustees[5] without even the courtesy of a hearing. In the fevered racial tensions on campus, the perception of the meeting as a kangaroo court proceeding was more than likely and the possible results of such an image were too serious to be dismissed.

The *Gater* office fight a year earlier loomed large in the trustees' minds. We argued that since George Murray had taught again in the spring semester, following inconclusive college action, to drop Murray for the *third* semester made little sense. In retrospect, the fact that the college appeared to condone the physical violence against the *Gater* staff may have made further coercion on campus more probable. Yet the not-so-subtle provocation by the student paper of black students prior to the assaults had gone unchecked. In fact, I recall not being at all surprised when the *Gater* incident was reported on campus.

Central to the dilemma facing trustees and college representatives alike is the fact that any effort to associate minority student programs with teachers of like racial and cultural backgrounds involves the college in questions of growing militancy among black and other ethnic groups and the limits within which such militancy can function. Those who meet conventional trustee expectations for restraint and circumspection are hard put to make it with today's students. They are viewed as Uncle Toms or traitors. Those who can speak in the idiom of ethnic consciousness and militancy are anathema to the relatively conservative orientation of most trustees and many faculty.

About midnight, in bringing the meeting to a close, Louis Heilbron, a senior trustee, asked if a move by the trustees to have Murray shifted to a nonteaching job for the rest of the semester would be workable for me. I said, "No, it would not." He said he had guessed as much. "What would be a possible approach?" I said it would help us most if the trustees publicly supported us for moving so determinedly into the conflict-ridden area of minority education. I asked that they take no action specific to Murray, clearly an administrative problem for which the local campus should be given latitude to work out on our own terms. We were excused and the response, as we left the room, seemed more relaxed and friendly than it had been on our entry. It was past midnight.

[5] Pete Lee, the only black member and only minority person on the twenty-one-member board, was absent.

The following day, both the finance and planning committees rejected the Student Union proposal despite our extensive presentation and three hard months of work that followed its failure to gain approval in the spring of 1968. The discussion continued before one committee for almost three hours. Russell Bass, student body president, said in shock, after the committees' actions, "They really want the students to tear up the campus, don't they?" Glenn Smith and I worked feverishly to convince the campus representatives it was worth another try before "taking to the streets." We were deluded.

The trustees called an executive session during lunch to consider Murray. Chairman Merriam said I would not be needed. Chancellor Dumke asked me to be available. I went to lunch with other presidents who were attending the trustees' meeting. Just as we were finishing our lunches, a chancellor's staff member hurried up to say that Dumke wanted to see me. He was waiting for me outside the trustees' meeting room and informed me that, *on his recommendation,* the trustees were to act in the general meeting to request that I remove George Murray from his teaching assignment and assign him to other duties. I said in anger, "Why the hell don't they *order* me to do it?" Dumke said, "Well, would you rather be ordered to do it?" My response was that the trustees had discussed it thoroughly with our staff the evening before. They knew my position. It was their decision to make. It was clear to me at the moment that if I did not take them off the hook on Murray, the special augmentation of the budget we had pressed for since June as well as the Student Union would somehow just not be cleared.

The mass media people would be swarming after lunch. I tried to hide out to figure out something constructive to say. Vice-Chancellor Mansel Keene hunted me up to comfort me and broke into tears, apologizing because he had been under strain from family illness as well as from severe pressure on the Murray controversy. Next came the chancellor's press officer to explain how I was to handle my role in a joint press conference with Merriam and Dumke. I suggested his plan was a lot of bullshit and I had no intention of making it one big happy family after being stabbed twice by the chancellor and the trustees. I said I would meet the press with Vice-President Garrity after the trustees' conference. He retreated saying he would bring me a copy of the trustees' press release. Because he did not, I pushed my way into the crowded press room to listen, then Garrity and I had our turn with the press.

In the subsequent general session, the trustees voted eight to five to request Murray's removal from the classroom. Dumke voted with the majority, then commended me for my "superhuman efforts" at San Francisco State. Governor Reagan, absent from the meeting, later told reporters, "The entire administration of San Francisco State should go along with the decision." Immediate objections to the decision came from all major faculty organizations, AAUP, ACSCP, AFT, CCUFA, the SFSC Senate, and the Statewide Academic Senate. Before the afternoon was over, Murray had received word of the trustee action, called a press conference, blasted the trustees as racists, and promised that police would have to come for him in the classroom. It was the first in a series of Murray's oratorical escalations to follow. It came as no surprise. The evening TV news programs repeatedly carried the trustees' action and close-ups of an angry truculent Murray referring to "racist pigs" and his determination to resist removal from the classroom. Reception of the news channel on which we received Murray's angry image was badly distorted on our color television set. His Panther headwear, his "shades," scraggly beard, and mouth twisted in rage struck fear and revulsion into my neighbors. Few knew that Murray was only twenty-three, the son of a minister, and a talented ex-square on a bad trip in the cauldron of race pressures.

The polarization we had attempted to avoid was now well under way: on one side, the governor, Rafferty, the chancellor, and the more conservative trustees; on the other, the college administration and most major faculty organizations, with the activist students certain to join them, along with the minority groups both on and off campus. Things looked bleak with the semester only two weeks old and a month of general election campaigning still ahead.

On campus, we moved as quickly as possible to a decision and public statement on the trustees' request to remove Murray. The dean of the School of Humanities asked the English department to review again on Saturday their action supporting Murray in the light of the trustees' request. A meeting was called for Sunday morning to include vice-presidents, deans, and the Executive Committee of the Academic Senate. The Sunday meeting, held at my suburban home, lasted three hours. It was marred by one incident reflecting the growing racial tensions plaguing the Bay Area and the college. One of the deans, who is black, arrived late and was driving around seeking a parking space. A neighbor called my wife to report a "strange Negro" acting suspiciously. Joe White rang the bell at that moment, having parked his car. Just then, a police car cruised by, the police watching the house, unusual action for a Sunday morning. White made a wry comment about "a nigger in a white ghetto" and joined the deliberation.

The assembled group reviewed the trustees' meeting and action, the English department's new report continuing support of Murray as an instructor, the legal and academic issues involved, the explosively tense campus and city and the alternative courses of action open to the president. It was clear that we had to act promptly and decisively in efforts to avoid possible ultimata from students, faculty, or community groups which would intensify conflict. There was almost total concurrence that Murray must be continued as a classroom instructor on the basis of present circumstances. We were aware also that the trustees' "request" was considered by some trustees as an order. We agreed to stress the fact that we accepted it at face value as a request in our rationale. It was recognized that our decision might result in my dismissal, and that Murray might well choose to escalate his activities. We would report the decision and discuss it with various groups scheduled to meet on Monday and inform the chancellor, the campus, and the press in that order on Monday evening or Tuesday. We expected to hold firm on our intent to continue Murray as an instructor.

All with whom we met on Monday supported our proposed action. There was some feeling by two of the college Advisory Board that they were faced with a fait accompli. We agreed and explained the time problem, promising to avoid further similar actions when possible. A lawyer on the board made clear his view that we had no other choice; if we arbitrarily transferred Murray from the teaching role for which he was hired, he said he personally would get a court order reinstating Murray. But the Advisory Board severely criticized our proposed public release on the matter, saying it might make sense to professional colleagues but not to people on the street. A board member, George Johns of the Central Labor Council, volunteered to help us reword the release before the 1:30 P.M. Tuesday press conference. He appeared at my office early the next morning with a much improved version of our position.

Murray had been informed he could bring two persons with him to my office in an attempt to accommodate his possible need for a witness. The meeting with Murray was brief. We tried to make it clear that we expected him to continue to teach, that the trustees' request had been declined and that all known groups in the college supported that position. The announcement would be made the following day. He spoke little, made it clear that the trustees were racists and that he would continue teaching. I asked him to consider the impact of any further public statements on the Educational Opportunities Program for which we were seeking community and state support and consider as well the problems facing us in defending his right to teach.

Tuesday morning, October 1, I sent a formal two-page letter to the chancellor, stating our decision and the reasons; I sent it by courier so that it would arrive ahead of the news conference by at least an hour or two.

Tension on the campus among the activist students and the minority students was reported severe. Some administrative staff felt the press conference should be held in one of the television studios to protect me, transmitted to another room large enough to accommodate all persons other than the press. We seemed prone to self-induced hysteria. Ferd Reddell, dean of students, advised against the closed press conference and I gladly supported him. There was no disturbance at the press conference. An overworked, threatened administrative staff, reacting to repeated examples of disorder, tends to develop a sense of danger that itself shapes decisions. The administration building tends to become a psychological bunker with little reconnaissance.

While the media people were setting up in a small theater, the expected call came from a key member of the chancellor's staff almost an hour later than anticipated. The plane had been delayed, apparently, stacked up over Los Angeles and the letter was delivered late. I was to cancel the press conference. The staff member, apparently under severe pressure, persisted. I made the case that the press were already waiting and that my statement was reasoned and nonflammatory, merely respectfully declining the trustees' request and stating the reasons; the decision had the backing of the college community and the lay Advisory Board. Irritated by the call, I read the statement that follows to a bank of newsmen, cameras, and mikes, not too effectively. In fact, I missed completely the last paragraph—my punch line! This oversight disturbed the black student leaders and caused them to ask just what this statement meant.

> I want to set the record straight with respect to the hiring of black instructor George Murray and the trustees' request that I reassign Mr. Murray to nonteaching duties. The vote of the trustees on September 26 was a request, not an order. I have responded in a

personal letter to Chancellor Dumke and today I intend to fulfill my obligation to the general public by clarifying the matter. George Murray is a part-time instructor in English in a program of vital importance to the entire community. He works with young adults from minority groups and with students who have some educational disadvantages. These young adults need instructors who can communicate in their terms and who can also teach standard English. This is an educational program that offers hope for young people who want to make their own way in the world. It may also be one way to ease tensions between races and between the disadvantaged and the more fortunate in our country. Mr. Murray was hired on the recommendation of the English department faculty, according to procedures used throughout the California State College System. He did a competent teaching job here for two semesters last year and the trustees have acknowledged publicly that his teaching qualifications are not in question. This brings us to the real question of public and official attitudes. The trustees' concern apparently stems from Murray's actions and statements outside the classroom. The exact basis for their request that I reassign George Murray has not been communicated to me in any written charges and his record at this college does not warrant action at the present time under our rules and procedures. Here are the facts and factors I must consider in response to the request to reassign Mr. Murray.

One: He was hired according to procedures used throughout the State College System and his status has been reviewed since the trustees' action. The finding is that no grounds exist for changing his assignment.

Two: Reassignment of a legally employed faculty member during the school term and without his concurrence can be considered professionally prejudicial. This action would require charges and an open hearing at which the individual has an opportunity to defend himself. No one outside or inside the college has suggested charges based on violation of law or regulations.

Three: Any action to change Mr. Murray's status must be based on rules and procedures that apply to all faculty members. His misdemeanor conviction resulting from a campus fight last year is not grounds for punitive action today, nor are his public statements and political philosophy.

Four: Mr. Murray is part of a critically important educational program. Reassignment on dubious grounds of any instructor in the Educational Opportunities Program would so violate the integrity

> and purpose of the program as to threaten its usefulness to the college and the community. We have undertaken an obligation to attempt to reach the young people who are the victims of national educational failings. It is a bold venture with built-in risks, including employment of some part-time people who aggravate some elements of the general public and please other segments.
>
> In summary, George Murray was hired according to established procedures and we have neither professional nor legal grounds to change his status. I assume that he is aware that as a part-time faculty member he is subject to the same action for personal or professional conduct in the future as any member of the faculty.
>
> For the reasons I have outlined, I have advised Chancellor Dumke that I respectfully decline the request to reassign George Murray.
>
> There is a concern beyond the Murray case that I wish to state in the strongest terms in closing. If we are to continue as a nation ruled by law, we must give all citizens the benefit of due process and the protection of the law. We cannot single out individuals or groups for special action.

A newsman approached Murray for a statement immediately after the close of the conference. He refused to comment. The reporter was surprised and irritated. He said to Murray, "Don't you have anything to say? You know, Smith laid his job on the line for you?" Murray turned away.

The radio was on in the president's office, as we returned from the press conference. The first newscast on the hour opened with: "President Smith defies trustees. . . ." Apparently, the term *declined* was not to catch on. A few stations used *rejected*. The report was repeated hourly and was featured on most evening newscasts, of course.

Turning to work at my desk, I picked up a number of documents that showed that our previous Sunday's projection of possible ultimata concerning Murray was borne out. The legislature of the Associated Students, comprising mainly elected student leaders, had extended their support in a resolution passed the day after the administrative decision had been made at the Sunday meeting:

> Be it enacted by the Associated Students Legislature of San Francisco State College in a meeting assembled on September 27, 1968, by a unanimous vote, that:
>
> *Whereas:* The present-day racist establishment has dictatorially placed itself in opposition to individuals' attitudes and

political beliefs regardless of their qualifications in incumbent capacities, and

Whereas: The existing educational system is outmoded, out of alignment with reality, and does not meet the needs of today's students living in today's world, and

Whereas: We, the Associated Students, feel that George Murray, instructor in English, is effective, qualified, and compatible with and within a viable educational system geared to today's student,

Therefore be it resolved:

That the Associated Students of San Francisco State College deem the request of the Board of Trustees of the California State College System for the removal of George Murray from his present instructional position because of his political beliefs; that said request is deemed a racist, fascistic, condemnatory, and condemnable decision that is consistent with the traditional suppression of the black people's struggle for liberation, and

Be it further resolved:

That the Associated Students of San Francisco State College supports the retention of George Murray in his present instructional capacity, and

Be it further resolved:

That the Associated Students Legislature urges President Robert Smith *not* to comply with the request of the trustees and

Be it further resolved:

That if President Robert Smith does support the rights of George Murray, the Associated Students will support President Smith in the face of any punitive action taken by the Board of Trustees, by mobilizing the campus community to take *any action necessary*[6] to accomplish said end.

Just below it in the pile of communications was a letter signed by five leaders of the "Program People," and the two campus papers, the *Daily Gater* and *Open Process,* key forces in winning the previous student body election:

> The recent trustees' request that George Murray be barred from teaching at San Francisco State College is an intolerable decision

[6] Italics added.

> by a group of reactionary fearmongers. Not only is this request a blatant violation of academic freedom but more important, it is also part of an official organized attempt to persecute the Black Panther Party. We cannot sit by and allow these men to arbitrarily punish black revolutionaries for their political beliefs and actions. We fully support the Ten Point Program of the Black Panthers and their right to participate fully in this academic community. Therefore, we urge you to ignore this racist "request"; in so doing you are guaranteed our full support should they attempt to bring the shit down on you. However, should you decide to abdicate to the trustees, we will be forced to oppose you and the trustees by *any means necessary.*[7]

The trenchant rhetoric and the commitment to "any means necessary" in both statements supporting Murray were not reassuring. Many of the same student leaders were doubtless reacting as well to the trustee action denying approval of the Student Union. The "*any* means necessary" phrase had steadily gained currency in speech and action on the campus, especially since the Vietnam War Convocation in November 1967. The same term, used by the governor, trustees, and chancellor was usually phrased, only a bit more gracefully, "by all necessary means."

Positive, supportive responses came by mail and telegram from the local campus and across the state, endorsements of our action by campus senates, departments, and individual faculty and administrators. The response from the public was heavily against my decision, though perhaps one-third of those were supportive. A few teachers and professors, some retired, expressed outrage that a person such as Murray should hold academic rank and teach. We worked hard to cool the aftermath in the press and the legislature. We met with key area legislators or their administrative assistants on October 3 to explain the context and rationale of the Murray decision. Our press officer, Harvey York, tried to interest the media people in other programs and events at the college.

While the trustees and chancellor were debating by telephone and caucus whether the Murray decision was an act of insubordination, Murray began to reveal his response to the conflict. He was reported to have said to the SDS in an off-campus meeting that my defending his teaching assignment was the worst thing that could have

[7] Italics added.

happened to him. On October 5, he spoke, along with several others, at a Speakers' Platform rally on campus of the need to prevent military recruiting on campus by "any means necessary." During the speech, he linked the U.S. with oppression around the world and called for black, brown, yellow, and progressive whites to struggle more in earnest. While the rhetoric and proposals for action were flamboyant, some of the content could have been drawn from General Cyrus Vance or Senator William Fulbright.

Referring to Max Rafferty, ultraconservative candidate for the U.S. Senate, Murray was reported in the press to have said, "The only way to stop him is to put a bullet through his head." On October 9 Vice-President Garrity, with my encouragement, filed with the chairman of the Academic Senate a request that disciplinary proceedings be invoked against Murray. Since the procedure had just been established, the Senate had not yet completed the process of selecting faculty members for service on faculty disciplinary panels. An ad hoc panel of three was appointed by the Senate chairman to begin the first of a three-stage process. In the meantime pressure from the Chancellor's Office built to suspend Murray. My staff and I continued to insist that as long as Murray was free of criminal or civil action, we would adhere to academic due process as established in the college and the system. It was part of a long-range strategy of mine to live within our laws and regulations as part of the effort to restore confidence among those faculty and students who still cared about the college as a place where reason and humane values were operative on the side of equity and justice. As is so often the case, civil rights and civil liberties and the principles supporting them must be supported in deeply adverse circumstances. Further, individuals drawing or provoking scorn and hate often become the seemingly unpromising agents for clarification of principle, process and commitment to such values, if anybody cares deeply enough to insist that our humane national traditions are supported.

The Military Information Day was successful in avoiding violence, almost totally unsuccessful in achieving the purposes for which it was planned since all branches of the service canceled their plans. I reiterated my support for "open recruiting" on campus and continuance of AFROTC. This aspect upset the doves among faculty and students, many of whom tend to be hawks in their willingness to war with administrators.

Because of the college position on Murray, a Chamber of Commerce official abruptly dropped his efforts to organize supplementary support for the year's athletic program. A senior state senator, friendly to higher education, telephoned me to voice his perplexity over the campus situation and his anxiety about growing constituency pressure on legislators to "move in on California higher education," especially since the public furor began over Murray and Cleaver. He said a number of legislators were considering closing the university and state colleges "until they are straightened out." But, he said, none of the campus chancellors or presidents could make clear to them what the exact consequences would be! I chuckled and replied, "I can tell you. The legislature will turn 300,000 angry young adults loose in the state just ahead of the election for one thing. By doing that, legislators will transfer the responsibility for working with the problems from college and university presidents to yourselves, and will relieve us of many of our problems."

It was becoming obvious that, following the trustee action in late September, Murray was beginning to make it as a black militant speaker in the footsteps of Cleaver, as the following press reports of his statements indicate:

> We don't need any more speechmakers. What we need is killers, political assassins. We've got to revolt and continue it until it becomes an armed revolution. [*Daily Gater,* October 7, 1968]

> They had a revolution with guns back in 1776, why can't we have one now? We won't put our guns down until everyone in the world is free. [*Daily Sundial* (San Fernando Valley State College), October 23, 1968]

Collecting media reports was one thing, getting eyewitnesses, who would report directly what they saw and heard was another. The sense of threat and fear that blocked restraining action had continued to grow on campus for at least a year.

Our staff departed for the next meeting of the Board of Trustees (at Fresno State College) facing triple jeopardy. The general election now less than two weeks away, the Student Union was up for what we assumed was to be the last chance, and trustee distress over my action in the Murray case and his escalating rhetoric were bound to pervade the meeting. The luncheon meeting was a grave, searching affair. There was the feeling that Murray's recent violent rhetorical attacks were what the college deserved for defending his teaching assignment. I thought it just as plausible that Murray's violent language was provoked by the trustees' action and the two months of attack on Murray by public officials including Governor Reagan.

I argued that the disciplinary due process under way should be adhered to, poorly adapted though it was to such a complex case; that the second phase of the proceedings would probably be completed by the next week; and that by mid-week we should be able to make a public statement either making formal charges, or dropping the procedure already under way. It seemed clear that events required completion of the hearing process both as a test case on the outer limits of faculty political-ideological behavior, and to clear or verify charges against the individual. Further, it appeared that Murray had set himself a course intended to force his suspension or dismissal. To take the bait and move arbitrarily, I argued, was to violate our own rules of process, further inflame the thesis of institutional racism, and in all probability precipitate disorders on the campus just prior to the November election. By making Murray a martyr in the eyes of the Bay Area minority community, we would also further polarize the whites and the minority populations. George Murray's situation had been blown up out of all proportion to its relative importance on the campus; excessive time and energy put into the Murray problem built the odds against keeping a step ahead of several other problems rapidly building on the campus. Further, there were several "Murrays" on campus who had not yet made it with the news media, or their constituencies. We needed to find ways of coping with highly militant minority leaders from several groups, rather than deciding to drive the first publicly controversial black figure from the college by arbitrary action, as though that were a solution.

I tried hard to set the Murray controversy in a broader context. There was clear evidence of the growing racial tension reflected in serious incidents in several higher education campuses of the Bay Area and elsewhere. A number of high schools were also suffering disruptions and two bombs were found on campus the previous Friday. We needed no action on Murray. We needed time to work on several acute problems if we were to be at all prepared for upcoming confrontations and disruption including the proposed student strike. Peace on campus depended on student and faculty attitude. If we were to gain the confidence of the majority of the students, we must work within our own rules. We had to find ways of curbing the intimidation, controlling the self-styled revolutionaries, and holding individuals accountable for specific breaches of regulations or law. We needed to respond to the basic problems that were generating frustration and disorder. The widespread campus resentment of the September trustee action argued against further action on their part. Moreover, the Berkeley students had begun a Sproul Hall sit-in the day before to protest the regents' action in the Cleaver issue.

The trustees reluctantly went along. Chairman Merriam's restrained news release said:

> We have received numerous questions concerning Mr. George Murray, instructor at San Francisco State College. President Smith of San Francisco State has advised us that the college is currently investigating certain conduct of Mr. Murray as reported to campus offices. In my judgment it is inappropriate for this board to take any action today which, while an investigation is being conducted by proper campus authorities, might interfere with the process of the investigation in a report from President Smith at our next board meeting.

Unfortunately, the chancellor demanded decisive action four working days later. Two issues remained for the day: (1) How would we fare on the re-presentation of the Student Union building? It was clear that Moshe Safdie's striking design was still opposed by Harry Harmon, the chancellor's architect and Governor Reagan's recently appointed state architect. (2) What the hell was Murray up to in his lunchtime speech to Fresno State College students—for he had been scheduled to speak on that very campus. The long discussion of the union was a nitpicking farce. College officials including myself were all but excluded from the muddle of conflicting information on secondary technical problems. James Thacher and Louis Heilbron, two of the San Francisco trustees, worked hard in support. A San Francisco news reporter informed me early in the meeting that it would be blocked by a tie vote unless someone switched. This was the estimate also of Vice-President Glenn Smith, who had worked in the corridors all morning. The fact that the building and program were to be wholly student financed, and had the total support of the various groups in the college and the local advisory board cut no ice. Much of the September state college presidents' meeting was devoted to a proposal presented by Chancellor Dumke and Board Chairman Theodore Merriam to strengthen the role and extend responsibilities of local advisory boards. Trustee Dudley Swim raised one objection after another. Russell Bass, student body president, had a hard time even finding anyone to accept his student petition carrying 6,000 signatures. The social, educational, and esthetic aspects of the project were dismissed to provide time to bicker over the cost of soap and labor to wash the extra windows and the way in which the ratio of usable square feet of floor space was figured. At different times, both Bass and I tried to link the severely overcrowded central campus area and the several years of student-faculty planning of the project with campus frustration and unrest. We were accused by one trustee of "holding a gun" at the trustees' heads.

During the union discussion just prior to the vote—an eight-to-eight defeat—the board received freshly dittoed pages of excerpts from Murray's violent speech on the other side of the campus. It crossed my mind that the lengthy bickering may have been a filibuster until the Murray report came in. One of my staff had already returned from the rally saying Murray was "pretty wild" and over half of the audience walked off on him. President Frederic Ness of Fresno State told me of intense efforts the day before among college personnel and students to avoid disorder in the wake of Murray's appearance.

What appeared to be a victory for the Student Union in the tie vote of the morning committee hearing became an eight-to-eight defeat. The tie vote in the committee coupled to a tie vote in the general meeting, with five Board members absent, on the face of it appeared calculated and contrived by caucus. Again Dumke voted for it after his chief staff man in building and planning, Harry Harmon, led the crucial assault against it in ways that systematically confused the issues.

Before leaving the meeting word came to me from the press grapevine that politically the Cleaver affair had been pumped almost dry and that Murray was in for a major build-up during the last ten days of the election campaign. Friday and Saturday, media reports of Murray's speech at Fresno and one two days earlier at San Fernando Valley State began to roll in. I asked a staff member to make every effort to get tapes of the speeches. While the reports seemed plausible, evidence to secure conviction for an actual offense differed from a news report of an alleged event, a point the chancellor and the trustees had ignored in September.

Murray did not drop the initiative. On Monday, October 28, he spoke on campus. Tuesday he was quoted in the *Gater,* "If a fraternity (black) takes up guns to defend our communities from the pigs, then it's doing something." And in the San Francisco *Chronicle,* "The only realistic way to deal with a cracker like Smith is to say we want 5,000 black people here in February, and if he won't give it to you, you chop his head off."

Tuesday, while waiting for the Fresno tape, I reviewed the ethical, racial, and legal problems of Murray's situation with key administrators and the chancellor's legal representative on campus, Larry Robinson. My staff was again finding it difficult to identify witnesses who would state what they heard Murray say. But other forces were also on the move.

By Tuesday evening, we arrived at alternative approaches to Murray. There was little remaining doubt of the accuracy of the reports on the Fresno speech. By day's end, I leaned toward filing additional charges of unprofessional conduct and suspension of Murray's faculty status for thirty days with pay. Some members of my staff were not in agreement with this solution. We decided to sleep on it and meet early Wednesday, September 30.

Up at 5:00 A.M., I wrote a rationale for campus and media release and began to project the probable consequences of suspension. It had become my firm conviction that Murray by his volatile and violent rhetoric urging violence, assassination, and revolution was, as a black leader, deliberately sanctioning and encouraging the type of violence the College of San Mateo had experienced the week before. Further, he was advocating homicide on our own campus, already tension-ridden, and naming specific persons as objects of violence.

A suspension would provoke consequences. The BSU-proposed "strike" would be assured. The student community program people would conclude that, as a white liberal, I had caved in to pressure on schedule. They would refuse to acknowledge Murray's escalating pattern of incitement to riot and violence against specific persons. The liberal to radical faculty would charge breach of academic freedom, despite my long association with that cause. I had been informed by the president of the campus chapter of AAUP that they were no longer supporting Murray, as they had before the trustees a month earlier. Finally, on campus, the charge of my being a racist president would be leveled, and campus disruption, involving both SDS and Third World students, was probable.

Reflecting on the last prospect, the constellation of the past week's events struck me. The hundreds of community program students on our campus were convinced that the Board of Trustees' rejection of the Student Union, coming after their aggressive summer hearing on the Experimental College, and newly proposed trustee regulations were meant to destroy their programs, the Experimental College, the Community Services Institute, and others. Subsequent events including the impounding of student body funds, proved them right. Six thousand petitioners had lost their Student Union. The Third World Liberation Front (TWLF) was already moving toward direct action. The state and national elections were just a week away. Rafferty was driving hard on anarchy and revolution in the colleges to enthusiastic ovations; as the polls showed he was trailing his opponent but gaining ground. Bay Area schools and colleges were requiring police action at one or another campus almost daily.

Our information channels continued to carry the word that action on Murray would spark disorder both on our campus and on other campuses. Events surrounding the Huey Newton (Black Panther) trial were extremely tense. The morning paper carried reports of the bombing of a San Francisco police station involving a "shattering" dynamite blast, scattered violence across the city, and the wounding of two firemen by sniper's fire.

It seemed crystal clear that a unilateral action by the college suspending Murray would be irresponsible. I decided to talk to Mayor Alioto as soon as I could get to the campus. He called me back at 8:30 A.M. (Wednesday) and, grasping the problem quickly, asked me how soon I could come downtown. Eleven o'clock was set so there would be time to review the situation with the administrative staff. Our staff agreed to meet at 2 P.M. to decide on action, immediately following my return to campus.

About 9:00 A.M. the first of a series of calls from the Chancellor's Office came in. A vice-chancellor was on the line.[8] Had I acted on Murray as I had "promised the trustees in Fresno that action would be taken by mid-week"? Apparently, 9:15 Wednesday was "midweek." I reminded my caller that the previous Thursday I was stating an expectation, not a flat commitment. He disagreed. A note of compulsive urgency on his end of the line struck me as we talked about my plans for the day. He objected to my talking to Alioto before acting, indicating he was in communication with Dumke and the matter must be cleared up without delay. I made it clear that the Alioto

[8] Dumke was in the East, rumored to be at an interview for a *Time* cover story. Reportedly, he was to become Secretary of Health, Education and Welfare in the event of a Nixon victory.

meeting would be held; that a campus staff meeting would follow; that perhaps by late afternoon, something explicit could be reported. The call ended on a high note of tension. Another telephone call, this time from Heilbron, brought the information that the several trustees who had steadily supported me had lost whatever clout they enjoyed with the board since the Murray speech at Fresno. Word was being circulated, he reported, that I had "gone back on my word given at Fresno." I thanked him for his support and explained what we were attempting to do.

I arrived at the weekly meeting of academic deans forty minutes late. The deans reviewed and endorsed a blunt, four-page letter drafted the Friday before, immediately following the Fresno meeting. It attempted again to state our needs and itemize the assistance we needed if we were to make it through the semester. Late in the morning, the mayor, two of his personal staff members, and I went over the Murray problem and my proposed action. We agreed that the meeting was to be "off the record" as far as possible. The mayor made it clear that he assumed the frantic pressure on me to act on Murray was related to the political campaign, and word that the *Los Angeles Times* was ready to blast the college and state college system on the issue of Murray as an instructor and advocate of violent revolution. He was clearly distressed about the possible consequences of action on Murray ahead of Hallowe'en and ahead of the election, because of the pattern of rising violence in the Bay Area. Telephone calls to the chief of police and district attorney, as well as the United States attorney, left us with information that more than enough disorder faced the Bay Area authorities without adding probable disorders at our campus. Alioto asked what it would take to dissuade me from action. We agreed that I would not act against Murray at least until Monday, possibly Wednesday, the day after the election. (Wednesday after the election was the day designated for the Black Students Union strike. Spokesmen for the Black Students Union said Wednesday had been picked partly to keep Rafferty from making more political hay from racist issues. It was also the anniversary of the BSU invasion of the *Gater* office the fall before.) Alioto offered to call the chancellor, Theodore Merriam (chairman of the Board of Trustees), and the local trustees to explain the city's problem. We agreed we both would talk to the *Los Angeles Times,* asking them to withhold or moderate their intended blast. They did, although our efforts may not have been decisive in that decision.

Mayor Alioto agreed to see if there were legal means of restraining Murray as an alternative to campus action. He said he would consider a possible grand jury probe of the Panthers including those operating on the campuses. Finally, because it was clear that violence was probable on our campus immediately ahead, I asked the mayor for three top police intelligence men to take an independent reading of what was building up on campus, and what, if any, additional security personnel the college needed. He agreed immediately. City police were not withdrawn from the campus during the remainder of the academic year. I had been brushed off earlier in the fall by the state attorney general, the district attorney, and the chancellor when I requested additional security personnel, I felt a lot better—temporarily. The "off the record" conference with the mayor was reported almost in full in the next issue of the *San Francisco Examiner*. It was not leaked by me. It helped the on-campus "Smith is a puppet" line and lent credence to the charge that I was turning to Democrat Alioto for support against the Republican-dominated trustee-governor combine.

Back to campus for the administrative staff meeting. So as to avoid interruptions, we met in the basement of the Creative Arts building to consider next steps. Just as we began the meeting, a faculty member found us to say there was an urgent call from another vice-chancellor that could not wait. I was unable to interpret my position to him effectively following the conference with Alioto. He suggested that I was using Alioto, at that time considered a probable Democratic candidate for governor, for political leverage to avoid what the trustees and governor knew I must do. The notion that the college had some responsibility for the urban area it served seemed not to register, nor did the possibility that campus social controls in a precarious situation depended on informed decisions.

I said that, nonetheless, the decision for now was made and we could talk further after the staff meeting. The meeting was a brief one —only long enough to review events and approve two statements for campus distribution. The first was a reiteration of my statement in September to the faculty defending the idea of an open campus, stating that "threats of violence are persistent, coming from several segments of the college community," and making clear the administrative position that "we will not condone violence and we will take what steps are required to meet disruption and violent action with responses calculated to ensure safety of individuals and property." The second statement, released to *Phoenix* (the campus weekly newspaper sponsored by the department of journalism) and later to be distributed on campus, summarized the extraordinarily rapid movement of the college in providing personnel and programs for racial and ethnic education despite the drastic budget deficit estimated at $750,000 for the fiscal year.

A late call from the Chancellor's Office brought news that I would receive an order the following day to suspend Murray immediately. I gently thanked the vice-chancellor and so went home to a very late happy hour with my family. En route I picked up an *Examiner* to find the first stated list of eight Black Students Union demands; the fifth of these demanded "that George Murray, a member of the Black Panthers and a part-time English instructor at San Francisco State, be allowed to remain in his current teaching position." Thus ended Wednesday, October 30, 1968.

Thursday and Friday were busy days. The chancellor's letter arrived by courier from Los Angeles while I was meeting with the Executive Committee of the Senate: "I am by this letter directing that you immediately suspend Mr. George Mason Murray. . . . This suspension is temporary . . . pending the preparation of formal charges and conclusion of an appropriate faculty hearing at the college." A California Administrative Code section was cited. "I further direct you to suspend Mr. Murray from his status as a student." The directive called for formal charges "for misconduct" and a hearing, "at the earliest practical date." The code provides a maximum suspension of thirty days. Hallowe'en was upon us, the election now five days away, the BSU strike six days away. Later in the day, Mayor Alioto telephoned to report that he had fared no better with the Chancellor's Office or the chairman of the trustees than we had. At 4:30 P.M., I sent the following wire to the chancellor:

> On receipt of your communication ordering the immediate suspension of George Mason Murray I have conferred with administrative and faculty advisors and with community leadership. In light of the unprecedented nature of your directive and certain ambiguities in your letter, I am requesting a meeting in San Francisco on Friday, November 1, with the chairman of the Board of Trustees, the general counsel of the California State Colleges, and you, which will allow the review of your order to take place in the context of the local situation with the participation of both campus and community officials who will bear the impact of the action.

A second wire followed:

> After reading the transcript of your letter directing me to suspend Mr. George Mason Murray immediately, it is my obligation to inform you that this action was taken against the recommendation of a wide range of administrative personnel at this college and officials in the San Francisco community. I, therefore, inform you that the possible disruptive consequences of this action, if they get beyond control, are a responsibility your office has assumed. I suggest that presidents of other urban state colleges be informed of your action concerning George Mason Murray without delay.

Concerned about my agreement with Mayor Alioto I finally reached him very late in the afternoon and told him of the two wires; I assured him we would take no further action until Monday as per our agreement. He startled me by saying I had no choice but to go ahead and suspend Murray and that my last wire was inadvisable. Joe, I thought, has a nice knack of assuming the role of counselor as he yanks on the rug! I concluded he did not want to admit that in San Francisco "disruption" could get "beyond control." I meant, of course, beyond control of the college administration.

Home very late again to find that my ten-year-old son and his mother had had a furious set-to and he was spanked and in bed without dinner. What a way to make a living! The next morning, he left for school without seeing anyone and without breakfast. Three days later we received a severe reprimand from his school because of his fighting on the school bus two days in a row. The principal's letter stated his amazement at my son's uncharacteristic behavior.

The chancellor's response to my request for an on-campus meeting was totally negative. Added to it was the threat of a special trustees' meeting to discuss my violation of what appeared to be a legal, if stupid, order. The Friday morning paper carried the results of the mayor's efforts to test Murray's behavior against the rules of law. The result, after checking with the U.S. attorney, the state attorney general, and the district attorney, was negative, a spokesman for the mayor said. Hallowe'en was behind us. The chancellor's attorney had prepared a letter of suspension in accordance with the previous day's letter, *from me to* Murray, suspending him. The chancellor had the authority to suspend Murray directly, but chose to direct me to do it. I insisted on two changes, opening the letter "By the directive of the chancellor . . ." and closing it "for the chancellor." A vice-president at the college commented: "The chancellor's action will assure Murray's clearance of disciplinary charges." Both San Francisco papers carried full and remarkably accurate reports of the Wednesday to Friday sequence, implying that I was attempting to buy time before acting against Murray. During the early weeks of the controversy, I attempted to hold off the trustees, leaving action until after recommendations from the faculty grievance procedures were completed. Following my own decision to suspend Murray on November 29, I was attempting to stall action until the city was prepared to cope with probable disorder arising from that action.

The *Los Angeles Times* on November 2 quoted Dumke: "The suspension of Mr. George Murray as a faculty member and as a student is action intended to ensure a prompt determination by San Francisco State College of his alleged conduct in recent weeks. Nothing less than the institution of formal academic proceedings, in my opinion, and President Smith agrees, will provide for an adequate solution to this problem." The article, by-lined by *Times* staff writer Daryl E. Lembke, continued: "The chancellor has been under great pressure from trustees, legislators, and others to take action on Murray." Examples of Murray's militant statements were cited.

On the same day, George Moscone, Democratic state senator from San Francisco, called for Dumke's dismissal during a speech at the St. Francis Hotel in San Francisco.

> The charges against Murray were being processed under procedures that provide for the fullest protection of Murray or any other faculty member. Unfortunately, however, this academic due process, and partisan political advantage were on a collision course. . . . The fateful election day is Tuesday: academic due process couldn't hope to render a verdict short of a month. . . . Into the breach plunged a panicked chancellor, Glenn Dumke, weak after being repudiated by his Academic Senate, and a board of trustees increasingly feeling the pressure of Republican desperation politics.

The next few days sharpened the battle lines. The specific act of trustee-chancellor suspension gave Murray increased stature as a martyr. It also triggered the raising of such "holy issues" (to use John Searles' phrase) as free speech, academic freedom, local autonomy, and racism.

On the following Monday, black students moved on the administration building at San Fernando Valley State College, holding college administrators and students prisoner under threat of violence. Two days later almost 100 black students staged a sharp disruption of the Oakland Merritt College cafeteria. The manager suffered a broken nose. The demonstration was in support of Murray.

At San Francisco State, support for the projected BSU strike grew. The Associated Students acted to endorse and support it. The executive committee of the campus chapters of AFL-CIO charged breach of due process and invasion of campus autonomy and supported the strike. A group calling itself Library Workers for a Strike called for a general student strike. The students from the activist programs who had promised in early October to use "any means" to oppose me if Murray were removed from teaching announced they would join the strike. Their flyer distributed on campus was attributed to the Experimental College, *Open Process,* MAX, the Community Involvement Program, and the Community Services Institute. Murray's "sudden" suspension was viewed as the first of a series of repressive acts by the trustees and the chancellor to "clean up" the college and perpetrate their own power. The proposed change in the administrative code bringing tighter control of student body affairs was cited to indicate the fight to support Murray was also a fight for their own survival. The "common enemy" was powerful and had no place for them, "unless it's one of total subservience."

The impact of the Murray suspension and my compliance was stated thus:

> When the chancellor and trustees put their foot down, something else becomes clear: the position of our college president. When the trustees originally requested that George Murray be fired, President Smith, realizing that such an action was bound to stir up trouble on campus, merely told them he was "investigating" the matter. In fact, no such investigation was taking place.[9] But when Chancellor Dumke turned that "request" into an order, Buffalo Bob changed his tune. Give me time, he pleaded, and I'll see to it that Murray is suspended—but according to the prescribed procedure of "due process." Murray will be charged with "unprofessional conduct," or some similar charge that is so vague that it's impossible to defend yourself against. The same thing happened last year to John Gerassi, Richard Fitzgerald, and Juan Martinez, three other professors whose

[9] Inaccurate. Garrity's action initiating disciplinary procedures, including fact finding, was taken October 9.

> dismissal was demanded by political climate of the moment. Making a pretense of legality when you're screwing someone looks less messy than an arbitrary order from on high. But it works the same way. When the heat is on, the college president—regardless of his conduct under normal circumstances—always sides with the chancellor and the trustees. If he didn't, they wouldn't have hired him.
>
> Murray's suspension, and the racism implicit in it, must be understood in its political context. Education at the state college level—and all other levels, for that matter—systematically prevents black people from getting the kind of education that is relevant to their needs. If black students set up a black studies department, their efforts are subverted by administrators whose orders ultimately come from above. Institutionalized racism is imbedded in the status quo of American society; to challenge it with that in mind is to challenge the very foundations of society. George Murray was suspended not because he is black, but because as a member of the Black Panther Party he has challenged the institutions which have always enslaved black people—including the educational system. And it is inevitable that white students who have also tried to challenge those institutions must be dealt with as well.

On a tense and volatile campus Murray's continued exhortations that problems be solved by murder—by assassination—became the major issue for me following my defense of his teaching assignment in early October. His willingness in speeches on campus to name specific individuals as justifiable targets in a state still not recovered from the assassination of Senator Kennedy appeared to exceed the bounds of professional ethics. Murray had also involved himself in confrontation situations accompanied by other black students involving threats, personal abuse, and obstruction of free movement. I intended to testify against him at his hearing. My own decision to suspend Murray was tempered with regret that I lacked the authority to suspend the chancellor and a few trustees, including Governor Reagan.

Murray left his class, after his suspension, without the necessity of police action. He was arrested during the first week of Hayakawa's administration, was suspended a second time, and was jailed as his parole was revoked. As we shall see presently, while in jail he played an important role in settling the student strike.

Chapter 8

Prelude to the Strike

Murray's "bring guns on campus" statement was almost a throwaway line in a more important pronouncement that stated that the black and brown students at the college set the date for the strike on November 6, the anniversary of the *Gater* attack. Official BSU press conferences (attended and legitimized by Nathan Hare and the new black Dean of Undergraduate Studies Joseph White) spelled out the goals of the strike. Beyond demanding the reinstatement of George Murray, the demands spoke to the need to move much more quickly with special admissions programs and black studies majors with control vested in the black community.

The call to strike was the prelude to events that were to overwhelm the college for four months, four months that saw classes on campus decimated, 300 faculty go out on strike, a change of presidents, massive police force on campus for over six weeks, and bloodshed and violence on numerous occasions. In view of these consequences and the confusions regarding the demands, some background is in order.

Under the urging of Jimmy Garrett and his aggressive BSU, and decisively supported at all levels of the administration and throughout the faculty, San Francisco State had been moving for the two years that preceded the student strike toward modifying its curriculum and structure to accommodate the vaguely developing desires of the black students. After the December riot of 1967, the pace had accelerated. Hare was hired with the expectation that he would coordinate through the various college departments a range of courses relevant to the black experience. The committee structure of the college addressed itself to analyzing the need for such a program, spelling it out and organizing it administratively. This became complicated by the emergence of a competing demand for wider-ranging ethnic studies. At the same time the administrative personnel of the college sought to take advantage of the new law that would permit 4 per cent exceptions to admissions requirements by developing a special admissions program for ineligible minority students and an educational program for these students. A significant number of courses addressed to the black experience were developed. Black students would have a full program, although not one under their domination.

This program development seemed in accordance with the thinking of Hare, who indicated in his first basic position paper on April 29, 1968, that no organized major would be needed until September 1969 and that not until then would he hope to expand the departmental staff, asking for three faculty in 1969. (This is to be compared with the 11.3 positions requested, and obtained, from the college Instructional Policies Committee in October 1968 and the 20 demanded by the BSU in their November 6 demands.) Hare did request that the various departmental courses be administered through a black studies department for the fall of 1968. The Academic Senate accepted the general goals and dimensions of the program and asked the administration to implement it. These actions were taken on faith since course descriptions or specific academic and ideological objectives were still in the planning stage.

Most of the college's administrative energies during the summer were spent in the difficult task of working with the various ethnic student groups to develop courses and to obtain tutorial help, counselors, and funding for the special admittees, usually referred to as the Educational Opportunity Program (EOP). This program had been the focus of the May sit-in, and it offered job opportunities in teaching and counseling or tutorial roles for a number of the militant ethnic leaders. No attempt was made to regroup the departmental black experience courses into an official black studies department. Such an action would have been largely an administrative arrangement within the purview of the vice-president of academic affairs, and communication between Hare and the other administrative officers in this area had become rather strained. Hare also had a considerable off-campus professional life and traveled around the country meeting speaking engagements. Failure to accede to this regrouping developed into one of the important symbolic issues in the BSU strike.

In mid-August leaders of the BSU began to press for a relatively autonomous black studies department. Working through other departments allowed the black community to control neither the course content nor the teaching personnel. Departments viewed the content and teaching methods primarily from a traditional perspective with emphasis upon "objective" academic approaches. With black leaders, however, the ideological commitment of the course and the instructor were important. They did not disguise the fact that they wanted such courses taught in a fashion compatible with militant black nationalism. As Hare indicated in his April 29 position paper, they expected that most courses would be exclusively for black students and would be taught by black, not Negro, faculty. Future experience with the Educational Opportunity Program would indicate that the BSU leadership expected some of their own number to be hired; two leaders of the BSU in the fall, Jerry Varnado and Benny Stewart, along with several others, taught in this program. Stewart had also been suspended for his conviction in the *Gater* attack.

This issue was accentuated by the appearance of a draft of an article that was to appear shortly in a magazine, *The Public Interest,* by the chairman of the political science department, John Bunzel. Bunzel had been active in state politics, had published widely in his field, and had a fine reputation for such works as *The Anti-Politics in America.* His article was a biting piece that chewed into Hare's position paper and the basic philosophy of black studies that he enunciated. Bunzel primarily attacked the absence of canons of scholarship or objectivity in this program, and he did it with the absence of tact that customarily accompanies academic debate in the journals. From then on Bunzel and his department became the "enemy," and Bunzel was subjected to a year of severe harassment—as will be described presently.

Whether it was working through a department, the college administration, or the Senate and its committees, the reality that angered the militant blacks more than anything else was that this meant pleading with "whitey" to achieve black needs—a rerun of their entire frustrating life experience. An independent black studies department would hopefully circumvent this indignity. But, as so often happens when the academic world confronts the desires of student activists, timing and procedures blocked the BSU ambitions. In mid-August many key administrators were taking well-deserved vacations (including President Smith) and the committees that would need to meet to consider this demand for instant departmental status simply could not be convened. In the eyes of some, this procedure was unnecessary since the Senate had given the administration the power to take what steps were necessary to facilitate a black studies program and since the "constructive alternatives" proposal that was written in the midst of the May sit-in stated that the college was committed to a black studies department. Others believed official procedures had not been followed and there was no institutional commitment to an operative department for the fall semester. Such conflicting views produced no confidence among the blacks that white educators should be entrusted with black needs.

In the minds of the black leaders there was no equivocation or doubt: the needs existed, whitey was welching once again, and so "you do what is necessary" to achieve your ends. There followed a series of confrontation-style meetings between groups of blacks and a few administrators, but nobody would commit the college until President Smith returned. On September 13 the issue came to a head. To give political muscle to their efforts the campus blacks had local Assemblyman Willie Brown work through Dean of Student Activities Elmer Cooper to arrange a high level meeting between key black community leaders, the administration, and the black students. Price Cobbs, psychiatrist and coauthor of *Black Rage,* Reverend Cecil Williams, and Willie Brown, among others, represented the community. Fifteen or so black students and the black administrators completed the group.

In this setting, with each administrator surrounded by blacks as if by prearrangement, another strategy was employed. "You new brothers and sisters, I want you to know who you are dealing with. This is Vice-President Glenn Smith, he's our enemy; over there is Vice-President Garrity who says he is our friend; Dean of Students Reddell says he's our friend also; that's President Smith, who, as of last week, was our enemy." Thus spoke Jerry Varnado, BSU leader. When President Smith asked the community leaders whether that was the way they desired to begin an important discussion of a complex issue, they declined to speak critically of their campus brothers but instead pressed for their demands. This pattern became standard throughout the year.

In addition to the immediate establishment of an independent department, they desired full professor status for Hare and a faculty allotment for the department so they could create and staff their own courses for the fall semester, now less than a week from registration. Neither the environment nor the timing conduced toward a favorable decision, although President Smith did commit himself to such a department and the policy that they could work toward the spring semester for a program. This was a critical decision: rational academic process and prerogatives won out at the expense of a "risky" commitment to action "now." History proved that the priority for rational process was even riskier and produced a confrontation that minimized rationality. Had a nonconfrontation style been employed, had the decision-making process been developed by the administration and the black community so that the president had not been placed on the spot so quickly in such a setting, a compromise might have been worked out. But the college did not sense the urgency of the demand; the black students did not trust the world of the honkies.

A parallel confusion and frustration in obtaining college acceptance of the specifics of a black studies major and a commitment of college resources and personnel to the new department during the first few weeks of the new semester contributed to the conflagration in November. Again the twins of administrative and Senate insistence on a modicum of deliberative process in making these decisions and the black community's impatience with this academic process produced the impasse.

To initiate a new major in the California State Colleges, an institution must obtain the approval of the Chancellor's Office and the trustees. Among the reasons for this procedure has been a deep trustee suspicion, sometimes justifiable, that academicians proliferate programs at considerable expense to the state. Therefore, once approved within the college, a black studies major must be presented to the trustees. In the case of this prospective major, proliferation was not of particular concern but the quality of the academic work and the issues of black separatism and possible indoctrination were. For these reasons the vice-president of academic affairs requested that Hare and the people that were working with him on the curriculum submit it to the Academic Affairs staff for review prior to taking it through the college committee structure.

Instead of working through the white administration, Hare and the new black Dean of Undergraduate Studies Joseph White chose to work closely with three faculty members who, through their membership on either the Instructional Policies Committee or the Executive Committee of the Senate, were in positions of faculty power that might allow them to expedite the college acceptance. All three belonged to the liberal, AFT segment of the faculty and were convinced that given the Murray setback and the noninitiation of a black studies department and program in the fall, the only possibility for preventing a black uprising was acceptance of this program quickly and an allocation of faculty to the department.

Unfortunately, these three faculty members—McGuckin, McDermid, and Miksak—did not communicate this basic insight to enough people in the administration and other faculty power centers, or, if they tried, they did not persuade these people of the cogency of their argument. Instead, they used their awareness of the faculty curriculum machinery to press for an immediate hearing during early October on the proposed major, secured its approval, facilitated the allocation of 11.3 faculty to the department, and ensured the early inclusion of the item on the Senate agenda. In the meanwhile it had become apparent to the Executive Committee of the Senate that the curriculum had never been cleared with the vice-president of academic affairs, that only course titles had been proposed for the major—black statistics, black economics, black psychology—and that some curriculum committee members had felt coerced by the large black audience that crowded the committee room. Consequently, in a hearing of all key parties except Hare it was agreed that the program would be reviewed by Academic Affairs and resubmitted to the committee within two weeks. It was also agreed that the Senate would act formally on the concept of a black studies major at its next meeting and on an accelerated time schedule to convince the black community that the college was committed to the initiation of the program by the spring semester.

To think that this action would allay black suspicions was an idle white hope. When the Senate did not act immediately on the Instructional Policies Committee's proposal after the blacks had bothered to deal with the faculty committees which it had been told were official college channels, no amount of procedural explanation could convince them this delay was anything but more racism. In the developing conflict everybody felt self-righteous: the administration had pressed for a quality program to ensure trustee approval; the Senate had ensured expedition and due process; the faculty sympathizers had tried to alleviate a calamity only to have villain administrators once again impede progress; and the black community's judgment that whites—whether faculty or administrators—were inherently racist and could only be handled by confrontations had been vindicated.

As the year began events in other sectors of the campus created tension and anxiety, but not in unusual degree for San Francisco State and not of the magnitude of the black frustration.

In fact, most of the student leadership energies were spent in defensive maneuvers rather than in revolutionary action. For several years the involved students had yearned to find release from the ugly wartime huts that housed student activities and they pinned their hopes on a Student Union building whose planning they had already funded with more than $100,000 and with hours and hours of energies. The far-out, hexagonal prism modules design of award-winning architect Moshe Safdie ran into conflict with the trustee principle of "compatibility," but then, given the neo-San Quentin style of most State buildings, this principle doomed almost any creative design. Since the building was being designed by "the people," with "the people's" money, and to meet "the people's" needs, the Student Union leaders worked hard for their own destiny and assumed they could win. Informal contact with the chancellor's representatives for the past half-year raised grave doubts they would. The issue came to a head at the trustee meeting when President Smith was advised to reassign Murray. At the same time the trustees rejected by a close vote the Student Union building design.

The student leaders were incredulous that absentee governors could so stifle an expression of the people's will, but since a way out was developed for one more hearing at the next trustee meeting, the students devoted their time to firming up technical problems and creating mass support. Neither did any good: at the October meeting the Union fell on a tie vote of eight to eight. The student newspaper speculated that had the college taken the "correct" Murray action during that ensuing month the Union might have been approved. Others shared this impression that the Union was a hostage in a bigger political battle. Though the student leaders lost their much needed center for community involvement on a commuter campus, they learned some valuable lessons on the uses of power. Trustee action confirmed radical predictions of establishmentarian philosophy and moved the student leaders considerably to the left.

A contemplated action by the trustees radicalized student government representatives even more than the Union vote. In several of the state colleges, student government organizations had the general legal status of private corporations. This gave them a freedom in the use of their almost half-million dollar budgets that some people in power thought was a major source of radical activity. In the minds of some trustees it was inconceivable that they who were given the public trust to govern these institutions should not be able to control the activities and use of funds of the Associated Students. And so an amendment to the system's regulations that would bring these activities and those funds under the control of the trustees and college presidents was promulgated. To the students, liberal or radical or even moderate, it seemed like the most blatant repression. Although Third World and radically inclined students largely controlled the Associated Students, trustee action on the Union and their contemplated amendment regarding the control of student funds ensured a radical Associated Students stance when the Black Students Union decided to strike in November.

While these actions of those in power were moving student leaders to the left, two campus events neither endeared the college to the public nor induced moderate faculty sympathy. Eldridge Cleaver spoke on the Speakers Platform on October 9, and immediately led the enthusiastic crowd of over 2,500 students in a rousing rendition of his song, "Fuck Ronald Reagan." For the public he said things like "Mickey Mouse Reagan, Donald Duck Rafferty, Big Mama Unruh, Meathead Humphrey, Bonenose Nixon, all these jive-ass regents, Smith, the pig who runs this prison camp; all of them need to be put in the penitentiary or up against the wall. . . . Up against the wall, motherfucker!" His message for students, which they rewarded with a standing ovation, was: "We want our own participation in the manipulation of the sovereignty that governs us. Nothing more, nothing less. Anything that stands between the people and the fulfillment of this principle has got to go, that's all, has got to go."

But these were only words, though threatening and prophetic ones. Ten days later, on October 18, two amateur time bombs were discovered, one in the Registrar's Office and one outside the office of the intellectual critic of the black studies proposal, John Bunzel. Many faculty interpreted the act as symbolic intimidation; the bomb had been timed to go off at 3:30 in the morning. Guards had begun to look around the buildings after one came across three black men walking across the campus at 2:30. The hand of one was bleeding and another cried, "Jesus Christ!" when he unexpectedly ran into the guard. Bunzel was to become a continuous target of the militant blacks. In addition to the time bomb, his tires were slashed and his car was painted while it sat in his driveway. One cannot overestimate the intimidating effect of this and other militant actions on academicians normally timid and confused when confronting force.

On other fronts, the college made no progress in filling the vacuum in disciplinary procedures despite the hiring by the dean of students of a black consultant to the process; the Senate moved into major policy revision of general education and faculty promotions procedures; and the AFT worked mightily, and with considerable surface success, in lining up faculty and departmental support for its nine-unit teaching load campaign that was to go into effect in the spring. In arbitrarily setting their own workload the faculty were pioneering in a new tactic for dealing with the power of the trustees and the Legislature in determining their professional working conditions. It was a determined but risky move to achieve power when consultation, faculty government, and legislative lobbying had failed, with the results totally uncertain. To maintain flexibility and obtain greater support from a professional group powerful with words but weak in action, the AFT-ACSCP hedged its commitment pledge with the following phrasing:

> We, the undersigned faculty members of San Francisco State College, hereby pledge not to accept a teaching load in excess of nine units as of the spring semester, 1969. We understand that this pledge

> obligates the signer only if a majority of the members of his department agrees to participate in the program, and that these members will have a final opportunity to decide, on the basis of the extent of faculty support throughout the system and on each campus, whether to implement the reduction.

Despite this hedging, there was a note of seriousness in the campaign as several significant departments began to submit spring schedules with reduced faculty loads and, of course, reduced departmental offerings. At some state colleges administrators responded with the tough line that they would recognize the faculty intent but would reduce the salaries of such pledged faculty by one-fourth. This produced particular anxiety since some departments at San Francisco State had virtually accomplished such load reduction for several years by skillful manipulation of the bureaucratic formula for allocating faculty to departments. This escalation of faculty tactics moved faculty into the confrontation style, educated many "withdrawers" at a bread-and-butter level to the power distribution in the system, and prepared many for placing their "bodies on the line" when the issues of police on campus, black student aspirations, Hayakawa legitimacy, and absentee control developed later in the semester. By the same token, this blatant power move by the employees educated the conservatively shifting power bloc in the trustees that the factory hands had to be whipped into line and even previous delegations of power withdrawn in the interests of a hierarchically managed system for the public good.

Another new phenomenon that linked the nine-unit load campaign and the AFT strike cropped up in the self-righteousness of those defying the system. In the words of the AFT president, Gary Hawkins: "People involved most deeply in the campaign are the ones who take their teaching most seriously." A similar claim was later made that the strikers were the most committed teachers and creative researchers. Neither claim endeared the activists to those faculty not choosing to join their ranks.

As early as the first week of October the administration received intimations that the minority groups had learned well their lesson from the previous season that the white academic power structure responded most rapidly when pressure was brought to bear on it; a Third World student spokesman enunciated their demands for the year: a School of Ethnic Studies, with bachelor's and master's degree programs and fifty faculty, 2,500 Third World students to be admitted by the spring and 5,000 by the fall of 1969, funding and jobs for all special admittees, and the retention of George Murray and Juan Martinez. Between the time of this pronouncement and the end of October, the summer frustrations of the black students had been multiplied by what they considered the racist treatment of their curriculum by the white administration and faculty committees and the obvious attempt to move on their English instructor, Black Panther Minister of Education Murray.

So, on Monday, October 28, they went on the offensive with a stomp around the campus and through the Administration Building in celebration of Huey Newton's clash with the police a year earlier. Standing on top of a cafeteria table, Murray himself called for the strike on November 6 that was to convulse the campus for four months in the longest student strike in the history of American higher education.

Within a week the BSU's Central Committee met and officially formulated the strike and their Ten Demands. The Central Committee represented a swing in the direction of centralized leadership and away from participatory democracy for the entire BSU or domination by a few charismatic leaders. A member of the committee, Terry Collins, explains its evolution in the BSU publication, *Black Fire:*

> In the spring of 1968 the Black Students Union saw that there was a need for democratic centralism. Before that time the Black Students Union had no formal structure. Dominant personalities of two or three people tyrannically reigned over the other students. Factionalism was rampant, potential revolutionary brothers were disillusioned, sisters were used and abused in the name of "blackness." It was the era of the bourgeois cultural nationalism, a stage of evolution that all black students involved in the movement move through, but must shake quickly. Bourgeois cultural nationalism is destructive to the individual and the organization because one uses "blackness" as a criterion and uses this rationale as an excuse not to fight the real enemy when the struggle becomes more intense. That is why we presented a new structure to the people in the spring of 1968 and called for the election of a central committee. In order to fight the enemy and win, we had to have a decision-making body of battle-hardened brothers who would be directly responsible to the people. . . . Because we use democratic centralism as opposed to ultra democracy and liberalism, we have been thrust into the vanguard position of college campuses. Whether we like it or not we must set the correct example.

In the same edition of this publication another Central Committee member, Clarence Thomas, explained the application of this leadership structure to the strike decision:

> If the Central Committee of the Black Students Union had put the issue of having a strike at State before all the black students for a vote, what would have taken place? Chaos. Some of the students would have been undecided. Reactionaries would have been against it due to their pursuit of a piece of toilet paper called a degree or their fear of losing their status as a student. The strike and the revolutionary struggle against the trustees, Reagan, Alioto, and Hayakawa for self-determination for all Third World people would never have been put into action with a democratic vote. The people on the Central Committee are selected by the students, give direction, leadership, and make policies for the students. In the final analysis, it is the people who control it, because the Central Committee has to make decisions on the basis of the needs and desires of the people. If it does not, the Central Committee will find itself without the support of the people who will either be indifferent or will replace their leaders with other new leaders, who will be responsible to their needs and desires as oppressed people.

Thomas concluded his article on "Where the Decisions Are Made" with a quote from Mao: "We must affirm anew the discipline of the party, namely: (1) the individual is subordinate to the organization; (2) the lower level is subordinate to the higher level; and (3) the entire membership is subordinate to the Central Committee. Whoever violates these articles of discipline disrupts Party unity." Thus, fourteen "battle-hardened brothers" planned the strike, its goals, and strategy. On Monday, November 4, they announced their demands and their strike at a press conference. Increasingly on the State campus when the BSU announced a press conference, the press attended in large numbers. The BSU and its leaders were an important source of the kind of news the Bay Area public feasted upon. To legitimize their strike the BSU leaders had two black administrators, Nathan Hare and Joseph White, appear with them at the conference and indicate their support. From this point on White, dean of undergraduate studies, became, in effect, dean of black undergraduate studies—an example of the difficulty of maintaining black administrators in all-college slots in the context of a militant black student organization.

Another all-college black administrator, Dean of Student Activities Elmer Cooper, spoke for the militant black students when he commented, "There are going to be a lot of disappointed people when they find out there will be no building taken over or any traditional crap like that. It's simply going to be a strike where black and Third World students and others don't go to class. That's it."

The BSU girded for action by holding a meeting of all Third World students in the auditorium on Tuesday to hear black militant leader Stokely Carmichael give a serious talk on the need for clear-cut objectives in revolutionary activity. Black guards stood at each doorway to the auditorium and permitted only Third World students to enter. A year ago when they had met to plan strategy after the *Gater* attack and to hear Ron Karenga, fiery black leader and orator, they had employed similar exclusionary tactics only to be told shortly by President Summerskill that this was prohibited on the campus. The guards were lifted then although not many white students volunteered to attend BSU meetings. By now no officials attempted to intercede, nor did they all year. One white student did get by the guards but he was attacked, bloodied, and thrown out. Carmichael's speech had a profound effect on the BSU and shifted attention from a one-day strike to the possibilities of prolonged confrontation.

That same day the administration continued its preparations for the unknown contingencies of a black student strike. Arrangements were made with the police to have approximately fifty plainclothesmen on the campus in communication with police headquarters in the president's office. Several squads of uniformed police would be nearby if needed. At the Senate meeting that Tuesday, Henry McGuckin, a former AFT president and antiwar leader, attempted to persuade his fellow senators to call for a faculty strike on the same day as the black student strike, November 6. He proposed that they would be protesting only the chancellor's interference on the Murray case. His motion was defeated, twenty-four to eight, with only the hard core of AFT members on the Senate voting for it. McGuckin then resigned from the Senate so that he could employ his energies more productively in support of the student issues, claiming the Senate was avoiding its responsibility to maintain the locus of authority on the campus.

For white activists and radical students the unilateral decision of the BSU Central Committee to stage a strike on its own terms posed a serious dilemma: What would be the position of the white students? In past confrontations they had developed coalitions with the blacks, realizing that black troops and black assistance slowed down the police and the administration in any repressive action. Besides, the activists might be able to play a role that would educate and radicalize the liberal white students during the confrontation, especially if they could induce a police overreaction. Some white radicals, on the other hand, resented the fact that black students demanded authority in deciding the goals and the strategy of the confrontation. By the end of the previous year the BSU was confident that the SDS did not dare oppose it on any basic issue.

In the mass participatory democracy meetings of the white students a schism developed between a new cadre, the by-now militant students in the Associated Students "programs" who feared the power structure was going to make them powerless, and the old-line SDS and PLP radicals. The "program" students initially assumed the leadership and organized the first key meeting, but their success was short-lived. After attempting to lead the group in embracing the goals of campus autonomy and student power, they were moved aside by the more experienced SDS leaders, who then persuaded the group to adopt the simple goal of eliminating racism on campus. This placed the power squarely in the hands of the BSU. When some students pressed for independence at least in devising tactics, the group was put in its place by a few blunt-speaking black students who told them they were welcome to come along only if they took orders from the blacks, because after all, radical or not, they were still honkies. This settled the issue. From that moment on the Students for a Democratic Society and the Progressive Labor Party never launched an indigenous movement of their own for the entire year but instead became shock troops and an auxiliary of the Black Students Union.

Chapter 9

Strike!

Faculty and students came to the campus Wednesday, November 6, with trepidation. Nobody knew exactly what to expect, including the rank and file of the black students. It was only when they met in the auditorium late in the morning that they got their marching orders. The tactics that chairman Benny Stewart spelled out indicated they had gone to school on the efforts of the SDS the previous May. No vulnerable building sit-in for them. Instead, Stewart, their leader, spelled out to them the "tactics of the flea" as they prepared to do battle:

> It just so happens that the members of the BSU Central Committee have been analyzing how student movements have been function-

> ing. Taking over buildings, holding it for two or three days, and then the thing is dead. Most of your leaders are ripped off and thrown in jail, or the masses are thrown in jail, and there's no one to lead them. From our analysis of this, we think we have developed a technique to deal with this for a prolonged struggle. We call it the war of the flea. . . . What does the flea do? He bites, sucks blood from the dog, the dog bites. What happens when there are enough fleas on a dog? What will he do? He moves. He moves away. And what the man has been running down on us, he's pysched us out, in terms of our manhood. He'll say, "What you gonna do, nigger?" You tryin' to be a man. Here he is with shotguns, billy clubs, .357 magnums, and all you got is heart. Defenseless. That's not the way it's going to go any more. We are the people. We are the majority and the pigs cannot be everywhere, everyplace all the time. And where they are not, we are. And something happens. The philosophy of the flea. You must begin to wear them down. Something is always costin' them. You can dig it. . . . Something happens all the time. Toilets are stopped up. Pipes is out. Water in the bathroom is just runnin' all over the place. Smoke is comin' out the bathroom. "I don't know nothin' about it. I'm on my way to take an exam. Don't look at me. . . ." When the pig comes down full force, ain't nothin' happening. He retreats. When they split, it goes on and on and on. . . . We should fight the racist administration on our grounds from now on, where we can win.[1]

Specifically, this meant classroom visitations to "ask students whether they support us, and if so, why are they attending classes." Stewart suggested that the classroom visitation teams keep their cool so as not to "play into the hands of those who will smash our heads, arrest us, and take our freedom away." When he concluded, approximately 120 Third World students headed for the classroom buildings in teams of from six to ten. This was the same tactic that had so offended faculty in the December riot a year ago, faculty who could countenance a variety of tactics but considered their classrooms inviolate. While the Third World students dispersed, their tactics were obscured by a large SDS rally at the Speakers Platform, a rally that attracted newspaper reporters and other mass media personnel who were to inhabit the campus for the next four months.

The specific incidents around the campus varied with the raiding team. The general format was to enter classrooms uninvited, tell

[1] Transcribed from a tape recording.

the class there was a strike going on and that they had better join it, and announce that as of that moment the class was dismissed. In many instances faculty and students resisted and were subjected to harsh rhetoric, threats, and occasionally physical intimidation. On a few occasions windows were broken and property destroyed. Soon knots of students gathered to challenge the black students; a few fistfights broke out. It was a tense scene. Education came to a stop in most of these buildings; the ingredients for a riot were there. As reports of the volatility filtered in from the deans in the various buildings, President Smith made the judgment that serious threat to the physical well-being of the students existed and decided to close the college for the day and bring in the police to clear the campus. Very few chants of "Pigs off campus" were heard as contrasted to the previous May. For the most part students were relieved to see the blue-uniformed symbol of order. No confrontations developed. After an hour of classroom education, the Third World students left.

The basic question now before the administration was, should the college be reopened the following day? To advise him on this decision, President Smith gathered most of the members of the Council of Academic Deans, his top administrators, and the Executive Committee of the Senate in his office for a prolonged analysis of the issues. This created an administrative structure for crisis problem solving that prevailed for most of Smith's tenure. It had the advantages of wide communication, varied input of ideas, and general support for the decisions reached. Yet, it was an unwieldy group where the individual could avoid responsibility by lapsing into obscurity, it lacked a sense of focus and precision, and significant groups such as the radical liberal faculty had virtually no representation. All of these qualities were manifest Wednesday night as the group struggled to make a decision on a serious problem beyond the experience of most in attendance.

From the beginning there was heavy support for keeping the college open while attempts were made to solve the problem. This thinking hinged on a respect for the right of students to obtain the instruction for which they had contracted, a deep resistance to the tactics employed by the Third World students in invading buildings and classes, and a feeling that closing the campus would enhance the power of the striking students. Negotiating under coercion was not attractive to the group, although most were aware of the Third World contention that this term, *coercion,* aptly described their life condition now and for hundreds of years. The political reality that keeping the campus closed would certainly produce a public and legislative outcry and pressure from the trustees and governor both to reopen immediately and to depose President Smith did not escape the group but did not dominate its thinking. In fact, when a chancellor's representative told them bluntly that such closing might cost Smith his job, Smith quickly interjected that that was the least important dimension of the problem.

Actually Smith, who kept relatively quiet during most of the debate, edged closer at the end to the point of view being voiced by black Dean of Undergraduate Studies Joe White and supported by about five others that a creative solution was needed, and that this could not be obtained during an insurrection suppressed by the police. Like many of the decisions during this troubled period, the answer was nudged forward by the omnipresent media personnel and their newscast and story deadlines. In the process of reconciling the differences in the group a significant point that had been raised earlier by several top administrators—whether any disciplinary action should be taken against the Black Students Union—fell between the cracks. The point was never seriously reactivated as other problems absorbed the group's energies; but once again, the impression was given that violation of the educational process could be undertaken with impunity.

While the administration pondered, so did the activists. The BSU retreated to an off-campus center and after extensive debate agreed to continue the strike. In the words of a key Third World leader, Tony Miranda: "When we called the strike first of all we needed to test our backing, our constituency. What happened was that we had more support than we thought we did. . . . We decided to have a one-day strike; following that we sat down and decided to have a continuous thing."

In view of this, one can wonder what might have happened if at the end of that first day: significant concessions had been made by the college; the police had never come to the campus and classes had continued; the faculty had united behind Smith and against the violence on the campus; significant disciplinary action had been taken on campus against the BSU and its Central Committee; and the politicians and trustees had stayed out of the scene.

Although the Ten Demands were listed as the focus of the entire four-month controversy, and they were enunciated, defended, attacked, explained, and explored in newspaper articles, partisan handouts, administrative pronouncements, Senate policy statements, Select

Committee compromises, and thousands of speeches and discussions, to this day nothing remains more obscure in the minds of the average citizen, student, or faculty member than these Ten Demands and their famous "nonnegotiable" status. In general they speak to the oppressed status of black students in American higher education and the necessity of remedying that situation by giving them power over their own destiny and education. But the strike and its resolution hinged on specifics and not generalities. Although announced at a press conference from which President Smith was blocked, the demands were not presented to him until sixteen hours before the scheduled strike. Not key Central Committee members but Leroy Goodwin and several "sisters" gave the demands and the ultimatum. Said Smith: "I was asked to agree to them on the spot. I was also told that the strike would proceed in any event. My proposal to use the meeting to establish communication with the strike committee was not accepted by the committee. In the face of the strike threat and because of the nature of several of the demands, including some which were beyond my authority to grant, I could not agree to the demands."

Although many groups addressed themselves to explaining and responding to the demands, the intent and feeling behind them are probably best enunciated in the BSU publication, *Black Fire*. To the academic community the BSU explained in one fashion; the *Black Fire* justification was intended primarily for the black community—for whom the demands were created—and it catches the anger, frustration, feeling, logic, and commitment that propelled the group in its intense struggle for most of a semester. After each demand the initial response of the administration is encapsulated.

THE FOLLOWING ARE THE DEMANDS OF THE BLACK STUDENTS UNION AT SAN FRANCISCO STATE COLLEGE. THESE DEMANDS ARE NONNEGOTIABLE AND THE SCHOOL CANNOT AND MUST NOT FUNCTION UNTIL THEY HAVE BEEN MET.

Demand #1: *All black studies courses being taught through various departments be immediately part of the black studies department and that all the instructors in this department receive full-time pay.*

Black Fire: At the present time, the so-called black studies courses are being taught from the established departments, which also control the function of the courses. We, the black students at San Francisco State College, feel that it is detrimental to us as black human beings to be controlled by racists, who have absolute power over determining what we should learn. Take for example the School of Behavioral and Social Sciences controlling the social welfare classes, the School of Humanities control over the English classes. In our social welfare classes our first downfall is that our instructors are completely ignorant of the ethnic backgrounds of black people. They are in some cases people who have never been married and have no children. They tell us, or try to tell us, the best way to raise our children when they have never in their lives raised one. As a matter of fact our mothers raised most of theirs. In our English classes we are taught to dig on writers such as Chaucer and Arthur Miller. These writers do not deal in any realistic manner with black people. Black people should be aware of our own writers such as Hare, LeRoi, Baldwin, Williams, Wright, and so on. We are taught in our English classes to speak differently, so that when we return to our communities we are not able to communicate with our people. Therefore a diversity among the race results. If there was a real black studies department there would only be qualified instructors who would receive full-time pay since they would be full-time instructors.

Administration: At first the administration stated that the new curriculum for the black studies department which was currently being approved through "channels" could not be implemented until the fall 1969 for legal reasons and that the current joint sponsorship between the regular departments and the black studies department would have to continue. Within days this was modified so that the new curriculum could be invoked in the spring 1969, thus making this demand a non-issue.

Demand #2: *That Dr. Hare, chairman of the black studies department, receive a full professorship and a comparable salary according to his qualifications.*

Black Fire: Dr. Hare is the only black administrator at San Francisco State who was selected and hired by the black students. And his loyalty is to the blacks on campus and not to the white racist administration. His salary bears witness to that well-known governmental fact that a black person with a Ph.D. earns, on the average, the same as a white person with a high school diploma. He is a noted Ph.D. who has been published in the leading black magazines, sociological journals, as well as the so-called "slick" magazines, and has authored a book about the black middle-class, *Black*

Anglo-Saxons. Because he is a revolutionary and not an Uncle Tom, the administration has thrown him a few crumbs, in spite of the fact that he is responsible for coordinating and administering the department, which has thirty-three courses scattered throughout various "sympathetic" schools and departments on campus. Therefore, it is immediately incumbent to pay Dr. Hare for his work and his qualifications.

Administration: The administration commented that Dr. Hare had agreed to his rank and salary when he came to the college less than a year before, that other administrators were also associate professors and that any promotion would need to be recommended by the faculty promotions committee.

Demand #3: *That there be a department of black studies which will grant a bachelor's degree in black studies; that the black studies department, chairman, faculty, and staff have the sole power to hire faculty and control and determine the destiny of its department.*

Black Fire: The black studies department should have the power to grant a bachelor degree to anyone who wishes to major in the field, and that black studies department, chairman, faculty, and staff have the sole power to hire and fire without the interference of the administration and the chancellor. Past experiences with the racist dogs have taught blacks to "do their own thing." The present black studies consist of thirty-three scattered courses throughout different school departments. It is most important that a credited department for the works of black people be formed on this college campus, to feed the needs of its black student body. The new black studies program does not allow a strong department of studies. The blacks recognize the urgent need for black studies that would tell the true nature of this decadent American society. The black students of SFSC have long struggled for three years to obtain a black studies program with little or no support from the faculty and administration. If our demands are not soon met, we will have to use force.

Administration: In responding to this the administration indicated its commitment to and progress with a black studies department and major, but on the autonomy issue stated that while departments have a high degree of autonomy, ultimately their decisions are "subject to review by appropriate faculty bodies and administrative personnel" and that the college is legally responsible to the chancellor, trustees, and Legislature.

> Demand #4: *That all unused slots for black students from fall 1968 under the special admissions program be filled in spring 1969.*
> *Black Fire:* Explanation: Many black students are unable to be accepted in a college because of low grade points received by taking the ACT or SAT test, for middle-class suburban honkies. But through the demands, hard work, and study of the BSU, black students are in this college. There were more than enough black students to be accepted into SFSC under the Black Studies Institute, OMFE, STEP, Upward Bound, and College Commitment Program (which is the so-called Educational Opportunity Program). But because of the hassle with the administration (that is, the administrators told many black students that their transcripts were late and the students who were receiving grants or loans were told that they hadn't come in) many of these students were accepted in other colleges where they were given their grants and loans—so that left 128 unused slots open. We have demanded and demonstrated to get the unused 128 slots filled by black students and Third World students who wish to be admitted in SFSC in the spring 1969.

Administration: At first the college stated that admission of 128 more special minority admittees depended upon funding and the resolution of the college's serious budgetary deficit, but soon it responded favorably and this became another nonissue.

> Demand #5: *That all black students wishing so be admitted in fall 1969.*
> *Black Fire:* By admitting all black students who apply, the state can make up for years of neglecting black people trying to get a college education. The current racist quota system must be abolished—not ten years from now, but by September 1969. Entrances based on high school grades are also unjust to Third World students; these grades were originally based on knowledge of a white culture that denied the existence of any relevant Third World cultures. We have hassled too long with racist administrators and their systematic exclusion of Third World students; we must change this now.

Administration: Here the administration merely stated that admissions requirements are set by the trustees and the Legislature, not the college. It further commented that the college was so short of facilities currently that more than 8,000 applicants per semester were being turned away.

> Demand #6: *That twenty full-time teaching positions be allocated to the department of black studies.*
>
> *Black Fire:* No department on any college campus can function unless it has instructors. A department such as black studies, which offers thirty-three courses, needs twenty faculty members to adequately teach these and more courses. The positions are there and all the administration needs to do is allocate them to the black studies department. At the end of the summer of 1968, there were forty-seven open teaching positions. Donald Garrity, the racist top pig in the campus, declared that these positions would go into other areas where he felt they were needed. He felt the money should go to other administrators' pockets rather than into the black studies department. The racist Garrity gave away positions that could have been filled by qualified, nationally known black men and women such as Harold Cruse, Sara Fabio, and Alvin Poussant. The administration had the positions and refused to give them to us, and we are again demanding that the black studies department be given twenty positions.

Administration: The college at first responded bureaucratically, using formulas and fund limitations to justify no more than four positions. Soon there was agreement to shift priorities and provide the 11.3 slots requested by the Senate.

> Demand #7: *That Dr. Helen Bedesem be replaced from the position of financial aid officer and that a black person be hired to direct it; that Third World people have the power to determine how it will be administered.*
>
> *Black Fire:* Dr. Helen Bedesem has consistently ignored the needs of Third World students, particularly black students. Money which has been given to the college for black students has been sent back by this power-mad woman with the explanation that she could not accept earmarked money or the outright lie that no qualified students applied. Yet this slavemistress has allowed similarly "earmarked" funds to be used by Chinese students. Dr. Bedesem, who it is rumored achieved her position not by the normal process of appointment, but by successfully staging a vicious power play when the position was vacated, has brought young black sisters to tears

with her verbal attacks on their personal lives. She has told black students that there was no money available just prior to her sending back funds allocated to poor students by the federal government.

Administration: On this personnel issue the college defended the work of Dr. Bedesem and stated unequivocally that this demand would not be given serious consideration.

Demand #8: *That no disciplinary action will be administered in any way to any student workers, teachers, or administrators during and after the strike as a consequence of their participation in the strike.*

Black Fire: We are striking because it is a necessity, a necessity for our education, for black people, and especially black youth and black children, throughout the Bay Area, this state, and all over the country. Already eleven students, black and white, have suffered disciplinary measures because of their devotion to this necessity. One white teacher has been fired because of his radical position. If the school chooses to use this as one of their methods of retaliation, we have no choice but to further escalate our struggle. The more students suspended and teachers fired, the more committed our efforts become, and the deeper our struggle. If any discipline is needed, run it on Pig Ronnie and Fuehrer Dumke.

Administration: The college response was brief: "The college cannot make guarantees regarding disciplinary action before the behavior occurs. The college follows standards of due process in all disciplinary matters."

Demand #9: *That the California State College trustees not be allowed to dissolve any black programs on or off San Francisco State College campus.*

Black Fire: The Tutorial Program, the Black Students Union, the Third World Liberation Front, the bookstore, the commons—all these and anything else which the students now control are due to be coopted and controlled by Reagan and his lackeys—the trustees. Title V if revised would eliminate student self-government, would give the trustees total authority to decide what activities are allowable and which ones aren't, and the chancellor would have to approve in writing any and all activities before they are implemented. They plan to control all the auxiliary organizations which are defined as (1) Associated Students organization, (2) any organization using the name of the state or the state college, (3) any organization which represents an official relationship with the college, (4) any organization in which college officials participate as directors as part of their official position, (5) any organization which provides services to the campus. Black people and other Third World students who need financial aid will be directly at the mercy of the trustees and the president. In short, the need the black people feel to determine their own destiny would be completely and utterly wiped out. Specifically, the trustees would have the power to: (1) eliminate the Experimental College and activities they don't like, such as the Tutorial Program; (2) censor any student paper, play, or film they wish; (3) raise the price of books and food without consultation and use the profits any way they desire; (4) use student money to finance any college program—whether it relates to students or not; (5) prevent students from working in the community.

Administration: After stating the legal authority of the trustees to dissolve any program, the college indicated it saw no reason for the dissolution of the black studies program and stated it would make every effort to protect this program if it reflected community needs.

Demand #10: *That George Murray maintain his teaching position on campus for the 1968–69 academic year.*

Black Fire: George Murray, who is a graduate of San Francisco State, is a well-qualified English instructor. He is able to relate to the needs of his black students, while most white instructors ignore the unique problem of black students on a white campus such as S.F. State. Black students on this campus need an instructor like George, who teaches students about black authors and their works, for those black authors talk to the student about his own experiences in the black community. George Murray's presence on this campus should not be determined by white people and their standards. Black people on this campus need to defend themselves against a power structure of which S.F. State is a part, because black brothers and sisters are killed every day, whether in Vietnam or in San Francisco by racist policemen who lay siege to our community. George's statement about students' defending themselves is not grounds for dismissal as an instructor. White administrators know little about the needs of black people and, therefore, should have no power to fire a man such as George Murray, who speaks truthfully about our needs as black people in white America.

Administration: "The question of the relationship of George Murray to the college is under investigation by appropriate bodies."

The overwhelming thrust of these demands was the indictment that institutions of higher education, along with most other American institutions, were racist: they were structured to admit few black students, and for those admitted they were organized so as to brainwash future bourgeois, middle-class leaders with white culture rather than give them education relevant to their black needs and experiences and one that would enable them to transform their powerless status. To correct this condition more black students must be admitted, they must be allowed to study a curriculum relevant to the black experience and taught by blacks, and, above all else, blacks must seize control of their own destinies. Leroy Goodwin, BSU off-campus coordinator, stated this point at one of the college convocations in unequivocal terms:

> Our major objective is the seizure of power. Power must come to the people and black power will come to black people. As things now stand, you must present your program to the pigs in power and they must approve it. Until we have power, everything is bullshit. The dog believes we want to participate in his political games and that if we demand ten things all the niggers really want is five. Each day the demands are delayed we will escalate our tactics. If armed struggle is what is needed for us to control our lives and our education, then that is what we will use. Peace and order are bullshit issues. They don't mean anything to us unless we have control of our lives. The pig administration has run down our attempts to win legitimate demands by peaceful means.

Specifically, the black students demanded control of the number of black students admitted, the size and governance of a black studies department, the choice of personnel for that department, the nature of their education, their individual student funding, their own discipline, and the nature of their life and off-campus activities. For the most part, the qualifications of their admittees, the nature and standards of their education, the background and qualifications of their instructors, the style of their teaching, and the criteria for their behavior contrasted severely with accepted college procedures, standards, regulations, philosophy, and mores.

Probably the most pronounced and significant schism between

black and white conceptions of higher education occurred at the level of the nature of the educational experience. This difference came to a head in the conceptualizations of a black studies curriculum. Across the nation programs were developing in this area that either employed traditional academic scholarly techniques to develop a new "area study" to describe the Afro-American history and culture or that focused on the specific, contemporary life experiences of the urban, ghettoized black. Both approaches underscored the need for black identity. At San Francisco State a more militant, revolutionary conceptualization of the goals of black studies emerged from the leadership group. Nathan Hare alluded to these goals in his numerous writings and speeches. Joseph White stated bluntly that, in searching for faculty, the department sought people who were committed to a militant black nationalist ideology. A quotation from an article on black studies by Robert Allen, founder of Afro-Americans for Survival, in a strike publication, *Strike Daily,* cuts to the heart of the matter:

> Just as the system could try to emasculate black power by turning it into a form of neocolonialism, it will certainly try the same thing with black studies. It will approve a "constructive" black studies program which is not "disruptive" of the school and society. It will seek to buy off those student militants that it can and will throw out the remainder. But a *relevant* black studies program cannot exist under these conditions. Black people *must* be disruptive because this society disrupts and destroys our lives. Hence, a relevant black studies department must be a home for the black revolutionaries, the George Murrays of the black colony. If it fails to do this, then it fails in its task of serving black people. Black studies cannot be complacent. It must punch and jab, always seeking to cut away at that which oppresses black people. It cannot be modeled after other departments because the function of these departments is to socialize students into a racist and oppressive society. The function of black studies must be to create enemies of racism, enemies of oppression, enemies of exploitation. This is a revolutionary task, but for black people and black students there can be no other choice. Either we revolt or we accept the spiritual and physical death of continued submission. But mindless revolt is not enough. We must always beware of the power structure's insidious efforts to channel our revolt into "acceptable" activity, to coopt our revolt and render it ineffective.

From the black perspective, the intent of the college responses to their demands could be just such cooption. Utilizing institutional values such as prior commitments, accepted college decision-making procedures, budgetary limitations, and systemwide rules and regulations, the administration stated clearly that it intended to control ultimately the educational and institutional experiences of the black students and to ensure that they coincided with state and college policies and accepted academic criteria and standards. The college was in sympathy with some of the black objectives but it reserved the prerogative of choosing which objectives were to be channeled into the overall college operation. With this the battle was joined both ideologically and tactically.

Chapter 10

Bloody Wednesday

The second day of the strike began with a standard tactic: fifty or so white strike supporters picketed the classroom buildings and urged students to show their support of the strike and resistance to racism by not attending classes. For the most part the picketing was peaceful though "persuasive" in the typical picketing fashion. Media men, pressed for incidents to satisfy avid reader interest engendered by headlines like "Terror Tactics Force S.F. State to Shut Campus," played up a brief two-student altercation in picture and word far beyond its significance.

At a morning press conference the Third World Liberation Front indicated its solidarity with its BSU brethren and added five demands of its own. In essence they were in the spirit of the BSU demands. For the Third World they demanded a school of ethnic studies, fifty faculty, and unlimited nonwhite admission, with control over all aspects in the hands of Third World students.

During the rest of the day tactics of the white strikers shifted from peaceful picketing to rallies, marches, and harassment, but no actions forced the president to utilize police beyond extensive infiltration by plainclothesmen. Toilets were blocked, fires started in wastebaskets and newspaper stands, and SDS-led "education teams" invaded classes seeking opportunities to explain the strike to the nonstriking students. Probably the most serious escalation came when a crude, homemade bomb blew open a locker in the Education Building and later a Nigerian student teaching in the EOP program was arrested with a bomb in his possession. The bomb scare did much to heighten the general campus anxiety, for rumor multiplied and enlarged the incident far beyond its original dimension. The rally-march-across-campus routine was blocked when demonstrators were told at the entrance to the Administration Building that disruptive acts would make them eligible for disciplinary action or arrest. To vent their rage they then marched through other buildings chanting and knocking on doors.

At the end of the day, the administrative crisis team assessed the damages, concluded that they were tolerable and that classroom attendance had not been significantly affected, and grimly decided to carry on the following day. A disposition to close classes and negotiate while coerced had totally disappeared.

Within liberal faculty circles there were uneasy stirrings. In the Humanities Building a petition was circulated demanding an open faculty meeting so that the issues could be discussed and faculty sentiment brought to bear on the administration. Among this group there were deep misgivings that their point of view was not represented in the administrative-Senate coalition making decisions. The AFT Executive Committee was already on record as being in sympathy with the objectives of the black students. The department of economics indicated a willingness to propose at the faculty meeting that the faculty go on strike on the Murray issue. The Senate Executive Committee resisted the call for an immediate faculty meeting, believing the absence of faculty from buildings during the noon witching period asked for trouble.

Probably the most important faculty development was an ad hoc meeting Thursday night and Friday morning of approximately sixty-five faculty members led by Mark Linenthal of English, William Stanton of economics, Fred Thalheimer of sociology, and the AFT leadership group of President Gary Hawkins, ex-presidents Peter Radcliffe, Eric Solomon, and Henry McGuckin, and Executive Committee member Susan Modell. The membership had its roots in the group sympathetic to student demands that met late one night in the May sit-in and then pressured Summerskill to make concessions before he flew to Ethiopia. Almost every one of the thirty-five signing the proclamation that emerged from the meetings were or would become members of the AFT. During the course of the next three weeks the ad hoc membership merged into a succession of short-lived groups—Faculty Organization for Responsibility in College Education, Ad Hoc II—until finally the members deemed it wise to recognize their basic allegiance and source of strength; they merged with the labor movement and went out on strike under its banner. By focusing upon issues rather than organization during the course of this evolution, the AFT leadership cadre attracted many faculty to its flag who might have resisted direct, immediate AFT control. Lessons had obviously been learned from the disastrous, ill-timed drive for power when the trustees attacked Summerskill.

In the early stages of this evolution the major overt issue was the trustee and chancellor intrusion into college affairs in the Murray case. On Friday the Ad Hoc Committee announced that if the order to suspend Murray were not rescinded by Tuesday at 5 P.M., the committee would strike on Wednesday morning. Thirty-five faculty signed the statement. The mood of the group was expressed by McGuckin when he said, "We have a long grievance of the chancellor interfering in the affairs of this campus and we have had enough." Despairing that the Senate with its polarized membership would ever take decisive action, the group decided to move out on its own. When asked if this action might not revive a failing student strike, Stanton reflected the spirit of his colleagues when he said, "We're not really concerned by that. . . . We're doing like the kids say—we're doing our own thing." The group was careful not to be overtly critical of President Smith, who had considerable personal support within the committee itself and still a wide following on the campus.

The Ad Hoc Committee's declaration was somewhat tarnished in the public's mind by the outbreak of hit-and-run tactics among the black students that happened to coincide with the announcement of faculty action. Displeased with the lack of popular support for the strike and the administrative resistance to negotiation or closing the campus, the Third World Central Committee decided to escalate the pressure by employing "the tactics of the flea." Under the cover of another large noon rally, several raiding parties dashed into departmental offices, scattered and destroyed equipment, and then fled within seconds. Three offices were hit by the stocking-masked raiders and two students were arrested. The mood of the campus was extremely tense, as over 5,000 people swarmed in the middle of the campus. A group of blacks with BSU leaders Jerry Varnado and George Murray among the membership moved menacingly on a black plainclothesman who had blown his cover; for a moment one had the impression of a lynch mob. A cool retreat saved the day. Off-campus individuals of many persuasions and with their own agendas began to be seen operating on the fringes of the mobs of students. That day for the first time Third World students joined the picketing, which gave it an entirely different tone. Many worried faculty, administrators, and students wondered just when the riot would come. All were glad that a three-day weekend loomed ahead.

During the week of November 4, several other events within the Bay Area and the nation did not augur well for the mood of the campus. At Merritt College in Oakland 100 blacks roared into the cafeteria and bookstore and left a trail of damage and disruption. The College of San Mateo, still rumbling from the black student attack several weeks earlier, bubbled up again when the board suspended popular black administrator Robert Hoover for failure to keep a militant student off campus as ordered. In the neighboring Daly City school districts both elementary and high school faculty initiated strike activity for one of the few times in California public school history. In San Francisco's Mission High a faculty member was stabbed attempting to break up a fight.

At Berkeley student leaders failed to mobilize a student strike on the Cleaver course issue but the faculty leadership continued to press the regents for a return of faculty authority on personnel decisions. Much more serious was the flare-up in Southern California at San Fernando Valley State College. Two days before the State strike, fifty students, mostly members of the college's BSU, held thirty-four members of the administration and staff hostages in the Administration Building for four hours to emphasize complaints similar to those at S.F. State. People were intimidated with fire extinguishers, knives, and fists. After a gun had been drawn by a plainclothesman, Acting President Blomgren ended the occupation by agreeing to amnesty. The following day he repudiated his coerced statement and a number of black students were suspended from the college and arrested on kidnapping charges.

And on Tuesday, November 5, President Richard Nixon rode to victory in an election that confirmed the activist student critiques of the nation. In California, both houses of the state Legislature went Republican for the first time in over ten years, thus giving Governor Reagan legislative support for his attack on rebel students and faculty.

The weekend seemed to take some of the sting out of the student strike. The Tuesday, November 12, rally had little fervor, picketing did not seem to cut down much on class attendance and the classroom visitations made few converts. These visitations did continue, however, despite a warning posted by a dean of students on classroom doors: "Individuals disrupting classes without the permission of the instructors will be subject to disciplinary action." The rule was new and simply was not enforced. A mediation attempt during the weekend by four faculty from the Department of Urban Studies was bluntly rejected by the BSU.

In reality Tuesday was the day for the collective faculty to "do their thing." They did it in characteristic fashion, although now the stakes were big. The most that could be gleaned from the unusually well-attended meeting besides fervid oratory and parliamentary quibbling was a motion requesting the resignation of Chancellor Dumke for his violation of due process in the Murray case. The vast support for the motion meant nothing; almost every official faculty group in the system had made similar requests in the past two years, but power rested with the trustees, not the faculty. Nothing was done to help solve the pressing internal problems, and the meeting was recessed until the next day. The Senate met and produced no constructive actions.

Wednesday, November 13, began in a low key. Attendance fell off at the faculty meeting and little was accomplished before the noon recess. Wild, varied, confused recommendations conveyed the impression that the faculty was so split and so inept at collectively handling student militant tactics that they were almost willing to abdicate and turn the task back to the administration. A small gathering listened to the customary SDS-BSU revolutionary pep talks at the noon rally. The only ominous note for the administration came when the Ad Hoc Faculty Committee created its own picket line at the front of the campus at 7:30 A.M. Sixty of various ranks, ages, and disciplines marched with their signs, thus giving the first tangible support to the striking students. The faculty group addressed itself only to the Murray issue, not to the other nine demands or the general charge of institutional racism, but nevertheless the "striking" faculty helped legitimize the tactic of students' striking for their objectives and gave a shot in the arm to a withering movement.

President Smith felt sufficiently encouraged by the pervasive peace of the campus that he left his office for lunch for the first time in a week. By the time he returned his battle was lost, his college was on the brink of disaster, and for all practical purposes his tenure was ended. Inherent in the approach of keeping a campus open by having police available to repress guerrilla tactics is the stark reality that the police ultimately decide when they will go where on campus to do what. Up to this point the administration and the police captains had cooperated easily in the command post that also served as the president's office. Scattered across the campus, police squads whiled away the time in a boiler room and in the corporation yard, and more than fifty plainclothesmen tried to look like students as they kept the militants under surveillance. For the most part, the police were bored by the inaction.

Then the mistake was made. It turned out to be tragic. On brief occasions squads of eight or ten police had moved in and around the Administration Building and surrounding classroom buildings, but they had wisely never ventured into the "student" section of the campus: the cafeteria, the adjacent huts housing student government activities, and the Speakers Platform area. But on Bloody Wednesday, a television cameraman had been roughed up by a black student and he requested some assistance from the police in arresting his attacker, believing he could identify him. Two plainclothesmen were sent with him to the area of the huts where the BSU was just concluding a press conference in which Murray announced that the historic welding of the people of color had produced such power that "you can tell every racist pig in the world, including Richard Milhous Nixon, that we're not going to negotiate until the demands are met." At the same time, close by on the other side of the cafeteria, the SDS militants were berating a group lounging around on the grass in front of the Speakers Platform for not controlling their own destiny by joining the strike.

Exactly what happened at the next critical juncture is still unclear, but either as a result of direct communication or the absence of communication, the Tac Squad came to the conclusion that their two comrades needed help and they sent a nine-man unit to their assistance. This action had not been cleared with the college administration, but it was hardly the type of situation where police would seek academic advice. The section of the campus on which they suddenly appeared had increasingly become dominated by the black students since their BSU hut adjoined it and had almost become considered their "turf." Thus, the "pigs" were invading the "ghetto," and all the blacks' fears and hate and rage and suspicions associated with previous encounters with the "pigs" in their lives suddenly focused on these nine beclubbed, helmeted, visored bluecoats.

What specific incident transferred the peaceful encounter to the wild, frightening, brawling riot that engulfed the campus for more than an hour is uncertain. Whether it was police brutality or black rage or the act of a provocateur who believed that the revolutionaries had finally put together the critical mass necessary to escalate a strike into a revolution, no one knows for sure. But the incident did occur, as it was almost destined to, and it triggered a violent, savage battle. White students came racing to the close confines between the huts and the cafeteria and surrounded the small band of embattled police. Rocks, bottles, plates, glasses rained on the police who then charged after individuals suspected of the violence. On occasion somebody was caught; on occasion people were clubbed wildly and blood flowed. The crowd screamed at the clubbing, then scattered in shrieking, panic-stricken mobs as the police charged in its direction. The cries, the shouts, the dashes, the rock-throwing, the police-student wrestling carried on for fifteen minutes. At least one scared policeman drew his gun when threatened. A relief squad plunged into the melee and was soon surrounded by taunting, chanting students. Blacks were zapped and fought back. People became hysterical and sobbed. Few doubted there would be serious injury or death.

Finally the police units began a retreat across campus with the students raging at their side, not willing to let them go. The old familiar chants were heard: "Pigs off campus! Pigs off campus! Pigs off campus!" "Oink-oink!" Again there were missiles, again there was club-swinging pursuit and shouts and mad scrambling to get out of the way and people falling and tripping in terror. As the two groups eventually squared off against each other with radical student leaders raging for an attack, suddenly the picketing faculty appeared and marched between the groups to prevent further bloodshed. At times there was no certainty that they would pull it off and might instead discover themselves directly in the middle of a fighting mob. Some students and some police were grateful; other students and other police were angered at the intercession. There was a historic scene when former legislator, now economics professor, William Stanton stood with arms outstretched urging the students to stop and return to the Speakers Platform for a rally. This they eventually did, and Stanton and a succession of the radical leaders used the occasion to whip up support. Said Stanton in a famous, widely reported and filmed speech:

> There are no more classes at San Francisco State! And we're not taking any more horseshit from the fucking trustees! The conduct of Dumke and the trustees has been absolutely criminal. . . . That man [Smith] is a damned fool for trying to work within the system. The trustees must act to restore Murray, guarantee adequate funds for black studies and the Third World people, and make a clear declaration that the faculty will be free to run this college. They must tell us what they intend to do to restore justice on this campus.

It was this speech that triggered a trustee and chancellor demand of both Presidents Smith and Hayakawa that Stanton not receive tenure.

Among the leaders to rage at the students were two PLP-oriented radicals who had been in the thick of every confrontation for the past two years, Hari Dillon and John Levin. Their mood was wild, hysterical, triumphant. The crowd roared at their cue lines. A movement was finally to be realized! Cried Levin, "George Murray was fired for saying students should bring guns on campus to defend themselves. After you saw those pigs walking around with their guns out, can you deny he was right?"

While the whirling battle raged across the campus, less than two hundred faculty sat patiently in the auditorium waiting for a quorum to show up so their morning meeting could be resumed. Then some of the striking faculty charged in to describe the violence that had just transpired. Stanton, emotional, almost hysterical, demanded that the faculty go on strike until the trustees gave the faculty full power to run their institution. Although the group was in no mood for this, there was an almost universal conviction that education could not be conducted in the violent atmosphere of the campus and the group voted overwhelmingly to close the campus until the problem could be solved. Later that evening Smith did just that, announcing to the massed press squeezed into his conference room:

> It's clear that as a result of the pattern of confrontation and violence occurring and the turmoil on campus we don't believe it's possible to carry on the basic instructional programs. . . . We'll keep classes closed until such time as we can reopen them on a rational basis. . . . Bringing in police as an effort to keep this campus open has not worked to my satisfaction.

From that point on decision making in California higher education, which had been increasingly influenced by political considerations in the past three years, became a major matter of public policy formulation. Executive and legislative concern shifted from such issues as the size of the budget, the question of tuition, and the overall governance of the various systems to precise administrative decisions on specific campuses. Who was hired to teach specific courses, procedures for campus discipline, how a president managed individual details of confrontation: all of these and many more administrative matters became the concern of politicians. They held press conferences to explain their posture, used these issues as major planks in their election platforms, and created more than 100 specific bills to handle these problems at the legislative level. They responded because their public solidly desired them to and because, having had to fight to become elected, most basically found it repulsive for society's institutions to buckle under pressure, especially student pressure, revolutionary pressure, black pressure, and long-haired pressure. When Smith closed the campus indefinitely while it was under student attack, in their eyes this told the world that violence and coercion paid off: militant students could close public, tax-supported institutions and force administrators to negotiate under militant terms.

On the other hand, those who were in the midst of the rioting and had basic responsibility and experience in educating, not riot control, became convinced that teaching and learning were impossible under these conditions and that a pretense of business as usual would produce only more rioting, serious injury if not deaths, virtually no learning, and polarized positions from which there would be no retreating. There were those in the faculty who agreed with the public and most politicians that the campus should never be closed, but they were relatively inarticulate and few in number at this time. In addition, many faculty and some administrators were convinced that the Third World students had legitimate grievances which might not be progressively settled without some such pressure. And so these faculty either were not too critical of the tactics or at least were not unwilling to negotiate under these pressured conditions. The educational Establishment contained such individuals far out of proportion to the general public, and this basic disparity in values and goals between these faculty and the public was to plague San Francisco State during this travail, and would hover over all colleges in the future as they addressed themselves to the social issues brought to their campuses by militant students for solution.

In the minds and guts of those who had observed or participated in the events of Bloody Wednesday at State, continuing education under these conditions was intolerable. Equally in the minds and guts of the majority of those who watched the events on television or read of them in the newspapers, bowing to these violent revolutionaries simply could not be countenanced. As usual on matters of such emotional appeal to vast segments of the California public, Reagan caught the pulse of the multitudes and his statement after President Smith had closed the college reflected this feeling: "I want to make it perfectly plain that as long as I am Governor our publicly supported institutions of higher education are going to stay open to provide educations for our young people. The people of this state, the people who pay the bills, want it that way." Furthermore, Reagan bluntly accused Smith of an "act of capitulation" and of having previously, in his handling of the Murray case, "kindled the fires of violence."

> For a school administration to deliberately abandon the leadership vested in it by the people of this state—at the expense of the vast majority of students intent on receiving an education—is an unprecedented act of irresponsibility. It is clear that the [college] administration, in its obvious quest for what was considered an easy way out, ignored other options which were available to assure the orderly continuation of the educational process.

And, justly disdaining to show favoritism, the governor voiced his opinion of militant faculty also—this "small, unrepresentative faction of faculty . . . determined to substitute violence and coercion for orderly grievance procedures available to all. . . . Professors are paid to teach, not to lead or encourage violent forays which only result in physical harm to persons and property. If they refuse to honor the trust our citizens have placed in them, they should look for work elsewhere."

Over and over these themes were woven into the public clamor: keep the colleges open, the people who pay the bills want it that way, the vast majority of the students want it that way, a small, unrepresentative militant faction of faculty and students dedicated to violence cause all the trouble, and spineless administrators capitulate to the militants by seeking the easy way out. Legislators, candidates for public office, supervisors, mayors, all felt compelled to show their colors on this issue. No more striking example of the incidental role the welfare of education plays in the ambitions of office seekers exists than the statement made by Reagan's expected opposition in the 1970 gubernatorial race, Jesse Unruh. Addressed to the governor, it commented: "You should not sit idly by as governor and permit San Francisco State College to close its doors. Such a posture would constitute a triumph for anarchy. It seems hardly necessary to remind you that the taxpayers of the entire state of California support this institution. They will not tolerate it if you allow riots and rebellion to dictate educational policy." The statement did not hurt Reagan, help Unruh, or facilitate the solution of the complex problem. A year before, Unruh had suggested immediately that Summerskill should be fired for closing the campus one half-day in the face of a similar riot. And it is interesting to note that Reagan himself, after four students were killed in a demonstration at Kent State, in May 1970, ordered a four-day closing of all state college and university campuses in California.

In the meantime faculty and administrators met separately and together in an attempt to seek short-term and long-term solutions to the problem so that the campus could be opened. Once again the resources and procedures of these college agencies of governance proved inadequate to the massive new problems. But although the flurry of resolutions and motions, the dialogue, and the continuous meetings essentially came to naught and left the college still trapped and unprepared to move ahead constructively, this period of two days represents a phenomenon in academic participatory democracy that is worthy of attention at least for its negative learning.

The setting for this attempt to utilize the collective wisdom of the faculty in solving student confrontation tactics consisted primarily of mass meetings in the college auditorium, although a brief period was allowed for departmental and school group thinking. For the most part there was no leadership. Since the intent of the meetings was to allow the faculty, not the administration or the Senate, to impinge on the crisis, the administration acknowledged these ground rules. It was fairly well preoccupied itself. The Executive Committee of the Senate went along with this antistructure, also, partly out of inability to organize any significant recommendations and partly in recognition of the deep feeling in some faculty circles that the faculty demanded to be heard. The Executive Committee did develop a recommended faculty response to the Fifteen Demands—ten from the BSU and five from the Third World group—believing that this was the heart of the short-term problem and that faculty action might give the Third World students an acceptable reason for terminating their strike; but the outpouring of militant suggestions for faculty action overwhelmed this basic attempt at leadership.

This failure of structure and leadership at a critical moment revealed some basic flaws that had been developing within the faculty governance system for a long time, but which more placid periods had not brought to the surface. Colleges which were able to respond to somewhat similar pressures with some success had effectively functioning committee structures; at State the committee system was almost defunct. At some other colleges, participation in faculty governance was widespread and respected; at State many able faculty focused their energies in their disciplines in teaching and research, leaving faculty political activities to a relatively small group.

The tone of the meetings reflected the deep and long-term discontent within the entire college with the system management of Chancellor Dumke and the trustees, particularly over the issue of system restrictions on the college's freedom of governance. This spilled over at this time on the issue of the chancellor's demand that President Smith suspend Murray, but there was a history of six years of fighting the basic problem of campus autonomy. As faculty had retreated to their disciplines and their suburban homes during the past decade, they became poorly informed on what was going on at the college and in the decision-making apparatus. In this crisis context they demanded to be informed and to be heard. Inherent in this communication problem were lurking suspicions that power groups were keeping information from them in order to manipulate affairs. And, finally, and most pervasively, the mood of the gatherings was colored by the wild, raging, bloody riot of the previous day.

Before the two days were concluded the faculty had had submitted to it a grand total of fifty-nine resolutions and recommendations for action. It is doubtful that higher education has witnessed a similar phenomenon of town hall democracy. Eighteen individual faculty members became so convinced that they personally had a unique contribution to make to the solution of the college's problem that they submitted their own resolutions. Twelve departments met and were able to reach sufficient consensus that they laid before the collective faculty their suggested actions. And beyond this, there were resolutions from two entire schools, three student groups, the part-time faculty, the student personnel administrators, and a variety of anonymous contributors. It took almost five minutes at one point to get past the individuals distributing copies of resolutions at the entrances to the auditorium. In the meetings the average faculty member usually discovered a particular motion in his collection of dittoed papers at about the time action was developing.

When it finally became apparent that no possible parliamentary procedures could fairly or expeditiously allow the assembled faculty to focus with wisdom on this massive outpouring of recommendations, it was agreed that a committee would work over the weekend to bring some order to the redundant or contradictory or impractical suggestions. But the faculty did not take this action without first rejecting the moderate leadership of the department chairmen and deans and instead accepting, by a slight majority, a more radical proposal from the department of sociology to the effect that the college would not reopen until the trustees had agreed to work through the basic problems of college governance.

In retrospect, this free-swinging total faculty attempt to solve complicated policy and administrative problems in the midst of a student strike dominated by militant black students was completely abortive. It was proposed that the faculty demand autonomy in its own governance, especially in Murray-like personnel matters, and if autonomy was not granted the faculty should go out on strike. Autonomy was not granted and the full faculty did not strike. A statewide constitutional convention involving the trustees and the chancellor was demanded to create new procedures for decision-making; nothing came of this idea. Within the college there was a call for a two day faculty-student conference to decide under what conditions the college would reopen; this conference never transpired. A conciliation proposal would have given a group of seven, including two BSU members, approximately one month to devise solutions, while the strike was held in abeyance; effective conciliation did not come until after three months of massive police intervention, a change of administration, a seven-week AFT strike, and full-scale arrests. Some resolutions saw inadequate funding as the source of all the turmoil and requested a review of and improvement in the college's funding, particularly as it affected black studies. This request proved to be highly visionary for the state was moving toward budget cutbacks, not supplements, for higher education. Nor did the college ever "work out ground rules for acceptable behavior for these times and proper methods for enforcing them on this campus" or shorten the information gap between administration and faculty that some thought was the source of much of the difficulty. The tenor of the militant utterances that were the faculty's first response to police enforcement of civil discipline and trustee governance of the campus is captured by one brief proposal:

> Be it resolved that this faculty refuse to open the campus for instruction under quasi-military control. When the college is protected from invasion by outside forces seeking to influence behavior by other than deliberative means, and these assurances are felt by students, faculty, and college administrators, instruction and conciliation conferences will be instituted immediately.

Most of the resolutions from departments and schools concentrated not on the behavior of the coercive students but rather on the repressive responses of the police and the trustees and also showed faith in the deliberative processes when focused on the "disease, not the symptoms." A few scattered individual resolutions demanded a hard line toward the striking students, but these were in the minority. The following phrases from their resolutions capture their intent: "resume instruction immediately," "affirm its refusal to be forced to consider demands from any group which are accompanied by threat, violence, intimidation, disruption, vandalism, or arson," "categorically rejects, until peace is restored on the campus, all the demands of the Black Students Union and the Third World Liberation Front," and "student and faculty found guilty . . . will be expelled or dismissed, and when released, placed on a peace bond which forbids reentry to the campus."

These meetings proved that the collective faculty could not respond effectively to the range of problems precipitated by violent student-police confrontations, and within a few weeks even those faculty members who had petitioned and demanded this process threw up their hands in despair and sought other means of influence or withdrew. One speech did make the headlines at these sessions. Although it did not precipitate any faculty action other than choruses of applause and boos, it probably endeared the speaker to the worried trustees and the governor. S. I. Hayakawa, professor of English, had become nationally famous as semanticist and lecturer, but at San Francisco State, where he had been teaching only part-time for a number of years, his influence on college affairs had been negligible. However, with the advent of student confrontation politics his interest became whetted—he became a prime mover in the conservative new Faculty Renaissance group and he ran and was elected to his first all-college position, the presidential selection committee that had recommended Robert Smith.

In rapid succession Hayakawa threw himself in the face of most faculty resolutions by criticizing the slovenly use of the term *racism,* the denial to the silent majority of students of a right to an education, and striking student violence. He demanded that the campus be opened immediately—with the help of police if necessary—and that students creating disorders should be suspended. In the eyes of the trustee majority this rather described the values of a top administrator who could whip the college into shape.

Chapter 11

Failure of Dialogue

If faculty had displayed no skills for crisis governance, neither did they need to bow to the skills of their "employers" as displayed at the special trustee meeting the following Monday, November 18. There was, however, one difference: since the faculty had made the historic move of sending its entire Senate to the trustee meeting, the faculty saw the ineptitude of the trustees, the chancellor, and the governor; their own slipped by unnoticed.

Chairman Merriam and Chancellor Dumke had at first mildly approved President Smith's decision to close the campus, but this approval was expressed before the governor made his views known. By now the governor had a majority of the trustees responsive to his values and power, and the governor chose to attend this meeting, his second since coming into office. The occasion of his first appearance had been the special meeting to evaluate Summerskill's decision to close the campus a year ago. He attended almost all meetings of the regents of the University of California. It became apparent in short order that Governor Reagan was the dominant figure in California higher education and that he was displeased with the type of management that capitulated to an anarchistic minority of violence-prone students.

Different views of the meeting emerged, depending on whether one believed in the hard-line or the soft-line approach. Most of those in power in the state as well as the vast majority of the general public supported the governor's insistence that the college open immediately and that the president not be allowed to negotiate except through ordinary channels until order was restored. This view was adopted as a formal resolution.[1] Trustee William Norris captured the attitude of many faculty who believed the problems were so important and complex that administrative flexibility was necessary when he commented, "This makes an impossible task [for Smith] even more difficult, if that's possible. It [the resolution] is a charade, that's all it is. You either have confidence in your administrator, or you remove him."

The truth, of course, was that the trustees by now did not have confidence in President Smith's approach of attempting to run the campus "without clubs," but they were reluctant at this moment to remove him both because of his popular following on the campus and because there was some dirty work he might as well complete before he was phased out. Smith's relationship with Chancellor Dumke had never been mutually appreciative or subordinate, and by now Dumke was convinced that Smith was the agent for the militant minority of faculty malcontents. The trustees, although many liked Smith personally, were of the belief that his impasse with Dumke and his refusal to take the hard line consistently made him a liability.

Smith had no illusions about what went on behind the closed doors in the personnel session and he arrived on campus Tuesday with the quiet conviction that his was a lost cause and that he was doing neither the college nor himself and his family any good by continuing. As an old schoolman, he knew that when you developed a "five-to-two majority against you" it was time to seek other employment. When he

[1] President Smith continued to seek "off-camera" avenues for negotiation without trustee approval. The trustees subsequently violated their own stance once Hayakawa's "whiff of grapeshot" failed to crush the strike.

expressed this intent to his administrative colleagues they were uniformly opposed and urged him to reconsider.

As the administrators worked through this problem the faculty met once again in mass session to hear the Senate version of the trustee meeting. Nothing served to radicalize the faculty more than the Senate attendance at the trustee meeting and the reports of individual Senate members for three hours on Tuesday. In the past the Senate leadership cadre had consistently attended all trustee meetings and reported critically through the faculty communication, *Faculty Issues*. At an intellectual level many faculty became aware that their professional and educational commitments and the values of the trustees were miles apart, but it takes much more than intellectual awareness to move most faculty to action commitments. The visible evidence of a group of trustees more concerned with the governor and his personal and political belief in repression appalled almost every member of the Senate. The overt disdain for faculty and their opinions, the simplistic approach to the intensely complex problems, the disregard for facts, testimony, and administrative perceptions, the attitude that "we have the power and we represent the people," the deference to Governor Reagan, the faith in a hard-line approach, and the lack of awareness of the educational and social issues, all made an indelible impression on the Senate members and one after another they rose to convey this. Few Senate members reflected the concern of a number of trustees that, for all of these complexities and social problems, society might have an obligation to resist this intimidation. Faculty feelings were influenced by the obvious attempt by a few archconservatives on the board to counterbalance the almost unanimous testimony of the Senate in support of Smith—"the continuation of formal teaching itself [might be] an irresponsible act"—by appealing to a few dissident Senate members, and to a representative of the nonacademic staff who commented, "As the sitting ducks in the shooting gallery that the president proposes to open . . . a majority of us want to know exactly what is going to be done to ensure our safety when the doors of the gallery are flung open and the guns are passed out to all save us."

The temper of the faculty was reflected in the two-minute standing ovation given to speech professor Nancy McDermid when she commented that the trustees and the faculty are so far apart on the basic issues of due process, campus autonomy, the meaning of duress, and black studies "that we haven't got the time to educate them or bring them *up to where we are* [italics added]. If there is any hope for this campus, it's got to be with us and not with them." Events were to prove that faculty were no more worthy of her faith than trustees.

Against his common sense and political inclinations, President Smith was persuaded to make one last stab at laying the issues on the line that afternoon to see whether faculty would unite behind him to preserve the college's authority to solve its own problems. He made the right speech to Mayor Alioto, who had unexpectedly appeared on campus an hour before the faculty meeting to see whether there was anything he could do; he made the wrong speech to the packed auditorium and the sixty media personnel and their dozen television cameras. The only possibility he saw for moving ahead productively under his leadership was for all parties to agree to a ninety-day cooling off period while the college attempted to utilize its full resources to solve the minority student problems. He indicated that he would employ all his powers to move in this direction, and that in the meantime classes would reopen the following day, and police would be available, if necessary, to contain any violence.

The faculty who were in attendance at the meeting, in no mood to resume education under the violent conditions that developed on Bloody Wednesday, still convinced that dialogue and a full understanding of the facts and issues could bring the faculty and the black students together, and feeling extremely hostile and rebellious toward Chancellor Dumke and the trustees following the faculty meeting, resisted Smith's proposal. In a riotous session—at one point students were asked to leave the auditorium to permit the faculty to vote, and some students refused, saying, "You will have to use violence against us"—the assembly roared approval of a resolution that would force the administration to confront the black leaders in a convocation the following day so the faculty could adjudicate the issues. Until this encounter was concluded, classes would not be held.

By openly defying the intent of the trustee directive to open immediately, the faculty at San Francisco State launched themselves on a collision course with the power system of the state. Before the smoke of battle settled three months later they discovered that the will of the public prevailed regarding black studies and police on campus, and that faculty powers they had taken for granted as their natural right were lost. When these faculty members made the issue closing classes until the black students were content with the resolution of their demands, they disastrously judged their support in the total faculty and ultimately placed the college's future in the hands of the BSU

Central Committee. In the showdown the total faculty did not support this position and the BSU showed no inclination, given their new powers, to negotiate any of their demands.

The Senate held a six-hour session in an attempt to reconcile the position of the trustees and President Smith and the faculty meeting vote, but no reconciliation was possible. Finally preparations were made for the convocation on Wednesday, November 20. Smith indicated that he supported the dialogue approach but that he was also committed to offering those students and faculty who wanted to resume their education the opportunity to do so.

Although the assembled faculty had demanded that the administration make its case on the Fifteen Demands in a face-to-face encounter with the Third World students so that faculty could weigh the evidence and the contending claims, few faculty showed up for this verbal confrontation. Most of the 800 seats in the auditorium were occupied by students, many of them committed to the student strike. Another 800 witnessed the argumentation via closed circuit television at other spots on the campus. Some students met with their faculty in classes. Most faculty pursued their professional interests at home.

At one point in the morning it was doubtful whether the Central Committee of the Third World Liberation Front and the BSU would agree to participate in the convocation, but they finally decided to use the opportunity to "educate" the white students on the racist nature of the institution. To cries of "Teach! Teach!" they rapped on in the morning session, with Smith pretty much alone in defending the position of the administration. Not many of his colleagues had a heart for this type of encounter. Besides, the Third Worlders wanted to deal with the top man. As the president outlined the budgetary and college and system decision-making difficulties in meeting the demands, the minority students over and over again said it was all a matter of which are your true priorities, that if you desired to eliminate racism at State you could do it despite these bureaucratic hang-ups and that you'd better support the demands or your institution will not open. The audience increasingly responded to the rhetoric and the philosophy of the minority students; Smith, to most, represented the Establishment that at every turn was giving the young people troubles, and they enjoyed listening to the blacks tell him off.

Many white students and some faculty also heard for the first time in their lives the deep discontent of the minority people and became more sympathetic toward their desires and their need to keep the institution under pressure in order to achieve these desires. Black Dean of Undergraduate Studies Joseph White touched a sentiment that kept cropping up in the views of a large segment of students during the entire four months of the strike when he said, to a large ovation, "I feel more education has gone on here since the strike started than the whole six years I was a student here." With the race and war issues so dominating their lives, many students preferred this education on these issues to the normal classes in Chaucer or statistics or historiography. Many faculty agreed, many did not; but few in the outside world appreciated this use of the tax monies.

When a poorly attended Senate meeting that night decided to carry out the will of the faculty meeting and pressure Smith to cancel classes for the remainder of the convocation despite Smith's reiterated position that he would support both the convocation and classes, the president decided it was time to determine whether his position or that of the faculty meeting and the Senate represented the views of the total faculty. Within twenty-four hours his office conducted a referendum on the question, "Do you support my decision to continue classes, yes or no?" In the largest faculty vote ever tabulated on the campus, Smith's continue-classes policy was supported by a better than two-to-one majority, 612 to 277. In posing the question he was clearly placing his own leadership—or what was left of it—on the line, and this undoubtedly influenced the vote. Nevertheless the vote obviously reflected the fact that the more moderate or conservative faculty avoided faculty meetings, that most faculty desired to resume teaching, that frenzied mass meetings with militant students in attendance were miserable settings for fundamental crisis decisions, and that the convocation had persuaded more faculty to resist the Third World strike than to support it.

Under normal circumstances this heavy vote of confidence by the faculty for his critical decision to continue instruction in the college might have shifted the balance of power at the college and moved the strike toward a solution, but at San Francisco State the pace of politics and the pace of the revolution had outdistanced by a thousand leagues faculty opinion on anything. In the political arena trustees and the governor were convinced that the faculty they had always considered the most radical, rebellious, and irresponsible were using the convocation idea to defy their authority, and this was a challenge they had no inclination to sidestep. Governor Reagan vowed that "appropriate action will have to be taken" if the closing of classes was a "childish attempt by the Academic Senate" to defy the trustees. Chairman of the board Theodore Merriam commented: "I am certain that this board will have to act further in whatever manner is deemed necessary to end this disgraceful, unprofessional, and unrealistic situation at San Francisco State." There would soon be an occasion to act toward Smith or the college "in whatever manner is deemed necessary"; the November meeting of the trustees was scheduled for Monday and Tuesday in Los Angeles.

The chancellor-trustee-governor mistrust of the faculty and Smith's administration had reached such a point that Governor Reagan voiced the suspicion in a speech that Smith might have been attempting to generate faculty support to close the campus and bypass the trustees' policy in his referendum; that is, that he really wanted a vote of *no* confidence! When Mayor Alioto broadcast a full-blown mediation proposal on the following day, the Chancellor's Office interpreted this to mean that Smith was using Alioto as his mouthpiece in an attempt to elicit Democratic political support to counteract Reagan's Republican pressures.[2] The communications gap between the college and the Chancellor's Office had widened to such an extent that even though the chancellor insisted on calling most important shots, there was virtually no significant, problem-solving, constructive dialogue. The chancellor had one basic representative on the campus; his suggestions, which at times were sympathetic to the college's plight and the administration's efforts, were often overlooked in the interests of cooperation with the trustee and executive will.

The fact that the faculty voted 612 to 277 to resume classes had zero influence on the Third World strike leadership. By now the job of waging a war had both centralized power among the minority students and given this power to those who were most militant. The black leaders who took on the role of moderate militants willing to spend some time trying to persuade the college it was both right and wise to give "power to the people" began to have less influence in strategic decisions or began to change and espouse the tough, no-compromise line. The brief history of the strike seemed to support the "On strike! Shut it down!" strategy. Had not the significant faculty been won over, the student base been enlarged, the administration been forced to submit to Third World excoriation in public, and the col-

[2] See American Council of Education report, page 197, in the chapter "Why I Resigned."

lege been primarily shut down for over a week? Why temporize with victory in sight? Power to the people!

The Third World strike leadership decided to force the issue at the second day of the convocation. In the previous day's session they had threatened to walk out unless Smith ordered the few classes in operation to shut up, but Smith called their bluff and they backed off. Backed now by the Senate's pressure on the president, the Thursday gathering was opened with a Central Committee member's insistent, blunt query, "All I want to ask President Smith is will classes be closed—yes or no?" When Smith refused to retreat from his educational conception of the convocation as a corollary to classroom instruction, the minority leaders and their supporters in the audience disowned both Smith and the convocation by walking out to strident shouts of "Resign, Smith! You're through here!"

The strikers immediately staged an outdoor rally in order to revive the guerrilla tactics of the strike. Speaker after speaker denounced Smith's commitment to continue instruction as an act of bad faith. "The administration has made us look like fools! They have shucked us!" "Yesterday we talked for six hours with that motherfucker. We want to deal with the issues and Smith says no." Why the Third World change of heart? Within the ranks of their white radical, SDS allies there had always been opposition to the convocation idea. As the SDS strike publication commented, it was felt by SDS and other students that the convocation would divert people's militancy and their commitment to fighting for the Fifteen Demands. This position had support with the strike Central Committee but at first it did not prevail. When Third World runners came back with the information Thursday morning that many classes had resumed operation, that what once had been a booming strike and a closed-down campus was drifting back to normal, a crisis presented itself. This time the hardliners won. "On strike! Shut it down!"

After the initial harsh oratory the large crowd at the Speakers Platform was given its marching orders: "We've been tricked! We've got to close this school down until our demands are met—by any means necessary! Now let's go march on that racist Business–Social Science Building and throw those scab students and faculty out of their classes!" Shattered were the hopes of those who believed reasoning together would lead to a solution. After a brief week's respite mobs were roaming, classes were being invaded, windows were being shattered, the police were back with their clubs, and blood was flowing. In many ways it was Bloody Wednesday revisited.

Reports to the command compound in the president's office from the buildings had a touch of panic to them as the marauders poured into the corridors to the accompaniment of wastebaskets turned into drums and the incessant chant, "On strike! Shut it down!" Doors of classes were thrown open, students were threatened, glass was broken, some instructors locked the classes in to escape the mobs. Again it was an issue of protecting people's personal safety by calling in the police with the risk of escalating the violence or letting the raids run their course and hoping that not too many people would get hurt and not too much property would be destroyed. Smith, with the support of his administrative colleagues, again brought in the police. Again it was a wild, raging, hysterical mob scene. Police dashed about in the heavily peopled campus attempting to trap the classroom invaders. Seldom were they successful. The odds were with guerrilla tactics, spread out over an entire campus. For many faculty this was their first exposure to a rioting college and they stood around, horror-stricken. In the words of the SDS, "Students attacked and creamed three plainclothesmen, dragging one down the steps of the Humanities Building." Two other policemen were engulfed by an irate mob when attempting to make an arrest and were forced to fire their guns into the air in order to make their escape. Hordes of students went racing and screaming across the campus after the gunshot, believing that the dreaded moment of full-scale battle and killings was at hand.

Inside the president's office as administrators, police, a few shocked faculty, and supernumeraries whirled about and peeked through the drawn blinds to catch the mob scene, a note of deep anxiety and pessimism began to creep into the conversation. "Were we right to reopen classes? Is somebody going to get killed out there? Will the blood be on our hands?" Confirmed hard-liners began to have second thoughts as they witnessed the impact of the bands of strikers and the burly police on the total college community. Education seemed impossible under these conditions. The president became a battle commander, not an educator. Some wondered whether rocks would come through the windows and whether the building would be ransacked.

At his jam-packed press conference that evening Smith, physically backed and surrounded by his entire administrative cadre, toughed it out and said classes would continue. But by the following morning,

Friday, Novemer 22, his deputy president was working out a conception of "classes" unique to any college. The goal of this tentative proposal was to turn the entire campus into a three-day institute on the pressing social issue of the day, racism, thus meeting the deep concerns of many faculty and students who were sympathetic to the charge of institutional racism, complying with the letter of the trustee directive to resume classes, ensuring that police would not need to come on the campus for a while, and buying a week's time through the Thanksgiving holiday to somehow negotiate a solution. By a pure quirk of fate three AFT leaders sought out Mayor Alioto in a desperate last-minute attempt to intercede with a somewhat similar proposal. But the plan Alioto announced at a press conference the next morning went far beyond classroom workshops on racism and would have involved fundamental negotiations between the parties in the state who had the power to respond to the Third World demands.

In the political climate of the state, plans by a potential Democratic gubernatorial candidate to solve the Republican issue of campus unrest had no chance of success, especially when they involved such widespread cooperation of separate baronies. But Alioto's public support of some form of campus discussion of the fundamental problem of racism as an alternative to regular classroom operation gave Smith a little more elbow room with his last-ditch proposal. Smith was encouraged in this direction by an unusual development Thursday evening after the day's rioting.

During the past weeks those faculty who believed that the only way to negotiate the demands was to close the campus increased their efforts. To meet both the educational needs of the students and the trustee directive while still maintaining no classes on campus, an indigenous movement developed to hold classes off campus in churches, private homes, faculty homes—any place. A flurry of activity centered around the Ecumenical House across from the campus to organize this effort and keep students informed where their classes might be meeting. Key AFT leaders were in the center of this activity, but it also attracted many apolitical faculty who had never been active in any organization.

Thursday afternoon a telephone appeal was made to this network of concerned faculty to come together that evening to determine how the faculty might intervene to stop the bloodshed and preserve the college. Two hundred and fifty faculty responded to this plea. What transpired ensured Smith's convocation, and gave the resistance movement within the faculty the broad base of activists that the AFT could soon tap when it took over the leadership of the movement. Symbolically the AFT took over at this meeting when its president, Gary Hawkins, eased chairman William Stanton out of his role and when its theoretician, Arthur Bierman, persuaded the thinning assembly late at night to follow his line of action.

The conduct of the meeting bore a striking resemblance to the participatory democracy strategy sessions of the SDS. Most of the faculty were troubled, angry, confused, and naive. Rambling, contradictory proposals emerged from a cacophony of shrill, critical oratory. Angry young faculty used the opportunity to denounce their elders in the faculty power structure for selling out. In this harsh, radical atmosphere few of the many moderate, uninvolved faculty spoke out. A state legislator who was in attendance commented later on the politically unreal, true-believer tone of the meeting. The psychic flow between the participants produced the momentary conviction that those right there in the room might well be able to topple the devil Reagan. The few radicals on the faculty saw the revolution progressing. Helpless, impotent people finally felt good inside that finally they might collectively be able to do something to stop the violence, the bond between them all. "We simply cannot teach under these circumstances! Only the faculty have the power to stop this bloodshed!" were the statements that drew most support.

Out of the welter of suggestions, Bierman's nicely timed proposal that the group picket the Administration Building beginning at seven-thirty in the morning emerged as the only agreed upon action. People went home with varying degrees of commitment to the plan.

Faculty approximately 100 strong showed up on Friday morning, some pressing into Smith's office demanding a meeting, some purely picketing as the Faculty Against Violence who would intercede should the police and students clash again. When the leaders pressed Smith to talk to the entire group, not just the chosen few, Smith agreed and the group flocked to a library conference room. The meeting was significant. Until this moment the president had heard from this powerful spectrum of faculty opinion only slightly; he conferred during the crisis decision making primarily with his top administrators and the Senate Executive Committee, and the articulate liberal-radicals had not sought to fill these positions. Many of these faculty members were faculty whom Smith highly respected and with whom he had identified on many other crusades. Over and over again they told him it was an impossibility to resume traditional classes, no matter what the governor or the trustees said. When he suggested the proposed classroom workshop on racism, they gave unqualified support.

People wandered around the campus all morning satisfied that police-student clashes had not been resumed and hopeful that out of the rumors of what Alioto or Smith or the Legislature might do would come stability. At one point several plainclothesmen were surrounded while drinking coffee in the cafeteria and chased in a lynch-mob atmosphere across the campus before they were able to escape into the library. A Tac Squad quickly came to their rescue and for a few ugly moments clubs flailed and a mob of 500 picked up their chant, "Pigs off campus!" More and more students began to believe deeply that the campus was theirs, that police should not be there under any circumstances, and that the police started most of the violence.

At mid-morning Mayor Alioto unveiled his plans for statewide arbitration to get at the heart of the system's problems. As skeptical students attempted to absorb this, others listened to several faculty on the Speakers Platform "tell it like it is." Then word of Smith's plan began to leak out and Smith soon canceled classes and told faculty and students to hold departmental meetings until a faculty meeting at 2:00 P.M. The department meetings turned out to be unusually productive as the rank-and-file faculty and students for the first time had the opportunity to try to come to grips with the problems convulsing the campus. This spirit of equality and camaraderie in the face of fundamental dangers, augmented by a variety of similar experiences throughout the remainder of the strike, began a ground swell of student agitation for new student-faculty classroom and decision-making relationships that might be the most important productive residue to the otherwise calamitous year.

At the faculty meeting President Smith announced his final effort at conciliation, the three-day classroom workshop on racism. The intent was to utilize the dialogue possibilities of the classroom encounter sessions between minority students and white students to explore the basis of America's race problem and come up with suggestions for eliminating the vestiges of institutional racism. Although overtures had been made to the Third World leadership to discover their willingness to participate, no formal acceptance had been received prior to the faculty meeting. At the meeting a group from the Third World demanded to be allowed to comment on the plan even though every effort had been made this time to exclude students. At the last minute agreement was reached, although the students' presence produced some angry blasts from some faculty.

Nesbit Crutchfield of the BSU laid down to the faculty several conditions that must be met if they expected Third World cooperation in Convocation II. One was that only the Fifteen Demands be discussed, not the abstraction of racism. And the striking students also insisted that all sessions be mass meetings and that there be no police on campus during the meetings. Elimination of classroom discussions and the wider problems of racism put Convo II right back where Convo I had failed and eliminated any pretense of classroom instruction as the trustees had ordered. The Third World demands were picked up by the faculty sympathetic to the minority students and desiring peace under any conditions—most of whom had agreed with Smith on his original conception of the plan in the morning—and they carried amendments to the plan that would make it acceptable to the Third World students. Tired and confused, believing they were somehow supporting Smith, the faculty gave almost unanimous support to the amended plan, 487 to 15. But many wondered why their president made such a proposal immediately after receiving a large vote of confidence from them supporting his commitment to keeping classes open. The referendum, though, had been requested before the wild action of Thursday.

The final act in the presidency of Robert Smith was a two-scene drama. Down in Los Angeles the trustees were meeting once again on the problem of San Francisco State. On the campus Convo II got under way. All weekend faculty, students, and administrators tried to work together to plan an ambitious workshop on racism that would be worthy of the problem and of excusing three days of classes. For almost the first time in three weeks of battle the striking minority leaders sat as equals with those in power in the college. In the end, they got pretty much what they desired, a repeat performance of Convo I, only this time classes were not in session and local television stations had given them the entire Bay Area as an audience.

A power struggle between the Central Committee and the conference planners held up the Convocation Monday for an hour and a half, but finally the BSU leader Jerry Varnado swaggered out to the microphone and took over. His first words were, "This pig Robert Smith . . . ," and the chorus of boos directed toward Varnado almost terminated the meeting. For the remainder of the day the Third World leaders used this forum to lash out at the administration with their radical rhetoric. Although the plans for piping the program around the campus were ambitious, few students beyond those in the auditorium showed up. Once again the campus was not truly open and those in power agreed with trustee chairman Merriam's observation that it appeared that the convocation was just a "device to delay the opening of the college further." From the point of view of the board and the governor, striking Third World students and rebellious faculty were running the campus as they pleased, and the administration continuously bowed to these radicals and exercised little control or leadership.

Despite these inauspicious circumstances, the college came off surprisingly well at the trustees' first-day marathon closed session. With nothing to lose, Smith decided the board needed to see new faces and hear new voices, so he sent Deputy President Pentony and Vice-Presidents Garrity and Smith to represent the college. He decided to hang on with the convocation. Drawing upon Pentony's experience with international relations briefing sessions, the group decided to go all out with charts and a full briefing. They carried it off successfully; some of the trustees were taking notes like students, they pushed aside a lunch hour so they could continue the educational session, and one trustee commented afterward that if somebody had moved at that point in the meeting to accept the administrators' plan, it would have carried. The group analyzed the constellation of student and faculty forces operating on the campus, they outlined the "tactics of the flea" guerrilla warfare strategy that the college had to contend with, and they suggested several positive steps that needed to be taken to improve the situation. For all of the headlines and all of the statements made by various parties about the San Francisco State predicament, the trustees were deeply confused and some honestly hoped to find some way to remedy a situation none of their experience gave them a background for understanding.

Once the briefing ended and the questions began and the board began to interact with itself, the college's proposal got lost in the dynamics of state politics and sixteen chiefs attempting to reach group consensus. Governor Reagan sat through the entire meeting. By the time the group gave up late in the evening to seek dinner and quiet reflection, the chancellor had made no proposals and the board had not been able to create any. The group did decide that it wanted President Smith at the meeting the following day, however, and his colleagues were told to make sure he was there at eight sharp in the morning.

Chapter 12

Why I Resigned

The blunt fact was that I quit as president mainly, but not exclusively, because we failed in six months of strenuous effort on the part of my administrative staff and me to get from the chancellor and the trustees the resources and kinds of decisions I felt we needed if we were to dig the college out of the institutional debris which my administration inherited.[1] Further, we could not get them to look past serious provocative acts to basic problems. Six months is more than enough time for a seasoned administrator to assess his prospects for doing a creative, constructive job. What was expected in a time of drastic ferment was to break the campus rebellion quickly using all necessary means, and to sweep revolutionary

[1] This chapter is a first-person account by Robert Smith.

themes under the rug and hold them there. That became a task for somebody who can take satisfaction from that pattern of operation.

Having accepted the presidency not as a career proposition, but as an effort to stabilize the college in a severe crisis situation, I had to press quickly forward with positive programs. Knowing that an institution of 20,000 people could not be expected to respond easily in any direction, including backing away from an educational abyss, I had pressed for a three-year appointment instead of an acting or an interim appointment, believing that three years would be none too long.

In the interviews of faculty, students, and others in connection with this study, as well as informed inquiries directed to the investigators, the question, "Why did I resign?" recurs. Many observers and participants in the affairs of the college have drawn their own conclusions. They differ widely and some, it is possible, are closer to the mark than mine. The views suggested to our study team range from "Smith lacked guts and had no staying power," or a black student's blunter statement, "Smith had no balls!" to "Smith was the best president the college ever had, but nobody wanted a president."

One student said that I seemed to understand the real problems of the campus but seemed unable to act decisively enough or forcefully enough while I still had time. This view was shared by some in the chancellor-trustee complex, but the action deemed appropriate appeared to be the reverse of that projected by the student. One trustee, who was consistently friendly to me, reported to a colleague that I was such a stubborn bastard, the trustees could not work with me. Some of the radical students reported that I was a puppet for the trustees and that I accepted that role willingly. Joe Burlas, who interviewed a number of AFT and student strike leaders following the end of the strike, concluded that the most prevalent feeling among them was that I had "copped out," thereby missing a historic opportunity to weld students, faculty, and a campus into a powerful instrument for social change. They believed there was a desperate need for the college to challenge the power structure of the state while there was still time to halt invasions of the college's autonomy. I could have led that challenge, they believed. One student, identifying himself as a revolutionary, complained about my resignation, which caught many of the radical dissidents by surprise—as did the quick appointment of Hayakawa. He could not figure out why I resigned, but by leaving office suddenly, I "blew their cover." He said the radical strategy for seizing power on campus was developed to take advantage of a liberal administrator not too quick to use massive retaliation.

Accepting the job was, therefore, a high-risk proposition. After ten years of administration in the college at the division, school, and dean's level, I had returned to teaching in 1964, with a public blast at the chancellor and trustees for mismanagement of the system (see *Journal of Teacher Education,* May 1964). One year prior to that, I had been proposed by a college consultation committee and then by President Paul Dodd as vice-president for academic affairs but was rejected by Dumke. From that date on, Chancellor Dumke had erroneously assumed that I led the forces of revolt among the faculty *vis-à-vis* the system. I had taken no central role in the ensuing four years of skirmishes, including the upheaval that followed my resignation. On returning from leave, September 1967, I found myself on four major cross-college committees: campus race tensions; international education; faculty action in opposition to trustee policies (in which my participation was negligible because of overextended commitments) adopted abruptly following the December 7, 1967, campus disorder; and the college promotions committee. These varying perspectives and several classes in social foundations of education, provided ringside seats to the build-up of disorder on campus, the student-faculty administrative conflicts involved, and the increasingly strained relationships between the several sectors of the campus and the chancellor-trustee complex that served as the common outside enemy for most of the groups struggling for self-determination and power on the campus.

It seemed clear, too, that the struggle over higher education between the California right, the New Left, and the ethnic militants was bound to continue with San Francisco State as one of two or three major higher education arenas, as had been the case during the last year of Summerskill's two-year stint as president.

Some thirty years in public education had annealed a few basic ideas that became a part of me and that I still believe are sound even in the current upheavals of thought and of circumstance. Specifically, the decisive one is that a person, a teacher, an administrator must have a range of choices that are his to make as *he* defines a problem, and for which he assumes the responsibility. Personal ethics, college regulations, and law help shape his choices in ambiguous situations; explicit emergency directives or ultimata cannot. If a president is to assume responsibility "for everything that happens on campus" the key is, what does he need in order to do it? That question was never asked by the chancellor or the trustees, nor was it seriously considered when posed to them by the college administration.

By mid-morning, November 25, the day of my resignation, I was down to about my last choice as president. That was *what to do about my role as president:* resign; stand against the majority of the Board of Trustees and be fired; or comply with their proposed directives and become in fact the puppet that state college presidents are increasingly accused of being. The chancellor had directed me to attend an 8:00 A.M. meeting of the trustees on Tuesday, November 25, against my judgment as to where I needed to be. On campus, the second day of the second convocation was scheduled for discussion of the demands of the Third World students. It promised to be a decisive day. Further, we had worked for some weeks to arrange a Tuesday study session with San Francisco legislators to talk about possible special support legislation for urban education programs as well as general financial needs of the college. That meeting could not be brushed aside. We had intended to split my time and that of our key staff members between the convocation and the legislative meeting. There was no time after the evening call from Los Angeles to fully salvage either campus situation.

On Monday, November 24, two vice-presidents and the deputy president had spent the entire day in Los Angeles describing to the trustees our analysis of the situation and our projected plans for working our way out of it. Reports were that things had gone well. It seemed gratuitous to demand that I leave the campus even more shorthanded to fly to Los Angeles to say, "No, my staff isn't lying. We really intend to do our best to get the campus open and settle the strike. And the staff plan is my plan."

It was a typical example of injecting the chancellor's and trustees' priorities into an already overstressed situation and thereby adding to the disorder, while publicly treating the president as a hired hand. At the urging of my administrative staff colleagues in Los Angeles, I agreed to fly down, arriving at the hotel by 11:00 P.M. By 1:30 A.M. we had reviewed the trustee meeting, the campus problems upcoming on Tuesday, plans for the legislators' meeting, and had outlined my presentation for the 8:00 A.M. trustee meeting. We had redistributed our thin forces and then went to bed for a few hours. Pentony, returning to campus, would leave early in the morning for the convocation. Vice-President Garrity and I would attend the 8:00

A.M. meeting of trustees. I would be on a mid-morning plane to appear at the convocation before lunch. Vice-President Glenn Smith would coordinate the legislative meeting.

Up at 5:00 A.M. (for the second day in a row) I took a walk in the pre-smog crispness of Los Angeles while reviewing my statement for the trustees. My head ached from fatigue, loss of sleep, and too many Toscanellis the long day before. With breakfast and coffee, I felt better.

Vice-President Garrity and I arrived for the 8:00 A.M. meeting. Instead of joining the meeting as scheduled, we were asked to wait in an office. The trustees met in executive session. By 9:00 A.M. my plans for a quick return to campus were shot. By 9:30, when we were called, I was angry. It was obvious that the aura of support reported to me at the close of the previous day's meeting had disappeared. There was no request for *our* plan of action, the purported reason for my unscheduled trip. We were given a resolution "directing" me to take several emergency measures and directing the chancellor to see that I complied. I was asked several pointed questions about my willingness to take arbitrary action in personnel matters and my willingness to guarantee that the campus be kept open at whatever cost. I insisted on time to read the materials and consider the issues with Donald Garrity. Back to the "bullpen"—a bit more angry.

A review of the directives, the supporting documents, and the "hard questions" convinced me that the chancellor and his staff and the majority of the trustees were again in process of imposing their specific solution on a problem situation for which they continued to insist I was "totally responsible." This was a repeat of the Murray case, the Student Union, the budget deficit, the directive not to negotiate while the strike was in process. In fact, I had a one-win, 5-loss record since my appointment in the crucial issues that came before the chancellor or trustees up to that time. Only one of the six, the Student Union proposal, had been placed on the trustee agenda at my request. The others were placed there with no reference to my judgment. The one win, the controversy on the Experimental College in July, was well on the way to being lost through the back door. One demand seemed merely stupid to me, that I keep the campus open "at all costs." As I reflected on the proposal, I thought of the day intelligence information carried a report of bombs timed to explode in three (undesignated) campus buildings, leaving us with only a short time to decide what to do. We toughed it out on a hunch that it was a ruse to empty all twenty buildings for the noon rally, although earlier, bombs had detonated with antipersonnel devices built in, fortunately without casualties. Another factor was the lack of time to do anything effective, except ring the alarms and turn people into the halls. Suppose I had been wrong and the bombings took place, with, say, seventy-five student casualties? The chancellor, the governor, and Trustee Dudley Swim would, I thought, have us run an unbroken class schedule around the dead and maimed. It occurred to me that the students and staff of the college, some 20,000 people, depended heavily on the president's judgment about the safety of the campus as no doubt did their families. Students and employees were not soldiers who were expected to die under some nameless officer's order.

Free men and women are not tools of someone else's political or moral purposes. Hayakawa, after two weeks with a thousand-plus police at his disposal, was forced to close the campus for an entire week. It was called a "revision of the calendar." This deliberate public relations distortion, and its acceptance without a public murmur, by Reagan, Dumke, and the hard-line trustees, demonstrated by itself the bankruptcy of the strategy some trustees were using to force me to go the paramilitary route.

The special meeting of the trustees on November 18, a week before, left me with a handful of resolutions I did not need plus an angered faculty Senate. A repeat performance, even more difficult for me to defend, was in the offing. It was not only that my colleagues and I were losing issues we had to win; the way we were losing them was distressing. This was the fourth crucial issue in which we had strongly put forth a position, with wide campus support, seemingly had it staked down, only to have the trustees or chancellor succumb between meetings to a negative final decision. In the September meeting—the first on Murray—the chancellor, in fact, presented the resolution "requesting" Murray's transfer from teaching to other unspecified duties. Yet, I had made it clear at midnight the night before that that was not a workable solution for our campus. After receiving the materials thrust onto me at the November 25 meeting it was clear they were unacceptable to me. Academia is strewn with administrators who, like Willie Loman, have become hollow men while trying to reconcile conscience with imposed job demands.

The question remained, Should I resign, or provoke my own firing? To be fired by the chancellor and trustees of the California State College System was to me the most appealing choice. But my dismissal, I thought, might well add to the disorder on campus, which was only a jump or so away from a riot, anyway, according to what I could learn by telephone. In low key seemed the best way to go for the safety of the campus and the people who would face picking up the pieces. If I leveled a blast of frustration at the trustees, every agitator on the campus would try to capitalize on the situation.

The second major reason for not upholding my faculty image as a chancellor- and trustee-baiter was that whatever my strength and weaknesses as a president, all fault did not rest with the trustees. During the previous week unilateral action by various faculty groups cut the ground from under my administration's strategy for ending the strike and maintaining the instructional program. Our plan was: use police only minimally to maintain safety and arrest lawbreakers; maintain instruction for all willing to attend class, despite disorder; continue to seek ways of mediating the demands, and so keep communications and decision-making open through department-student meetings, convocations, and other means; and close the campus temporarily if hysteria and violence threatened injury and loss of life. I learned, through a call from the mayor asking advice about how to handle them, that a small AFT-oriented faculty group, without consulting with me, went to Mayor Alioto to persuade him to propose publicly a specific plan for a major convocation while the deputy president was working through campus avenues to reopen discussions with strikers. The faculty and Senate between them also took unilateral action to try to force the closing of classes and to stack the Planning Committee for the convocation, thereby guaranteeing two days of confrontation rather than any possible conciliation coupled with continuation of instruction. I saw that as total capitulation to the most arrogant supporters of the fifteen "nonnegotiable demands," several of which just could not or should not be granted. My insistence on continuing classes was accepted temporarily by the Senate only after I suggested I resign. Although two-thirds of the faculty backed my decision to continue classes in a campus poll, the other third won the decision through Senate and faculty meetings. Nor was this all.

The more conservative wing of the faculty, the Renaissance ad hoc group led by Hayakawa, gave me something of a mandate late Monday afternoon on what must be done to cool the campus. They insisted on meeting with me immediately while I was still involved with the convocation and while the chancellor's staff man was trying to arrange for my Tuesday meeting with the trustees, the state college presidents wanted my telephoned views on a resolution for financial support, the faculty members of the Convocation Planning Committee were waiting to tender their resignations, and I was instructing my secretary about what to pack for the flight to Los Angeles. Insisting the meeting was impossible before Tuesday noon, I asked them to leave me a memo. A further reason for not blaming the trustees totally for their Tuesday stance was the too-close similarity between the line of pressure the chancellor and trustees pushed Tuesday morning and the Hayakawa-Renaissance memo I had in my briefcase. (None of the Renaissance propositions was to be successfully employed, even though Hayakawa was appointed president before the day was out.) At the special trustee meeting the week before, members of the same group dissented from a strong statement offered by the chairman of the Academic Senate revealing a split faculty which conservative trustees quickly exploited with delight.

Nonetheless, I believed the conservative majority of the trustees and the chancellor during the previous weeks had played the key role in eliminating any small margin for successfully dealing with the multiple crises on campus short of massive police action. In my view, they had accomplished the same result in destroying the effectiveness of Dodd and Summerskill within the first three semesters of *their* terms.[1] I also believed that the faculty's inability to govern themselves coherently and with some aplomb in a period of sustained crises left me with a campus situation I could not successfully interpret or defend. My request at the general faculty meeting a week before, that we all back off from the barricades for ninety days and stop supporting a strike that used guerrilla tactics and other disruptive means, brought me censure—my speech, hastily prepared, poorly done, and lacking in clarity, missed the mood of the meeting—rather than support from a large enough number of the faculty to stall supportive action for my proposal. Rugged as the student disruptions appeared, I believed they were less difficult than my relationships with the chancellor and trustees and my growing problems with ad hoc faculty groups after the forced Murray suspension.

While chairing the Summerskill Consultation Committee dur-

[1] Lest the impression be left that San Francisco State's problem of maintaining administrative leadership is unique to that one campus within the California State college system, Summerskill's sudden departure marked the first of *eight* presidents to leave seven colleges in the nineteen-college system within fifteen months.

ing 1965–66, I urged the committee not to make nominations for the presidency until we had assured ourselves that there was a role for a president and that we could make a clear statement of what his powers and responsibilities were in fact to be. Our failure to face that responsibility preceded by just two years Summerskill's failure in his nonrole. What we did, in fact, was to describe the major problem areas confronting the new president. We were unable to assure him of the authority, the chancellor support, and the resources required to gain the initiative. Perhaps there is poetic justice in the fact that I suddenly found myself the third experienced educator-administrator in a self-chosen nonrole in an administrative situation that had steadily deteriorated for a decade. My insistence on a three-year term by gentlemen's agreement and then no further reappointment proved a feeble effort to beef up the role. The same was true of the effusive verbal assurances of the chancellor and a dozen of his staff that I could count on them for "all possible support." Legally, of course, I still served only "at the pleasure of the trustees." The Donahoe Act creating the state college Board of Trustees makes clear that the "state college system shall be *administered*[2] by a board designated as the trustees. . . ." Chairman of the trustees Merriam asked who was running the college when I "declined" to act on a trustee request to reassign Murray. He reflected strong trustee intent to assume the literal meaning of the unfortunate mandate to trustees—to *administer the system* rather than to *provide for its administration.* Trustee prerogative should not extend past the president to the personnel and administrative decisions within a campus.

The alternative assumption was stated earlier, that my administrative colleagues and I were, in fact, administering the college within the policies of the trustees and broader considerations of state and federal law. This is an untenable position at San Francisco State. The need for local administrative discretion and elbow room for real choices becomes more rather than less crucial when campus problems become acute or complex. Yet, the tendency of the chancellor and his staff is to usurp the decision-making process on the campus before the trustees can do so every time a tough problem arises, especially if the problem has been aired in the press and has political potential. This report has cited example after example of that process. And in our system the chancellor must move fast if he is to intervene first because key trustees

[2] Emphasis mine.

and elected state officials have become habituated to second-guessing specific administrative decisions at every level and to pressing for special meetings of the trustees each time a handful becomes agitated.

An administrator with any depth of perspective on his job and himself must serve not only "at the pleasure of the trustees" but at his own pleasure, and to a large degree at the pleasure of the faculty and the students. Of all these, his own satisfaction with the role must be primary, and his family's experience with it has an important bearing on his satisfactions. By eleven o'clock on November 25 it was clear that none of the warring groups, especially the majority of the trustees and the most militant faculty and students, cared much for any position other than their own. My own "pleasure" in the nonrole of president of San Francisco State was approaching zero.

It was also obvious that the chancellor, the trustees, and the governor were preoccupied with "breaking the back" of the student strike and of radical campus groups. How to get it done quickly was the overriding consideration, and with the National Guard, if necessary. They needed a man who concurred in that approach, who could watch the ebb and flow of 1,000 police and 3,000 demonstrators on the verge of assaulting each other, and with pleasure assume responsibility for the scene *while the police controlled it*. The "lightning counterattack" employed by Hayakawa did break the strike—three months later.

One further perception grew as I worked with the chancellor and trustees. It is not much of a trick to find out just about what a president or dean cannot in conscience do, and then demand it be done. If the trustees assume the board is a gentleman's club with little responsibility to distinguish between policy functions and administrative interference, the shortage of administrative leadership will grow even more acute. Even in my initial interview some trustees pressed me hard to make clear just what I intended to do about specific controversial personnel and program issues for which I obviously did not yet have the facts. I tried to make clear the process by which a decision would be made, gave examples of my previous handling of similar problems, and explained my unwillingness to prejudge specific problems in the interview setting. Later word came that some trustees saw me as evasive. Trustees cannot acquiesce in each other's excesses. Only four of twenty-one trustees appeared to see this issue. Campus officials and faculty face similar problems at their level and often fail to insist on restraints as well.

Not only were we not solving the crisis problems in a manner defensible to me, another year was slipping by without movement toward the needed long-term development of the college.

When my request was made to return immediately to instruction, most of the trustees and the chancellor appeared greatly surprised. The chancellor urged me to stay at least until a replacement could be designated, or until the end of the semester. On my refusal, he raised the question of my professional ethics, which surprised me a bit since the question of my dismissal had been before them for some weeks and as recently as the previous day. One of the trustees, whose views of higher education I viewed as essentially destructive, expressed what appeared to be real concern for my professional future, although he was highly instrumental in my decision to resign. At the executive level, even the worst kind of hatchet job should be done with elan and without destroying the person, whom the hatchet wielder may actually like in a personal way.

Review of a variety of documents since my resignation dramatically highlights the massive confusion in the decision-making structure, both within the state college system and within the college, much of which I sensed during the final two weeks before my decision to resign and which I failed to surmount. The lead-up to the disorder of November 1968, as well as its duration for four months, must be set in a disturbed decision-making structure that had a long build-up. Here are excerpts from a preliminary report on the San Francisco State crisis made by a team of higher education observers who studied the situation in late November 1968, under the auspices of the American Council on Education. The report was not intended for general circulation, but despite the intent to keep it confidential copies were circulated in various quarters.

> The chancellor is personally detested and distrusted by the bulk of the faculty and student body—even by those that are "conservative" or "rational."
>
> The trustees are perceived by the majority of San Francisco State College as hostile, contemptuous, unreasonable, intractable, vindictive, incompetent, and so on.
>
> The college . . . is perceived by the trustees as rebellious, unreasonable, sick, temperamental, egomaniacal, and even lawless.
>
> The conservative trustees (that is, most trustees) perceive the chan-

> cellor as an impotent man who tries to please everybody and who has no position of his own. Even the liberals are critical of him in this respect.
>
> The San Francisco State College President Robert R. Smith is perceived by the trustees as rebellious and incompetent and by the chancellor as deceitful, evasive, and defiant. . . . Dumke believes that his "act of statesmanship" (in appointing Smith) has been repaid with ingratitude, personal disloyalty, and outright conspiracy; he feels that Smith has deliberately fanned faculty disloyalty and disorder.
>
> President Smith is perceived by the radical students as a tool of the repressive power structure. He acts in "bad faith" and "tries to play on all sides at once." Bob Smith is personally liked by the majority of faculty and by many students. His sincerity is not seriously questioned by the middle and conservative groups, but his every decision is considered fair game for debate and review by the multitude. The Black Students Union, of course, doesn't trust or respect anybody, and their commonest public reply to Smith's attempts to relate the facts of life is "bullshit!"

Perhaps the characters in the above cast are not quite as venal as depicted. I think it is a plausible description of the perceptions of the individuals of each other.

The report asking *So What To Do?* includes the following mischief-making statement: "All the real choices are unpleasant. The ideal solution, as one trustee suggested to me, would be to find the funds needed, fire Dumke and Smith and get on with it." In the summary of the report "historical" factors purportedly causing the crisis are cited. The past three presidents at San Francisco State College are labeled "weak." Despite a number of inaccuracies included in the draft of the report, it is a highly significant document produced by knowledgeable outsiders viewing a climactic event in higher education. The major distortions and gaps in communication are identified more sharply than I had perceived the problem during President Summerskill's last turbulent year. The examples cited below demonstrate the stark caprice introduced into the decision-making process when conflict breeds deep distrust among those who must resolve the struggle. Here are some examples included in the report:

> One of the observers sat through the trustees' Los Angeles meeting November 18, 1968, which the San Francisco State College Aca-

> demic Senate attended en masse. The next day the same observer sat through the faculty meeting in consternation while the Senate reported back to the faculty. Their reports were not only emotionally colored but also filled with misrepresentation and distortion—and those reports were the only sources used by the faculty, in addition to the untrusted press. When one faculty representative stood up and said that he thought the trustees were sincere men, trying to undersand the situation and do their best, he was booed and heckled so fervently that the chairman had to gavel the audience into silence.
>
> A report of an investigator's telephone conversation with Chancellor Dumke, a few days later, adds another dimension: Dumke stated his angry conviction that Mayor Alioto's "mediation" proposal,[3] announced early Friday morning after a conference with four radical faculty members who came to visit him after Thursday's violence, was simply a "front" for Bob Smith. "All Bob is doing is using the mayor as a dummy to mouth his own ideas."

The observer had convincing proof that such was not the case, which he reported to the chancellor. In fact, I saw the above action by the four faculty members as a betrayal of the faculty and administrative leadership of the college. I thought the mayor was well intentioned but had bought a prepackaged bill of goods that was unworkable. We *were* concurrently working on a possible plan to resume the interrupted convocation. The Alioto proposal, attributed to me by the chancellor, in fact forced the college administration's hand and helped put the initiative for structuring the convocation in the hands of strike sympathizers.

Another example helped convince the observers that outside observer-mediation teams have promise in helping resolve campus conflicts and struggles. It has to do with a luncheon conversation with two "liberal" trustees, Friday, November 20, five days before I resigned.

> They said they saw Smith's action [acceding to the demands for a convocation to discuss the issues with students] a "defiance of the board." I told them that classes had been in operation, by Smith's order, since 8:00 A.M. Wednesday, that they had continued until stopped by the rioters on Thursday afternoon, that they had resumed later on Thursday and were running, as far as I knew, at that very moment. [They were.] Furthermore, I said, evening classes

[3] Proposal for a three-day convocation.

> had been running on an almost normal basis, the exceptions being those teachers physically afraid to be on the campus at night, with full Tac Squad protection. The two trustees were amazed and delighted. Their impression from news reports was that the campus was "closed down." I also described for them Bob Smith's very firm stand, in the face of angry and emotional faculty pleading, to keep classes going at all costs. This was news to them.

Thus, almost the last of the trustees who had strongly supported the college administration's efforts and strategy also decided on fragmentary false information that I was an insurgent.

The study team stated that

> the basic *immediate* problem is financial. . . . The state (that is, the Legislature, the Department of Finance, the governor) will not talk about augmented funding as long as the campus is in disorder.[4] On the other hand the radical student-faculty group will not cease the disorder until the relief is granted.

The charge of minority students is "If we are quiet nothing, but nothing, happens, baby! If we tear things up, no demands can be met because such action would reward intimidation." Another of the reversals of fact turned on who was responsible for the fiscal deficits facing the college. Feedback from the trustees and chancellor blamed me for the crisis. Yet the vice-president for business affairs advised me before my appointment to deny responsibility for the upcoming fiscal crisis for my own protection. I chose not to do so to avoid disparaging the work of the previous president and the college administrative staff, who probably did as well as they could given the recurring campus disorder of the previous year. Every major commitment contributing to the desperate fiscal situation that fed the fall disorder was inherited by me from actions by the Chancellor's Office or the prior college administration.

There is nothing extraordinary in a new administrator's picking up a load of problems accumulated by his predecessor[5] during a

[4] Four months of intense administrative effort prior to the outbreak of disorder had failed to bring a shred of financial relief, even as the state's unexpected financial reserves exceeded a half-billion dollars.

[5] In fact Hayakawa inherited almost all those left over from Summerskill, as well as a potful of new ones I had accumulated. He did receive approximately $300,000—which I had requested in June—during his first weeks in office.

period of institutional disorder. But such accounts must be settled quickly if possible, so that the new administration can have a fresh impact on an unstable situation. Not only did my administration fail in achieving this through the chancellor and trustees during the first weeks of the summer 1968, but I also ended up being cited as a prime *cause* of the unresolved problems, and a conspirator in fomenting new disorders. This surprised me, somewhat.

PART THREE

S. I. HAYAKAWA

Chapter 13

The Hayakawa Appointment

To the vast majority of the faculty at San Francisco State College the appointment of S. I. Hayakawa to replace Smith was unbelievable, a bolt from the blue. For the past eight years he had taught infrequently, usually one course a semester, sometimes on the campus and sometimes at his Mill Valley home. Although nationally distinguished in the field of semantics, he had no experience in college administration and slight awareness of the operation of the college. No one could remember his ever having taken on essential committee membership, and never a position of leadership or one that demanded administrative skill or executive talent. Many colleagues closely associated with him in the School of Humanities were also convinced that his style and personal characteristics were not of the order required for a successful college leader in the current era of democratic involvement of faculty and students.

But those so amazed at Hayakawa's appointment had not been listening to his pronouncements since the Free Speech Movement at Berkeley in 1964 nor had they observed his political activity within the newly formed Faculty Renaissance. The tendency of militant students to eschew rational dialogue and conventional decision-making channels in favor of mass disruption, physical coercion, and violence disturbed Hayakawa greatly, and he expressed his feelings and beliefs from the podium with a skill sharpened by years of public lectures. He saw the movement as being neofascistic in the tradition of Hitler's Germany, and he viewed the radical leaders as a home-grown Mafia. For administrators to bow to the arrogant demands of these "thugs" in the guise of dialogue was an act of craven cowardice that could only ensure continued academic disruption and youthful tyranny. Hayakawa moved from professorial articulation of these views to political action when he joined the Faculty Renaissance. He was a welcome addition to the ranks of this indigenous college political organization, for his liberal reputation of the past counterbalanced the group's pronounced conservatism. For Hayakawa the organization represented a potential base from which to launch his transformation from a man of words to a leader of men and a man of action.

As the AFT became the coordinating agency of most faculty sympathetic to the demands of the striking students, the Faculty Renaissance began to serve as the instrument of those faculty who believed the actions of the striking students struck at the very heart of the college. Meetings were held, pronouncements were issued, and the group tried strenuously to persuade the college and President Smith that only a tough, hard line could restore order. These random activities came to a head when a delegation headed by Hayakawa attempted to talk with the man Hayakawa had helped put in the presidency, Smith, on Monday, November 25, while Smith and the college engaged in the second convocation with the Third World strikers. Smith did not have time for the delegation but his office, at his request, did receive from the group a plan for reversing the tide and containing the militants. What Hayakawa and his friends proposed in their document the trustees proposed to Smith at their summit meeting Tuesday: deliver ultimatums, restrict due process, suspend students, and fire faculty. Acting President Hayakawa did not deviate significantly from Professor Hayakawa's advice. This strategy became the central pillar of his administration.

The philosophy of the approach is reflected in one of the concluding paragraphs in the Faculty Renaissance document: "There is no way of getting out of our current mess, Bob, unless you take the aggressive initiative and put the strikers and disrupters on the defensive. They are at the moment accustomed to appeasement—to getting everything they want. It will really stop them in their tracks if you change the direction of events. Liberal indulgence of extremist Negro demands and whims are killing the future of the Negro."

To set a positive tone, the Faculty Renaissance leaders—most of whom were to become Hayakawa's chief aides—proposed the "immediate formation of a black studies program with autonomy in hiring, firing, decision making, and so on, with promise to go to Reagan and California Legislature, for funding. *Director to be appointed.*" If the black community would not respond to this initiative, a get-tough policy was proposed:

> (2) Call a meeting of black deans, Stanton, and so on. Tell them they are leaders and channels of communication between administration and activist students. Tell them they have until December 2 to cool the students and campus. They are professors and deans, and they are fully responsible. (3) Tell them if campus is not calm on December 2, they (black deans and professors, white professorial strike leaders, and so on) will be suspended (with pay) and charges will be brought against them of unprofessional conduct. Injunctive procedures will be used to keep them off campus while under suspension. As professors and deans they have neglected their obligations to the student body as a whole, in order to pit part of the student body against the rest. Some have been personally involved in classroom disruption and in the encouraging of strike action on the part of faculty and students. (4) If campus is not restored to calm on December 2, if disturbances break out, suspensions of professors and deans involved in the disturbances will be announced to the press. Such suspensions will have the full support of Dr. Dumke, the trustees, Governor Reagan, Unruh, and so on. (5) Faculty will be asked to declare themselves on December 2 whether or not they are on strike. Teachers who are not in their classrooms as scheduled

on December 2 will be presumed to be on strike. Five days on strike will be considered a declaration of resignation, and all resignations will be promptly accepted. (6) Students will be notified that they are to attend classes December 2. Those remaining on strike may picket peacefully. However, those interfering with the studies and activities of others will be subject to immediate suspension. Police protection and/or injunctive procedures will be used to keep off the campus students or nonstudents who interfere with educational activities.

Ed Duerr (Business)
Frank Dollard (English)
Earl Jones (Music)
James Sweeney (Biology)
William Harkness (Physical Education)
Howard Waldron (Industrial Arts)
S. I. Hayakawa (Secretary) (English and Speech)

It is interesting to note that Dollard became Hayakawa's executive vice-president (to be replaced by Jones in the fall semester), Duerr took on the difficult task of administering student justice, and Harkness became the dean of student activities in the fall. Waldron became their man in the Academic Senate.

It was later learned that this Faculty Renaissance group and Hayakawa had been making various overtures to Chancellor Dumke and conservative board members for some time. The first strong public move came, however, at the first special board meeting to interrogate Smith. Several from the Renaissance attempted to counteract the Academic Senate's overwhelming support of Smith's policies—obviously on cue from the board chairman. To the board, forced unexpectedly by Smith's resignation to pull a president out of the hat at a moment's notice, Hayakawa seemed a logical choice. His philosophy for handling militant students and faculty coincided with theirs. At long last the rebel campus would have a tough leader who would show one and all who was in charge. He could persuade the silent majority of the faculty and students to assert their dominance. His liberal reputation might placate some liberals. His Japanese ancestry might please some Third Worlders. His national academic reputation would give an added luster to the appointment. Even the faculty could not complain, for Hayakawa was from their ranks. So, with no interview, no faculty consultation, and with very few of the trustees having even met the man, Hayakawa was appointed as acting president—the college's seventh president in eight years and third in less than one year.[1]

Nothing illustrates the huge gap in understanding between the trustees and faculty more than the appointment of Hayakawa as San Francisco State's acting president. When the news of this emergency appointment reached a meeting of an ad hoc faculty group of over 125 members, it produced an instantaneous chant of "Strike! Strike! Strike!" To this group of liberal, concerned faculty the trustees' choice was incredible. The only appropriate response was the ultimate weapon, withdrawal of services. After three weeks of fumbling for a strategy to reduce the violence, the trustees had made the choice for them. Even moderates were unbelieving. The only real enthusiasm came from Faculty Renaissance colleagues.

Many in the ad hoc group came from Hayakawa's own department of English or from other departments in the School of Humanities, and they believed they had deciphered his true talents and true character. Within these ranks his personal and academic reputation had deteriorated. Although some of these faculty had basked in the reflected light of his national fame in the field of semantics, many had concluded that Hayakawa was a mere popularizer who might have been at the forefront of a significant intellectual movement at one time but was now trading upon cliches, timeworn ideas, old speeches, and past glories. His capacity to construct a verbal edifice of vivid words, polished phrases, and attractively oversimplified ideas few denied him. The fees he obtained in this major professional endeavor of making popular speeches to a wide range of audiences attested eloquently to this skill.

But whereas the audiences were awed, many of his colleagues believed Hayakawa, if not semantics, had been cast off on the shores as the intellectual mainstream swept past him. They also believed he recognized this and that he was seeking a new intellectual hobby-horse and a new career. The phenomenon of student unrest might catch the

[1] In *Ronnie & Jesse: A Political Odyssey,* Lou Cannon states: "Reagan and Alex Sherriffs, his educational adviser, had discussed the question of a replacement if Smith did quit and they had agreed that it should be someone from the faculty if possible. 'I said we would be far better off if we found someone on the campus among the ranks because of the efforts of the radicals to make it appear that their autonomy was being invaded,' Reagan recalls. 'I said what about this man Professor Hayakawa? I do not know the man but he has been quoted . . . as saying that the college should be kept open and all that' " (p. 252).

public concern for the next decade as semantics had for the past twenty years. If so, they believed, Hayakawa's task was to become visibly identified as the leading authority on student disruption and college control. The fact that this isssue had both theoretical and political ramifications gave it an additional attractiveness, for some believed that Hayakawa had been toying with the possibility of using his mastery of the spoken word and the personal image before the electorate rather than just the paying quasicultural audience.

An amalgam of Hayakawa's previous liberal sentiments with an establishmentarian, law-and-order posture on student unrest would seem to have a cogent political appeal in the current political climate. Hayakawa had consistently capitalized upon this possibility by emphatically stating that the real enemies to a liberal social view and to all that higher education represented were the radical tyrants, and that preservation of liberalism and academic freedom demanded containment of those who pressed for their goals by any means necessary. However, among most of those faculty who drew the sacred academic cloak of liberalism around their shoulders, Hayakawa's liberalism was suspect. They believed he used the trappings of liberal thought to conceal a basic authoritarianism. Although he had dabbled with the phenomenon of group dynamics and sensitivity training in his industrial consultancies and educational workshops, his detractors among the faculty claimed he did not subscribe to the humanistic motivations behind this movement but rather used the techniques in a manipulative manner to further his own ambitions.

Beyond his alleged tarnished academic and liberal reputation, the faculty who believed Hayakawa's appointment was a disaster were convinced that a characteristic and fundamental egotism along with these authoritarian traits would totally incapacitate him in dealing with faculty and students in the modern era of democratic administration. Thus, Hayakawa took on the extremely difficult and onerous task of administering a liberal, chaotic, polarized, militant campus with probably the largest coalition of sworn faculty enemies to oppose any president in the history of the state colleges. The question in his administration was whether enemies such as these would be a hindrance or a help.

Among those who either took a blood oath to destroy Hayakawa, the "trustee puppet," or simply would not give him their allegiance were the faculty who had dominated the college's governance ever since Chancellor Dumke had been the college's president. They had been active, articulate, and liberal. But their total, self-righteous domination of the college had begun to alienate increasing numbers of formerly apathetic faculty. The congruence of this liberal coalition's philosophy and some of the ideas emerging from the student activists led to the disenchantment of still larger numbers—those who belonged to the 626–247 majority support of President Smith's decision to keep the college open while negotiating with those students with grievances. Although many in this large group had grave doubts about the inexperienced president's ability to administer a complex college, they halfway admired Hayakawa's courage in challenging the disrupters, and they had no intention of actively opposing him in the early stages of his almost impossible assignment.

Given the dominant student dissent issue of the campus, faculty support or lack of support was soon to become a secondary concern. Unbeknown to those faculty still living in an earlier era of faculty hegemony, control had quickly passed from their hands to the power structure of the state and its representative on the campus, Hayakawa. For a long time the majority of the trustees, the public's representatives in charge of the state colleges, had been waiting for just such an opportunity to challenge these faculty activists who had "usurped" some of the powers of the trustees and the administration. Now, with the public and the legislature aligned against these faculty who refused to control the student troublemakers, with what they believed to be the silent majority of the faculty finally activated, and with a leader who derided these faculty liberals and had the power to make his orders stick, the long-awaited opportunity was at hand. The fact that the perennially fractious campus, San Francisco State, offered the object lesson delighted these trustees and the chancellor. Hayakawa, who had not led the parochial academic life of most of his colleagues, was far more aware of this shift of power and the freedom it would give him if he could create a more convincing public image than that of his faculty detractors.

Acting President Hayakawa also undertook his duties in the face of the united opposition and disdain of the then-elected student leaders. They saw him as a mere extension on the campus of the "corrupt Establishment" ruling the country and therefore a perfect tool for radicalizing the liberal students who had yet to accept the radical analysis of society and the campus. They seemed to reason: you reveal the repressive Establishment by violent dissent; you expose Hayakawa by accelerating the pace of campus disruption. When he overreacts with mass police power, each day should see an increase in the radicalized legions. The reform liberals then in control of the student government had been listening to their own rhetoric on the need for student power for so long—and had been witnessing the national campus trend to enfranchise more students—that it was inconceivable to them that what they viewed as a reactionary, repressive puppet of no administrative experience and slight faculty support could blunt their movement.

In addition to the considerable and devout faculty and student opposition, the jaunty new president transformed himself from professor to administrator in an atmosphere of grave skepticism from his administrative colleagues. Although some were pleased with the prospect of firm punishment for student militants, they were all aware of Hayakawa's total ignorance of the operations of the system, of the college, and of their jobs. And whereas Smith had earned their respect and affection with his team approach to constructive problem-solving, Hayakawa was obviously a lone wolf operator. A number viewed the difficulties of trying to solve the impossible problems of the chaotic campus under the new president as so great that they talked of resigning. Eventually most stayed on, embedded in and dependent on the status and pay of their positions and believing that only their experience could keep the college afloat. Hayakawa's relations with these key aides were not improved when he began to surround himself with a new palace guard of loyalists from the Faculty Renaissance group.

But as events were to prove, neither faculty nor student nor administrative resistance could prevent Acting President Hayakawa from keeping the campus open (most of the time) and eventually defeating the rebel faculty and students as long as he had the taxpaying public and the state's power elite behind him. The first two weeks of Hayakawa's term were devoted to ensuring this public support by the strategy of tough opposition to the strikers made visible by skillful use of the mass media. What was begun as a tactic mushroomed into a phenomenon never before witnessed in American higher education—a phenomenon that would make Hayakawa persona non grata on his own campus but such a folk hero across the nation that a poll later indicated he was the most widely respected educator of the year.

Hayakawa faced the first test of his leadership when he wandered into a gathering of the college's top administrators late Tuesday evening, November 26. The official announcement of Smith's resignation and Hayakawa's appointment had yet to permeate the campus, although a few in the group were aware of this development. Those in on the secret were leading the rest in a game of twenty questions to see who could name their next leader. Then in walked small, perplexed Hayakawa. All sensed that there was no need to continue this guessing game.

Within the space of half an hour Acting President Hayakawa displayed three characteristics that were to dominate his administration. First, he revealed his total isolation from the operations of the college by needing introductions to all but a few in the room, despite fourteen years on the campus. Then he asserted his bedrock administrative philosophy for handling confrontations. He stated with some passion that the situation could be cleaned up as soon as he could suspend one hundred or so student troublemakers and fire the forty or more faculty radicals who worked hand-in-hand with them in destroying the campus. When asked if this meant that he subscribed to the philosophy of Max Rafferty, he said, "Yes." He added, "I intend to be a son-of-a-bitch." And then he demonstrated his own personal decision-making style when the group was contemplating whether to continue the agreed-upon three day convocation which had one day to run before the Thanksgiving holidays. The new president arbitrarily declared that the convocation was ended, that the college would have a holiday instead on Wednesday, and that classes would resume on Monday after the Thanksgiving break. In a way, this decision had been made for the college by the Third World students that very afternoon. Seeing that they would obtain no concessions from the administrators sitting on the stage with them, tiring of the endless haranguing, and fearing that talk could soon become a substitute for revolution, thus slowing down the momentum of their strike, the Third Worlders decreed at the end of the Tuesday session that the convocation was over and that the following day would be spent in a one-man, one-vote referendum to determine whether the people were "for or against" the Third World demands. It was also becoming apparent to all that the locus for decision-making for many of the demands did not rest with the campus authorities but was tied into the total power structure of the state through the trustees, the governor, and the Legislature. The Faculty Renaissance group had all along opposed the idea of the convocations, claiming they were not intended for rational deliberations but rather were used to intimidate the administration by closing the campus down until the demands were met. One of the hopes of Smith's administration, that the radicals would expose their true aims and thus facilitate faculty, student, and public resistance to their more extreme demands, had hardly been tested, but it was obvious that with support or not, the strikers were going to continue to close the campus down.

The five-day extended holiday proved to be a very busy period for all parties. The perennial leader of the Senate, lawyer Leo McClatchy, set a pattern for his and the Senate's relations with the new president when he immediately held a press conference to denounce the Hayakawa selection process, claiming that the agreed-upon procedure of working such appointments through the college's Presidential Selection Committee had been bypassed. Indeed it had. To many faculty this became a fundamental moral issue since Hayakawa was a member of that five-man committee and all members had agreed to the policy that none of them would be a candidate for president. Hayakawa dismissed this criticism on the grounds that these were emergency conditions and that he was only acting president. Several faculty members later brought charges against Acting President Hayakawa for this "unprofessional" act, and although the charges were sustained by the faculty's new disciplinary process, Hayakawa and Chancellor Dumke simply dismissed them.

This incident epitomized one of the central moral dilemmas that has developed at State and across the nation as a concomitant of the student dissent movement. A moral battle cry of the dissidents has been victory "by any means necessary." Utilizing "any means" has given them considerable advantage in an academic milieu committed previously to other moral principles, including due process. To combat this advantage the power interests have become less squeamish about higher principles and often have acted on their own version of "by any means necessary," believing their obvious identification with the greater moral good justified inconsistent means. Thus, Hayakawa simply stated that the previous agreed-upon committee rules did not apply to him because he was allied with the moral forces attempting to root out the anarchists taking over vital American colleges. This same taint of expediency and self-righteousness was to complicate many of his actions, just as it had also compromised the activities of the militant, self-righteous students. Some faculty who reacted in moral indignation to these traits in their new president overlooked or quietly supported them in the militant students.

This faculty anger and shock over the Hayakawa appointment provoked a rash of ad hoc faculty gatherings during the holidays. Faculty, used to being rulers of their small classroom worlds, could not believe that such a blatant offense could be committed against them with impunity. Somehow, somewhere, there must be a method of redressing this egregious grievance. Articulate denunciations and visionary plans for battle were a surfeit on the market. One group decided to ask their colleagues not to teach on the campus until the administration implemented the Fifteen Demands and until Hayakawa's appointment had been officially sanctioned or rejected by the Presidential Selection Committee. Another group quickly proclaimed itself the Faculty Organization for Responsibility in College Education (FORCE), vowed to set up a vigil around the campus Monday and to press for their demands through department meetings. Among these demands were college autonomy, trustee rescission of their recently enunciated system rules for student conduct (immediately dubbed the Ten Commandments), no police on campus, special funds for a School of Ethnic Studies, elimination of the college's reputed $500,000 deficit, a nine-unit faculty load in the spring semester, a new method of trustee selection, and financial aid for any needy students.

The AFT also met during this period and began to formulate its plans to ask the Labor Council for strike sanction. Frequently the membership of the ad hoc groups, FORCE, and the AFT were almost identical, and it seemed inevitable they would coalesce to ensure better organization and more power. Since the essential leadership cadre in all the groups consisted of AFT leaders, and since the AFT had an organization, money, power, and some experience, the month-long random involvement of concerned faculty members kept pointing toward AFT leadership. Politically this proved to be a very astute strategy for the AFT, for instead of having the AFT proclaim to the faculty that they should immediately strike under the banners of the AFT—as had been done disastrously a year before—this slow simmering of faculty discontent allowed more faculty to become involved and eventually to seek out the AFT. Although this swelled the ranks of the AFT and made its leadership more palatable, it also introduced a new group into the AFT who were neither dedicated trade unionists nor committed to the basic AFT purpose, collective action for economic gains. These new faculty members passionately desired to reduce the violence and to assist the ethnic groups in obtaining greater educational opportunities. Both groups cooperated fully in the conduct of the strike, but the basic schism opened in early March when the organization had to decide whether to return to work with the student issues still unsettled. Whether it was the ad hoc groups, FORCE, the AFT, or even the Academic Senate, the primary thrust was against the Establishment, and none of these groups felt obliged to be critical of the militant students or to take responsibility to rein them in. Only one faculty group fell outside the congruence of these organizations: sixty-seven members of the Faculty Renaissance pledged their support to their fellow member who had brushed aside the faculty political structure and taken control of the college, Hayakawa.

For the new president these five days were a welcome respite for pulling his thoughts together on administering a college and repressing a rebellion, and for making the contacts necessary in the state and higher education power circles that would validate and facilitate his administration. The bubbling, fanciful, creative—and naive—facets of the new leader were revealed when rumors began to circulate during his first full day in office that he planned to contain the revolution by transforming it into a swinging, loving, be-in. Among the ideas that he floated with his administrative colleagues were inviting his close friends among black entertainers, Mahalia Jackson and Duke Ellington, to come on campus and coopt the Speakers Platform with joyful music instead of revolutionary rhetoric; allowing acquaintances among the Japanese florists to saturate the campus with horticultural symbols of peace, beauty, and love; asking bands of nuns to circulate around the campus and disarm the militants with their Christian radiance; and demanding the silent majority of students and faculty to come out and assert their values by wearing blue armbands. Of these fantasies, only the blue armband campaign saw the light of day, and by identifying the Hayakawa supporters these armbands made them prime targets for the militants. After a few days blue armbands were as scarce on the campus as were trustees (few ever came to view the problem firsthand).

After toying for a few days with these imaginative techniques for instituting a new, peaceful, swinging order, Acting President Hayakawa got down to the business of administering the college. On Friday, November 29, he had his first full-scale meeting with the chancellor and his staff. It is difficult to say who was the most surprised, Dumke or Hayakawa. To all of the officialese that all presidents were expected to be aware of—budgets, staffing formula, FTE, tables of organization, line relationships, Title V provisions, trustee regulations—Hayakawa reacted merely with inscrutable silence. Somebody else could handle these trifles, he had more important things to do. Awed though they were, the headquarters staff had to live with him; he was their choice for better or worse. When the public soon placed him on its shoulders and proclaimed him a hero, he obtained even greater leverage with and independence from the chancellor. Some of his succinct retorts to Dumke in the ensuing melees (for example: "Well, you stay down in your bunker and keep your head covered; I'll run things up here!") would have delighted the large anti-Dumke faction on the campus if attributed to anybody else.

More important, Hayakawa formulated and cleared his ideas for opening the campus. They were consonant with both his Monday recommendations to President Smith and the trustee proposal that Smith rejected. They came forth as regulations true to his hard-line philosophy: (1) Declare emergency conditions so that inappropriate due process procedures and regulations can be set aside and punishment expedited. (2) Prohibit any classroom interference or disruptive behavior. (3) Outlaw unapproved use of the Speakers Platform or bullhorns. (4) Suspend immediately any student charged with a violation of these rules. (5) Provide student hearings within seventy-two hours by a hearing officer. (6) Demand that faculty meet their classes on the campus at scheduled hours. (7) Suspend temporarily faculty that disobey this rule. (8) Accept immediately the resignation of any faculty member after five consecutive days' absence without leave (for example, striking). (9) Prohibit firearms or other weapons.

Acting President Hayakawa announced his new regime in a manner that was to become his trademark, at a full press conference on Sunday, December 1. His clear, strong words delighted a public weary of compromisers, conciliators, and capitulators. The new president also embroidered his regulations with his philosophy: Order had to be achieved at any price before the college could address itself to the basic problems. Revolutionaries and anarchists were behind most of the disruption and, although they complained about police on campus, tactically they desired the police so they could incite them to repressive measures. Colleges have as a prime function rational discourse, not social action. The black community has legitimate grievances against society and higher education, but the militant blacks do not speak for the majority of this black community. Nevertheless, he would always be willing to talk with the black militants and had sent them a telegram to this effect. As a Third Worlder himself he might be able to mediate these grievances.

One other mark of Hayakawa's eventual public posture, castigation of certain of his faculty colleagues (faculty radicals in particular), was not highlighted in his first pronouncement but hit the headlines the next day when he announced refusal to grant tenure to economics professor William Stanton. This he did despite prior supporting tenure recommendations from the department of economics, the dean of the School of Behavioral and Social Sciences and the vice-president of academic affairs. In agreeing with what had been an implicit demand from the trustees, Hayakawa gave notice that activist faculty might well be laying their jobs on the line and that, unlike his predecessors, he, not democratic faculty procedures, had the final word.

For all of his prior statements on how to handle the phenomenon of student dissent, for all of his emerging hard line as an administrator, Hayakawa still needed a tangible, visual image of a tough, no-nonsense leader that the public could relate to. The aggressive students, chance, and his own instinct for notoriety and risk-taking provided him with the opportunity to fill that need within the first hour of his active presidency. Over the holidays the striking students had been equally active. Monday, they predicted, would be a day of trial: who would survive, the strikers or Hayakawa? If they could attract sufficient support on Monday to their causes, they dreamed of closing the campus for the rest of the semester. Rallies, classroom disruption, organization in the departments, guerrilla tactics: they would try anything to make the "puppet" admit defeat.

When Hayakawa arrived at the campus he discovered not only that the students had not submitted to his edict against amplifying equipment, but that they had stationed a sound truck only 100 yards from his adminisration offices. Hayakawa did not meet with his Council of Academic Deans or consult the Academic Senate to plan an appropriate response. Instead, within minutes he personally charged the truck with minimal protection, tried to speak, and, when shut off, abruptly silenced the truck by yanking out its wiring system. Students and some faculty challenged his precipitous, "violent," illegal action; Hayakawa responded that he would do it again every day if necessary. After some pushing and shoving he strode in victory back to the campus.

All of this performance was documented by the ubiquitous TV cameras. By nightfall the image of the feisty, diminutive prexy topped by a colorful tam-o'-shanter while taking on the shaggy-headed militants went out to the nation. For once the words and actions of an academician coincided. Here was a tough leader who simply would not capitulate to the mobs. Even though most of his academic colleagues were appalled at this conduct, the public loved it. From that moment on, his image was clear. It seemed to many of his colleagues that Hayakawa devoted all his skill and energies for the next six months to the enhancement of this fortuitous beginning. In the new context of forces operating on campuses engulfed in turmoil, image proved more powerful than words, policies, or faculty or student support. The success of this image proved that Hayakawa (or any other president willing to pursue his line) could turn away from his campus and all the confused forces on it. He could get his support from the public and politicians who never set foot on the campus, who usually look for simple answers, and who do not have to live with the pedagogical wreckage, the simmering hate, the return to the soft power of apathy and the tyranny of the absolute.

Chapter 14

Keeping the Campus Open

Monday, December 2, saw the enactment at San Francisco State of the basic scenario that was to be duplicated with minor variations for the next two critical weeks. It was a scenario more appropriate for a Haymarket riot than a Mr. Chips. Pitted against each other were two resolute forces: the striking students versus Hayakawa and the local police. The students were determined to close the campus and achieve their demands at whatever cost; Hayakawa and the police were equally determined to use whatever force was necessary to keep the campus open and to repress the militants. These two fierce forces became locked in a battle of wills and bodies.

Although there were occasional brief skirmishes before noon, the gathering of forces usually began around twelve o'clock. Until then most students were in classes, but by lunchtime State's unique student body began to assemble expectantly around the perimeter of the large greensward that was the hub of the campus. Strikers roamed about casually, exchanging small talk, passing out shrill literature, smiling confidently. Cameramen and reporters saturated the campus but found little to report before noon. The action commenced with a drift toward the small, redwood Speakers Platform on the northern edge of the lawn as the scheduled orators took up their places. On several days the ceremonies began more dramatically when the leadership cadre assembled across Nineteenth Avenue at the Ecumenical House and then heralded the day's festivities by marching in a tightly knit group between the Humanities and Administration Buildings chanting "On strike! Shut it down! On strike! Shut it down!" As they marched confidently, an excited shiver would go through the crowd. In official ranks, behind doors and windows, it was recognized that another zero hour had arrived.

Typically, on the Speakers Platform, speaker after speaker tried to outdo one another with bitter condemnations of the racist institution, the pigs, Hayakawa, Reagan (contemptuously pronounced "Reegan"), and the corrupt Establishment. The white radical students had a basic position piece as did the black, brown, and yellow leaders. "Bullshit!" "Motherfuckers!" and other standard street talk sounded so constantly it was difficult to determine whether they were being used as nouns, adjectives, adverbs, verbs, or all at once. As one striker replied when interrupted by a request for the time: "Don't shit me, mother; it's three-fucking-thirty!" On cue a group of fifty to one hundred strikers packed in front of the platform would raise their clenched fists and again and again shout "On strike! Shut it down!" in choral response to the fiery incitements and indictments.

While the revolutionary temper of the crowd was being inflamed, blue-coated policemen were rather inconspicuous. For the most part, plainclothes policemen had been called off except for intelligence gathering and had been replaced by small groups of San Francisco's "friendliest"—the cop on the beat—in each building. A complete reversal had been effected on the proposition that the bluecoats would incite rebellion, especially since it had been proved in the Smith era that plainclothesmen could make arrests in the mobs only with considerable threat to their own personal safety. Such action also always seemed to incense the student crowds. The Tac Squad and other mob-control platoons remained on the periphery of the campus awaiting marching orders. Although Acting President Hayakawa's regulations prohibiting such unscheduled rallies and the use of amplifying equipment were blatantly mocked, the police did not take overt action to enforce these orders. Later in the day Hayakawa occasionally swore out warrants against key leaders who had defied his rules.

The second act of the battle scenario began when a strike leader called a halt to the speeches and exhorted the crowd to show its defiance of Hayakawa the puppet and its support of the strikers by joining in a parade on the circular walkway that bordered the greensward. As the strike cadre set itself at the vanguard of the marchers, a surprising number of the relatively uninvolved spectators joined in until frequently the entire campus was encircled with marchers eight abreast and numbering 1,000. For many of the students at State, marching and chanting became an important personal testimony of opposition to the violence, the Establishment, Hayakawa, and Reagan. For the strike leadership this parade was a basic strategy for obtaining some useful, though token, commitment from the swelling ranks of students either sympathetic to their goals or hostile to their enemies. Many students thus signed a pledge card for the strike in a manner reminiscent of the many who have stood up and promised their souls to Jesus at a Billy Graham revival. The oratory, too, had a revivalist, fundamentalist ring. The contrast with the standard styles of academe was startling. Bearing witness to their convictions by walking in the parade were a sprinkling of the more dedicated faculty, although many faculty sympathizers simply could not bring themselves to this public display of their feelings. Of the 700 or so black students on the campus few beyond the BSU leaders participated. Equally large crowds stood mutely watching the marchers and were taunted for not participating; and some individuals stepped forward and joined the happy ranks.

After a circuit or two the third act began when the leaders climbed back on the platform. This time the speeches were brief and harsh. When the Third World guerrilla general sensed a climax had been reached he would cry "Let's get the Puppet!" or "Let's pull those racist scabs out of their classes in the BSS Building!" Then he would grab his bullhorn and lead a small strike cadre toward the target.

The battle march represented the last act of this staged piece.

From then on it was mostly random improvisation. As the strikers moved on their objective an electric impulse seemed to actuate the spectators. Danger and bloodshed were close at hand. People looked over their shoulders for the imminent arrival of the police. The wary scurried out of the line of battle. Some took ringside seats in the upper stories of the adjoining library building. Others who were tempted to do battle or at least observe it close at hand converged on the arena.

Within the ranks of the strike troops the movement was also predictable. As the attack group turned from the platform and surged toward the target the leaders who had been rhetorically whipping the crowd to action now began to drift toward the outer fringes. Few of the BSU, TWLF, or SDS strategists remained at the point or were ever arrested in these raids. A token cadre led with the bullhorn. But as the time for violent rock-throwing, glass-breaking action arrived, as the moment of conflict with the police in the buildings approached, those bearing the brunt of battle and risk were largely the new recruits, recent converts who had been caught up in their rage against the despised Establishment.

When the building target was clear, one of the police observers immediately warned the off-campus command post through an efficient walkie-talkie system, and troops would be dispatched—and their deployment recorded on the plastic overlay of the battle map. A quickening of pulses, a murmur of expectancy signaled the cadenced arrival on campus of the police. By then usually the front door of the target building had been smashed and a few windows broken. Desecration of property was an important, conscious, symbolic act. Quickly the bluecoats placed a protective cordon in the front of the building, the mobs retreated, and then the individual and small group forays began—taunt, invective, obscenity, rock. Then a sudden police charge into the mob after a particular culprit. Hysterical screaming, scared running, thumping clubs, blood, students and police wrestling on the grass. Groans, curses, attempts to free students who were now restrained roughly with batons gouging their necks or arms pinioned behind their backs. If one platoon of police appeared endangered by the mobs, new squads swung into action. In the early days 200 police saw action. Later they numbered as many as 700. California Highway Patrolmen and reserve units from nearby cities supplemented the San Francisco police. At times the mixed commands were difficult to coordinate. Students and faculty gasped at the overkill in numbers and tactics.

Soon the battle of maneuver began. The goal of the police was to clear the center campus of students. The goal of the militants was to frustrate the police, hopefully provoke them to more retributive violence, and shut down the campus. The police moved in coordinated sweeps across the total campus. Grudgingly the students retreated, haranguing and taunting. Then came another clash, wild chases, incipient riots, and always the ubiquitous three-foot club.

Nothing radicalized the San Francisco State student body and faculty as much as the sight of the brawny, helmeted Tac Squadder chasing a single student, felling him with a truncheon blow, then striking him several times on the ground as blood spurted out. This treatment was not typical police behavior but it happened enough, in sight of thousands, to transform many in the silent majority into strike sympathizers and police-and-Hayakawa haters. Occasionally innocents received equally rough treatment, for the police often had neither the ability nor the desire to make fine distinctions. Clergy, medics, faculty protectors, taunting students, bystanders—they looked alike to the harassed police. Although women were seldom clubbed, they did not escape manhandling if they got in the way. Some sobbed, some clawed, some shrieked. The cameras whirred and the thousands of spectators obtained their vicarious thrills while deploring the violence. Or they died a little inside.

For some police the crowd control was merely another job, a day's pay. For others the clash with students had obviously been long awaited and was pursued with fierce joy. No love was lost between long-haired militant and burly trooper.

During lulls the voice of Acting President Hayakawa would be heard over the powerful public address system atop the Administration Building. "There are no innocent bystanders. Go back to classes. There are no innocent bystanders." The utter incongruity of these injunctions reminded most of the people of Orwell's Big Brother—as did other activities of the new president. It is doubtful that many obeyed and probable that hundreds were incited to further resistance. Still the repeated command rang out: "This is your acting president. This is an unlawful assembly. Please disperse. If you want to make trouble, stay where you are and the police will see that you get it."

There were moments when small squads of ten or twelve police became surrounded by pressing mobs of hundreds. A mass student attack seemed inevitable. But usually the police kept calm and were eventually freed by a fast organized relief squad. The police did not escape injury from rocks, bottles, and clubs. At times these student attacks were admittedly deliberate attempts by the radicals to provoke, for a violent police counterattack produced converts and escalated the revolution. Any box score of injuries, however, showed that angry students were no match for trained professionals. Stitch by stitch the students lost, twenty to one.

This swirling ebb and flow of two or three thousand individuals encircled by thousands of spectators and a chain of buildings often lasted well into the afternoon. Then, on signal, the leaders marched off again down the narrow corridor between the Humanities and Administration Buildings. If the day had been violent the mobs might hurl rocks and bolts through windows as a parting hostile gesture. Miraculously few students or office workers were hit or cut. When in a particularly ugly mood, the mobs tied up traffic on the corner of Nineteenth and Holloway Avenues, thus provoking one last police chase. Several times mounted troops were used for this clean-up in the streets. Neighboring householders stood in their doorway remarking, "Get those dirty hippies!"—but occasionally, "Cossacks!" This calloused use of horses against people was particularly galling to the strikers. By three o'clock the police had usually withdrawn, the film had been sent to the studios for the early news show, and Hayakawa was preparing for his customary press conference. In early days he appeared for these meetings garlanded with flowers.

As the days wore on the police modified their tactics. Commanders were quick to sense the inflammatory affect of freely swung clubs and all police were ordered to swing only at the legs. For the most part the head-splitting disappeared. Crowds were kept off balance by continuous maneuver and pressure with outstretched clubs. There were occasional days devoid of any combat, but these were rare, usually the rainy days. One clear day a large student raiding party invaded the Administration Building and threatened to break down the president's door. They had to be controlled with Mace and drawn guns. A student leaving the building carelessly left his attache case. Inside police found a gun and primitive bomb ingredients. In one of the more incongruous moments of the strike, the student later knocked on the president's door to ask if his case had been found and was promptly arrested. Attache cases were the rumored hiding places for weapons and as such became a symbol of status and threat.

The sum total of property damage during the two weeks and for the total strike was minimal compared to the damage to humans incurred in the protection of property—several arson attempts blackened a few areas, many windows were broken, and toilets were frequently clogged; at one time the damage was estimated at $30,000. The police did not endear themselves to the crowds when they rigidly refused to allow the white-coated volunteer medics to attend the injured demonstrators. According to police regulations, it was said, only official doctors could have business with individuals injured during police activity. No one ever determined how official doctors were to give immediate first aid.

Equally provocative to students and faculty was the police technique of sending a squad into a group of strikers to arrest a student for whom they had an outstanding warrant. Invariably, when this happened, the peace was broken and a violent clash followed. The police response to the criticism was simple: we had a warrant to serve, it was difficult to locate this student off campus, he was spotted so we arrested him, like any other alleged criminal. The fact that the student arrested was usually a noted strike leader created the impression that these raids were deliberate strike-breaking techniques. But then, on the other hand, the TV coverage so carefully sought by students had ensured police familiarity with these leaders.

Over the two weeks approximately 148 arrests were made, mostly one at a time. (A mass arrest, it was feared, might well have produced a full-scale riot. The mass-arrest tactic had to wait until January, when enough students had been kept off campus by the strike that those arrested were deprived of mass support.) The police made several early morning charges on small groups of pickets; but they made few arrests. This disruption of relatively peaceful though noisy picketing again infuriated the strikers.

The cause of the Third World strikers was greatly enhanced when a dozen recognized leaders from the black community joined the young militants in placing their bodies on the line. The appearance on the platform and in the vanguard of the marching ranks of Assemblyman Willie Brown, Dr. Carleton Goodlett, Reverend Cecil Williams and others gave a degree of legitimacy to the protests that could not be ignored. In December, Acting President Hayakawa had attempted to dissuade these leaders by engaging them in dialogue on their own grounds, but the meeting turned into a loss for the college. To the black leaders Hayakawa seemed patronizing and uninformed. When he attempted to magnify his personal living experiences with blacks during the 1940s to show his sympathies and understanding—and to certify his awareness of the ambitions of the average, not the militant, black person—he met loud and articulate criticism. When he attempted to outline a "deal," black rhetoric engulfed him: the academic specialist in communications and the practitioners of gut-level black communications made no constructive contact with each other. Hayakawa stalked out of the meeting, his liaison with the black community in tatters.

One of the central motivating forces behind this community support for the strikers is reflected in a statement by Reverend Williams: "We of the adult world are not going to see these youngsters go down. . . . They are going to realize our dream in their lifetime." Not to have supported their brothers would also have meant political suicide. Originally these community leaders came on the campus during the first weeks "to interpose their bodies" between their brothers and the police. To make certain of this commitment, observers agreed, the BSU leaders created incidents where this interposition could not be avoided. This led to the arrest of Goodlett and others. Undoubtedly their presence served as a restraint on both the police and the more violent strikers. It also galvanized San Francisco's civic leaders who had no intention of creating a Northern California Watts.

Central to this broad response from the San Francisco community was Mayor Joseph Alioto. During the Smith era he had conferred frequently with the college in an attempt to defuse the crisis. Originally he had advised Smith not to accede to the trustee request to suspend Murray, believing it was a politically inspired act designed to create an incident that might influence the November elections. Advised by college AFT leaders, he later proposed a campus convocation involving all people in power positions in the state who could make the decisions to solve the college's problems. Not only did he sympathize with the plight of the college but he was also cognizant of the impact of a race riot on his gubernatorial ambitions. It was also the police of his city who were being drained off for the college action and his city's strained budget which would have to pay. He could hardly refuse to insist that the police protect state property and the education and even the well-being of the students, yet this law-and-order posture did not distinguish him from the man he might have considered running against for the governor's office, Reagan. It also was not consonant with his deep commitment to mediation as the technique for solving the problems of strikers. His commitment was grounded in experience.

Barely had the strike become full-blown under Acting President

Hayakawa than Mayor Alioto began to use the full force of his office to effect citizen intervention. In this he was propelled by the active concern of organized labor. San Francisco is well known as a labor town, and Alioto had depended heavily on labor support in his mayoralty campaign. When the college's AFT chapter requested strike sanction from the Labor Council on the second day of Hayakawa's tenure, December 3, this translated the strike from a campus to a city issue. The Labor Council was not particularly anxious to appear to the rank-and-file laboring man to be encouraging long-haired student revolutionaries, black militants, or faculty dissidents, either; yet it could not cast itself in the role of rebuffing a union or playing hand-in-glove with Governor Reagan. Mediation seemed the answer. Working together, Mayor Alioto and George Johns, executive secretary of the Labor Council and long a member of State's local advisory board, created a Citizens Committee led by Bishop Mark Hurley that eventually helped conclude the student strike.

One of the principal deterrents to mediation was the growing confidence of the BSU and TW strikers. Many classes were either closed down or being held off campus. There was wide variance between the administration and student statistics on the extent of the disruption, but in such major schools as the behavioral and social sciences and humanities attendance was conservatively judged to be down below an overall 50 per cent during the middle of the day. Massive police intervention was both rapidly radicalizing the uninvolved students and faculty and costing the city a heavy price. Black community support offered the possibility of a force the college administration simply could not contain. And now a large sector of the faculty, the 250-member AFT,[1] contemplated lending its support to the strike. How could a man for whom they had so much contempt, Hayakawa, hope to blunt their force?

When Hayakawa held a press conference at the end of his first week in office, Friday, December 6, to announce his endorsement of the combined Academic Senate–Council of Academic Deans response to the Fifteen Demands, the BSU-TW leaders showed utter disdain for what they considered an attempt to buy them off. "He's offering us tidbits! He's trying to divide us!" Amidst these cries, the response

[1] Variations throughout this account of the size of the AFT membership and the number of faculty on strike stem from the large, almost daily, increase in the membership during late November, December, and early January and the fact that not all AFT members were active in the strike.

that had seemed most logical and reasonable to the faculty and the administration was categorically shot down. Three months, hundreds of arrests, and thousands of dollars later the striking Third Worlders were to settle on the terms they now so vociferously rejected. The irony of this situation was accentuated by the fact that the college under President Smith had been in agreement on these same points even before the strike had been instituted on November 6. The academic community recognized that it needed to enlarge the ethnic enrollment and programs but it would not concede total power to the ethnic students in determining which and how many Third World students should be admitted, who should be hired to teach in the program, or what the nature of the studies should be.

In rejecting the Senate-administration-Hayakawa response to the demands, Juan Martinez, the nontenured lecturer in history who had emerged as the Chicano leader, reflected the emerging Third World confidence when he commented, "We will continue the struggle —if necessary—all year long—or as long as it takes to win all these demands." Leroy Goodwin claimed, "We see our momentum growing and now we have the largest college strike in the history of the country." Inspired by this growing strength, Goodwin, the BSU Off-Campus Coordinator, announced on December 10 "an official declaration of war. . . . Under this state of war all ad hoc rules and regulations set up by the acting president, Hayakawa, to hamper freedom of speech or freedom of assembly will be disregarded, and the battleground tactics and time sequences will be determined by the central committee of our revolutionary people."

At the same time that they declared war on Hayakawa, the TWLF and the BSU announced what was to prove to be the greatest roadblock to the Alioto-Hurley-Hayakawa mediation efforts, a series of preconditions that would need to be met before the strikers would even consider negotiations. The closing of classes and the removal of police prior to negotiations were old demands, but when a hard insistence on total amnesty was made a precondition, "talking" negotiations were delayed or sabotaged for the next three months. The TWLF-BSU demanded that those arrested be granted amnesty, that charges be dropped against those scheduled to be arrested, and that those suspended by college authorities be reinstated with a clean record. Although various elements in the power structure were willing to reconsider specific types of violations, the idea of total amnesty for criminal or college charges was completely unacceptable to Hayakawa, the trustees, Governor Reagan, Mayor Alioto, and the general public. From this point on, the protection of valiant strikers became a more important issue for the militants than the original demands that had led to the arrests and suspensions. The TWLF-BSU simply could not abandon the troops. They also believed their strike was so successful that they could insist on these preconditions.

As the new array of forces pressed on the college during its crisis—the striking students, the AFT, the Labor Council, Mayor Alioto, the Citizens Committee, the trustees, Governor Reagan, and Hayakawa—the college's formerly strong policy-making body, the Academic Senate, found itself continuously reassessing its role. In times past it had taken for granted that its constitutional authority was sacred and that it did indeed possess the power to govern the college, though crucial tests of the thesis had been avoided. To its dismay it learned from the December experiences that both the striking students and the Establishment were unwilling to recognize this authority on an issue of this magnitude. No one seemed to challenge the Senate's decisions on general education policy or the college's grading system, but student dissent quickly became a matter of public, not educational, policy formulation—and an area where academics were viewed as inept.

The advent of Acting President Hayakawa's administration in this confrontational period presented an excellent opportunity to make this shift in the balance of power. After a brief testing period of a few weeks Hayakawa clarified his position on proper Senate-administration relations when he was challenged by the Senate for his policies "for resolving conflict on campus." First he indicated that he would "not yield to any form of gangsterism, whether exerted by blacks, whites, yellows, or browns." Then he bluntly told the Senate off:

> Ask whether your actions help to solve problems or serve only to perpetuate and complicate them. Ask whether you are willing to take bold new actions for the good of the entire institution, to break precedent if necessary, to limit your own powers if required. Ask whether the roadblocks you have placed in the paths of my predecessors have been the product of a realistic concern for the problems of the college or of a simple desire to keep anyone but yourselves from having any effective power.

Hayakawa concluded his comments by rejecting the Senate policy for student disciplinary procedures. Thus, within two weeks the Senate was transformed from an authoritative body, on the verge of voting no confidence in its new chief executive, to an auxiliary group of advisers, which was suspect in the mind of Hayakawa. Ensuing events for the year confirmed Hayakawa's hegemony.

The Senate dilemma also derived from two other factors: the deep polarization within its ranks on the strike issues and its natural orientation toward educational policy development, not crisis administration. As the Senate struggled to redefine its role under Hayakawa during this student revolt it drifted toward a mediating role between the TWLF-BSU forces and the college administration. For most of the Christmas holidays it attempted to reassess the college response to the Fifteen Demands as it listened to a trio of negotiators from its ranks who had been in continuous dialogue with various Third World leaders. Its reassessment pleased few in the academic community.

As an example of its dilemma, originally it had responded to the demand for unlimited nonwhite admissions by pledging that the college would "encourage and facilitate in every way the admission of more students from the black and other ethnic communities" and specifically would ask for a larger enrollment quota for the college in the fall 1969 to effect this enlarged ethnic admissions. In the renegotiated response the Senate agreed to "make every effort to admit students to reflect the ethnic makeup of the urban area served by the college." Given the ethnic makeup of the San Francisco area, this was quite a shift in policy.

The Third World students were not impressed. Possibly they realized that the faculty did not have the power to implement such a decision. On the other hand, the conservative forces in the college resented the Senate's attempt to play a mediating role and disapproved of the nature of some of the concessions. When the Senate refused to conduct a referendum to determine whether faculty supported or resisted the impending AFT strike, these conservative groups, and others, became convinced that the Senate had fallen under the influence of the AFT and liberal faculty forces, and they therefore undermined its influence.

As the Senate with its liberal majority continued its ineffectual challenge of various Hayakawa policies, the AFT thesis that the Senate was impotent and could not serve faculty interests in restraining the campus bloodshed came to be accepted by more and more concerned faculty. For this formerly uninvolved group the AFT became the only available rallying point for those who desired to have some critical impact on the disastrous trend on the campus. The Senate did force Hayakawa to rescind his ill-conceived, barrel-head student disciplinary procedures, and it did protect students whose academic records were threatened by the college confusion by offering any student a "pass–no report" option for any course. This act might have protected the student but its often indiscriminate use did not enhance the college's academic reputation when the regional accrediting team visited the campus in the spring.

Chapter 15

Local 1352 Mobilizes

Given the vacuum in faculty ranks when the power structure ceased to acknowledge the authority of the Academic Senate, it was inevitable that the campus local of the California Federation of Teachers, Local 1352 (usually referred to as the AFT), would move to fill this void. For years its theorists had been maintaining that nothing short of countervailing power achieved through collective bargaining and a contract could protect the faculty from the overwhelming and hostile force of the Establishment. At several points in the preceding two years it had appeared that the consistently threatening and nonsupportive actions of the Reagan administration, the Legislature, the trustees, and Chancellor Dumke had finally convinced a reluctant faculty that it must opt for the pains and joys of collective bargaining to ensure minimum protection. But just as the faculty came close to biting the bullet, militant student ventures threw the college and the system into turmoil and torpedoed the collective bargaining drives.

Beginning in the spring semester, 1968, the AFT had joined with the other large, aggressive faculty organization, the Association of California State College Professors, in a novel attempt to enhance its power not by a collective bargaining election but rather by exercising the faculty's putative power to organize its teaching responsibilities according to professional judgment. Thus, the AFT-ACSCP combine launched a pledge campaign that produced widespread support to reduce teaching loads from twelve to nine units in the spring semester, 1969, on the faculty's own authority.

As December 1968 loomed before the college the moment of truth in this bold challenge was close at hand, for the trustees and the chancellor were not inclined to support this autonomous faculty takeover. A salary reduction of one-fourth had been discussed in some administrative circles for faculty who unilaterally reduced their teaching loads. A showdown between the AFT and the system in the next two months was therefore inevitable. The disruption of the educational process by the student strikers and the police and the resultant violence and incipient riots merely added to the AFT grievances and the possibility of additional faculty support. One other issue had been added to the AFT agenda when the administration began to talk about the option of laying off 125 faculty in the spring semester in order to counterbalance the college's unusual deficit for the academic year of around $750,000. Since the system and the administration had incurred the deficit, not the faculty, and since faculty who might not be teaching in the spring would be the younger members, who were heavily represented in the AFT, this was a natural issue.

As the college confronted the student strike under President Smith, the sympathies of the AFT clearly belonged to the strikers. For the past year the issues of racism and student power had been incorporated into the economic and faculty power goals of the union. When the strike began the AFT declared itself on the side of the strikers and in favor of closing the campus and removing the police so that dialogue and negotiations could begin. It was particularly incensed at the absentee control of the college affairs by the trustees and governor, as illustrated in the command given to Smith to suspend Murray. Campus autonomy had long been a flag that the AFT, and most faculty, automatically saluted. At no discernible point had the AFT ever condemned the student strike tactics or taken an active role in attempting to maintain some order and discipline on the campus. These were Establishment, administrative roles and AFT wanted nothing to do with such seemingly repressive acts. This avoidance of any responsibility for the difficult task of containment while always stressing correction of underlying causes blackened the image of the union in public, trustee, and some faculty circles.

Prior to Acting President Hayakawa's ascendancy the AFT had been unwilling to oppose President Smith openly, but most of its leaders had worked through the many ad hoc faculty groups that were constantly enlarging the base of faculty discontent. As these groups discovered that they had neither the organization, skills, nor muscle to impinge on the striker-administration impasse, they continued to turn toward the AFT. The trustee selection of Hayakawa as acting president facilitated this drift. The AFT emerged after the Thanksgiving weekend as the focal point for faculty desiring to have some opportunity to influence the tragic events at San Francisco State.

The fatal decision by the AFT to commit itself to the strike tactic was reached at a meeting on Tuesday, December 3, the second day of the Hayakawa regime. After long debate the union voted eighty to twenty-two to request a strike sanction from the San Francisco Labor Council. The specific reasons for the sanction were not included in the resolution passed but were left to the Executive Committee to develop. The intent of the action was to use a threat of a strike and the force of the labor movement in San Francisco to pressure the trustees and the college administration to negotiate student and faculty grievances. Not only might these grievances be settled by this process, but, also important to the AFT, it might receive recognition by the trustees as an organization that could demand negotiation for its members. Such a strategy is the important first stage of collective bargaining progress with an agency that has declined in the past to recognize the bargaining principle.

A second resolution passed that day spoke to the faculty distrust of Acting President Hayakawa's use of his emergency powers:

> The San Francisco State College Federation of Teachers, Local 1352, will strike when any faculty member of the San Francisco State College faculty is suspended without due process of law, or is suspended or dismissed for peaceful demonstration, suspension of

> classes, picketing, or striking for redress of grievance or in furtherance of campus tranquility, or union policy, provided that: The Executive Committee of Local 1352, after investigation of the incident, finds such dismissal or suspension to be unjustified in accordance with the above. And be it further resolved that this local will stay on strike until said faculty member is reinstated and the relevant administrative bodies enter into meaningful negotiations to grant and ratify a written agreement to ensure that such suspension or dismissal becomes impossible in the future.

Clearly the AFT intended to encourage its members to suspend classes or hold them off campus "in furtherance of campus tranquility," and to protect them with a strike if any were arbitrarily suspended for this action. This act in itself placed the union in collision course with the trustees and a president determined that faculty could not cooperate with the striking students by suspending or rescheduling their classes. Idealists at the AFT meeting urged an immediate strike on the grounds that teaching under the chaotic conditions was impossible. Hard-headed pragmatists insisted that the support of organized labor was essential to any victory, and they prevailed.

The initiative now shifted to the power structure of the San Francisco labor movement and its experienced executive secretary, George Johns. As stated previously, organized labor did not desire to endorse a strike involving militant black students and white radicals, but it was aware that it was in a strategic position both to help mediate the tense situation on the campus and, in the process, to gain some recognition for the AFT as a negotiating unit with the trustees. Bringing white-collar professionals into its ranks could more than compensate for various defections. To achieve these purposes, Johns and Mayor Alioto conceived the idea of a large-scale mediation session under labor's auspices on Monday, December 9, that would involve the AFT, the college administration, San Francisco State legislators, representatives of the trustees and the Chancellor's Office, organized labor's hierarchy, Mayor Alioto, and media representatives. Hopefully such a group would have the status and the resources to solve the college's problems and to influence the trustees in granting some type of recognition for the AFT demands. To ensure labor's dominant role in the mediation, Johns invited one of the country's top mediators, Ronald Haughton of Wayne State University, to spearhead the conciliation effort. Johns expected that the trustees would respond in the fashion of the many reluctant management groups he had had to deal with in his long career, for most of the trustees had management experience. However, should the trustees not enter into meaningful negotiations, Johns persuaded the Labor Council to grant the AFT's request for a strike sanction. The leadership of the AFT stated that it was determined to proceed with the strike, with or without Labor Council sanction, if the trustees would not negotiate in good faith. The executive committee of the union also urged Hayakawa to close classes for three days while the mediation effort got under way.

Events soon proved that the Labor Council and the AFT had completely misjudged the posture of Governor Reagan and the trustees. Over the weekend the governor had made one of his privately funded, periodic reports to the people of California, and for his topic this time he chose campus insurrections. The governor said, "Disorders which disturb or disrupt the work and educational activities of any university or college campus can no longer be tolerated. . . . Never can we capitulate or surrender . . . to the vocal, abusive minority of the militants." These militants he described as anarchists and revolutionaries and indicated that the trustees and the regents should never abdicate to a coalition of these students and faculty lusting for power. Again he reiterated the position that he had previously urged on the trustees, that there should never be negotiations with students and faculty as long as the college was being coerced with disruptions.

On the governor's request, Chairman Theodore Merriam of the trustees took a tough position on the Labor Council's mediation offer:

> I must point out, and clearly, that the overall problem is a problem of higher education in this state and that the Board of Trustees, by law, is the governing body, and that the members of this board are the representatives of the people of California. It is not appropriate for other agencies, either official or unofficial, and no matter how well intentioned, to attempt to intrude in an authoritative manner in affairs outside of their true area of responsibility.

Governor Reagan said, "I don't think there is any mediation needed. . . . The college administration must make the policy and can't share that with anybody." To ameliorate this seeming intransigence, Chairman Merriam appointed a trustee liaison task force for the San Francisco State College problems consisting of four Bay Area trustees: Louis Heilbron, James Thatcher, Albert Ruffo, and Karl Wente. This act was to prove critical in the final resolution of the strike, but not until two months had elapsed and the college educational effort had approached almost a standstill.

Merriam's tough line was such an obvious slap in the face to Johns' well-intentioned efforts that he and his Labor Council began to think more seriously about strike support. Sophisticated industrial management seldom had been so adamant. The trustee nonnegotiation approach also accelerated the strike activities of Local 1352. Tuesday night, December 10, it agreed to institute informational picketing on the campus. More important, it made the fateful strike decision. By an overwhelming vote the local decided to go out on strike Monday, December 16, with or without Labor Council support, unless the trustees had begun meaningful negotiations by 2:00 P.M., Friday, December 13.

This action did not satisfy the militant Third World strike leaders who were sitting in on the meeting. In their eyes the mediation efforts were a "shuck" and they demanded that the AFT walk out immediately. Said Tony Miranda: "You're selling us out! We're out there getting busted every day and beaten by the pigs while you're sitting around waiting for a strike sanction." A large group in the union felt this criticism was justified. When the Executive Committee was enlarged by three members to form the Negotiating Committee, the membership chose three from this critical sector: Eric Solomon, Henry McGuckin, and Fred Thalheimer.

A working relationship with these striking students proved to be one of the most difficult tasks for the AFT. The student grievances were central to the college crisis, and many AFT members were placing their bodies on the line primarily because of the issue of institutional racism. Yet, the vital Labor Council endorsement would certainly not encompass student demands. To walk this tightrope the AFT agreed to a set of economic demands that would ensure Labor Council support and form a basis for negotiations but took the equivocal position that the student grievances "must be resolved and implementation assured" by the administration. This latter compromise avoided bitter AFT debate on the specific demands, gave the Labor Council a way out, and could be justified as a nonpaternalistic attitude by the faculty toward the students and their issues. Most of the public interpreted the posture as tacit support for the disruptive students and consequently criticized the striking faculty bitterly.

With fifty or so AFT members picketing alongside the raucous students in front of the Administration Building Wednesday and Thursday, December 11 and 12, and being jostled unceremoniously by unimpressed police on occasion, the zero hour on Friday loomed ominously ahead. Preparations for the strike on Monday were launched with total commitment by the union. All the complicated support activities were planned, a headquarters office was rented, picketing stations were allocated, jobs assigned, and locals on other state college campuses were urged to stage sympathy strikes.

But Friday produced a surprise. On the initiative of the Academic Senate and his administrators, Acting President Hayakawa quickly agreed to begin the Christmas holidays one week early and make up the week at the end of the semester. Many neighboring junior colleges and high schools would already be into the holiday season on Monday, December 16, and the strikers were urging these students as well as people in the community to mass on the campus as the faculty strike began. The prospect of the complications this would create for the police and the administration was the reason given by the president for his early holiday pronouncement. Striking students and soon-to-be-striking faculty were not sure whether this was a tricky maneuver designed to outwit them or a heaven-sent opportunity. Both decided to capitalize on its advantages. With Acting President Hayakawa now at the helm, Governor Reagan raised no question about this closing of the campus.

To those hopeful that men of goodwill could somehow settle these nettlesome disagreements if only opposing parties could gather around the negotiating table, this unexpected respite cleared the air. Since the trustees resisted conferring while strikers disrupted the campus, the vacation created a peaceful condition that allowed discussion. The trustees quickly decided that they could indeed meet, for a section of the law stated they were authorized to confer with employee organizations on request. The AFT, which had been resisting negotiations while the campus was in turmoil, now had the closing of classes, which it had advocated. Stretching before both parties, as well as all other interested agencies and people, were three quiet weeks to seek a peaceful settlement. This became the agenda for the holidays. In case the mediation failed, the AFT engaged in heroic efforts to ensure the launching of a successful strike.

A sizeable delegation of union members met on five different days during the three-week holiday period with Assistant Chancellor Mansel Keene and Norman Epstein, the chief legal counsel for the

California State Colleges. Various other parties, including mediator Ronald Haughton, AFT lawyer Victor Van Bourg, George Johns, and representatives of the statewide AFT and ASCSP organizations, also sat in on the meetings. Although much time was consumed by union representatives elaborating upon various grievances, it became quite clear that the AFT's basic objective was to initiate some semblance of a written agreement between the trustees and the union on some issue while at the same time placing pressure on the Establishment to settle with the students. It was also clear that the trustee representatives had absolutely no authority or powers to negotiate or sign anything and were there "to meet and confer" and listen to the AFT grievances. Other meetings were therefore doomed from the very beginning. The AFT representatives reflected this pessimism in their basic communication to the members of Local 1352 on December 29. They commented that it was their unanimous conclusion that there had been "no meaningful negotiations and no progress on our strike issues."

At the termination of the December 28 meeting Van Bourg attempted to persuade the trustee representatives to initial, as a tentative agreement, a statement summarizing two steps which the trustee representatives said had already been taken by the system prior to the AFT demands. The AFT felt such a written agreement would at least show that the trustees intended to proceed in good faith with the negotiations. Since negotiations or agreements were by definition beyond the authority of the trustee representatives, no initialed agreement was produced at this time.

The meetings were held in mock negotiating style with the union representatives frequently recessing for prolonged caucusing and with mediators shuttling back and forth between the AFT room and the trustee representatives' room. With serious issues before the college, the union requested, as a negotiating position, an automatic progression salary schedule, the right for faculty to schedule nine-unit loads for themselves, as much sick leave as might be needed, automatic sabbatical leaves of one year at full pay, $1,000 per faculty member for graduate assistants, faculty autonomy in determining college admissions requirements, and one-man faculty offices. These demands were offered as initial bargaining positions on economic issues in order to convince the Labor Council of the union's sincerity.

In addition to these visionary working conditions, the union stated emphatically that it desired a written contract as a bare minimum, and that it would strike on January 6 unless amnesty were granted to all arrested or suspended for strike activities. The dismissal of charges was specifically requested even for individuals charged with a crime involving violence to the person of another. Such excesses, according to lawyer Van Bourg, could be attributed to "the enthusiasm of the moment" and should be excused. In taking such a position the AFT Negotiating Committee was acting for the student strike Central Committee, which had developed this demand as a precondition to negotiations, and was endorsing the historic labor posture that strike settlements should protect prior "illegal" strike activity. To those in a power position, most of whom had been deeply offended by the vision of militant student strikers presented to them nightly on TV, the idea of no punishment for these tactics was outrageous. And faculty asking for such amnesty were considered equally culpable.

Under such conditions—trustee representatives having no power to negotiate, the AFT making impossible economic demands, no one being in a position to speak to the vital student grievances, and the amnesty impasse blocking everybody—it became a question only of when the discussions would cease. The meeting on Thursday, January 2, was so fruitless that the AFT Negotiating Committee announced to its membership, "It is the unanimous opinion of the Negotiating Committee that nothing has happened. Despite this, we will play this string out to show our good faith by returning Saturday morning for another session. We must be prepared to strike on Monday. Only a miracle could turn Saturday's meeting into a negotiating session."

Saturday witnessed no such miracle. On Sunday night the faculty turned out 250 strong to make the decision no other college faculty group in California—and few in the nation—had ever made: Strike!

An electric excitement, almost an elation was in the air as the casually dressed faculty members strolled into the YMCA hall close to the college on January 5, 1969, to consider joining the student strikers. The hall was jam-packed. A series of speakers spelled out the issues, declaimed on the historic nature of the event, and summarized the extent of support from labor, other campuses, and a variety of Bay Area community groups. As the emotional pitch swelled, Arthur Bierman, father of the AFT and chief of the negotiators, gave a detailed analysis of the patient, constructive efforts of the negotiating team to attempt to produce one glimmer of willingness to negotiate from the trustee representatives and of the consistent rebuff of these reasonable suggestions time after time after time. It was a masterful cheerleading performance, and the membership performed on cue with great enthusiasm. Then a note of seriousness was added by lawyer Van Bourg, who drew from his extensive labor experience to spell out in detail the precise nature of a faculty strike, the risks, the legalities, the price. Immediately it was moved from the floor for unanimous consent to approve the strike that had been pledged before the holidays if no serious negotiations developed. With a mighty roar and not one quiet "no," Local 1352 of the California Federation of Teachers declared itself on strike as of 6:00 A.M. Monday morning.

The only divisive note intruded when it was moved from the floor that a prior position that would have allowed faculty to strike yet still hold classes off campus be rescinded, and that the official union position become a commitment to total withdrawal of services. Some faculty thought this resolution was both unfair to students and unfair to faculty who had come into the strike according to the previous ground rules, and they reminded the group of this commitment in passionate terms. As the group debated the resolution the small number of BSU Central Committee members in the back of the room galvanized into action. Both George Murray and Jack Alexis laid it on the line. "Listen, you motherfuckers! This is our strike, we are the ones getting our heads busted and going to jail. The least you can do is quit teaching. If you defeat this motion we'll take your Executive Committee and line them against the wall and shoot each one of the motherfuckers!" roared one BSU leader.

In the uproar that followed a timid voice demanded a secret ballot on the resolution. Once again the black students were testing the true commitment of the white faculty to the black student demands, a commitment they continued to doubt for most of the next six weeks. And they were testing it with the coercive rhetoric of the ghetto and black student meetings, not with deliberate, dispassionate academese. After about a three-to-one vote by the militant membership to support the resolution, a jubilant faculty group marched out of the hall singing "Solidarity Forever," proud of their tough idealism, hopeful of victory, but slightly tense in the stomach.

What moved normally individualistic, passive, rational, risk-avoiding intellectuals to lay their bodies on the line, to gamble with their jobs and salary losses from $2,000 to $4,000, to incur the wrath of most of the public and many of their colleagues, and to take on the total power structure of the state of California? With about 250 faculty making the decision, a similar number of personal motives existed. But a few loomed larger than the rest. In interviews,[1] over and over again one heard passionate references to the violence and bloodshed. Until the relentless, massive confrontations during Acting President Hayakawa's first two weeks of leadership, most faculty had merely heard of the two or three serious near-riots in November, or had seen quick documentation on TV. But with classes seriously impaired regularly from 11:00 A.M. to 3:00 P.M. for the two weeks of December, many faculty members stood by in total consternation as they watched the mob scene of the strikers and police that had transformed their quiet academic retreat into a bloody battlefield. Many were almost physically sick. Most could not conceive that a major race riot could be avoided or that somebody would not be killed. In post mortems among the striking faculty you heard the statement, "At least we saved some student lives," repeated continuously. Most felt both incredulous and impotent. This inability to find any other constructive outlet for a gut-level drive to put a stop to this insanity was undoubtedly the unifying force that drew this disparate collection of individuals together under the wing of the AFT. Here at least, unionist or not, was an action alternative. No other campus base seemed to offer this option. Many were also deeply convinced that the massive police intervention was a fundamental desecration of the academic environment, and that it contributed to rather than prevented the violence. Police on campus under any circumstances was simply something they could not tolerate, no matter what the administrative justification. The occasional police brutality reinforced this attitude.

A preponderant number of the striking faculty sympathized entirely with the plight of the Third World students and desired to see their demands met. Most were convinced our country and our colleges are truly racist, and that we will continue to discriminate against our black brothers for another fifty or more years unless action now is forced by the black youth. Contributing to integrationist causes had not seemed to modify significantly 400 years of social prejudice and servitude. Now here on their own campus they could strike out for

[1] Most of the view from within the AFT was obtained by the authors in extensive, frequently taped interviews with both leaders and striking members. For a more detailed view from within the striking faculty, see Arlene Daniels and Rachel Kahn-Hut, *Academics on the Line* (San Francisco: Jossey-Bass, 1970).

black youth and, in so doing, hopefully bring peace to their college. Thus, their heavy guilt feelings over complicity with racism and police repression could be assuaged. For tactical reasons in dealing with an unsympathetic labor movement, however, this motive had to be couched in ambiguous terms. But most striking faculty were convinced their painful efforts would be wasted unless they helped force administrative negotiations with the BSU and the TWLF. This was a somewhat hidden but dominant item on their agenda. And it was an item that alienated most colleagues who resisted bowing to black student coercion, especially since these colleagues believed the institution had been moving as rapidly as possible in the past year to meet all legitimate ethnic demands.

A corollary motive to the desire to avoid bloodshed was the conviction of the striking faculty that the delicate, trustful nature of education made a mockery of teaching on a campus in continuous tumult. Many of the striking faculty had already transferred their classes to churches or homes. For teachers to teach and students to learn in an atmosphere of chaos and violence was a delusion and a fraud to which they would not contribute. A moderate state senator, James Wedworth, who had virtually lived on the campus for two weeks, made the categorical comment in a press release, "To my knowledge, despite attempts at instruction by some faculty, no true educational processes are going on. . . . No one can learn in an atmosphere of fear, destruction, and brutality." Wedworth believed the conditions were serious enough to justify his radical proposal that the campus be fenced in like a defense plant, with only individuals showing authorized identification badges permitted beyond the gates.

Both the fear that their illegitimate new leader, Hayakawa, would attempt to fire them if they balked at his edict against teaching classes off campus and a basic hatred for Hayakawa and his dictatorial administrative style were other major unifying concerns within AFT ranks. Hayakawa had made it quite clear that he believed a sure cure for the college would be the firing of fifty or so faculty troublemakers. To counter this possibility the AFT communicated to Acting President Hayakawa and the trustees in their original strike vote that they would go out on strike if any faculty member was punished for deciding he simply could not teach or meet his responsibilities to students on the embattled campus. This embittered hatred ran deep in most AFT members and sustained them when all else failed during their struggle. What they could not forgive in their nonstriking colleagues was the nonstrikers' willingness to demean themselves by teaching for a man they saw as a petty dictator.

Some AFT members saw the issue as stretching beyond the campus and encompassing dangerous tendencies in our broader society. Some agreed with the radical analysis of our capitalistic system and believed our society is fundamentally imperialistic, repressive, and corrupt. This view found more favor among the younger faculty. In the course of the strike the AFT developed a fierce radical caucus. For this group the strike was an opportunity at last to launch a blow against an Establishment they saw ever dehumanizing our culture and leaving the individual citizen impotent. These radically inclined faculty had their liberal counterparts among the large numbers of faculty, strikers and nonstrikers, who finally recognized that college autonomy, faculty prerogatives and power, and higher education in California as they knew it and desired it were under severe attack from conservative forces that were now dominant and moving within the trustees and other state power circles. For the past seven years these faculty had occasionally heard the wailing of their more politically inclined confreres, but the events of the past year had finally alerted them to the "enemy." Morally incensed and politically unsophisticated, they demanded action. The Murray suspension, the police intervention, the Hayakawa appointment had all convinced them that their college, their students, their higher education were being used as pawns on the larger political chessboard. As with many sudden converts, some took on the zeal of the true believer.

In the center of the AFT decision makers stood the small cadre of dedicated trade unionists for whom faculty power and economic gain had been powerful drives for at least the past decade. Although they shared with their fellow strikers a revulsion against a violent campus, police intervention, racism, and Hayakawa, above all else they looked to the day when faculty could get off their knees in their dealings with the power structure and negotiate as equals under the protective wing of collective bargaining. The confluence of the student strike and the other issues both validated their constant theme and presented the golden opportunity. In their eyes, when would you have a better issue for large-scale support and pressure on the power structure? With dedication, skill, and luck an organization that represented a minority on only one of the eighteen[2] campuses might be able to force the trustees and the Legislature and the governor to deal with the union, to recognize it, to negotiate, to sign a binding agreement.

The faculty strikers were a "mixed bag" not only in their motives but in their ages, disciplines, and personality styles as well. Their preponderant strength came from the humanities and social sciences, with spotty support in education, science, and the creative arts, and virtually no members in business or physical education. In the speech and philosophy departments almost the entire faculty struck. English was a bastion of rebellion with about sixty of ninety faculty members supporting the strike. Various social science departments such as psychology, economics, anthropology, and sociology were split. The normally apolitical art faculty became instant rebels while their brothers in music were pillars of the loyalist faction. As the faculty went so often went the students—and vice versa. Rank and age were highly mixed, although a much higher portion of the younger faculty struck. Using either the student evaluation of faculty handbook, *MAX*, or the record of research grants to faculty, one would have to conclude that many of the most creative, productive faculty were on strike. For the most part they faced the rigors of the strike and survived. Colleagues more dependent on authority, order, and structure found the ambiguity, hostility, and risks of the strike devastating.

This was the array of mixed motives, diverse personality types, and potpourri of ages and disciplines that marched from the YMCA hall Sunday, January 5, to the picket lines Monday in a historic confrontation between faculty and their bosses. The power struggle that developed during the following six weeks decimated classes, threatened careers, enshrined Hayakawa, cost faculty in the neighborhood of $325,000 in lost salaries, and evoked high public hostility toward faculty members, colleges, and San Francisco State College. The struggle contained the violence, had little impact on the resolution of the student demands, polarized and embittered the faculty, established a precedent that college faculty could strike and not actually lose their jobs, and ultimately was lost by the 300 or so striking faculty after a monumental conflict.

[2] In this account the California State College System is referred to as one of eighteen campuses. A nineteenth, California State College at Bakersfield, did not open until fall 1970.

Chapter 16

A Hero's Image

In the history of American higher education one would think that the withdrawal of services and active striking of 300 out of a 1,300-member faculty for four weeks of one semester and the beginning two weeks of another would constitute the major historical event of the Hayakawa administration. Future years may confirm that this is indeed the case. But in the here and now the emergence of probably the only folk-hero college president in the memory of academic man was a more startling phenomenon. Not since Robert Maynard Hutchins at the University of Chicago in the 1930s had a college prexy so captured the imagination of the general public. Parlaying a consistently punitive hard line against militant students and faculty with a politician's skill with rhetoric and the media, Hayakawa projected a nationwide image as a spunky, feisty educator who had the guts to tell the militants to "go to hell" and the courage and tenacity to make his orders prevail.

A Gallup poll picked him as the nation's top educator. The National Council of Churches selected him Man of the Year along with President Richard Nixon, Averill Harriman, and Bayard Rustin. At the Washington Gridiron Dinner he received the greatest applause of the night and was seated between General Westmoreland and Senator Edward Kennedy. Political polls indicated that he had greater name recognition than any political figure in the state except Reagan and predicted a heavy voting appeal were he to run for senator or even governor. His mail came in bagfuls at the peak of his notoriety. Seldom did he receive fewer than fifty speaking requests a week, many of which were for high fees before major national organizations. When he appeared with bat in hand and tam-o'-shanter clad for a VIP-media celebrities softball game, 10,000 people paid him the surprising tribute of a ten-minute standing ovation. Trustees and the governor listened to his comments as they never had to any other college president. His name and his image glutted media responsive to his popular style. Thus, his implacable enemies, the striking students and faculty, discovered that paradoxically their hostile attack had created a "monster" that alone had the power to defeat them.

By the end of the first month in office Acting President Hayakawa revealed clearly the philosophy, the tactics, the TV image, and the personality that were to be characteristic of his eventual administrative style and that the warring students and faculty would have to overcome. His philosophy and actions once he became president corresponded closely to those which he had proposed in his speeches as a faculty member and which have been previously recounted. In brief, he saw an institution that relied upon dispassionate, objective teaching and research being fundamentally threatened by those who would enshrine power commitment, social action, and doctrinaire beliefs. To him an inability to keep the academy distinct from the pressing world about would contribute to its demise. And democracy could not afford this. He was particularly shocked at the timidity of those faculty members entrusted with this sacred institution, and professing belief in it, who refused to take action against those who, in his view, would overpower it, debase it, and obscure its vital distinction from the world about it. Convinced that the silent majority of faculty, students, and the public were hostile to this takeover, he enlisted himself in what became almost a religious crusade to repel the new barbarians. His basic theme became: Under no circumstances will we capitulate to these thugs and gangsters and close the college.

With glee he grappled with the enemy, students and faculty, black, white and brown. A cry he emitted in an administrative meeting captured his sentiments: "We'll have their heads on a pike!" Good guy–bad guy distinctions were easy for him, and he was convinced that you defeated the bad guys by bringing overwhelming force against them and then punishing them. The police became his army; arrests, jails, fines, and suspensions were his weapons. Beneath all of Hayakawa's actions ran a deep belief that he alone stood at a critical historical crossroads for higher education, and that by defeating the enemy he could turn the threatening tides of anarchy and rebellion. No other college president in America had so unremittingly declared himself in favor of a repressive, law-and-order philosophy. But what college presidents had eschewed, two California politicians—Reagan and Rafferty—had embraced with great popular appeal. Acting President Hayakawa not only duplicated their basic beliefs but also employed their proven techniques of tough, one-dimensional rhetoric and mass media image development. His success in this virgin field of administrative behavior was so great that political polls hinted that this previously obscure professor could conceivably defeat either Reagan or Rafferty in political battle.

With most of his faculty and student constituencies arrayed against him, Acting President Hayakawa's only chance for success depended upon his ability to tap the reservoir of massive public resentment against those militants who had disrupted sacred, tax-supported facilities with their violent tactics. The example of Reagan and Rafferty gave him a model. His years on the academic Chautauqua circuit soliciting converts for general semantics provided him with the skills for vivid, oversimplified appeals to the head and the heart. And a conservative "angel" in Chicago, multimillionaire insurance executive Clement Stone, underwrote his appeal to the multitudes with a bankroll and Stone's own press agent, Mike Teilmann. Commenting on the group that appeared to be attempting to destroy the college, Stone stated, "It's communistically inspired." In a flurry of press conferences, speeches, and television presentations, Acting President Hayakawa was projected before the national public as an earthy, witty, gutsy little Japanese professor who was more than willing to take the mobs of bullies on—and who would beat the hell out of them in the process. From the truck driver having his beer at the corner tavern to the children-dominated parents watching the evening newscast, a uniform, exultant cry of "At last!" sprang forth.

The image Hayakawa had to create was quite clear. First, he had to plug into the American morality act, the good guys versus the bad guys. This turned out to be quite easy, given the rhetoric and actions of the striking students. They became "anarchists, gangsters, hooligans, yahoos." Some were "Maoists," many were "high on drugs." Faculty opposition was infiltrated with "crypto-commies." Second, Hayakawa had to identify with American virtues of courage, fearlessness, toughness. His raid on the offending sound truck launched this image. When he continuously proclaimed in various forms, "I will not yield to any form of gangsterism," he had this identity captured. "Get the hell out of here!" he shouted before the media when black faculty and students surrounded him on the stage as he addressed a portion of the faculty. The public loved it. Also of high importance was his disassociation with the conventional, disparaged vision of an academician: abstract, dull, thoughtful, intellectually arrogant, and humorless. With this Hayakawa had no trouble. His rhetoric was terse, vivid, and earthy. He described the large number of students still going to classes as "voting with their behinds." He prohibited "parades, be-ins, hootenannies, hoedowns, and shivarees." When asked what was in his large orange and plaid bag he commented, "That's my lunch. I eat a hell of a lot." Good middle-class profanity liberally laced many of his utterances.

Whereas most of his academic colleagues considered it a professional virtue to keep their tempers under wraps, Hayakawa told some needling, liberal KQED television reporters that he would not take any more of their snide, hostile questions and stalked out of the studio. Faculty were appalled at his behavior; but the highbrow educational television station received a massive mail response two to one in support of the feisty president. When taunted by militant students during a speech at the University of Colorado, Hayakawa improvised a dance step to groove with their chanting. Naturally this provoked them. Quips flowed from his ready wit at a steady pace.

"I won't allow it" was his answer to a question rather than the academese, "Under the circumstances the complexities would seem to indicate that it would probably be preferable if we did not proceed." Although his response to the query of how he felt after the first day of panic and head-busting—"It's the most exciting thing since my tenth birthday when I rode a roller coaster for the first time"—became a legendary Agnew-type gaffe among students and faculty, the masses in the TV audience paid it no heed. Time and again the intellectual community was amazed at the noted semanticist's crudeness in language, but it failed to realize that he was speaking to a far different audience for quite different purposes. An active hostility toward these faculty enemies became another facet of the Great Warrior's image. As faculty attacked him, Hayakawa used his podium to respond in kind. He denounced their soft lives, their gutless stands, their radical tendencies, their unwillingness to stand up to student militants, and their naive view of the world. Underneath all of these utterances was a shrewd awareness that faculty were not appreciated by the masses and that implacable opposition to them won votes off campus though losing them at home.

Out of all of these TV clips and these thousands of words emerged that strange creature, an intellectual with whom the public could identify. Identify and adulate they did. Bob Hope telegrammed him, "All the world is behind you." Another typical telegram read, "You've got the anarchies and the commies on the run. Keep it up . . . and you will continue to be a national hero." All of the hostility welling up in the deeply disturbed middle-spectrum American against militant blacks, radical whites, long-haired hippies, their own rebellious children, communists, and anarchists found a release in the conduct of this unusual college administrator, and he was lifted to their shoulders, for the moment, and made an instant hero. His speeches attracted standing-room-only audiences. Everywhere he went people came up to congratulate him. His shrewdly chosen tam-o'-shanter trademark connoted Hayakawa across the nation. "The people of the state are behind me!" he confidently proclaimed.

Although an acclaimed image would give him the support necessary for engaging his enemies, these enemies still had to be engaged and the college had to be administered. Again the first thirty days witnessed the evolution of a style, a style distinct and at great variance from anything displayed in earlier years at State by its previous presidents—Dumke, Dodd, Paulson, Summerskill, or Smith. All of Hayakawa's energies focused upon the primary task of keeping the college open and defeating the enemy. He evinced few of the traits or interests normally associated with the top executive of a complex urban college of 18,000 students. Administrative structure, budgets, reports, curriculum, the Academic Senate, the ongoing functions of the college: little of this meant anything to Acting President Hayakawa. At critical meetings of his administrative colleagues he would answer phone calls, read congratulatory telegrams, clip articles for his scrapbook, leave the room, or snooze. This was not his "thing." His view was that his experienced vice-presidents and deans should be able to administer the college. For his own personal support and advice he surrounded himself with a coterie of Faculty Renaissance loyalists none of whom had administrative experience. In working with the conservative student Committee for an Academic Environment and his own Faculty Renaissance group, Hayakawa acted upon the assumption that those opposed to him were primarily a militant minority and that his leadership task was to mobilize the vast number of silent faculty and students to rally around his standard. In neither case did the fact correspond with the hope. Both of these groups did, however, give him a nucleus for support.

The politics of consensus was not Acting President Hayakawa's style. Rather than working constructively with all groups in order to obtain a policy that represented diverse views and would be widely supported, Hayakawa operated by means of edicts. Power did not scare him; unlike many of his fellow academicians, he thrived on it. Since the Academic Senate and the Associated Students had already declared themselves as his enemies, "to hell with them." "I believe we can do better in finding student representatives than to depend on the utterly irresponsible and rebellious body of student officers now claiming to represent the student body." From that point on Russell Bass and his Associated Students disappeared into oblivion. Hayakawa's predecessors gave them an open door to their offices; he gave them the back of his hand. Though the student government gleefully joined the fray, it discovered it had no muscle. On the radical front, the SDS, BSU, and TWLF had bypassed the student leaders and assumed power.

What these student officers might have been able to contribute through reformist activities and the Associated Students funds was soon denied them when Hayakawa moved powerfully on their budget during the holidays. As stories leaked out that student funds were being used by the BSU to purchase rifles and underwrite their strike, the attorney general decided to audit the entire enterprise. This move was in line with a growing concern throughout the state that militant students had taken over some student governments and were using the student monies to finance their struggles. At the chancellor's level a resolution had long been under consideration that would eliminate the private corporate status of some of these auxiliary organizations and place them directly under the control of the college president. Use of Associated Students funds to bail out student dissidents had raised the ire of several trustees.

The attorney general's investigation soon led to placing all funds in a receivership pending final auditing. Although Acting President Hayakawa originally stated that the investigation was routine and he had nothing to do with its initiation, he was later to tell groups that his cutting off of the "bread" from the strikers was a fundamental strategy in bringing them to heel. When its funds withered the Associated Students became a shadow organization and its president, Bass, disappeared from the local scene. With the demise of the student government and the castration of the Academic Senate, centers of moderate, liberal power disappeared and the action moved to the right and the left. Militant Third World leaders who had been on the tutorial and other payrolls soon felt the squeeze at a moment when they most needed financing. In dealing with the striking students, Hayakawa alternated hard-line public statements and taunts with behind-the-scene attempts at negotiation. While his hard line produced public support, as it was obviously designed to, it also ensured a credibility gap that made negotiations fruitless. Besides, during December the TW strikers were convinced that they would certainly prevail, especially with the AFT joining their side in January.

The Academic Senate did not loom large on Acting President Hayakawa's horizon. As he saw the distribution of power in state and in his college he must have had Stalin's famous query flick through his mind: How many divisions do they have? To the Senate's dismay it was to discover that under the new circumstances it existed primarily at the indulgence of the new president. It also learned that the faculty was so polarized and shattered that the Senate could not turn to the total faculty for legitimizing. Here and there the Senate could expose a flagrant edict or force a slight retraction of a poorly conceived policy, but in the final analysis Hayakawa treated it as a vexing mosquito buzzing around his head that needed an occasional swat at most. In short, the style and strategy of Acting President Hayakawa transvalued "all power to the people" to "all power to Hayakawa." Whether this regressive approach will become a trend or an aberration in the college and the system remains to be seen.

Although the hopeful, the idealistic, the concerned had thought that three weeks of quiet, behind-the-scenes negotiations might well unsnarl the tangled web of relationships on San Francisco State's campus, events did not support this optimism. Each side felt self-righteous; each side was confident of victory; each side believed a soft compromise solution would be interpreted by their constituencies as damaging loss of face. There seemed only one answer: a test of force. And so, as in a Greek tragedy, each side took predictable, compulsive actions that were destined to elicit predictable, compulsive counteractions, with a predestined, doomed future being equally certain and inevitable.

After the mass disruptions and near-riot conditions of the first two weeks of Hayakawa's regime, the striking TW students and their white allies could not conceive that they could not close the college down and bring Hayakawa and the trustees to their knees. Although some might have had some qualms about the effect on their momentum and style of the impending AFT strike of 300 faculty, on the surface it seemed that this legitimizing influence and increased power would only make it much more difficult for students to attend classes and faculty to teach. And all during the holidays support from the TW community had been drummed up. Almost without exception, these communities and their leaders told the college, "Give the students what they are asking for. It's right."

On the other side, the determination of those in power had been equally fortified. The new symbol of their resistance to anarchy and violence, Hayakawa, had been able to elicit a public outcry and mass support beyond fondest dreams. With ultimate power backed by large public endorsement, there seemed to be no need to negotiate, even if this stance meant a prolongation of the confrontation and even the possibility of the institution's demoralization or destruction. In the minds of both parties, it was a historic "vanguard" occasion. Under such conditions institutional well-being became incidental. One of the most dedicated and skillful of those attempting to mediate the dispute, Bishop Hurley, caught this march toward Armageddon when he wearily commented a few days before the resumption of the struggle, "Nobody's ready to make any change in course and arrest the confrontation."

The AFT faculty were equally committed to the proposition that it was basically a battle between good and evil, and that as preceptors for the idealistic young they had no alternative but to throw themselves into the fray in an attempt to curb the violence and bloodshed and to secure justice for the TW demands. Few were deceived by the facade of economic demands that the union had to enunciate in order to obtain desperately needed organized labor support. In essence this band of 300 faculty was also fighting a holy war. To many it seemed inconceivable that ultimately the great majority of their colleagues and students would not join them to produce a victory. Six weeks later they were to emerge with an embittered view of these same colleagues as well as a much more realistic assessment of the power structure of California.

The ideological justifications for the opposing camps were quickly communicated to the public as the campus prepared to resume its operation. Acting President Hayakawa took the initiative for the Establishment when he began his war of words with a biting press statement:

> A new picture is becoming clear as the troubles of our college are prolonged. The battle is between the forces of anarchy and the citadel of reason. Our enemies are cowards. They must resort to violence, lies, and deceit to gain what they cannot win by reason or exercise of the democratic processes. We cannot allow them to win at San Francisco State College or higher education throughout America is in danger.

To ensure that the citadel of reason would prevail, Hayakawa proclaimed some tough rules for the operation of the campus. The most drastic outlawed the traditional student battle technique of mobilizing the student legions through a rally or parade. Use of the Speakers Platform or any other substitute location on the central campus was prohibited. In addition he warned that "persons who interfere with the peaceful conduct of the activities of San Francisco State College are subject to arrest" and that students engaging in disruptive activity might also be suspended or expelled. Exterior picketing was to be allowed but not interior picketing. Faculty were jolted when Hayakawa proclaimed that all classes would need to be held on campus except under unusual circumstances that had departmental chairman support. Rebellious departments granted this support quite casually and there was little the new president could do about it. Typical is a statement from Chairman Caroline Shrodes of the militant and powerful English department to her colleagues:

> Since my reading of the situation is that our circumstances are indeed exceptional, I submit for your possible use this memorandum

> of permission to teach off campus. The circumstance is exceptional since never before has a significant number of our colleagues gone on strike as a matter of conscience. It is extraordinary that faculty members should be asked to cross a picket line manned by their friends and colleagues. Finally, our "inflamed literary imagination" notwithstanding, many of us sincerely believe that the safety of our students and of ourselves might be in serious jeopardy were we to attempt to hold classes on campus. And the governor's offer of protection "at the point of a bayonet" is hardly reassuring! Except for the time I shall conduct my own class at Newman Center or attend meetings off campus, I shall be working at home.

Such was the disdain within the faculty power structure for Acting President Hayakawa's ultimata. Whether his student prohibitions could be enforced remained to be seen, but the gauntlet was definitely thrown down. Governor Reagan's vow to keep the campus open "at the point of a bayonet, if necessary," reinforced Hayakawa's stance and earned a national notoriety all its own.

The AFT made its counterappeal in a direct mailing to all faculty. The tone of self-righteousness and "our ends justify our means" resembled that of Hayakawa and Reagan. After spelling out how the trustees had not negotiated in good faith during the holidays, President Gary Hawkins stated:

> This means you will have to make what may be the most important decision in your life: Shall I or shall I not support the strike? The AFT, in all fairness to you, must say that we will consider anyone who goes through our picket line to be a threat to the success of our strike and a threat to our jobs and future livelihood. . . . The AFT has presented the trustees and the local administration with several demands. You may not agree with all of them, but if you agree with most of them, we believe you are obligated to be on our side. Violating our picket line will be interpreted to mean that you have chosen to be with the trustees and against us. Despite the many issues the AFT has presented to the trustees, in a strike situation with jobs at stake your options become simplified and deep. You will not have the luxury of nice distinctions or Byzantine excuses. An ancient distinction will be involved with all its emotional connotations—friend *versus* enemy. He who observes our picket line is a friend. . . . We do not plan to bodily prevent anyone from entering or leaving the campus, but anyone who plans to cross will be subject to moral force: they can expect to be considered SCABS.

It is difficult to assess the impact on the total faculty of this "Byzantine excuses" letter. It probably received as much attention as Reagan's bayonet comment. In its true-believer fervor it had a similar tone. It certainly introduced a new and disquieting style of persuasion, but this is implicit in a strike-picketing operation. For the large numbers of faculty who had long seen the AFT as a hotbed of radicalism, the threatening tone rekindled and energized their hatred.

But probably its more pervasive influence was felt among the moderate, uncommitted men and women who considered themselves moral, independent, rational, and liberal. Although opposed at a verbal level to the violence, to Reagan, and probably to Hayakawa, they had not yet been persuaded of the wisdom of joining ranks with the striking students to close the college. To this group the simplistic reasoning, the true-believer zeal, and the explicit threats of this critical AFT communication were offensive. It cast grave doubts about the leadership of the AFT and the wisdom of joining it. Although coercion is not alien to academic circles, its raw nature is usually muted by the rhetoric and convoluted processes of promotion and tenure procedures and rarely reaches the overt "friend versus enemy" stage. As these individuals crossed picket lines Monday, January 6, they were to discover in the words and actions, in the moral suasion and implicit threat, that the letter had not been too inaccurate in describing the new campus strike climate.

The sense of strife and tension remained when San Francisco State resumed operation on Monday, January 6, but it also became apparent that tactics and strategy had been radically altered by the intrusion of striking faculty into the scene. On that day, and on most succeeding days, the locus of dissent shifted from the interior quadrangle to one of the main entrances to the college at Nineteenth and Holloway Avenues. Instead of roving mobs and mass police sweeps, one found a solid, continuous line of 2,000 picketers chanting and waving signs under the wary surveillance of relatively small numbers of the constabulary. All strategy focused upon making it morally and almost physically impossible for a student or a faculty member to enter the campus at this central point. To solidify this blockade, smaller groups of pickets, usually faculty, paraded in front of all other entrances.

Although this tactic had never been the basic plan of the BSU and its "war of the flea," its leaders decided to join the line and see if their new faculty allies might have a point. Students provided the bulk of the massed pickets, and the solid swarm of marchers did pose an ominous threat to the neutral student who descended from the M-line streetcar just a few yards from the human barrier.

For almost three weeks this labor strategy became the fundamental battle plan for the strikers. Implicit in the student-faculty coalition were certain basic tensions, especially since the AFT was committed to nonviolence and control of the line. Even from allies many student strikers could not take this paternalistic domination, especially when it did not seem to produce instant capitulation. One day the students defied the AFT picket captains and left the peripheral picket line to resume their marching in the interior of the campus outside the Administration Building. On other occasions there were pushing and shoving between faculty and students when students asked for trouble by refusing to meet police demands for a pathway in their midst. Acting President Hayakawa, ever eager to discredit his enemies, the striking faculty, commented at his press conference:

> Today for the second time radical students took charge of the teachers' picket line and the professors acted like true puppets. The AFT picket leaders lost control, if they ever had any, in the marching circus. For two days pickets have threatened, intimidated, insulted, and hampered peaceful people trying to enter this campus to teach or to study. Today AFT picket leaders were given more than ample opportunity to establish a walking corridor at Nineteenth and Holloway for people arriving by streetcar and bus. In minutes it became obvious who was in charge of the picket line because more student radicals joined the march. They closed ranks. They sang. They became defiant. Then the police read an official notice to all pickets, ordering the participants to obey the law. After waiting a reasonable time, the police moved to enforce the law and we made the news again as the national target for radical teachers and students who are determined to destroy higher education.

The tense coalition between TWLF leaders and the AFT is reflected in a TWLF release at the same time as the Hayakawa statement:

> The strike at San Francisco State began on November 6, 1968. It was called by TWLF. It has been directed by TWLF. It will continue to be directed by TWLF. After two months of intensive struggle by TWLF and white students to win the TWLF demands, the AFT finally decided to go on strike. This in itself shows the difference in political consciousness between the faculty and students. . . . We view it as positive that the AFT has finally gone on strike.

> It must be clear, however, that the AFT is, by their own admission, striking primarily for their own demands and only secondarily, under pressure, for the fifteen demands of TWLF. Further, it is we the students who have initiated this strike to fight against racism. Because of the strength of our strike the AFT has taken the opportunity to gain some long outstanding demands. . . . We will not compromise the commitment of the thousands of courageous students by allowing the militancy of our struggle to be held back by anyone.

Despite this rhetoric and these complications, the AFT did a remarkable job of conducting an independent strike which essentially coopted the TWLF strike and still commanded the respect and support of these TW strikers. Although there were a few fierce police skirmishes with students on the line as the police responded to provocations, invaded picket ranks to arrest a leader for whom they had a warrant, or insisted on nonviolent picket activity or a path through the line, the post-holiday, AFT phase of the campus strike bore no resemblance to the shrieking mob scene that preceded the AFT intervention. The basic AFT strategy of taking command with a strong picket line worked and, for the most part, the police-student confrontations and potential for injury, loss of life, and rioting diminished. However else the striking faculty might have created problems or failed to reach their stated goals, this shift in the tempo of the strife was a heroic contribution for which only they deserve the credit. Even Hayakawa was later to admit that the AFT "consciously did try to restrain students from violence." Once the Labor Council endorsed the strike, the San Francisco police treated faculty pickets with the same patience and respect they show for all pickets in this labor town. Police-AFT conferences were held each morning to clarify strategies and the rules of the game.

Nothing that the AFT, the police, or the administration could do would ensure peace and tranquility, however. At one stage a group went on a tire-slashing foray in the faculty parking lot. Acting President Hayakawa's new administrator of student discipline, Edwin Duerr, barely escaped his fire-bombed house, and John Bunzel, perennial BSU target, was to come out of his home one morning to discover all his tires slashed and "Fascist Scab" painted over his cars. Toilets were stopped, stench bombs emptied classes, and the library was sabotaged with a "book-in." More seriously, a time bomb that failed to go off at midday at a traffic center in the Administration Building was discovered and defused. Few of these incidents could be attributed to any specific individual or organization.

Beyond containing the mob violence, the most important contribution of the AFT picket lines was the decimation of classes. This in itself cut down the riot potential; there simply were not many students around the campus. Many students sympathized with both the student and faculty strikes and refused to cross the picket line and attend classes. Frequently classes either were closed because the faculty member in charge was on strike or were shifted off campus by faculty who refused to cross the picket line and would not force their students to make this moral decision. The desertion of the campus was facilitated by an Academic Senate decision that allowed any student to take a pass–no report grading option in any course, a decision aimed at protecting helpless students caught in turmoil not of their own making. Since a "pass" grade encompassed *A* through *D* effort, it allowed a student minimal attendance or effort yet a respectable record.

The extent of this boycott is difficult to measure. But whether one were to take the AFT figure of 80 per cent nonattendance or the administration guess of 40 to 50 per cent, the fact is undeniable that the basic, traditional process of education had been seriously interrupted. Acting President Hayakawa continuously attempted to obscure this point in his press releases, but it was undeniable. Hopes of the AFT were pinned to the prospect that the power structure would be so threatened by this attrition of the college operation that the trustees would be forced to the bargaining table. This hope rested on the assumpion that there would be a public outcry against this withering of a major educational institution. But such a major outcry did not occur, and instead the public's outrage was directed at the AFT for having provoked the crisis.

Acting President Hayakawa led the attack on the striking faculty. He was joined by the editorial writers of most of the state's newspapers, three nonunion faculty organizations, many politicians including Reagan, and Dumke. The basic theme developed in this criticism was that the AFT had been opportunistic in using the student strike to further its own economic and power interests. Hayakawa said he considered the striking faculty "a militant minority of the faculty" which has "hitchhiked on the militant, violence-ridden strike for a vicious power grab." This theme of opportunism was reiterated in a joint statement by three faculty organizations at San Francisco State, the American Association of University Professors, the California College and University Faculty Association (a CTA affiliate), and the California State Employees Association. They called the strike "a cynical attempt to hitch faculty bread-and-butter issues onto the problems of minority students." The CSEA had previously stated, "To capitalize upon campus unrest, to deliberately make more difficult an already difficult situation, to use the students' militancy as a means of increasing a faculty group's power is wholly irresponsible." A *San Francisco Chronicle* editorial asked, "What kind of professionals are they who would set out to do irreparable damage to the already battered and damaged college?" Said the *San Francisco Examiner,* "It is a strike by opportunists, malcontents, and academic ne'er-do-wells. . . . They did not approach the strike in the normal union manner but instead seized upon the opportunity presented to them by the strife of a student strike." In truth, even strikes in "the normal union manner" appealed very little to the Hearst-owned *Examiner.*

Try as they might, the AFT was never able to escape this opprobrium of "hitchhiking," "riding piggyback," being "blatant opportunists" in the view of the vital public. Obviously this public was not enthusiastic about the basic idea of striking public employees; however, this resistance had been mollified in other situations. But when it could be made to appear that faculty were attempting to feather their own nests, increase their fringe benefits, and improve their working conditions by both taking advantage of legitimate student grievances and confusing their solution, the hue and cry echoed up the state and into the halls of the Legislature in Sacramento with a shrill blast.

This highly moralistic posture in condemning the AFT encountered an equally moralistic response. Most of the striking faculty were risking their style of life, their paychecks, and their jobs not for economic gain but rather to provide some faint hope of deescalating the campus warfare. To have their courageous idealism condemned as self-centered opportunism was the ultimate irony. Most were bitterly incensed, especially since many of those trumpeting the charge were risking nothing. As has been said before, economic demands had been inserted into their grievances primarily as a realistic maneuver to obtain essential labor movement support. Some old-line AFTers were certainly deeply committed to these demands and pragmatically believed you pressed for them when the chance offered itself. But they were in the minority. In retrospect one wonders how the public and the total faculty might have reacted if the AFT had taken the truly high road and withdrawn their services in a nonadversarial way on the simple issue that, as professional educators, they could neither teach effectively on the disruptive, dangerous campus atmosphere nor be a party to risking the health, even lives, of their students. Both the criticisms of self-serving opportunism and aiding and abetting the militant students could have been mitigated by such a stance. And since the charge of unsafe working conditions appeals to trade unionists, the Labor Council would have had a valid excuse for a strike sanction. This approach might also have been a banner that would have attracted more colleagues, thus providing the larger strike base that the AFT desperately needed.

Not only did the focus on Labor Council support result in the long list of economic demands, but it also ensured a strike strategy in the classic labor union mold. This strategy has little subtlety; it does not take into account the academic culture and it is predicated on economic losses to management and adversarial warfare. But at San Francisco State there was no management to lose profits by the strike but only faculty to lose essential salaries. And the adversarial relationship on the line between faculty and faculty, faculty and student, student and student infuriated many. "Scab," "Reagan-lover," were among the milder epithets. Students crossing picket lines were often insulted by student pickets and occasionally harassed physically. For many, going to college became a traumatic experience. Faculty verbal intimidation of both students and faculty was not unknown. Among academic men this left a residue of hate, guilt, and fear that did not conduce toward AFT support and that has strained relationships since the end of the strike.

High in the minds of college faculty throughout the system, and certainly with the striking faculty, was the question of whether those faculty on strike would lose their jobs. In California the right of public employees to engage in collective bargaining, including strike sanction, had never been enacted into law. However, there is the by-now famous Section 24311 of the Education Code which provides that a state employee's resignation is automatic if he is "absent without leave . . . whether voluntarily or involuntarily, for five consecutive working days." Given the history of this particular statute, there is general agreement that it was never intended for strike absences but rather was designed to protect institutions when employees simply ceased appearing for work. For the next two months, and particularly during the six weeks of the faculty strike, this piece of legislation was to prove critical. Chancellor Dumke sounded the warning when he declared on the first day of the strike that this section of the code would be fully enforced and faculty absent five days would be considered to have automatically resigned. Acting President Hayakawa reiterated this posture and added, "Simply, the striking faculty will soon eliminate itself, and at least one of our problems will be solved." Governor Reagan added his voice to the chorus after the faculty heads. Interviewed striking faculty consistently stated that they considered it a real possibility that in view of the law and the punitive nature of their adversaries, they might be fired. Still they struck.

But as the first five days of the strike wore on two realities began to emerge: the college had little capacity to prove that a faculty member had been absent five days, especially since the duties of a professional college teacher were only generally understood in the profession, but nowhere precisely defined; and the firing of such a large group of distinguished teachers, including almost the entirety of some departments, would probably do more to strengthen the faculty resistance than any other act possible. Many conservative professors within the college were openly stating that though they disagreed with the issues and timing of the strike, they deeply believed that faculty members should have the same right to withhold their services as any other employees. The Academic Senate went powerfully on record as resisting any severance of employment for strike activities. More important, the statewide Academic Senate, after six years of resolutions and rhetoric in most crisis situations, overwhelmingly declared that it would encourage the faculty of all of the eighteen colleges to withdraw their services for one day should any state college faculty member be dismissed for striking.

Behind this emerging criticism of the imposition of Code Section 24311 was the basic policy statement of such a prestigious organization as the American Association of University Professors: "Participation in a strike does not by itself constitute grounds for dismissal or for other sanctions against faculty members."[1] This academic posture, accompanied by the hostility of the San Francisco labor forces to management firings of strikers, forced some high-level rethinking. The rank-and-file union member had little enthusiasm for the Labor Council support of this strike, but united opposition to firings could be counted upon. Teamster official Tim Richardson stated this position clearly

[1] "Statement of Faculty Participation in Strikes," *AAUP Bulletin, 54* (1968), 157.

when he declared that the labor movement "would polarize behind" the striking faculty if they were fired. As a result of this overall support and the legal snarls associated with Section 24311, Chancellor Dumke, President Hayakawa, and even Governor Reagan began to hedge on their earlier threats to fire the strikers. The bluff had not worked; now face had to be saved.

A major force behind the college's equivocal position on firings was the Council of Academic Deans. Although relatively critical of the striking faculty, this group of administrators knew full well that the elimination of the strikers would destroy the college. Besides, many of the strikers were their friends and colleagues of long standing. As a group they prevailed upon a reluctant Acting President Hayakawa not to act precipitously. Between a delay in securing accurate faculty attendance data and the utilization of a technicality that seemed to allow the administration the power to grant involuntary leaves of absence, the issue of automatic resignations was strung out during the entire course of the strike. Eventually the technical loopholes of rehiring "resigned" faculty immediately after they quit striking and finally obtaining reinstatement for them resulted in the almost universal avoidance of this sticky issue. But, in fact, 122 were fired, although rehired with full status.

Whether a faculty member was teaching or "in attendance" became a matter of considerable controversy. Strike conditions imposed circumstances that had not been envisioned by lawmakers or college administrators. If a faculty member were conscientiously teaching his classes off campus, was he "in attendance"? Various seminars and other types of classes had frequently met in faculty homes in the past. How did current off-campus teaching differ from this never-questioned previous practice? Since meeting classes is only one of a faculty member's functions, if a striking faculty member were to counsel students on "the line," or attend department or Academic Senate meetings, or carry on his research and study, would he not be meeting some of his professional responsibilities and be deserving of some remuneration? And, of course, in the view of ardent AFT members, striking against the impossible working conditions and the illegitimate authority of Hayakawa and the trustees itself symbolized the highest form of professional behavior. The automatic resignation statute was further complicated by the critical phrase "five consecutive days." Many faculty members did not have classes every day and customarily remained at home working in their studies on these off days. Could they not be construed to be in attendance on these days, thus breaking the consecutive nature of even their admitted absences? Attendance figures were crucial since both state payment of salaries and the automatic resignation issue hinged upon it. Some individuals in the state were far more agitated over the prospect of taxpayers' funds going to rebellious faculty who were providing no services than they were about firing these faculty. College practices throughout the country have always depended upon faculty voluntarily communicating absences, but under strike conditions members of the union had been advised by its lawyer not to admit to being on strike. Thus, there were the questions: Who was on strike and who was teaching, who should be paid and who should not be paid?

The college administration realized that it must face these questions squarely, especially after it had been communicated from various sources that the individual school deans were responsible for the attendance reports upon which payment was based. Reluctantly these deans reversed the traditional process and required the faculty to sign a weekly statement indicating that they had met their responsibilities rather than simply report when they had been absent. With this decree all hell broke lose. Anguished cries of "loyalty oath" rang through the halls. Even many nonstriking faculty vowed not to demean themselves by signing such reports. The difficulties of administrators seldom had elicited faculty sympathy in the past; in strike conditions, the chasm was widened. Even many in "middle management" refused to cooperate: almost half the department chairmen dragged their heels at complicity with the new punch clock system. Deans began to make various exceptions to the formal signature process, yet they were conscious that they needed accurate figures for payroll purposes. To add to the confusion, faculty strike leaders who had been clandestinely meeting classes off campus reported that they had been in attendance and were paid. This provoked consternation both in administration and union ranks. Strikers losing as much as $2,000 a month did not look with favor upon fellow picketers who received full paychecks, even if some of the latter did donate additional funds to the common strike fund. The attendance "scandal" came to a head late in January when the official payroll roster had to be prepared. Earlier one trustee had been so infuriated by these unbusinesslike procedures that he proposed a regulation for the entire system that would demand faculty certification of attendance each month and would subject the faculty to criminal prosecution if they made a false certification.

Not only did the trustees attempt to invoke the dubious Section 24311 but they also tried to break the strike through the injunction process. Encouraged by their lawyer, who asserted that California law did not speak to the issue of the right of public employees to strike, the AFT ignored the injunction and it was never sustained. In a labor town this proved to be a rather safe strategy.

While the AFT struck, the power structure retaliated, and the educational program deteriorated, most of the remaining faculty withdrew or cast about for some means of settling the dispute. In this they were encouraged by a poll conducted by another faculty organization, the Association of California State College Professors. With 80 per cent of those professors legally defined as voting faculty responding, the poll discovered that 64 per cent were opposed to the AFT strike. This figure sharply contradicted the AFT estimates of only about 25 per cent opposition. Among part-time faculty the figures were 57 per cent opposed, 43 per cent supportive.

For most practical purposes the Academic Senate had become of little value in any conflict resolution. Deeply split, eliciting little support from either the total faculty or the administration, the Senate floundered. This impotence was compounded by a cadre of AFT members who were allowed by the union to cross the picket line and attend Senate meetings so that they could carry out union policy. Eventually the Senate became aware that, as a group, it was handcuffed and so it decided to focus its efforts in a five-man committee given the task of somehow helping to resolve the strike. Much of this committee's energies were wasted, but it did conceive of a select committee process for mediating the student grievances that led to the final settlement.

Around the fringes of the faculty, random ad hoc groups formed, made suggestions or pronouncements, and then tended to vanish. One amorphous group, the Coalition of Concerned Faculty, did focus sufficient energies to engage in a rather effective information program with the California Legislature. Teams of from three to five faculty members, chosen from the small minority that might be able to communicate cogently with legislators, made over twenty-five trips to Sacramento to "tell it like it is." In a general way this did quite a bit to assuage the Legislature's fears that too many faculty were radical or did not live in the real world. The overwhelming conviction of these concerned faculty, and of most of their silent colleagues, was that the educational process was impossible to pursue on the campus, that the college was slowly being destroyed, and that something had to be done. Many were sympathetic with most of the demands of the striking students and faculty but, although guilt-ridden, did not believe the technique of striking could settle the issues. Among some a move to delay the opening of the spring semester gained currency as the only act of wisdom. Everywhere gloom, despair, and powerlessness enveloped the faculty and the campus.

The hope of the AFT had always been that serious impediment of the educational operation of the college would force those with power on both sides to reach a settlement. The concept "those with power" encompassed the BSU Central Committee, the BSU, the TWLF Central Committee, the TW community, the trustees, Acting President Hayakawa, Governor Reagan, Labor Council Secretary George Johns, Mayor Alioto, and a few key figures in the San Francisco Establishment. That such polar extremes could even physically associate, let alone engage in productive dialogue that might lead to a settlement, was a visionary ideal. Both the TW strike leaders and the California power structure were convinced that they alone possessed the essential power and that history was on their side. For either, to lose face by compromise and seeming capitulation to the enemy appeared to invite political suicide. Yet, to continue the battle of attrition would lead only to no black and ethnic studies programs and, quite possibly, to only a shell of a college. It was the starkness of these options that forced elements within the trustees, the San Francisco power structure, the Hayakawa administration, and the labor movement to work assiduously to discover some means of mediation and some basis for a compromise.

The first gropings toward a detente occurred during the first week of the post-holiday period. A new force had tentatively emerged within the BSU ranks in the person of Roscoe Blount. Although not a member of the BSU Central Committee, Blount had been active in the convocations, and he took it upon himself to engage in several serious negotiating sessions with Acting President Hayakawa and his staff. His apparent goal was to produce a package that he could sell to the total BSU constituency. Since it had become obvious that the negotiating room within the original fifteen demands had narrowed, and that several of these demands would be met in part or in their entirety, the focus of discussion centered on the crucial issue of amnesty for those arrested or suspended during the crusade. In addition, some symbolic act such as the retention of Murray in a nonteaching role was pressed.

This blatant challenge to the power structure of the BSU and the status of its Central Committee had inherent dangers, yet a settlement that might protect those arrested—a tacit guarantee that might not always be available—had appeal. A combination of violent resistance within some factions in the BSU and premature publicity for the plan in the San Francisco newspapers, either inadvertent or skillfully arranged, led to the demise of this effort and the disappearance of Blount from the scene. The TW strike leaders emerged stronger than ever and reiterated their position that not only were their demands nonnegotiable but that talks "to implement" them would be initiated only after total criminal and institutional amnesty had been arranged. At one point in the tenuous negotiations centered around Blount, Mayor Alioto was persuaded to enter the scene and to take the political risk of guaranteeing in writing his support for the dropping of minor, but not major, charges against those arrested students, but this offer also carried no weight with the militants. The strike leadership simply could not believe that their virtual closing of the college would not induce greater concessions, and they also could not agree to desert those in their ranks who had been arrested for so-called major charges.

Another abortive effort at mediating the teacher grievances was initiated by the unusual coalition of Chamber of Commerce leader Robert Cardinal and Teamster secretary Tim Richardson. One of the impediments in any reconciliation with the striking AFT was the fact that the AFT represented only a minority of the San Francisco State faculty. Thus, it was felt that some machinery must be developed so that the other faculty organizations and the official Academic Senate could cooperate in a consideration of the AFT demands. In this way any agreements that could be reached with the college administration could have a comprehensive impact. Nothing came of this venture either.

Probably the negotiations that offered the most sanguine prospects for success centered around Executive Secretary George Johns of the Labor Council and trustee Louis Heilbron and the Trustee Liaison Committee. Johns desperately wanted the union movement out of this mess. All he needed to withdraw strike sanction was some slight recognition that the AFT and the Labor Council had been able to achieve some progress for the faculty members. After all, it was a wildcat strike of a minority of the total faculty, and Johns recognized from his extensive labor experience that such a strike had minimum leverage and should be satisfied with minimal gains. A minimal gain that appeared achievable centered around college and systemwide faculty grievance and disciplinary procedures. Other minor concessions might be granted but these procedures were central. For five years the Statewide Academic Senate had hassled with the Chancellor's Office and the trustees over a comprehensive set of rules and procedures, and now mutual agreement seemed assured. With the possibility of punitive action against its striking members prominent in the AFT thinking, these grievances and disciplinary procedures had become critical to the faculty union.

The procedures which the statewide Academic Senate and the trustees had agreed upon provided that if a decision reached on a campus were not satisfactory to the faculty member involved, it could be appealed to a statewide panel of faculty members and the decision reached by a subcommittee of this panel, chosen by lot or by the chancellor with Senate chairman concurrence, would be final. Not trusting the faculty members who might be chosen by some colleges for this panel, and who might emerge with the power over an AFT member's career, the AFT insisted among its many demands that a more common labor method of arbitration be available as an option. This system would allow the faculty member and the administration each to choose a panel member and then the two chosen would agree upon a third member. To Johns this made sense. To Heilbron and his committee a variation of this system might be acceptable. The leadership of the Statewide Academic Senate indicated that if a similar process had been suggested by the AFT during the five years of policy development there would have been no objections, and that they would be willing to recommend its inclusion now. With this seeming concurrence of opinion, Johns saw a distinct possibility for the union to claim some success on a vital issue, and this could provide the Labor Council with a rationale for withdrawing its strike sanction. Were this done the AFT would be in perilous position, for without Labor Council sanction it was politically and physically vulnerable. Yet this settlement would not speak to the student demands whose arbitration had driven most of the striking faculty to their desperate measure.

Other forces within the state intruded to make this a nonissue. One of the major concerns of Governor Reagan and some trustees had been that the settlement of the dispute should give no appearance of significant concessions to the troublemakers, especially if such a settlement might give the impression that the trustees had negotiated with the strikers, and negotiated under duress. The faculty and student strike was certainly pressure, if not duress, and a written memorandum of understanding between Johns, Acting President Hayakawa and the Trustee Liaison Committee could surely be construed as negotiations. Such negotiations had the further liability in the minds of the governor and many trustees that they could set a precedent of collective bargaining by public employees. This, of course, was a major goal of Johns and the labor movement.

As Johns and the trustee committee were on the verge of an agreement, Governor Reagan telephoned Chairman of the Board of Trustees Theodore Merriam and insisted that this operation be canceled because it violated board policy not to negotiate under duress. Merriam agreed that the union and trustee representatives were "coming close to negotiations" and called a halt to the meeting.

With the Merriam telephone call the hopes for an early settlement were shattered. Johns was bitter: "If we had had that meeting we would have undoubtedly settled the strike." One month later, a month that produced deep personal alienation and further college deterioration, the forces involved came right back to this point of negotiation and settled the strike on similar terms. But it took that month of dogged, destructive struggling to convince both parties—for there was no assurance that the college AFT would have gone along with the earlier Labor Council settlement—that this represented the minimal compromise.

Attempts to reconcile the differences between the conflicting parties and to return the college to its educational mission were vitiated by the self-righteous attitudes of the participants once they became ensnarled in the adversarial relationship. Both sides attempted to bombard the public with a rhetoric that alternatingly castigated the enemy and heaped praise on fellow crusaders. To Hayakawa, the AFT strikers were a "disgrace," they were engaged in a "vicious power grab," they "placed personalities and factionalism ahead of the institution," and they were attempting to devise "new ways to sabotage education and bug the administration." Later Hayakawa kept reiterating in his many speeches (fifteen to twenty a month) that the disease extended beyond the striking faculty and infected academic ranks in general. Much of his invective showered upon the faculty in the humanities and social sciences, areas which also happened to be the center of most strike activities. Not content with ideological critiques, Acting President Hayakawa told the receptive taxpaying public that "a twelve-hour teaching load is one of the nicest, softest jobs in the world. . . . We all know that very often you glance over your notes ten minutes before you go into class and you are all set." This last barb completed the total alienatiton of most faculty who had known Hayakawa as a teacher.

The striking American Federation of Teachers also identified with the pure and the good and could find little in the performance of Acting President Hayakawa or the trustees and their minions to congratulate. Beginning from a basic assumption that its strike was intended "to improve the quality and the quantity of education at San Francisco State," the union told colleagues that strike support was the "last chance to remain a college at which you can be proud to teach." "All of us on strike could abandon the state college system and take higher paying jobs elsewhere. It is only our commitment to the people, the students, and the city of San Francisco that keep us on the picket line." All antistrike activities were designed for a "constructive solution." "Showing good faith" was the test of all negotiations and strategy. Rather than concentrate their barbed epithets directly on Hayakawa, the AFT collected the president's most distorted comments and issued them in the widely read *Quotations of Chairman Hayakawa.*

Loaded words, distortion of fact, emotional appeals became standard stock-in-trade of these parties formerly committed to the exact opposite. The detachment and objectivity of the scholar-professor apparently applied only to inconsequential research, not action commitments to vital social issues. In a pallid way, Hayakawa and the AFT took on the rhetorical characteristics of the SDS and the BSU. While adversary assailed adversary, the image of the academic profession plummeted to a new low. This climate had, of course, been set by the militant students. Their harsh recriminations pervade this entire account. Beyond their language, their intransigence on nonnegotiability and their establishment of politically impossible preconditions created effective roadblocks to all mediation of the student demands. What flexibility they hinted at in private dialogue did not move the conflict any closer to solution as the state officials responded to their inflaming speech and their disruptive behavior.

Any disposition toward further trustee and Hayakawa compromise on the Fifteen Demands was effectively eliminated when the faculty leader of the black movement, Nathan Hare, confirmed on

January 14 all the fears of those who believed the basic goal of the strike was to give the BSU total license to preach revolution. Hare told the press that he desired faculty for the new black studies department who could work within a black revolutionary nationalist framework. "I don't want assimilationists." As examples of the type of individuals he was seeking, Hare named several leaders of the BSU strike: Jerry Varnado and Benny Stewart. For many months key trustees had believed that black self-determination and "power to the people" were code phrases for the indoctrination of revolutionary propaganda. Taxpayer support of a program aiming to destroy traditional economic and political beliefs, all under the guise of academic freedom, such trustees as well as the larger public vowed never to condone. That many faculty would glance aside when these political criteria were applied to hirings while at the same time decrying any other intrusion of political selectivity in appointments, as suggested by the governor, only led to further diminution of academic prestige and credibility.

Chapter 17

Behind the Scenes

Whatever one might say about the wisdom, the effectiveness, the success of the San Francisco State College strike by Local 1352 of the California Federation of Teachers, there is little room for criticism of the amazing organization, the vast flow of energies, the selfless dedication, and the creative, innovative spirit. Most in the labor movement scoffed at the possibility of pampered, unrealistic intellectuals actually engaging in full-scale industrial warfare. Many thought that when the crunch came, an excuse would be created. If not, if the faculty actually did go out on strike, hardened labor leaders envisioned a disorganized protest of a few days and then a quick, face-saving return to work. When it eventually seeped in that the faculty would fight for ideals, not just remuneration, that they would sustain themselves for six weeks at a paycheck deficit of around $325,000, without a strike war chest, and that they would pound the picket lines in rainy weather under the threat of the Tac Squad, they were incredulous. In particular Johns, a seasoned labor veteran, began to see glimmers of the long-disappeared idealism of the 1930s, clasped the union to his heart, and used up a number of his blue chips with his less enchanted labor colleagues.

The AFT entered the battle with great handicaps. No withdrawal of services would diminish the profit of management as in the industrial world—it would even provide savings, thus papering over the desperate budget deficits inherited by Smith and Hayakawa. This left the union with little actual leverage. At a previous point in time, a mild public sympathy might have developed for vague, seedy academicians taking risks for principles. This current struggle did not project this image, and the California public was aligned heavily against the faculty. Quite simply the masses saw the faculty as complicit in a violent revolutionary takeover of the college, even scurrying to add to their own economic comforts in the process. Therefore the striking faculty became the enemy. Nor did the media depict the strikers as heroes.

Within general faculty circles, a quiet guilt, bitter criticism, and even some hatred prevailed. Local 1352 was engaging in a wildcat strike. It was a minority group in only one of the eighteen colleges in the system. Continuously the trustees questioned, "How can we make agreements with you when you do not even represent your own faculty, especially agreements that would extend to the systemwide faculty?" To this the AFT responded, "That's your problem." For years the AFT had organized to achieve bargaining status by majority vote but events had conspired against the union. Now this same unpredictable course of history had offered the union an unusual opportunity for power through bold, unilateral action. The moment was grasped. Let the rest of the faculty cope with the AFT power.

Originally the AFT had grand hopes that other locals would rise to its support, strike their colleges, and create such a mess that the governor would have to come to terms. This hope proved naive. At San Jose State the local did indeed go on strike and did picket San Jose State and send support to San Francisco State. Yet the numbers were minimal, the picketing ineffective, and the local finally settled even before San Francisco State. At other campuses there was considerable agitation. Strike sanction from the county labor councils was actually obtained in several instances. But other than at San Jose, no significant strike activity developed. As sympathetic as many state college AFT members were with the valiant efforts of their San Francisco colleagues, the issue was still not one that touched their daily lives and therefore was not worthy of the risks of job security and financial loss.

As a test of strength the State Council governing the locals in the state colleges organized a one-day boycott in support of their San Francisco brothers. Even the most ardent trade unionists had to admit the boycott fizzled and threatened the power structure in no manner. This absence of united support by statewide AFT members on an issue that Local 1352 felt transcended their campus and was vital to both the future of the system and faculty rights embittered many of the striking faculty. In their view at least their union brothers could have dipped in deeply to provide essential financial support, for the local had no strike fund. Unionized high school teachers were more helpful than college colleagues. Failure at such a critical juncture has threatened the future of the AFT as a power in faculty ranks.

To allay these anxieties, improve the public image, elicit support, discover funds, and organize the complicated daily activities of approximately 300 striking faculty, the union unleashed a cyclone of energy and creative activities. The attempt to counter the statewide power structure with local community support was massive. At least a dozen speakers daily gave the AFT side of the story to community groups. Established organizations, especially in the ethnic communities, were urged to take public stands. Faculty associated with other community organizations were told to get their groups involved with the San Francisco State issues. Local legislators and politicians were contacted, church groups approached, labor enjoined. Daily task forces traveled to Sacramento to obtain a quiet legislative audience. Broadsides were published and circulated, calls to radio talk programs and letters to editors were pressed. During the holidays and between semesters, delegates toured the nation or spoke at professional meetings to give the "true" side of the controversy. Few stones were left unturned in the effort at least to neutralize a hostile public. Polls indicated that a phrase from Hayakawa or a newsclip of a mob scene counteracted much of this grass roots activity.

Money was central to the strike. Most faculty lived from paycheck to paycheck and a weekly strike benefit of from thirty-five to fifty dollars met few bills. Insurance premiums, credit installments, mortgages, and rent and food bills had a compelling urgency. Another task force fought this battle. From all sources contributions were solicited. Part-time jobs took some of the pressure off as a dozen or so professors went to the docks and worked with the longshoremen. Wives went to work. Loans were arranged. Any way in which the state's largess to the unemployed might apply to striking faculty was explored. Some money came in; much more went out. In the final analysis the union simply could not counteract the enormous economic pressures and after six weeks ran out of resources. Individuals who had passionately shouted, "Aye!" to the strike vote on January 5 discovered the lonely, adversarial role of a striker living on borrowed money or on dwindling bank accounts a harrowing existence. As one leader commented, "I think to some it was a shattering experience. I know a lot of people whom I feel very warmly toward. They couldn't cut it. They didn't have the financial self-confidence. That is really what it was because they could have done it. Anybody could borrow enough money if they had to to go almost a year, but you have to believe you can do it." Even for the majority about whom it was said, "This was one of the great exhilarating experiences of their lifetime," the individual financial pressures caused some second thoughts. The penurious conditions of their lengthy graduate indentureship had left scars on most that a month without a check quickly reopened. And then there was always the threat of having to seek employment elsewhere, if fired, in market conditions that did not welcome associate and full professors.

Yet group morale remained at a surprisingly high level. Despite anxieties when the institution failed to buckle under their massive attack, most "knew their cause was just and no matter what personal sacrifices might come, they were going to do it." Picketing hour after hour, day after day proved to be even less congenial for the academic man than for the average union worker, yet the strike maintained its momentum. Assignments were met with regularity, each did his part as was ordained by the strike leadership. One of the unexpected insights of the strike was the capacity of highly individualistic professors to subordinate their customary autonomous self-direction to the orders of their peers in leadership positions. "Joe, you've got the midnight-to-eight shift" and off went the professor of art to his scheduled duty. Men and women who seldom in the past acknowledged even the existence of the college administration and its rules and regulations, trudged back and forth in rough clothes and inclement weather or performed menial tasks if that was the desire of the union Strike Committee. For many students the sight of one of their professors in this incongruous role of a committed activist served as a major influence in shifting allegiance from passive resistance to total involvement.

Credit for this group solidarity, complex organization, and dedicated effort clearly belongs to the AFT leadership. Although the strike was hardly won, and future historians might well conclude that the decision to strike in conventional labor style at that time was a grievous error, Local 1352's expanded Executive Committee did sustain a strike with unexpected skill and imagination. Thrust into roles completely contradictory to professing, this congerie of English, speech, sociology, and philosophy teachers rose to the occasion. Here and there individual union members criticized a specific act or decision, but for the most part a following accustomed to criticizing any authority remained relatively satisfied. One member seemed, when interviewed, to reflect a common sentiment when he stated, "The membership was quite satisfied with the general way the strike was run. The organization was well done. The important decisions were always by the membership." This balance between leadership authority and constituency decision-making proved difficult in an arena that emphasized action, strategy, and timing. Not all were as pleased with the democratic functioning as was the member quoted, but at least, at the time, the vast majority seemed to recognize power for many decisions had to be vested in a small, representative group. Said another member, "The leadership was a good team, they balanced out."

Youthful Gary Hawkins, in only his fourth year on the campus yet president of the union, was the visible symbol of the union. Within the membership it was said, "He really instituted confidence, he was a kind of father figure." Arthur K. Bierman was the other major force. He finally had the strike he had been waiting nine years for, and he dedicated himself during sixteen-to-eighteen-hour days to his crusade. The sentiment that he and Hawkins "performed brilliantly together" was shared by many in the union. To those nonstriking faculty who bitterly opposed the union, these same leaders became the men in the black hats, capable of no enlightened act. The entire Executive Committee met almost daily to engage in the vital but academically foreign activity of planning strategy. With the stakes large and resources diminishing, unusual stress was placed on this group. Many, many more within the union shared the extensive burden of leadership, for sustaining this labor warfare for the first time against such an array of Establishment power demanded much organized effort.

Whether the union would have been able to strike for two months, obtain a trustee signature on a settlement document of sorts, and protect its membership during the rehiring period without the services of its dedicated, experienced legal counsel, Victor Van Bourg, is dubious. One astute member assessed Van Bourg's contribution as follows: "Van Bourg was the shrewd politician lawyer. He's one of the best in the country; you feel confident in him. He's absolutely honest, he said it the way it was. Sometimes he'd speak from a lawyer's point of view, sometimes from his own, but he always let you know what position he was speaking from. He separated the issues more clearly than anyone else did." One issue that he attempted to clarify in the early deliberations pertained to the style of an academic protest. Said one member, "He advised us that there were better and more creative techniques to use." The union's employment of the ultimate weapon, massive withdrawal of services, in traditional adversarial labor-style striking remains a strategy deeply questioned. Undoubtedly the economic demands and the picketing tactic alienated many within both the academic and general community. Striking also made the union highly vulnerable. In reflection, one leader commented: "If this should come up again and, God willing, it won't, but if it should, we would use more creative methods like teach a couple of days, strike a couple of days, not say anything in class, find ways that could accomplish the same protest purpose but could make it easier to protect ourselves financially." But to obtain agreement on sophisticated protest strategy at a moment of passion and violence from 250 individualistic, non-action-oriented academicians was a challenge beyond the capacities of most in union leadership. At this time the major goal remained to deescalate the police-student warfare in the middle of the campus. This the labor-style strike did.

For some in the union the camaraderie, the new, intimate level of interpersonal relationship with fellow faculty and students, the sharing of action for an idealistic cause transcended all the fear, anxiety, and economic loss and gave the strike a quality that makes the comment, "It was probably the finest moment that most people have ever had in their entire life" seem not far-fetched. The union had always attracted a membership and leaders responsive to celebration as well as cerebration, and islands of revelry dotted the sea of sacrifices.

For all of these energetic, dedicated activities, the San Francisco State AFT found itself in a precarious position after two weeks of pounding the pavement. To be sure, the violence had abated, a strike had been sustained, nobody had been fired, and the educational process had been badly crippled. But these achievements were merely tactics aimed at the ultimate goals of a settlement of the student strike and some form of trustee negotiations with the union. At this basic level the power structure had been adamant. Nothing productive had developed with the striking students since the abortive negotiations involving BSU member Blount. The nibble at faculty negotiations with the Heilbron Liaison Committee had been coldly terminated by Governor Reagan and trustee chairman Merriam. Thus, the AFT was faced with a Pyrrhic victory of sorts: a sustained strike that appeared to have little chance of achieving the goals that had set it in motion.

In a manner consistent with historical union-management adversarial relations, the AFT moved to increase the pressure and make it more painful for the trustees and the college administration not to settle. First, the striking faculty resolved to fill out their grade reports for the fall semester but to hold them in "escrow" in the union headquarters until the administration had come to terms. The administration countered by assuring all students that their academic advancement would not be jeopardized by this "unprofessional" tactic and that department chairmen and school deans would be authorized to grant them at least pass grades should such a freezing of grades occur. The union tactic neither worked nor endeared the AFT to faculty and administrators who believed it unethical to "use" students, and their legitimate right to grades, for union advancement. But such opinions claimed little respect among those who took credit for stopping the violence.

The second AFT escalation of pressure concentrated on the critical college task of mounting a spring semester schedule of classes. With a distinct possibility that the strike might not be settled prior to spring registration and beginning instruction, the administration was confronted with the dilemma of whether to schedule classes for those faculty who were apparently striking. To enroll students in classes without instructors would pose severe problems for the college. From the AFT point of view, this was the administration's dilemma, not theirs, and it stemmed from refusal to negotiate. The union would give no assistance; if the strike were settled, faculty would teach; if not, they would continue to strike. The administration strategy to blunt this tactic was sidestepped by the union. When the Council of Academic Deans demanded that all striking faculty sign a statement promising they would be available for meeting their teaching functions in the spring semester, strikers blithely answered on their attorney's recommendation that, yes, they would be available to "meet their professional responsibilities." Lawyer Van Bourg assured them that signing the letter did not create a contract, that it would assure them a schedule of classes to return to, and that "meeting one's professional responsibilities" could have many meanings. Behind this facade of toughness the union Negotiating Committee maneuvered energetically to establish some form of negotiation. Time was running out, morale was sagging, funds were dissipating, widespread support had not materialized, and the moment of truth was not far distant. Then three events took place within three days in late January that eventually broke the log jam.

On the positive side, the trustees, meeting in Sacramento, reversed the Reagan-Merriam position prohibiting the Heilbron Liaison Committee from continuing discussions with the AFT and the Labor Council. With Governor Reagan injecting a heavy political tone in the meeting and insisting that no impression be given to the public that the board was negotiating with the rebels, it took two and one-half hours merely, in effect, to ratify the existing formal arrangements. Implicitly, though, this action recognized that it had been a mistake to break off relationships two weeks earlier and that a serious step needed to be taken to resolve the differences threatening the college's opening for the spring. In setting the stage for additional dialogue, conservative board members also seemed to acknowledge that the AFT essentially would be suing for peace in these talks and that the entire board had the power to negate any "agreements" reached by the committee if it so desired.

Trustee Heilbron, the senior statesman of the board, who was obviously doomed not to be reappointed by the governor when his term concluded in March, was a powerful moral force in this decision. More than most of the other board members, he recognized the AFT effort as a legitimate employee strike, as is reflected in his comment, "It is not in accordance with American practice to demand that strikers return to work before there can be a discussion of the issues." The initial appearance before the board of eloquent black student and community spokesmen from San Francisco also influenced the decision to resume the discussions.

If this action created the opportunity for concluding the faculty strike, an incident on the campus on January 23, 1969, provided the incentive for the students. Ever since the strike had resumed on January 6, after the holidays, the militant black and white students had chafed at the AFT domination of campus tactics and had resented the consequent subservience to Hayakawa's dictum that all campus rallies were outlawed. Three weeks of endless picketing, with no obvious gains, convinced the student strike leadership that new tactics—or a return to old ones—must be ventured. Therefore, after lengthy leadership debate, a rally was announced for January 23 to "see where we are now"—but also to test the limits of Hayakawa's decree. This casual gathering proved to be a turning point in the termination of both the faculty and student strikes and in the eventual pacification of the campus for the entire next year.

To most students the occasion appeared to be merely a repeat performance of standard strike "participatory democracy"—an assembly around the Speakers Platform aimed at boosting morale by denouncing the system. The assembly of over 500 contained radical strike leaders, liberal sympathizers, and curious onlookers. For ten minutes they listened to the customary fiery rhetoric. Then came an announcement over the public address system on top of the Administration Building that declared the gathering illegal. After a brief pause, another voice proclaimed: "This is an illegal assembly. I order you to disperse immediately in the name of the people of the State of California." To most who heard the warnings, there seemed to be little danger. Hayakawa had made a similar statement often in the past and nobody had enforced it. So students sneered, shouted back, and continued their rally.

Within five minutes those in attendance discovered they had been had. Police in an obviously well-planned maneuver poured in from all directions, surrounding the gathering and making escape almost impossible. After a few fruitless gambits to break the encirclement, the group settled down to a lengthy mass arrest.

For three hours paddy wagons waddled into the campus, picked up a jam-packed cargo of "criminals," and rattled off to the jails. By midnight 453 individuals had been arrested, booked, and incarcerated. Included in the bag were many of the Third World and white student strike leaders as well as almost a dozen sympathetic faculty. By mistake one of Acting President Hayakawa's staff observers got caught in the net and his plea, "But I represent President Hayakawa!" could not save him from the ride to jail. Knives, pool balls, clubs, and even a gun remained on the ground after the students had departed.

In retrospect, the campus rebellion was broken by this police and administrative gamble on a mass bust. So successful had the student strikers been in closing classes that few students remained on campus to challenge the action. According to militant leaders, a massive radicalization of students would be precipitated by such repression. They vowed to be back again and again, even if it meant being arrested again and again. Cried Nesbit Crutchfield of the BSU Central Committee to the crowd after a night in jail: "Not only will there be masses as there were yesterday, but they will be doubled and tripled. If you are not ready for revolutionary change—not reform—then you better step back because we are coming fast, fast, fast."

But Acting President Hayakawa was intoxicated with his success. The following day he gleefully told another standing-room-only crowd at the exclusive San Francisco Commonwealth Club, "When we arrested 483 [sic] of them, that took care of an awful lot of them. They refused to disperse so they all got busted. The skill and finesse of the police was an amazing and beautiful thing to see." It was a characteristic speech, and if his wildly applauding slice of the San Francisco power structure had had occasion to choose a governor on the spot, Hayakawa would soon have been taking up residence in Sacramento. In typically colorful language he excoriated the off-campus "pinheads from Sonoma State, knuckleheads from San Jose State, and savages from Berkeley" who added fuel to the fire. His strategy of separating the blacks from the white militants had a trial here, for he stated that the real purpose of the dissidents was to keep the minorities at a disadvantage so there would be "moral grounds to advocate revolution" in the land. He concluded to a standing ovation, "The entire episode is an attempt to seize power, to ignore the ballot box, to instigate mob rule, which is called 'participatory democracy' in left-wing circles."

Hayakawa had good reason to be elated. For almost the entire next year the defense of those arrested would absorb the funds and energies of the movement. (It also, incidentally, totally disrupted the San Francisco court schedule.) Unrefunded bail desposits cost strike supporters over $20,000. Average trials of ten-student groups took between four and six weeks. By the end of a plodding year 109 students had been convicted of one or more charges of unlawful assembly, refusal to disperse, and disturbing the peace. Many received jail sentences. Two hundred and forty-two others chose to plead guilty or no contest in return for a suspended sentence and probation. The militant students badly miscalculated the power of the Establishment. Moreover, instead of propelling all of those who had been arrested into overt revolutionary activity, the bust, jail sentences, and prolonged court hearings had an opposite effect on many. It deeply embittered them and taught them to look out for themselves. The mass arrest also served as an example to those who had so cavalierly violated college regulations. Ironically the occasion for the arrest was one of the least disruptive events during the strike. In the future a hostile peace prevailed.

The more immediate stimulus to the AFT to use the new trustee opportunity for discussions came that same January week when the union tried to mobilize a one-day sympathy strike on all the eighteen campuses for the twenty-eight faculty at San Jose State who had been terminated (later to be rehired) under the five-day automatic resignation law. By all standards the mass strike failed. Many colleges failed to recognize it. At others token pickets marched for an hour or two. Only at Sacramento State did there appear to be an appreciable impact on the academic program. Instead of threatening the trustees, the ill-timed walkout convinced them that the faculty would not really stand up and be counted on either the automatic resignation law or the San Francsico strike issue, despite occasional outpourings of strident rhetoric and hostility. Whereas the students misjudged the intentions and power of the Establishment, the striking faculty confused their own moral indignation with physical and financial faculty support. After the week of January 20 the road was all downhill, even though it took six more weeks to traverse it.

The events of late January did not place pressure on the AFT alone to negotiate. Facing Governor Reagan and Acting President Hayakawa was the possibility that either San Francisco State would not open for the spring semester or, if it did open without the AFT faculty, the educational operation would be much more seriously crippled than it had been at the end of the fall semester. To initiate a semester with virtually no courses in key departments and with students and faculty attempting to disrupt an already shaky registration process occasioned no joy in administrative circles. Such a prospect had a ring of reality, for the AFT had yet to decide to go back to teaching. Some trustees talked ominously with college groups about actually closing the college. Such a drastic step had considerable attraction for some officials who would have liked to make of San Francisco State an object lesson to students and faculty at other colleges who contemplated use of confrontation tactics to achieve their goals. In view of the limited education that the college might be purveying in the spring semester, shutting up shop might have been justified, at least for a period of several months. Looming large on the other side of the ledger, however, was Governor Reagan's vow to keep the campus open "at the point of a bayonet, if necessary." Both the governor and Acting President Hayakawa had much face to lose by closing the campus. Yet, if they could not terminate the strife and open the semester with a semblance of a normal educational operation, the public might easily begin to question the strategy of massive repression no matter how emotionally attractive.[1] So, despite possession of most of the high cards, the power structure had much to gain by a negotiated settlement.

Racial strife at Berkeley and San Fernando Valley State College also pressured officials to conclude the San Francisco State strike. At Berkeley a low key but threatening TWLF strike had begun over many of the same issues that convulsed State. Within a few weeks the same scenario of picket lines, fights, mass marches around campus and through buildings, fires, and full-scale police intervention would be enacted. San Fernando Valley State had been tense ever since a band of TW students had imprisoned college officials in the Administration Building and physically threatened some. Subsequent protests and arrests raised the specter of an extensive confrontation. Although Governor Reagan had profited in public opinion polls so far by student strife, widespread disruption might convince the populace that he was not actually in control of this social institution, higher education, upon which both the parental hopes and the state's economic future were pinned.

Burgeoning police expenses were an additional inducement for the state to seek a conclusion to the academic disruption, though on its own terms.[2] When in January the statewide Academic Senate took a tough position in support of the right of faculty to strike and seriously considered the alternative of terminating its official relationship with the system so that it might offer itself as a private collective bargaining

[1] In Cannon's *Ronnie & Jesse: A Political Odyssey,* Governor Reagan is quoted as saying, "If this [campus discipline] is still an issue come election time, it certainly will reflect badly on whoever permitted it to go on that long" (p. 324).

[2] As of January 7 alone, the cost was estimated at $662,704. Over the entire period at least $1,000,000 was spent by the city of San Francisco and surrounding communities. Legislation was introduced to spread this cost to the state in the future.

agent for the faculty, faculty rebellion could no longer be considered purely a San Francisco phenomenon.

Additional pressures concentrated on the faculty and students. One month after the California Legislature convened at the beginning of January, more than thirty bills had been introduced by irate legislators aimed at controlling and punishing militant students and faculty. By now the San Francisco Labor Council was not enthusiastic about supporting the battle much longer. On the campus, the state's attorney general moved to place the Associated Students funds in receivership because of alleged financial irregularities. This action undercut both financial support of the TWLF and strike-sustaining activities of the student government. And as the strike continued, the future of the black studies department, the reason for the struggle, became dimmer and dimmer. Then, in late January, Murray was arrested for possession of a gun in his car.

It took only a few days for the protagonists to jump at the opportunity presented by the trustee shift in position. By Monday, January 27, labor officials, the AFT Negotiating Committee, the college administration, and the Trustee Liaison Committee resumed the negotiations that had been terminated two weeks previously by the governor's intervention. For three days the parties met face to face, with the labor officials and mediator Ronald Naughton attempting to find points of agreement between the college representatives and the striking faculty. Although guarded statements indicated progress was being made, a subsequent memorandum of understanding issued by Johns and his labor hierarchy on February 7 revealed very significant differences when compared to the final settlement document. And at no point was reference made in either document to the primary issue that provoked the faculty walkout, the TWLF's Fifteen Demands.

When the trustee committee refused to agree that the memorandum represented any real meeting of minds, Johns blasted the trustees and the governor for refusing to allow a settlement even though Acting President Hayakawa and his staff had stated publicly that they could "live with" the document. But many of the understandings had statewide implications, and the trustees were not going to allow Hayakawa to commit the system just to solve his problems. Although Johns commented that the only issue holding up agreement was a difference on grievance procedures, there was much, much more at stake. Heilbron so indicated when he stated that "no understanding has been reached with respect to the paragraphs as contained in this draft memorandum." Close analysis of the Johns letter reveals that on almost every point it was couched in terms that were about as advantageous to the union as it could conceivably hope to expect in the current situation. From the trustee point of view it would have been disastrous to accept it.

The union gambit did not work. For the next week behind-the-scenes maneuvering took a more realistic turn with Johns concentrating on the point of statewide grievance procedures. This was an important concern of the striking faculty. Should Acting President Hayakawa or the trustees invoke any punitive reprisals—and the union leaders were convinced management always punished in order to diminish the possibility of future strike reoccurences—such grievance machinery would be the last line of defense for the aggrieved faculty. For five years the statewide Academic Senate had been attempting to develop such procedures. Now all major disagreements between the chancellor and the Academic Senate had been sufficiently ironed out that the trustees had on their February agenda final action on the document.

But the AFT was not satisfied with the protection provided in the procedure. All parties were agreed that should the grievant not be content with the final action taken at the campus level, he could appeal it to a final appellate body at the statewide level. Reluctantly the chancellor and the trustees had even decided to delegate their powers to this final group. The issue was joined in the composition of this group and the process for choosing the committee which would have final authority for adjudicating the aggrieved's complaint. The Senate had been satisfied with a process for forming the panel by selecting academic personnel from the individual colleges by procedures acceptable to the campuses, and then choosing the final committee either by chancellor appointment or lot.

From the union perspective this local autonomy selection process could not guarantee that administrators at some campuses might not dominate the choosing of the college representatives to the panel. A final selection of a three-man committee by lot could conceivably produce a group oriented toward a management bias. To counter this the union proposed an alternative system whereby both the president whose decision was being challenged and the aggrieved could each choose one committee member from the entire system, not a panel. Then either these two parties could agree on a third person from any background or, in case of an impasse, the critical third member could be chosen from a list of five persons provided by a "proper court or the California State Mediation and Conciliation Service." Grievance procedures had always been important to unions, and since this process reflected a common organized labor practice, the Labor Council representatives supported it. If the Labor Council officials could ensure this protection for the striking faculty members, it would be willing to withdraw its strike sanction so that labor could pull out of the troublesome battle and the college could resume relatively normal operations.

A process that so clearly intruded a fundamental organized labor practice into academic disputations was, however, both unpalatable to the trustees and to the statewide Academic Senate officers. Could a compromise be developed? Around this prospect hinged the entire settlement of the agonizing strike. The campus union remained deeply split on the question of agreeing to any settlement that disregarded the student demands. A rapidly enlarging faction painfully began to recognize that the union was losing its battle and that it might be best to accept an agreement that protected against reprisals and that, by ensuring rehiring and reinstatement, at least proved that faculty unions could both strike in the state of California and negotiate with the Board of Trustees.

Into the breach stepped the leaders of the statewide Academic Senate. They proposed a compromise process for choosing the final appellate committee that did still restrict the choice to the panel of statewide academic or administrative employees, but it did allow, along with other options, the alternative that the aggrieved party and the president involved could each choose one committee member. Then these two could either agree on the third member or he could be chosen by lot from the panel.

Out of such fine distinctions are wars of attrition terminated. When the statewide Senate and trustee representatives gave Johns and his colleagues assurances that their groups would indeed endorse this amended process, the Labor Council officials pressed the AFT Negotiating Committee to conclude the strike. This grievance process and the other points of agreement between the trustee committee, President Hayakawa, the Labor Council representatives, and the AFT Negotiating Committee were incorporated into a letter addressed to Johns and signed by trustee Heilbron and Executive Vice-President Frank Dollard, acting for Acting President Hayakawa. It then became the challenge to the Negotiating Committee to sell its constituency on these terms.

For an evening and a day the massed faculty strikers debated the terms. Harshly opposed to such a settlement was a group composed mostly of those members who had never been seriously concerned about the technical union issues but rather had joined the union and had struck in support of the student demands and against Hayakawa and his police repression. Obviously the student strike had not been settled, and one of the most important AFT demands had been that "Black Students Union and Third World Liberation Front grievances must be resolved and implementation assured by the trustees" before the union would go back to work.

When it had earlier appeared that the AFT local might be forced to forsake this objective, BSU and TWLF leaders had heatedly threatened the lives of members of the union and had told them at the meeting, "We'll follow you even if you leave the state." But now some of the TWLF strike leaders became aware that the power structure simply was not going to bend and that the union was rapidly running out of money and commitment. The adamancy of those in power was underscored when a black municipal judge, Joseph Kennedy, sentenced six students arrested in the mass bust to ten-to-thirty-day jail sentences because they had violated the terms of their probationary status given them for a prior arrest at the May sit-in. These TWLF leaders saw wisdom in the new AFT strategy that an acceptance of the terms might be qualified with the phrase "if a peaceful and free academic atmosphere prevails on the campus."

With this proviso incorporated into the final union action, Local 1352 tentatively accepted the settlement plan and its lawyer, Van Bourg, announced this action on Monday, February 24, at a press conference attended by Mayor Alioto and the labor hierarchy. Acting President Hayakawa and Governor Reagan expressed themselves as skeptical of the union posture for, with the student strike certainly not terminated, there was the ever-present threat of an academic amosphere that would be far from "peaceful and free." The union refused to elaborate on the meaning of this qualification, but it served several essential union purposes. First, it allowed the split union membership to otherwise support the terms of the pact without coming to final agreement on the student demand issue. Second, such qualified agreement was urgent so that the trustees would act on the grievance procedures. Now the ball was thrown to these trustees at their Los Angeles meeting on the following Tuesday and Wednesday. Third, it kept the pressure on Hayakawa and the trustees for a few more days to attempt to reach a compromise with the striking students, for with this provision there was the alternative that the union might not return to work if peace and a free academic atmosphere did not actually prevail on the campus. Finally, this qualification left open to the union membership a reconsideration of its action after the trustees had acted.

The spotlight now shifted to the trustee meeting. Governor Reagan cast gloom on this meeting when he announced at a press conference that he certainly would not, as one member of the board, vote to support the document since it committed the system to illegally recognizing the AFT as a collective bargaining agent, it went far beyond the authority of the Liaison Committee, and it guaranteed the striking faculty they would still be paid even though they had been out on strike. Much of the meeting was spent assisting the governor in extricating himself from these comments which bore no relationship to fact. As with most of the trustee and regent meetings of the past three years where Governor Reagan had been in attendance and student unrest issues had been central, the delicate task of the meeting became one of taking the requisite action to solve the problem without giving the outward appearance that the board or the governor had in any way compromised with the rebels. This process frequently involved motions, amendments, substitute motions, and hours of convoluted debate on actions that had no substance but could torpedo the fragile understandings. In this instance the governor insisted on a statement that said that in the future the trustees would talk with employee organizations such as the union only if the members "are meeting their employment responsibilities and not disrupting the academic process." Implicit in the resolution, of course, was the admission that in this instance the trustees had talked, through their Liaison Committee, with faculty out on strike.

When at times it appeared that the issue might be in doubt, Acting President Hayakawa and trustee Heilbron came to the rescue. On one occasion, Hayakawa told the governor, "I implore you to worry less about appearances and more about the reality. We have all the cards in our hands right now." No state college president had so bluntly lectured the governor in public, but with the words coming from the bantam battler of the militant hordes, the governor chose only to nod and smile. Trustee Heilbron cleared the meeting of much of the obfuscating underbrush when he frankly stated that all of the points in his letter to Johns either represented current policy or were within the discretion of the college president, with the exception of the revised grievance procedures. These procedures, which were basic to the agreement, received virtually no explanation or debate. With the air cleared, the Board voted fifteen to two to adopt the new procedures. Although Governor Reagan voted with the majority, Chancellor Dumke abstained, using the old political argument that agreement might indicate to other teachers that "this type of pressure" could be successful.

The final act in the most prolonged and involved faculty strike in the history of American higher education shifted back to the Buchanan Street YMCA in the heart of San Francisco, where Local 1352 faced its moment of conscience. No longer could the question of faculty return while students still struck be avoided. But while it could not be avoided, it could be faced with an added awareness of several stark realities.

By now the spring semester had gone into its second week and union members had acted upon the strategy of agreeing to come into the fold, but only for the two days of teaching necessary to ensure the existence of their classes should they finally agree to end the strike. This action was deeply resented by the administration, fellow colleagues, and some students. After having signed a statement agreeing to resume their professional responsibilities for the spring semester, AFT members left the college in the lurch by walking off with their IBM class cards. Although most AFT strikers had told students they were taking some risk by signing for AFT classes, and most striking faculty had been identified in a circular by the conservative student Committee for an Academic Environment, departments were faced with the problem of either closing the classes or having colleagues cover them for a while. Since some of these faculty members had been covering strikers' classes during the past semester as well, ill-will was promoted. Some departments shifted nonstriking faculty to these classes and gave the strikers less desirable schedules when they returned. AFT members were incensed by these actions and believed their fellow faculty were in league with the administration in its strike-breaking tactics. To students the AFT explained that the short-run discomfiture was a necessary price for the long-term benefits that the union was ensuring by its struggle.

Events of the first faculty meeting during the registration week added to the hostility of many in the faculty toward both the AFT and the BSU. The union picketed this meeting and verbally harassed colleagues who attended, calling them Hayakawa stooges. At the poorly attended meeting, Acting President Hayakawa employed a typical baiting technique when, in commenting on a fishing expedition during his holiday trip to Hawaii, he stated that "we began surrounding and catching opelu not one at a time, but 453 in a single sweep. The sight made me so homesick, I started out for San Francisco that night." Immediately a claque of black faculty and BSU leaders in front began to harass Hayakawa with chants of "Down with the puppet! Down with the puppet!" Within a few moments a group led by Hare marched onto the stage and interrupted the president's speech. TV cameras flocked to the bait and recorded Hayakawa angrily telling Hare to "get the hell out of here!" Police finally calmed the scene with several arrests as agitated faculty shouted shrilly from the audience. The incident made the 6:30 news and front pages, as all parties had desired. Hayakawa fired Hare as chairman of the black studies department and then suspended him with pay pending a disciplinary hearing. (The hearing eventually sustained Hare's contention that his actions were motivated by the highest conception of professional behavior for a committed black faculty member.)

Hayakawa announced Hare's removal from his chairmanship duties while standing in front of the recently bomb-blasted windows of his Administration Building. He commented, "This pattern of intimidation is of a piece with Dr. Hare's disruption of my speech to the faculty." This bombing as well as one that earlier had caused the closing of a student lounge added to the public and faculty distaste for the strike. One more source of support for the union disappeared when the San Jose State faculty sympathy strike was ended by the San Jose AFT over the objections of the union president and bitter students in attendance. Now Local 1352 was indeed all alone.

Added pressure was placed on the student strikers when Acting President Hayakawa prepared an edict forbidding any department to hire any student or faculty member who had been arrested in connection with strike activities. Since this would lop off at least one-half of the thirty-two individuals scheduled for instruction in the Educational Opportunity Program for disadvantaged TW students, it represented a serious attack. Were it carried out, a decimation of the EOP program accompanied by the failure of Hare and the black faculty to implement the black studies department would represent a tremendous loss for the striking students. The edict also communicated Hayakawa's consistent tough line and willingness to take whatever actions he felt were necessary to quell the rebellion. Later the president relented somewhat in the final implementation of this decree, for it was pointed out that arrests did not assure convictions or guilt. Some regular faculty had themselves been arrested in the mass bust.

It was in this context of administrative pressure and public and faculty hostility that the AFT met to make its historic decision. The agreement was a bitter pill to swallow after such wrenching personal sacrifices and such visions of grand success. Faculty gains were minimal, with the chief concession an amendment to the grievance procedures that was primarily important only to protect against reprisals. Beyond this, the understanding, as stated earlier, did authenticate a first college strike in California by guaranteeing rehiring and reinstatement of tenure, status, and privileges, and it did represent a tentative first step toward faculty-trustee negotiations. But all of the remainder of what had escalated to fifty-two specific AFT demands had met powerful trustee resistance. Most important, the student demands had not been met.

At this juncture one optimistic campus development occurred. The special committee of the local Academic Senate, casting about desperately for some new technique for resuming college-TWLF communication, decided that such dialogue would never eventuate as long as Acting President Hayakawa had to be central to the deliberations. Working on this assumption, they met with the Council of Academic Deans and produced a proposal whereby Hayakawa would delegate his negotiating power to a six-man committee of his own choosing. The president picked up on this idea immediately and appointed what to the AFT and the striking students was a surprisingly balanced committee. Chaired by Curtis Aller, an economics professor with mediating experience, the committee had a membersship that was prestigious, tough, generally sympathetic to both due process and the plight of the disadvantaged, and determined to make an all-out effort to conclude the debilitating strike. Because this group was invested with putative powers for reaching a college rapprochement with the TWLF Central Committee, hopes were raised that the AFT would not be totally abandoning the student strikers. These hopes were fanned in the mass membership meeting that attempted to decide whether the union should come in from the cold or continue to wage labor warfare. Most of the union Negotiating Committee, including Hawkins and negotiating chief Bierman, urged termination of the strike. They and many of their colleagues believed that the union had reached the end of its rope: personal and union funds had diminished, morale and loyalty were withering, and no potential gains loomed ahead. A continuation of the strike would lead only to the firing of a fair share of the strikers and the crumbling of their college. Although challenges to the legality of these firings might eventually be sustained in the courts, this offered little immediate hope for the faculty, the students, or the college.

On the other side lined up those who all along had urged that the students simply could not be abandoned and that you could not trust the power structure either to settle the student strike or to carry out the terms and spirit of the faculty agreement. When all of the arguments had been concluded, the 216 in final attendance paraded up and cast their votes. By a count of 112 to 104 the strike was ended. On Wednesday, March 5, almost four months to the day since the student strike had been initiated, most of the union faculty walked back into their classrooms. Some of the 104 who voted against returning met and seriously considered staying out, but BSU representatives helped convince them they would be of more assistance on the faculty than fired.

Our narration of the faculty strike would not be complete without some assessment of the AFT's gains and losses during this traumatic period. The union's contribution to the reduction of violence has already been described. The influence of its individual members in ad hoc groups on the failure of the Smith administration to contain the student militants has also been depicted. Several references have been made to the fact that the faculty strikers defied a state law supposedly prohibiting a faculty strike of more than five days and were eventually returned to full employment and rights. And a "first" of quasinegotiations had been forced on a stubbornly resisting Board of Trustees and Governor Reagan. Among the indefinables will be the final impact of the AFT activities on the future of collective bargaining for state college faculty. But clearly they influenced the public and legislative backlash, the trustee and chancellor imposition of management controls, and the attenuation of faculty government, institutional autonomy, and faculty independence. There is no doubt that the college and the system are in much worse shape than before the strike, but cause and effect relationships are difficult to weigh. To attempt to blame the plight of the system on the strikers is to ignore the accumulation of unresolved problems and frustrations that prompted the strike as a last resort. Whether the union ultimately provoked more student gains than losses remains for history to decide. Gains were slight in the final student settlement. Without AFT support the student strike most likely would have been terminated earlier.

Much more susceptible to a precise analysis are the specific demands of the AFT. One could use as an expression of these goals the exact wording of the union's official position. A more realistic interpretation of these expectations would be the language of the Johns memorandum of understanding dated February 7 that culminated the three days of late January negotiations with the Trustee Liaison Committee. The following paragraphs compare the Johns' statement with the actual Heilbron-Hayakawa agreement with the Labor Council and the AFT. (Item numbering refers to the language of the final settlement document from the Heilbron committee.)

Item 1: Union Recognition. By law the trustees are required to "meet and confer" with faculty organizations desiring such communication. At both the public school and college levels the California Federation of Teachers has never been content with this law and has constantly pressed for union recognition and the power to negotiate, not just confer. With the legislature in no mood to change the law, the union has attempted to change the situation with de facto recognition and negotiation. This was one of the major union aims of the faculty strike, and was twice incorporated into the Johns memorandum. Its Item 1 hoped to commit the trustees to the statement that "a proper request [to meet] will be, has been, and will continue to be honored." The trustee response: "Any future meetings with the union would have to be consistent with the obligation to meet and confer with other employee organizations." The trustees were not about to commit themselves for the future to the process of serious negotiations with only one group at one of the eighteen campuses. In Item 8 the Johns memo took another stab at this goal. "With the above understanding a direct relationship is established between the AFT Local 1352 and the state Board of Trustees and with the administration of San Francisco State College. This understanding does not include nor is it concerned with other faculty groups. These groups should enjoy an equal recognition and autonomy." The Heilbron committee did not even bother to respond to this reiteration.

Item 2: Amnesty, Arrest, and Discipline. Earlier the AFT had insisted that general student and faculty amnesty and administrative withdrawal of its emergency regulations were preconditions to even talking with the board. This insistence evaporated in the real world of negotiations. Yet these were still important concerns of the union and they were incorporated into Item 2: "All matters of amnesty and matters relating to suspensions, discipline, arrests, warrants, tenure, and emergency regulations shall be referred to meetings and discussions between the representatives of San Francisco State College and AFT Local 1352, with the right reserved to any grievant or his representative to submit such grievance to the grievance procedure as established herein." In this delineation of this goal the distinction between student and faculty amnesty is blurred, and a whole range of concerns is spelled out. The trustee committee specified that only "any matter of amnesty, arrests, and warrants affecting members of AFT Local 1352" would be referred to meetings of the San Francisco State administration and the union. No mention was made of emergency regulations or student actions, and the range of faculty concerns eliminated specific reference to "suspension, discipline, and tenure" as matters for administrative-union arbitration. Throughout the strike, amnesty for those involved in the strike was a fundamental union concern. For both Hayakawa and the trustees college and court punishment of convicted violators of law was basic to future containment of rebellions and to public support. Although those in power recognized that neither the collective faculty in the college or the system nor organized labor would countenance mass faculty firings, they were not inclined to sidestep due process hearings in favor of union-administration arbitration.

Item 3: Grievance Procedure. The final compromise on this grievance procedure that had been made critical by the threat of punitive action toward faculty strikers is delineated in a previous section. The union considered this compromise a fundamental accomplishment. Since in all probability the gain could have been achieved by the AFT by working within the Statewide Academic Senate framework, it proved to be an expensive achievement. The final action did shore up a weakness from the faculty perspective that the Senate had precipitated when it failed to ensure how individual colleges would select members to the system appellate body. The trustees, however, did not agree to the early union demand to eliminate the panel selected by the colleges, they did not support a process that would have allowed the third member of an appeals committee to be chosen outside of academic circles, and they did not allow an instrument of labor-management disputes, the California State Mediation and Conciliation Service, to become involved in academic grievances.

Item 4: Possibility of Faculty Layoffs. At one point in enrollment and budgetary deliberations during the 1968–69 academic year, the chancellor gave consideration to the possibility of solving the college's extensive budgetary deficit by reducing spring faculty employment by as many as 125 faculty. Naturally this became a major concern of the union. Most faculty severed under such circumstances would be part-time faculty with only one-semester contracts, and in this part-time group the union had heavy representation. Prior to the January faculty strike the Chancellor's Office discovered funds that could be reallocated to the college to cover this deficit and thus avoid layoffs. In the Johns memorandum the union attempted to take some credit for this saving of jobs. The trustee committee was quick to point out in its letter that the decision had been validated in a document dated December 16, 1968, from Vice-Chancellor Brakebill to the college. Whether the union pressure facilitated this action is problematical.

Item 5: Ethnic Studies Staffing. When the Academic Senate and the Council of Academic Deans agreed during the early fall semester to provide 11.3 professorial positions for the black studies department in the spring semester, an understanding was reached that these positions would come from the original fall allocations to the various schools, if necessary. This was not a significant concession. Since the black students who would be enrolling in the black studies department would be leaving other departmental courses and thus reducing student attendance and concomitant faculty need, it was in the order of things that other departments would have a reduced faculty allocation and the black studies department would earn a normal faculty budget. In many cases the departmental loss was only an accounting process, for the same faculty member in the regular department teaching, say, black history, would now be credited to the new black studies department. Again the Johns memorandum implied this state of affairs could be credited to the strike and the union. Again trustee Heilbron and his colleagues were careful to underscore the fact that this was a normal process and was the "long-time policy of the college."

Item 6: The Nine-Unit Load. A hidden agenda item of the entire faculty strike had been the AFT's attempt to use the student disruption to further its commitment to reduce the faculty teaching load in the spring semester to nine units by independent action of individual faculty members. This power play had been threatened by the chancellor's decree that such faculty might well have their salaries reduced by one-fourth. The document that came out under the auspices of the Labor Council attempted to bring the arbitration services of some person of stature in education, such as former Secretary of Health, Education, and Welfare John Gardner, to bear on the problem. In the interim it proposed that the trustees commit themselves to the proposition "that no academic employee who has been assigned a reduced teaching load during 1969 should be docked or otherwise have his pay reduced as a result thereof." The trustee response was extremely careful to state that there would be no such docking or pay cut "so long as said assignment was made in accordance with college procedure and the staffing formula." Needless to say, "college procedure and the staffing formula" would not encompass the arbitrary reduced loads envisioned by the AFT. On this vital matter, the AFT gained nothing. Considering the cost factor that would be added to the system budget were all faculty to have had their teaching loads reduced one-fourth, the union ambition was highly visionary, especially in a tax-conscious state governed by a man committed to reducing costs and bringing college faculty to heel. But compared to the teaching load at similar colleges, the nine-unit goal seemed plausible.

Item 7: Open Personnel Files. A year prior to the San Francisco State strike the Statewide Academic Senate had developed a policy which the trustees had approved and which was designed to alleviate faculty concern about personnel files that might contain derogatory information of which the individual faculty member had no awareness and no opportunity to refute. The process was simple: personnel files were to be open to the individual concerned. In the customary ways of the system and the college, this policy had not been implemented fully, especially at the departmental level. The AFT included this item as a fresh demand in its list. The trustee committee saw no disagreement since the trustees had already enacted the demand into policy.

Item 8: Rehiring and Reinstatement. At both the college and the chancellor's level agreement had been virtually assured that striking faculty considered resigned under the five-day automatic resignation section of the Education Code would be automatically rehired if the AFT returned to work shortly. It was also agreed that the college and the system would urge the State Personnel Board to reinstate these faculty with all their rights and privileges. This had been a major but almost inevitable accomplishment of the union, supported by most of the total faculty and all of organized labor. Trustee Heilbron's letter confirmed that this was a college issue and that the college would communicate the rehiring commitment in a memorandum to the union and had already stated its support of nondiscriminatory reinstatement. Labor and the AFT had pressed for a process whereby the respective union and trustee lawyers might "take whatever steps are required to resolve this issue, and no formal action shall be taken by the parties until said attorneys have rendered their final recommendation and resolution." By this means the union hoped in some way to nullify the Educational Code provision which allegedly allowed the trustees legally to fire striking faculty. Believing the law was on their side, the trustees took such "formal action" by separating the affected faculty from their employment. But they also supported the college in rehiring and in seeking reinstatement. Although many in power would have preferred getting rid of the troublemakers as a means of purging the colleges and intimidating future faculty who might consider the use of the strike weapon, this was not a realistic method of bringing peace to the campus or system. As trustee Heilbron commented in a document to the authors, "If the trustees had not made their own effort, if the college had not extended itself to accept a return of the striking faculty, labor might well have considered that its prestige had become so involved that it had to support the strike the full way and withhold all services from the college." This could have shut down the total college. Never did the Labor Council employ its full power during the strike. Union members worked on a variety of college projects all through the strike period.

Item 9: Reprisals. Whereas the union attempted to ensure "no recriminations or reprisals against any member of any labor organization who participated in or supported the strike," the trustees made a more restricted response: "There will be no reprisals against a returned teacher simply because he participated in the strike; there will be no reprisal against any member of any other labor organization who participated in or supported the strike. The college so advises." Hayakawa, with trustee support, was careful to point out that avoidance of such reprisals would be assured only for faculty who returned, and that this protection applied only to the faculty member's strike activities. Conceivably the striking faculty member might engage in other conduct which might warrant college action. This was to prove a crucial distinction when Hayakawa moved in and reversed unanimous English department and School of Humanities recommendations for rehiring seven AFT members the following year. Of course, the real reasons for personnel decisions are frequently difficult to ascertain.

In the concluding paragraphs, Acting President Hayakawa and trustee Heilbron were careful to point out that most of the items in the communication dealt with matters within the discretion of the college itself, and that even those understandings would be contingent upon the striking professors' returning to their duties for the spring semester and the San Francisco Labor Council's withdrawal of strike sanction. The union had an additional point in its memorandum of understanding which attempted to commit the trustees implicitly to supporting "legislative powers" for local Academic Senates, but the trustees avoided this trap by eliminating any reference to this item in their letter.

In summary, the union lost on nearly every aggressive thrust in its memorandum and the trustees gave away virtually nothing that had not been previously settled. Except as has been stated earlier, the union failed in most of its economic demands and in its commitment not to return to work until there was a resolution of the student grievance. But the college did open in the spring semester, nobody was killed, and only one late-returning faculty member was fired. And the issue of faculty power through collective bargaining is still a matter for the future.

Chapter 18

Back to School

The return of the AFT solved only half of the college problem: the Third World students, who had initiated the strike, talked as though they were no closer to settling their grievances in March than they were four months previously. Their leadership once more vowed to "carry on the struggle" until all demands were met. Roger Alvarado daily hinted at new modes of resistance: "We are definitely going to pick up the tempo in the near future. When it comes—whatever the change in tempo is—it will come suddenly." But to any sensitive observer it was transparent that the tides had drastically shifted in this battle as well. Two months earlier, in January, the striking students truly believed that they had the college administration and the state's power figures literally on their knees.

Nonnegotiable demands did not seem a far-fetched goal. Now, in March, all was gloom. Most important, momentum had been lost. In all of the confrontations of the past two years, timing and pace had proved to be vital factors. When the Third World students agreed to a shift in tactics away from the highly successful rally-march-raid techniques of December to AFT peripheral picketing strategy, they lost a dynamism they were never able to recover. The striking faculty, in effect, coopted them. The Third World naively accepted the union assurance that few faculty would cross a picket line and therefore the college would be closed. But faculty did cross this combined student-faculty line. The abortive attempt to shift back to the rally-raid tactic on January 23 culminated in the mass arrest of 453 and made their position more precarious. A challenge from the left had forced the Central Committee to this dubious tactic. When the strikers were not able to fulfill their threat of an even greater illegal rally a week later but instead played it safe with a huge picket line, Hayakawa became fully aware that he had them licked. The semester break also played into the hands of the opposition. Students scattered, to return with little zeal for additional confrontations. Many of the rank-and-file black students came to college with ambitions of economic mobility. Disruption of the college threatened to delay their graduation and their economic advancement. Few of these students had given other than token support to the strike. Four months of inactivity were difficult for them to endure.

The basic realization that slowly seeped into the thinking of the Third World student leadership was that the authorities were determined not to lose this battle no matter what the cost. The $662,704 that was estimated on January 7 as the cumulative cost for police protection of as many as 200 a day did not discourage the taxpayers or city officials. A decimated educational program scared few. If, indeed, the college needed to be closed for the spring semester, the price was not too great. All segments united in tough support of this position: Acting President Hayakawa, Mayor Alioto, Governor Reagan, Chancellor Dumke, the trustees, the Legislature, a majority of the faculty, and most of the California citizenry. This citizen adamancy is verified by the results of a poll conducted in February 1969 in California by Mervin Field. Seventy-two per cent of the sampling agreed strongly with the statement: "Students who challenge and defy university and college authorities should be kicked out to make room for those who are willing to obey the rules." Only 6 per cent disputed this position vigorously. A year before only 58 per cent had been this positive about eliminating the troublemakers. Forty-seven per cent were equally dedicated to the proposition that faculty in state-supported institutions should not be allowed to strike, while only 12 per cent would strongly support this right. On one of the major demands of the Third World students, an open admissions policy for San Francisco State, a mere 7 per cent strongly backed this idea and 6 per cent were mildly supportive. Sixty-seven per cent strongly disapproved and 17 per cent disagreed somewhat.[1]

With the public overwhelmingly against them, momentum lost, and the rally-raid technique coopted, Third World student leaders vainly sought new strategies. Two such initiatives failed completely. When Third World leaders turned to internal academic disruption by enrolling en masse in a class taught by their favorite faculty target, John Bunzel, and then harassing Bunzel for three straight sessions so that he could not lecture, college arrests drove the disrupters out of the class. Faculty support of the strikers plummeted to new lows after this venture, and the Academic Senate finally affirmed "the right of the student to learn and right of the teacher to teach in the classroom as the sacred prerogative of an academic institution," and repudiated "the denial of these rights by any means as unjustified for whatever reasons. . . ." The vote was nineteen to four. Eight abstained from this fundamental declaration, causing great bewilderment and hostility among those who wondered if some of their colleagues had become so enamored of the strike that they would not even protect each other's right to teach.

Far more disastrous to dwindling sympathy was an attempt on March 5 to blow up the Creative Arts Building. In the past, several bombings had been thwarted, and in only a minor incident had an alleged bomber been arrested. Nevertheless, the threat of such drastic action loomed ever in the consciousness of those responsible for the welfare of the college and those teaching in the buildings. Bombings were the ultimate guerrilla fear technique, and strike leaders had generally embraced guerrilla warfare. Chief of Police Thomas Cahill predicted, "It's only a matter of time until someone loses his life." This incident verified the fears of those who believed the statement "by any means necessary" was not an idle threat. On that evening a pipe filled

[1] Mervin D. Field, "Tougher Line on Students," *San Francisco Chronicle,* March 4, 1969.

with blasting powder exploded prematurely and severely wounded a young Black Students Union member, Tim Peebles. A search revealed two more bombs in a suitcase in an adjacent room. One appeared to utilize six sticks of dynamite. An official said this explosive device could have destroyed much of the building.

The Black Students Union rallied to the support of Peebles and his associates. Chairman Benny Stewart held a press conference and proclaimed Peebles "the innocent victim of the racist, oppressive society" at the college. A day later members were soliciting contributions for his hospital expenses in a campaign across campus. But the rest of the community was aghast. Previous bombings could not be attributed to any single group. This attempt appeared a conscious tactic of some of the desperately battling Third World students. Morale in the BSU declined with this injury to one of their own. In one of the strange incongruities of the strike, Peebles was described by his high school faculty as a mild, popular leader of both white and black students before coming to San Francisco State and being inducted into the militant BSU. Fifteen months later, in June 1970, young Peebles prepared to stand trial for this incident. In the meantime he pursued his studies at State in surprisingly good health. In this case, as in most, when the glare of publicity had dwindled, Acting President Hayakawa refused to prosecute prior to court action.

The AFT settlement diminished the chances of student strike success by greatly reducing the pressures on the college administration. Now classes were assured and all administrative attention could be devoted exclusively to defeating the students. Hayakawa was confident that he needed to concede nothing and that he had the militants licked. By withdrawing from the picket lines the AFT made the student pickets vulnerable. In the past, the police of this labor town had been circumspect in dealing with faculty and student pickets. Despite court injunctions, arrests were token. Now, with Labor Council sanction withdrawn and the AFT back in the classroom, the police moved in on the line of endless chanters and told them simply that they would be arrested if they did not disperse. The message had gotten across to the students, especially since Third World community leaders had gravely warned them that there was no money left for bail bonds after the January 23 fiasco, and they quietly faded into the campus.

A culminating blow to the strikers was the withdrawal of financial support. Not only was the community drained, but Acting President Hayakawa shrewdly moved in on the strikers' major source of campus funding. The freezing of Associated Students funds robbed many Third World leaders of their basic means of survival. When Hayakawa announced that no arrested students would be eligible for work in the Educational Opportunity Program, still more strikers faced financial starvation. Many things the students could do without, but "bread" was a necessity. The dismal prospect of long, expensive legal defenses stemming from the January 23 mass bust made the financial picture even gloomier.

Strike morale and strike unity are not difficult when a string of victories lights up the TV screen and has a harassed college on the run. Such morale and unity, however, become difficult to sustain over a period of four months of increasing frustrations and dwindling hopes. As the educational program disappeared, as financial resources dried up, as the enemy became stronger and stronger, inevitably voices in the ranks questioned the leadership and wondered aloud why it had not settled when ahead. In a post mortem on the strike, labor mediator Ronald Haughton commented that the Third World strike leaders were skillful at mounting a strike but did not know how to conclude it. Many BSU followers wondered whether they had been misled. This dissension within the midst of the Third World students is bitterly delineated in an article entitled "Why We Settled" by BSU Central Committee member Leroy Goodwin in *Black Fire,* May 1969. White administrative circles had always believed schisms and power plays in the BSU heavily influenced the course of strike activities, but reliable data had not been available. After admitting to several basic errors, Goodwin launched into a scathing attack on five categories of black brothers and sisters who had not displayed throughout the strike the proper revolutionary dedication.

> Well, through observation we saw the determination and support of the people rapidly decreasing due to a distant political level, communication gaps, and paranoia or fear of the Central Committee. And as the chairman of the BSU often says, "The only way a people can be defeated is when they lose their determination to fight." Beside the above-mentioned reasons for our diagnosis, was also the high and blatant rise of "opportunism" among our "so called" ranks (i.e., SLICK-NIGGER MENTALITY). In this class there were contradictions of all sorts:
>
> I. There were those who knew that the Central Committee was so busy directing and struggling with the strike that they had a golden

opportunity to run all around the country making speeches as authoritative leaders, and picking up the purse (anywhere from $25–$500 a speech) for themselves rather than returning it to the organization. These I call the leeches or money motivated.

II. Then there were those who saw all the other people struggling in what appeared to be an endless strike, and also were aware of the fact that BSU had secured substantial grades for strikers, so they seized this opportunity to take an "early summer vacation," and would return after the battle to share in the spoils. These were the forefront proponents of the "Slick Nigga Mentality."

III. There were also the old frat boys who had lost their prestige to the dynamism of the revolution. This segment is perhaps the saddest for they still carry with them their bourgeois ideology, and see leadership as a series of flashy speeches, rewarded by an onslaught of pussy (sex) and TV appearances. They fail to understand the seriousness of people's lives, or feel the fear and agony of seeing seventeen-year-old men and women have their skulls crushed and hurled into jail for something that you taught them was essential for humanity.

IV. Then there were the "shit slingers." This was the elite group of (primarily women, but not exclusive of men) people who could not wait for us to pull the pigs' boot out of their ass, so they could stick their finger back in and thump shit at you. Some did this out of habit or ignorance, others out of revenge and intentional.

V. Then the last major category was the so-called communist organization of PL [Progressive Labor Party] who could, I'm sure, quite logically and effectively criticize the formation of clouds or the counterrevolutionary sound of the wind. These were the intellectual lunatics, who seem to always appear at the height of battles initiated by "other" groups with a blueprint for the revolution. They also had other incomparable qualities; they seem to be professional at meeting disruptions, coup de tai (overthrown) manufacturers, and they appeared to always voice the criticisms of the people, but for different reasons. The people usually criticize to strengthen the organization, but PLP criticizes to politically show why the people should transfer their allegiance from their present organization to PLP. What has PLP ever initiated, or started of their own accord? Who or what revolutionary people or organization has PLP not criticized? A bunch of armchair revolutionaries and nit-picking politicians with suicidal tendencies.

> So due to the increasing contradictions within, as well as outside, the BSU, it was necessary to "negotiate" what we said was "nonnegotiable," the demands (SPACE). Perhaps it was not until then that we realized our mistake, that we saw that we were trying to make a tactic (demand-strike) a principle (nonnegotiability and no compromise). The penalty for our mistake was clear, we would have to "lose face." Then we began to wonder if our face was more important than the lives of people who believed in us. Or if the truth was subordinate to "saving face." But we came to grips with the reality that the struggle of oppressed people was more important than fourteen individuals walking around with the myth of the revolution going on in their minds. Imagine a flea worried about losing face.

For all of this accelerating predisposition to conclude the strike and get on with the task of winning the new battle of the black studies curriculum and the black studies department, some medium needed to be devised to allow the Third World students some minimal "saving of face." A graceful exit had to be arranged, for despite all the handicaps of continuing the strike, the students were not inclined to come crawling to Acting President Hayakawa on their knees to sue for peace. No matter what the power realities, negotiate with Hayakawa they would not consider. Out of the labored, torturous activities of the Academic Senate such a mechanism did develop. When all else seemed to fail, the Senate appointed a five-man committee and commissioned it to seek a solution to the college's travail in whatever fashion seemed wise and prudent. Jordan Churchill, Jules Grossman, Ray Simpson, Ted Kroeber, and Ann Paterson struggled with this burden. After more than a month of trial balloons that quickly became deflated and endless discussions with all faculty groups, the committee became aware that the college administration had become rigid and incapable of taking new initiatives to settle the student strike. Trustees seemed more sensitive to this lethargy than the faculty: "When is the college going to do something?" In desperation the committee turned to the Council of Academic Deans. CAD was receptive, and within a few days a new college posture on the issues had been formulated and the idea of a neutral Select Committee emerged. Hopefully, Acting President Hayakawa might delegate his powers to negotiate to such a group if he picked it, and this could introduce new faces and relegate old ones to the sidelines. Both CAD and the Senate saw the risks of this blank-check approach as necessary given the widespread impasse.

On Thursday, February 21, at the end of the first week of instruction in the new semester, a group chosen primarily by Executive Vice-President Dollard met with Dollard and Hayakawa. Dollard had chosen an old office mate in English, John Edwards. Edwards said he would serve if Curtis Aller of the economics department, an experienced labor negotiator who had been away in Washington, D.C., for three years and was therefore relatively uncontaminated, would participate. The deans chose Dean DeVere Pentony from international relations and the Senate selected philosophy professor and former Senate chairman Jordan Churchill. Donald Barnhart of interdisciplinary social science had Latin American associations, and so he was added to the group that Dollard hoped would advise Acting President Hayakawa on the wisdom and composition of such a Select Committee. But fate took strange twists during these final weeks, and on this occasion it chose to call Dollard out of the room for a phone call. When he came back he discovered that Acting President Hayakawa had impulsively told the group that it would be the Select Committee itself, not an advisory group to the president. This explains the relatively liberal cast to the group that, as Acting President Hayakawa was to discover, expected to act with the full authority of the president and to work night and day to end the strike with honor to all parties. He was to regret his hasty decision. The hard-line, conservative point of view was not represented among these professors. Throughout all negotiations they pressed for an innovative, viable ethnic studies program and for compromises, not victories and defeats. Eventually they earned the respect of the Third World students and brought the strike to a reasonable conclusion.

Early efforts were not sanguine, however. Reluctantly Acting President Hayakawa accepted the committee's statement that it had "authority to speak for the president on all issues where he had final authority." Such delegation was indispensable if the group were to have any credibility with the suspicious Third World Central Committee. Even this putative power and the new college stance on the demands, as enunciated by the deans, gave the committee slight legitimacy when it first met with the strikers in a gloomy basement hall in Chinatown on Monday, February 24. Anticipating the beginnings of negotiations that AFT associates had predicted the weary students desperately sought, the committee instead was served with an ultimatum of three impossible preconditions. George Murray and Paul Yamazaki—an arrested Third World leader—must participate in the negotiations, in jail or otherwise, disciplinary hearings must cease, and the committee must bring to the table those who had authority to implement all of the Third World demands. There was no need for further discussions. After a few questions, the meeting broke up.

An exchange of correspondence and counterproposals brought the sides no closer together. The students claimed the Select Committee had no powers and was only a part of the "pig structure's tricknology." With the AFT final response to the trustee and Hayakawa settlement drawing to a close on Sunday, March 2, the negotiators made every effort to mediate the student strike first. After an AFT settlement, little leverage could be exerted on an administration confident with its victory. But even AFT leaders who had the respect and affection of the Third World Central Committee could not persuade the black and brown brothers to bargain. Nor could they convince the faculty mediators to cut down their bargaining power by taking specific positions on the famous demands. In an effort entailing considerable risk, Mayor Alioto had given to Bishop Hurley a signed statement indicating he would use the powers of his office to minimize prosecution of students arrested for nonviolent crimes if peace could be restored during the weekend. Hurley carried the statement, but he could not find the students. By the weekend of March 1–2 the committee had not heard from the students and concentrated instead on a statement that might hold forth the hope of future progress and thus influence the AFT to settle even though the student issue remained unresolved.

The Third World Central Committee spent the week of March 3–7 digesting its new circumstances now that the AFT had settled 112–104, Peebles had been injured in the midst of a bombing, and the police had broken up their normal picketing with the threat of an arrest. Clearly the strikers were in trouble. And so was the divided union. In the final showdown, Third World students had helped the union accept its defeat and return to the college as a resource for the activists. Only twenty-two faculty, mostly part-time teachers, did not return. The Select Committee remained in business but with slight hopes. Varied advisers suggested more constructive action, including a radicalized cadre of fifteen to twenty department chairmen headed by Steve Rauch of psychology, Caroline Shrodes of English, and Kai Yu-Hsu of world literature. Even a stray Third World leader dropped in to suggest the dire personal consequences to the individual negotiators if the students' goals were not fulfilled.

On Sunday, March 9, a telephone call by Jack Alexis to Bishop Hurley of the Citizens Committee broke the log jam. For three months Hurley had worked fourteen hours a day seeking a solution to this impasse that threatened to destroy the college and project into San Francisco itself. Patiently he had tried to facilitate dialogue by walking the lines with the student strikers, but they were so certain of victory, suspicious of each other, and dubious about a cleric who was associated with Mayor Alioto and the Establishment that they never accepted his quiet suggestions. But finally, when it appeared they were defeated, Hurley seemed to have the least to gain by settlement leadership and the greatest leverage with the city powers for potential amnesty. In this judgment they were reinforced by AFT leaders such as Bierman, who by now lived the strike twenty-four hours a day and was in continuous midnight telephone contact with the bishop.

Despite the inauspicious beginning Sunday at the St. Francis Rectory, when police questioned the influx of black brothers into the sanctuary, the meeting initiated discussions. Contacts were frequent in the succeeding days and it was finally suggested to Bishop Hurley that it might be fruitful were he to contact Murray in his jail cell. This the bishop did. The confidential interview and a subsequent gathering of key Third World, AFT, and city representatives convinced Bishop Hurley that meeting the precondition of Murray's involvement in negotiations might be the key to final settlement. This insight led to a critical meeting in the jail which included Hurley, Aller, and BSU leaders. Once Murray had given his jail house blessings to the specific terms of the settlement and told his brothers, "Settle," final arbitration was in sight. The Murray demand was eliminated, the patron saint had spoken from his incarceration, and Select Committee Chairman Aller had gone the last mile.

But although the students were on the verge of being reconciled, Acting President Hayakawa was not. While Hurley had been making the major breakthrough on Wednesday with Murray, Hayakawa had threatened to call off all negotiations. Why should he negotiate? The students had clearly run out of steam and offered no threat to the college now that the AFT faculty had resumed teaching and the college was in full operation. No peace offer was necessary, and it might actually reinforce the BSU and Third World militants who had caused all the trouble. Let them face their constituencies as beaten men. Maybe a more moderate leadership would emerge that would work constructivly with the administration in creating a high-quality ethnic studies program. This was both Hayakawa's view and that of his key advisers, who had recently become familiar with the emerging terms of the Select Committee. Faculty Renaissance leaders said he should silence the committee; Hayakawa's retired-colonel public relations man, Harvey Yorke, advised against any concessions; and the man he had chosen to invoke law and order, business professor Edwin Duerr, saw his disciplinary hearings undercut by proposed campus discipline terms. Only persuasive rhetoric by the committee obtained a forty-eight-hour reprieve.

By midnight, Thursday, March 13, the strike was virtually settled. The committee met continuously with the Third World Central Committee after the Murray meeting and concluded terms acceptable on almost every issue except amnesty. Hare and Murray had been disposed of as issues by the implication that a community board might generate quasilegal personnel powers, this same board held out the hope of "power to the people" on all other matters, and open admissions for black, brown, and yellow students was conceded to be beyond the powers of the college. But since many of those wandering in and out of Third World lawyer Franklyn Brann's kitchen sampling his food and beverages could conceivably be eliminated by disciplinary action from the college they had delivered from its racist attitude, amnesty remained the pivot point. The threat of SDS disruption of a planned hearing later in the afternoon—it now being Friday, March 14—magnified this impasse, for such disruption could quite conceivably torpedo the almost completed negotiations.

As a last desperate gesture now that the spirit of goodwill was evaporating, the Select Committee decided to call Hayakawa at his home and request a delay in the hearing. On this point the tough president was adamant: the hearing would proceed. Stalling for time, Edwards grasped at the prospect of a morning meeting between the actual adversaries: Hayakawa and the Central Committee. "But I'm leaving for a meeting with President Nixon at 9:00!" "Well, how about 7:30?" With this wild gambit, one more chance piece fell into place. Hayakawa agreed, and before the militant brothers could object to facing the Puppet, their enemy, Brann, sealed the offer and sent them on their way.

In a face-to-face encounter as dramatic as the jailhouse meeting with Murray, the black, Chicano, Chinese, Japanese, and Latino representatives walked into the president's office at 7:30 that morning. No Chinatown basement this time; rather it was the enemy's turf.

After four months of reviling the diminutive Japanese hardliner on every occasion, the Third World leaders lost their assurance and aggressiveness in his presence. Words were halting, the eloquence of Thursday night had disappeared. It took Brann and Hurley to move matters along. Hayakawa spoke little, paced the room, took an orange from his refrigerator and began to peel it as he sat on the edge of his desk listening to the arguments. Finally a point got to him. "All right. You say you are leaders. Well, let's see if you can lead constructively as well as in confrontations. I'll give you a month, until April 11, to prove you can keep this campus peaceful. In the meantime the disciplinary hearings will proceed, but I'll defer action on their recommendations. If all is quiet by April 11, I'll consider your recommendations. Now, if you'll excuse me, I have to catch my plane for Washington. Good morning."

The committee chased after their president to iron out points on the way to the airport. The students exploded in street language at the effrontery of The Man! But Hayakawa had won the day and dominated his first encounter with those who had harassed him continuously for three long months.

Once the emotions had been drained, representatives of students and of the college proceeded with their negotiations. In their own way, the BSU contained the SDS uprising. Saturday and Sunday saw the talks concluded. Relationships were amicable and the reasoning was sharp and to the point. For the BSU, it was all settled except for amnesty. The other ethnic groups wrangled procedurally for the establishment of a School of Ethnic Studies that would ensure Third World control. Constituency support was checked several times by the BSU representatives. Sunday night they claimed to smell a trap, and with tape recorder running, challenged Pentony and Hurley for engineering a stab-in-the-back sellout to rivals in the BSU. When Pentony and Hurley demanded a meeting with the accuser, the ploy was swept under the rug and negotiations proceeded. For almost the entire strike student leaders seemed wary of sellouts.

Late in the evening the issue of college disciplinary action became focal again. Brann's genius at face-saving language had helped the group skip by the other tangles, but the students deeply believed they should not be penalized for their virtuous actions, and the faculty were convinced they had to pay some price for their disruptive activities. When it finally seeped in to the students that amnesty was impossible, the debate revolved around specifics. The Third World bargaining position became dismissal of nonviolent charges, a maximum of six months' probation for disruptive or violent convictions. Although the faculty were inclined to believe that educational disruption should warrant a greater penalty than physical attack, by three in the morning they settled for a maximum of two semesters' suspension for violence, one semester for disruption. Nonviolent convictions such as the January 23 bust would warrant only reprimands. Embroidered with a string of qualifications, these became the disciplinary terms of the recommended settlement. On all other points the Select Committee assumed it acted for the president, but since Hayakawa had committed himself firmly in the Friday meeting against blanket amnesty, all agreed that the committee could use only its persuasive influence at this point. To all intents and purposes, this solution concluded the college–Third World warfare of four months.

The protracted struggle was not to end that easily, however. When Acting President Hayakawa was provided his copy of the terms Tuesday, March 18, he exploded. It had been his understanding that his four-week cooling-off proposal included a freezing of negotiations. By continuing the discussions, he felt, the Select Committee had betrayed him. It had agreed to terms when no compromise was necessary. The committee was incensed at this last-minute backdown. It had never occurred to the faculty to discontinue the almost completed settlement. This had been their charge that they had pursued in good faith and with high skill. In one of the ironies that continuously haunted their efforts, Hayakawa missed his chance of cooling the negotiations by flying off in another of his publicity efforts, this time in the brightest spotlight. He paid for his picture on most front pages engaged in serious talk with Nixon by having to let the students off the hook. Had he been in the vicinity over the weekend, undoubtedly he would have been consulted and would have had the opportunity to impose his view of the understanding. But he left with the words, "If you need me, call the White House."

When the Select Committee decided to sign the document on the assumption it represented the president, this placed Hayakawa in an untenable position. Fortunately, the terms of the agreement varied so little from his and the Senate's offer during his first week in office, except for the disciplinary recommendation, that his acceptance of the academic understandings presented him with a constructive image that he believed in. In typical political doubletalk at his Friday press conference, Hayakawa took the hard line that "I cannot agree prior to any hearing what the limits of the penalty for a given offense will be," while at the same time agreeing that he would not take any action on important hearing recommendations until after the April 11 peace period. This would give "the TWLF-BSU the opportunity to demonstrate their leadership in establishing peaceful conditions on campus." He also refused to remove the police from campus or discontinue his emergency prohibition of rallies, as recommended by the Select Committee, until this student good faith could be exemplified.

In a denouement worthy of the entire enterprise, Churchill and Barnhart walked into the president's office on the day before, Thursday afternoon, after finally obtaining the student signatures, laid the document before Hayakawa, and triumphantly stated, "You sign here." The president was dumfounded. "I'm not going to sign it! You know damn well I'm not signing it!" To place his signature on a statement indicating concessions when his image and instincts embraced noncapitulation was unthinkable for the bantam battler. This he had made clear to members of the committee earlier in the week, but in their jubilation at wrapping up the lengthy and delicate negotiations, individual members blocked out his comment. Since it seemed fitting, a typist had added space for his signature at the bottom of the page. Nobody questioned the inclusion, and so the faculty members placed it before him.

Although there were rumblings that the absence of the president's signature would negate the entire negotiations, the students obviously desired to terminate the conflict and begin the development of their programs. And so, after a few customary rhetorical challenges to Acting President Hayakawa's integrity, the strikers officially announced the termination of the strike and the initiation of curricular development of the ethnic studies programs. The Select Committee held its peace, hoping for the best although privately incensed with the president's ambiguous treatment of the authority he had previously delegated to the group.

The eventual disposition of the question of amnesty for the strikers in their civil court suits provided a final ironic postscript to the entire four months of turmoil. Third World leaders had been highly perturbed about the fate of those among their ranks who had been arrested on the campus and were scheduled for court trials. College discipline disturbed them, also, but not as much as the threat of jail sentences. Early in January Acting President Hayakawa had seized upon this point in his private attempts to settle the strike quickly, and he actually worked out a statement, in the presence of Bishop Hurley, that would have had the college pressing charges only in those instances of overt violence or classroom disruption. Flushed with victory, the students did not deign to consider these terms. Then, during this same period, Mayor Alioto played the role of peacemaker by indicating publicly a willingness to support a similar position—a general amnesty for the nonviolent cases. He later signed a statement to this effect and gave it Bishop Hurley to use if he thought it might make a difference.

Once the students finally acknowledged that they would need to negotiate, however, civil amnesty became a central concern. Bishop Hurley, with his wide city associations, held the key to this hope. He pledged his support. But as the strikers strung out the negotiations for three weeks, the district attorney's office informed Bishop Hurley that the period during which the college authorities might decide to withdraw certain charges was fast disappearing. Within a matter of days cases would go on trial, and at that point there would be no room for reconsideration. The city could hardly prosecute some students for an act such as the January 23 bust and then allow charges to be dropped for other students arrested for the same act. Once the AFT had settled, Mayor Alioto also withdrew his statement. Acting President Hayakawa by then indicated no willingness to alienate himself from the police by first pressing for arrests and then not following through on the prosecution. Summerskill had tried that route, to the great displeasure of the San Francisco police.

Still, on Sunday, March 16, Bishop Hurley had hopes that he might yet gain some concessions from the city authorities. But the Third World Central Committee refused to sign the settlement until their constituencies had had their say. They finally settled on Thursday, March 27. Bishop Hurley arranged one last-chance meeting between Mayor Alioto and the Central Committee. But they had delayed too long. As fate would have it, the man on whom their cause rested, Bishop Hurley, had to leave the meeting with a bleeding ulcer which removed him from the scene for the following weeks. With the bishop gone, a full range of court trials except for those who would plead *nolo contendere* was inevitable. Several Third World students went to jail when they might well have avoided it, and many received fines and probation sentences probably because the Central Committee deliberated several days past the point of no return.

An analysis of the terms of the settlement to which the Select

Committee allegedly committed the college reveals little that the striking Third World students gained by continuing the confrontation three months beyond the occasion of the first Academic Senate-CAD-Acting President Hayakawa offer on December 6. In fact, a strict accounting would probably indicate an overall loss. Amnesty might have been achieved and Hare and Murray might well have been employed at the earlier date. These "nonnegotiable" demands were subsequently lost. The college never agreed to autonomy in hiring and curricular decisions. The black and ethnic studies departments were to be treated like any other department. In November the Academic Senate agreed to 12.3 faculty for the black studies department (including Hare) rather than the twenty demanded, and exactly 12.3 were hired in the fall 1969. Ethnic studies demanded thirty, obtained ten in the settlement, and actually hired ten.

On the crucial issue of open admissions for all ethnic students who applied, the Academic Senate at one time agreed to seek a college population distributed roughly in proportion to the ethnic composition of the Bay Area community. This idea became lost in the Select Committee document. The college did pledge itself to develop "parallel admissions standards for Third World people" and to seek changes in the state law which would both accommodate these new standards and allow increased special admissions exceptions. Such parallel standards have yet to be created and the college would appear to possess little leverage for persuading the trustees or the Legislature to follow these recommendations. The college had no impact in dissuading the trustees from shifting ultimate control of student activities from student-managed corporations back to the college president or in persuading the attorney general to lift the freeze on Associated Students funds. Both had been held out as hopes by the Select Committee.

Elaborate plans were agreed to in the settlement document for the creation of a School of Ethnic Studies, but this had been preordained in November. The arrangement to have Third World administrative personnel responsible for the processing of financial aid to Third World students, again, had never been at issue. The specific demand to replace the Caucasian coordinator of student financial aid with a black person never received serious attention.

In actual practice, Acting President Hayakawa did follow most of the Select Committee's recommendations for the processing of campus discipline. Once the glare of nationwide attention had shifted from Hayakawa and his hard-line policies, and after the Third World students did prove that they could pacify the campus, reprimands did become the basic college practice for nonviolent actions, no students were expelled, and no students were suspended for more than two semesters. Double jeopardy for those involved in both court cases and college cases was generally respected by the president for most of 1969–70. For the most part, campus discipline reverted back to its moribund state after the irregular and heavily challenged efforts of the first coordinator of internal affairs, Edwin Duerr.

In an addendum to the specific responses to the Fifteen Demands, the Select Committee made an additional eleven recommendations. These included the establishment of an ombudsman, an arbitration process for terms of the settlement, a constitutional convention, and the elimination of the state of emergency on the campus as of March 20. No constitutional convention has been convened, no ombudsman has been appointed (although both had been agreed upon prior to Hayakawa's term), no arbitration panel settled differences between the president and the Third World students, and the emergency was not lifted until April.

Thus, in almost every instance, the students who had decided to close the college in order to force the Establishment to deal with them as equals, equals with legitimate rights that could not be compromised, were defeated. What they gained would have been theirs months earlier when they exerted only pressure, not force. What they lost could be attributed to their faith in the inherent virtue of their cause and their consequent commitment to "any means necessary." A seemingly fragile, vulnerable institution had been bent and distorted but not quite broken. After months when it appeared that only a massive blue line stood between Hayakawa and those clamoring for his elimination, the feisty hard-liner prevailed over both the militant students and the rebel faculty. Whether these same tactics can keep the opposition subdued, and whether normal educational activities can be resurrected and sustained under this leadership, remains for the verdict of history.

Epilogue

Aftermath

San Francisco State College entered the 1961–1969 Summerskill-Smith-Hayakawa period a proud, creative, liberal, and democratic institution, an institution reputed to be one of the better state colleges in the nation. It emerged into the poststrike era a shattered college, fragmented, withdrawn, demoralized, and authoritarian. The destructive impact of this revolutionary, confrontational style of conflict resolution on the extremely fragile structure and relationships of an academic institution remains one of the major lessons of the San Francisco State experience. Whether wiser, more committed action on the part of the system and the college administration and faculty could have muted this conflict is a matter for conjecture; the deleterious consequences, however, are becoming a fact of history.

A democratic academic community became transformed into an authoritarian, management-run college. A student government that had become a national symbol for progressive styles of educational reform and community involvement lapsed into limbo. A faculty that had earned the right to govern itself and had become a leader in the battle for appropriate institutional autonomy in the rapidly centralizing system divided bitterly during and after the strike, withdrew to the isolated classroom or to the cozy home study, and silently tolerated presidential rule. Shimmering hopes of educational transformation adapted to the critical times became lost in layers of mistrust, disinterest, and maladministration. Other colleges proceeded on plans to redistribute power between trustees, administrators, faculty, and students. San Francisco State, which had been on the verge of a constitutional convention for these same important purposes, jettisoned the idea after the chaos of 1968–69.

The esthetics of the campus, never a cause of delight, increasingly reflected Haight-Ashbury tastes. And looming ever in the forefront, and rarely challenged, were the new directives of Big Brother, whether emanating from Governor Ronald Reagan and his responsive trustees, the Legislature, Chancellor Dumke, or President Hayakawa. Repression and managerial controls were the order of the day. Students sullenly went to classes; faculty taught and picked up their paychecks. Few desired a return to the trauma of strikes, violence, chaos, fear, and massive police intervention. It was easier to "do your own thing," avoid commitment, and shrug off restraints.

From deep involvement in a revolutionary cause, the striking students, the silent but supportive majority of the San Francisco State student body, the AFT 300 and their sympathizers within the ranks of those who continued to teach—all gradually peeled off to go lick their wounds and seek other sources of fulfillment. Only the black students and their Third World compatriots continued the struggle. Together they proceeded with zest, enlarged ranks, and developed flexible strategies to work within the institution rather than without to achieve their goals of self-determination and a relevant, revolutionary educational program. Their struggle with President Hayakawa, his administration, and the Establishment of California dominated the events of the college in the immediate poststrike period and gave promise of being central to the college in the next decade.

During the strike one continuously heard from responsible parties the assertion that San Francisco State College had become the staging ground for a trial battle between militant, revolutionary confrontation tactics and the repressive techniques of massive police involvement, authoritarian controls, and punitive reprisals. "All the world" was supposedly watching. As went San Francisco State, so would go at least California's institutions of higher education, if not the colleges and universities of the nation. President Hayakawa reiterated such a warning in his many public appearances. Funds, support, and even personnel were allegedly flowing into the camps of the strikers and the administration to ensure respective victory at the academic Armageddon.

If this analysis is accurate, if the year of the strike should turn out to be a watershed in revolution versus repression, the lesson to be learned is clear: the Reagan-Dumke-Hayakawa style of law and order is the answer to student anarchy and revolution. Both the student and faculty strikes were broken with virtually no significant concessions, both student and faculty strikers paid excessive prices in money, energy, and psychic stress, the public and the power structures as well as many students and faculty repudiated this disruptive style of change, and democratic decision-making procedures were replaced with a concentration of power and managerial controls.

Radical theory anticipates such escalation of repression and forecasts a reciprocal upsurge of revolutionary commitment and zeal. Within the black culture on the campus, commitment has certainly accelerated, whether in response to the tactical losses and repressive administrative countermeasures or in spite of them. Elsewhere—the radical students, the concerned liberals among the students and faculty who joined the struggle and got burned, and the AFT—occasional heated rhetoric obscures the fact that the campus has not become radicalized and the new power relationships have become reluctantly accepted. It remains to be seen whether the victors will become overconfident and overzealous with their restrictive controls and will produce a new wave of more committed radical and liberal opposition.

Clearly the Black Student Union and its Third World allies lost in its war with Hayakawa, the trustees, and Reagan. Nothing achieved in the final "settlement" could not have been theirs three months earlier. In the process of the struggle their black studies program was delayed a semester, students went to jail, large sums were spent in legal defenses, and the public and the power structure were alienated. Yet, a final reckoning might well conclude that the black revolution was enhanced by the strike. From this long-term perspective, financial losses, arrests, delays, and busted heads might prove inconsequential when placed alongside revolutionary commitment and black community support. As the black brothers and sisters work to utilize their black studies department and Educational Opportunity Program beachheads as bases for furthering the cause of "power to the people," this commitment and this support can hardly be doubted.

In black and ethnic studies, this aftermath period represents an attempt to achieve the basic goal of the strike, self-determination with its resultant revolutionary curriculum, through exploitation of the legitimate departmental trappings such as personnel, funds, a curriculum, and student majors, rather than by a signature on a settlement document. According to both administrative statements and testimony in *Black Fire,* the black student power structure has moved to shape faculty behavior, student behavior, and educational activities in accord with a revolutionary philosophy. By this strategy the blacks have wrapped themselves in the sacrosanct faculty shibboleth of departmental autonomy and have put this cloak to new uses. Faculty are expected to serve as instruments of the students and the community. Although President Hayakawa vowed through the media that the faculty in the department would reflect an academic perspective and that their selection would not be controlled by the BSU Central Committee, once the strike was over the BSU largely achieved its goal of a faculty responsive to a radical point of view by shrewdly and doggedly carrying on the struggle while the administration relaxed during the summer months with its television victory.

The events of the strike clearly communicated to prospective black faculty the circumstances under which they would be working, and thus few applied who anticipated customary faculty authoritarian control of a course of study replete with syllabi, texts, footnoted term papers, frequent multiple-choice examinations, normal curve grading, or neutral perspectives. Those who did slip by the BSU–black faculty screening process had it communicated to them by vivid language and action that in the black studies department there was truly "power to the people" and they would be expected to behave accordingly. To ensure the revolutionary perspective of the curriculum, correct faculty behavior, and a democratic student-faculty climate, the BSU Central Committee used Educational Opportunity work-study funds to select for all the courses teaching assistants who would serve as political commissars. In *Black Fire* the task of these teaching assistants was bluntly outlined:

> Each black studies course has a teacher's assistant who has been selected by the Central Committee to politicize the class and to develop the student control over content. Recognizing the need to have student and faculty moving together in the struggle against fascism, capitalism, imperialism, and racism, the teacher's assistant will not be acting as an authoritarian figure indoctrinating the students and perpetuating miseducation to prepare students to fit rather than change the system. The job of teaching assistant is: (1) To fully educate the students to the political need for student control over content, which involves developing initiative and awareness of self-determination. (2) To inform the students of the local, state, national, and international news—past, present, and future. (3) To organize the students to form collective student power, with the teacher, not to focus on the teacher as the enemy instead of the pig power structure. (4) To inform the students about the Black Panther Party, its functions, how it is meeting the needs and desires of the people. (5) To inform them of the moves of the power structure at State, specifically Hayakawa. (6) To help the students with the problems they have with the administration at State. (7) To stress the need for the students to work on the different commitees: legal defense, public relations, curriculum, administrative, revolutionary arts and culture, and so on. (8) To talk about the strike if necessary—tell how the students got their heads beat in and how they are now facing unjust charges because they were fighting for their beliefs—the troubles they are having in the courts and jail. (9) To assist the teacher with the administrative duties of the class and to learn the skills from the instructor.

A major strike figure, Nesbit Crutchfield, was chosen as administrative assistant for the department to ensure BSU control of faculty and students. Crutchfield, a member of the BSU Central Committee, had been arrested three times during the strike and was under indictment for allegedly connecting fuses to automobile gas tanks in the parking lot. Nevertheless, the Hayakawa administration appointed him to this important position. When his appointment came up for renewal in December 1969, it was terminated.

It is difficult to obtain any accurate or objective assessment of the learning activities or styles in the black studies courses. Historical precedents do not exist in American higher education for such a revolutionary, community-oriented curriculum, and so much is experimental. Yet, were one to give much credence to the rhetoric of *Black Fire,* revolutionary goals and curricular philosophy appear to be congruent. A recent statement of the goals lists six:

> (1) a cultural identity, because we live in a society that is racist, that degrades and denies cultural heritage of Third World people, specifically black people; (2) to educate our people to understand that the only culture we can have is one that is revolutionary (directed toward our freedom and a complete change in our living conditions), and that this will never be endorsed by our enemy; (3) to build a revolutionary perspective and to understand the need for using the knowledge and skills we have and get only for our liberation and the destruction of all the oppressive conditions surrounding us; (4) to educate ourselves to the necessity of relating to the collective and not the individual; (5) to strive to build a socialist society; (6) to redistribute the wealth; the knowledge, the technology, the natural resources, the food, land, housing, and all of the material resources necessary for a society and its people to function.

Several fall editions of the paper also carried extended course descriptions by the new faculty. The overall tone would support the general intent of these six goals. For a course in black oratory, instructor Thomas Williams states, "The student should hope to attain tools which will teach him how to go about effectively changing his community; to attain revolutionary consciousness. He should hope to become an advocate of change in relationship to everything that is oppressing humanity." For black history there is the comment, "The course will deal with reevaluation of black history so as to achieve a certain political awareness within the student. History is important only in that it educates to the point of political awareness." In black politics, "The goal is to understand what there is as well as to change it." Fieldwork to fuse theory and practice and ensure desirable change becomes a part of the course. "To put a paper together which relates to the community and the local, state, national, and international struggle against oppression" is the goal of black journalism. Obviously a dispassionate account of the history of black people or the circumstances of black politics or black economics is not a major aim of such faculty and such courses.

As if these goals and educational activities were not enough to frighten the power structure, one of the black theorists extended the ultimate strategy:

> Black studies is only a microcosm of any particular college curriculum. The overall strategy of the department must be to unite all of the revolutionary forces of all of the departments of the college so we will be able to decentralize the colleges and the schools and return the knowledge and the control of its use to the people. . . . It is absurd to have the black studies department take the correct perspective and not move to bring about the same consciousness in other departments on campus. It is absurd for a student to be very active, vocal, and struggle-oriented in black studies and then go to his U.S. history class and sit passively while a racist professor mis-educates thirty or forty students. Black studies is a base from which to move like a mighty storm on all of the other departments to revolutionize them also.

Since this philosophy, this educational offering, and this classroom style violated most of the mores, ethics, procedures, and regulations customary to academic life, it was inevitable that the black students and their department and the college would again assume adversarial roles. As rumors about the nature of the educational operation, student power, and alleged coercive techniques used to bring faculty into line bubbled about, the college through President Hayakawa took the department head-on once again in the media. "A reign of terror" existed, stated Hayakawa at a press conference (which the deans, his administrative staff, and the Senate leadership had all warned against). When new Dean of Undergraduate Studies Urban Whitaker confirmed a wide range of student coercion of faculty which had led to the resignation of the student-selected department chairman, Lucy Jones, this allegation achieved considerable credibility. Later the BSU student coordinator of the black studies department, Clarence "Buz" Thomas, commented:

> The actions of Lucille Jones, in conjunction with her husband, Woodrow Jones, clearly show that they are in fact our enemies. The Central Committee and a few other students have known Lucille and her husband for about two years. We do not think this time that she is an agent provocateur, but the Joneses' ignorance and political naiveté are causing the same results as that of the pig, so therefore it does not make a damn bit of difference if they are pigs

> or not. The Black Students Union Central Committee takes the position that Lucille Jones and her accomplice, Woodrow Jones, have committed treasonous acts and are definitely our enemies at this time. You, the students (the people) must decide what must be done. The power is in the hands of the people.

Both Whitaker and Hayakawa also challenged the subprofessional character of the student-controlled department and the revolutionary perspective of the curriculum. A paragraph from a letter sent by President Hayakawa to a few members of the still unformed community advisory committee for black studies catches the substance of the administrative charges:

> A small group of militant students are insisting on controlling the administration and the content of the program, intimidating faculty and students, taking over classes for political indoctrination, resisting the faculty's right to select its administrative chairman, excluding nonblack students enrolled in black studies from attending departmental meetings, and a variety of other tactics. These tactics add to the already almost insurmountable difficulties we face in establishing a viable and distinguished program of black studies.

As the tactics of escalation were resumed, the administration threatened to drop all teaching assistants and faculty from the payroll unless the faculty would meet with the administration to clear lines of responsibility. It also considered closing the department and distributing the courses to other departments unless the black students obeyed college regulations. President Hayakawa was within hours of announcing this dissolution before he was dissuaded by his academic administrators. Through all of these alleged violations of academic freedom and professional ethics, the faculty of San Francisco State remained strangely mute, either in a comatose state after the horror of the previous year or simply not willing to challenge the black students and thus appear to be on the side of Hayakawa.

Thus, the poststrike period reveals that few of the fundamental issues that separate State's black students and the academic world have been settled and that the college continues to be dominated and convulsed by this conflict. To this point the militant black students have chosen to use the momentum of their strike and their large power base to openly challenge the system in peaceful ways and to dare it to cope with them. After avoiding the problem for a long while, the administration finally picked up the gauntlet. Whether a combination of irreconcilable positions, the constant exposure to and use of the media in the conflict resolution, and the face-saving needs of both parties will lead to a gradual escalation and another mass confrontation remains for future determination. Spring enrollment in the black studies department dropped 52 per cent. Apparently the redundant, revolutionary curriculum lost some of its appeal for a group still somewhat economically upwardly mobile.

The black community could still choose to go back within the system and use the system and its relative freedom and obscurity to achieve many of their goals, but at a slower than "now" pace. The academic community, on the other hand, could choose to modify some of its past imperatives in a way that would accept many of the black desires as legitimate needs for an admittedly highly oppressed segment of the population. The politicization of this issue and all of higher education makes a rational and viable choice extremely difficult.

A major casualty of the year of the strike was the activist, reformist student government that had so attracted national publicity in prior years. Associated Students President Russell Bass began the year with the most extensive and progressive goals of any student leader of the past decade. By December the Associated Students was scarcely visible amidst the smoke of battle. By January Bass and Company had apparently packed their tents and quietly stolen away. The death blow was dealt by President Hayakawa in the spring semester when he facilitated the government's freezing of all student body funds. Without "bread," programs could not be sustained and student energies could not be enlisted. For all practical purposes the official student body government then became defunct.

Students learned what faculty were slowly grasping: in the new style of conflict resolution through confrontations, the official governmental structures that students and faculty had been gradually developing in more peaceful times simply had little purpose or capacity. Whatever they were designed to produce—with their committees and constitutions and resolutions and minutes and parliamentary procedures and dialogue—had little relevance once a hard-line president, the police, and the governor had joined battle with the black communities, radical students, and striking AFT faculty. In such a context the slogan "you're either for us or against us" seemed to apply and left little neutral territory for those who desired to be above the fray. Such neutrality was no great temptation for the reformist student body leaders: not to join the student strike in opposing Hayakawa and the police would have left them with absolutely no credibility. So Bass and his student leaders allied with the white and black radicals—and got lost among the revolutionary legions. Their style had little contribution to make to a physical struggle. And, in making the token gesture of strike support, the official student body organization became the sworn enemy of the power structure.

When the students attempted to use their funds and some of their prior powers to further the strike, President Hayakawa stopped them cold. Funds were impounded, the student mouthpiece, the *Daily Gater,* was gagged, and the legitimacy of Bass and his student government was simply not recognized. Cries of illegality fell on deaf ears. The faculty, which in times past might have taken procedural "civil liberties" stands, was so polarized and entrapped in its own struggle that it had neither the inclination nor the power to aid the students.

Prior to their strike support, the Associated Students had troubled the chancellor and the trustees with the range and style of their activities. For instance, student control through private corporations of the college cafeteria and bookstore and their large budgets did not seem efficient or desirable to the business-oriented board. Use of profits for bail funds for students accused of militant campus behavior might be currently legal, but the trustees did not condone this action—and the laws could be changed. The Hayakawa assertion that the black militants were using student body funds to buy guns and further the revolution met with sympathy in power circles. "Pornography" in the student press made some trustees wonder who was running the shop. Now official student government support of a revolt against the system settled the issue in the minds of many trustees. They moved in powerfully to create rules and regulations that not only governed specific student activities but also vested ultimate control of student corporations and their activities in the president of the college. Thus, student freedom to control many of their own institutions and their own behavior, while progressing in other systems, regressed in the California State Colleges. No small contribution to this regression was made by the Associated Students at San Francisco State and their testing of the limits before and during the strike. Much that was hopeful and enlightened disappeared in the strike rubble. The Experimental College ceased to exist. The new permissive general education experiment that in many ways was a response to student leadership went into operation in the fall semester, 1969, without the supportive machinery of the student government or much faculty enthusiasm. Student evaluations of faculty performance through *MAX* terminated. Under Summerskill, students had a significant majority influence in all cases of student discipline; under Hayakawa, student perspective might well have slight influence on the final decision. The Student Union was another casualty of the struggle, as were the *Daily Gater* and *Open Process*. Without college funds the *Gater* has limped along and taken on a severe radical cast. The weathervane student personnel services reflected the new dispensation when the recently appointed black Dean of Student Activities Elmer Cooper was replaced by the Faculty Renaissance president, William Harkness of the physical education department. Permissiveness, student power, and the soft line in this central area of student aspirations were replaced by laws, order, and a philosophy receptive to President Hayakawa. The monopoly of hip activities counselors was broken by recruits from the Hayakawa youth organization, the Committee for an Academic Environment.

After the spring 1968 outbreak, during the final days of the Summerskill administration, the Academic Senate and the administration had responded with the prospect of a constitutional convention to reassess the power distribution between faculty, students, and administrators. The obvious intent of the convention was to forestall future confrontations by recognizing the new campus climate across the nation and giving students a more responsible and powerful role in policy determination. As the Year of the Strike rolled on, the constitutional convention appeared to be a mere reformist hope that was desired by neither the newly powerful radicals nor the management-oriented administration. Like many "policies" and resolutions during that period of action, the convention slipped into the limbo of pious verbalizations. While Stanford, Princeton, Columbia, Colby, and many other colleges were moving into more cooperative faculty-student-administrative stances to ameliorate the growing tensions, San Francisco State slipped back into a rigid, hierarchical posture that could produce only sullen acquiescence or adversarial relationships. The emotions of the strike, the rigid, self-righteous use of blatant power by both sides seemed to leave no alternatives. Faculty and administrators had been both slow to respond to legitimate grievances and reluctant to apply restraints to egregious excesses. When the lessons finally were grasped, a point of no return had been reached.

An ironical postscript to the incident is provided by the fact that the Senate persuaded the administration to invest more than a half-time faculty position in planning the convention, yet the person chosen for that leadership employed most of his energies during the period leading the AFT strike.

Hayakawa applied the coup de grace to the Associated Students when he vetoed on procedural grounds a student body election that returned an activist slate responsive to the radicalized student body and ordered the administration, not the students, to conduct a second election. This interference with their own lives proved too much for the activists and they proceeded to boycott the Hayakawa election. Naturally this guaranteed the election of the slate responsive to the president. In choosing to challenge through the courts President Hayakawa's authority to take such action, these same activists assured their own ultimate defeat. San Francisco State's student body affairs, such as they are, are being governed by a group of dubious legitimacy, possessing virtually no funds and receiving little student support.

For the administration this could well turn into a Pyrrhic victory. Most analysts of the student unrest phenomenon on American campuses recognize that the most constructive way to avoid confrontations involves more, not less, student involvement in the governance of student lives and the campus. By virtue of the excesses of recent student body leaders at State, the cooption of these leaders by the radical movement, and the consequent administrative repression, this option of cooperative student-faculty-administrative efforts to construct a college adequate to the times seems to be disappearing. The alternatives of apathy and disintegration or alternating confrontations and repression loom starkly before the college.

Throughout the spring and fall poststrike semesters of 1969 the radical white students were an inconsequential force on the campus. The student strike had been essentially the black students' operation: SDS and allies acted primarily as an auxiliary unit, the shock troops, the masses—not the vanguard. Serving in a peripheral relationship for such a long period enhanced neither the power nor the organization of these white radicals. Their style responded best to crises, emphasized spontaneity, and focused on short intervals. When the AFT intervention in the strike lessened the confrontation and produced a deserted campus, the best the radicals could do was march aimlessly in the picket lines, wondering what happened to their revolution. Settlement conferences ignored them. Much of their energies in the spring and summer were spent in their abortive legal defense in the courts. What they had fervently hoped would be a spotlighted pulpit to expose the repressive tactics of the Establishment turned into a cross for their crucifixion. Instead of redirecting their newly radicalized student legions against the perfect symbol of repressive control, Hayakawa, they day and night scrounged money and support for their trials. Many leaders received fines, jail sentences, and probation. Once in the spring the radicals marched on the Administration Building in hopes of reviving the struggle, but even the media gave them scant footage.

The chaos, the disruption, the prolonged struggle, the punishment, the costs: all had proved too much. Massive police intervention had produced the cherished radicalization of thousands of students but the movement had no strength or status to capitalize on this new disenchanted base. Everybody had been burned, and all pulled back from the flames. The essential strategy had failed. Middle-class white students had too much to gain by acquiring their degrees and becoming part of the system on their own terms.

Ideological splits completed the disarray of the white radicals. A Joe Hill caucus warred with a Worker-Student Alliance. Some preached the campus was not the proper seedbed for the revolution and that even racism and the Vietnam war were not the prime issues. Instead, an alliance of all the oppressed—workers, students, women, the black, the brown—which could be aimed at the repressive power structure and its capitalistic-imperialistic economic base had the only hope of revolutionary success. As SDS fractionalized into at least three or four segments nationally, San Francisco State radicals split, attacked each other, withdrew, and wandered aimlessly. Battle strategies were replaced by the war of the leaflets. General Electric or Safeway replaced President Hayakawa as a visible target when the diminished radical leadership attempted to project itself into a national revolutionary posture.

Nary a bullhorn was heard throughout the campus. John Levin was nowhere to be seen; Alex Forman obediently marched to class rather than on the Administration Building; Greg deGiere did his time in jail. Only a few, such as the ubiquitous rebel Gene Marchi, continued unabated their careers as full-time activists. Those who had made the faculty and administrators quake for over two years now had blown the scene or were lost in the mass of 18,000. Repression gained a triumph, if only temporarily.

When Local 1352 voted to go back to teaching it was with the full understanding that only the locale and tactics of the struggle would change, not the goals or the intensity. "We'll operate within rather than without!" proclaimed the AFT Executive Committee. But these union leaders had not calculated correctly the emerging general faculty hostility toward the AFT, the shift toward administrative control and new rules, or the diminished enthusiasm within their own ranks for continued disruption and attack. Sustained warfare is not a comfortable academic stance. By the end of the semester the thrust of the AFT had been so blunted that its membership had dropped from about 390 at the peak of the strike to an August total of 201. Once again the union found itself a small minority of the faculty, a base for the young, the dedicated, the embittered—a broad-spectrum radical group fighting the battle of the Vietnam war, racism, student power, civil rights, capitalistic repression, local campus autonomy, and due process as well as the traditional organized labor objective of collective bargaining for economic benefits.

The first disillusionment for the AFT members came when they returned to the college and attempted to channel their new-found strike power into the decision-making procedures of the college. They persuaded the Senate to oppose Hayakawa's student disciplinary process only to discover that the Senate no longer had power. When they took the same issue before the faculty and won a resounding faculty endorsement, they learned that their acting president was not swayed even by faculty meeting votes. When they attempted to dominate the grievance and disciplinary panel and committees with devoted union members and to use this intricate legal machinery to indict Hayakawa's behavior or to protect their own membership against charges of unprofessional behavior or nonrehiring, they sadly found out that the president considered these "final" adjudications only advisory to him. And finally, when their two representatives on the Presidential Selection Committee became a leading force in the unanimous opposition to Hayakawa as permanent president, they and the faculty discovered that the trustees had changed the rules of the game and faculty were no longer important in the choice of their leader.

Even in the protected departmental and school domains union faculty were to learn that they could dominate the vote but lose the war at an administrative level. In the past the entire faculty would have united in protection of these Senate, faculty, grievance committee, or Presidential Selection Committee privileges. Following the trauma of the strike, faculty would unite effectively on nothing, act against administrative hegemony never. The battle from within became shadow-boxing against an elusive opponent, an empty gesture that produced few victories but many angry statements and resolutions.

One other union effort to control the faculty machinery proved misguided and naive. Although the Academic Senate had lapsed into impotency during much of the strike and did not loom large in President Hayakawa's view of the levers of power, its domination could at least have some nuisance value in the vendetta between the AFT and President Hayakawa and some moral leverage as faculty attempted to reclaim their rights. With this in mind the union proceeded to attempt to capture the body by running a slate of nominees for the spring at-large elections. All strikers were told in writing where their loyalties lay, a unique gesture in the college's political history. This party-line politicking and the AFT's strike actions touched off a conservative backlash slate which overwhelmed the AFT nominees. Although there were other candidates in the election, ballots tended to be party-line choices. The majority of the faculty again indicated that they disapproved of the strike and its sponsoring agency, even to the point of voting for conservative or unknown representatives. For San Francisco State College's faculty, this was a major reorientation.

The union had burned its bridge to the middle-ground faculty. When those who had joined the union primarily to protest the police violence, the impossible teaching conditions, and President Hayakawa's repressive leadership abandoned the organization in large numbers, leaving the leadership basically in the hands of those for whom unionism was a way of life, this leadership and its supporters among the new faculty continued to alienate many faculty with shrill cries and adamant, one-dimensional policies. All literature, all acts, all energies were focused on Reagan-Dumke-Hayakawa atrocity stories. Although in many cases these indictments had much basis in fact and considerable potential for faculty sympathy, AFT advocacy in typical AFT militant style ensured faculty inaction. The faculty appeared to prefer castration by the power structure to common allegiance with the AFT in quest of potency. Striking under the strike's circumstances, picketing, self-righteous advocacy, hostility toward nonstriking colleagues, antiinstitutional tactics, and common cause with white and black student militants had alienated large numbers of average academicians. When President Hayakawa addressed the faculty at the beginning of the fall semester, the auditorium was virtually filled.

Even within loyalist ranks, the AFT discovered energy, devotion, and commitment rare qualities. The young seemed most involved. In recognition of this fact the membership chose four nontenured unionists to serve on the Executive Committee and to provide leadership against Hayakawa during the critical poststrike year. Late in the fall semester, 1969, this presented the union with its next serious challenge: President Hayakawa overrulled the department and school reappointment process in three of these cases and gave these faculty terminal appointments pending thorough investigations of alleged unworthy conduct. The fourth nontenured Executive Committee member, President Erwin Kelly, was terminated within the school administrative levels. Along with seventeen other cases of AFT members who were denied reappointment or tenure at some levels of faculty and administrative power within the departments, schools, or college, these instances of alleged union-busting threaten to ensnarl the college in another full-fledged confrontation. President Hayakawa's enmity toward the union is a matter of the record; frequently he has stated that heads must roll because of unprofessional activity and as a lesson to the AFT. His unhappiness with the decision pressed on him by the Council of Academic Deans and the Trustee Liaison Committee not to fire the entire group of strikers is substantiated by many in responsible positions. And the AFT lawyer, Victor Van Bourg, had assured the union that reprisals were a common form of poststrike intimidation and that nontenured strikers would be particularly vulnerable. Never in recent years had San Francisco State's president employed his final powers on personnel decisions so decisively. Much of the union's energies were of necessity employed during the spring semester, 1970, challenging these decisions just as the militant students' force was concentrated in the spring semester, 1969, on the legal defense of those arrested during the strike.

In the issues of political reprisals and the concentration of ultimate personnel powers in the hands of one man, especially a man not chosen by the faculty as its president, the entire faculty has an interest. Whether from its defeat in the strike the union learned that it needs to work in a style that can enlist majority faculty support will be tested in the ensuing battle. Early signs indicate a rededication to union tactics and student alliances, tactics and alliances that tend to split the faculty not in terms of the issues but along the old, emotionally laden prostrike, antistrike axis. Whether the middle-ground faculty learned the lesson that AFT-Hayakawa polarizations leave them no rational recourse will be reflected in their posture and active response to this vital problem.

At the statewide level the dangers of wildcat action and the need for 50.1 per cent faculty support in order to achieve the power of collective bargaining have had their influence. Both the AFT and the ACSCP organizations are promoting a merger to eliminate jurisdictional hassles now that they both are committed to collective bargaining as a primary goal. Faculty support has been halting. If such a merger occurs, the new organization should be well on the path toward majority faculty membership and in a position, if it can maintain party discipline, to press for a collective bargaining election. The eventual alignment of such a Union of Associated Professors with organized labor remains to be thrashed through, but the AFT is convinced it is the most dynamic group and that it will prevail. Ultimately faculty might need to choose between an unofficial organization of this nature and the comprehensive, official Statewide Academic Senate if such an election is forced. The power structure of California naturally is not receptive to modifying the law so as to make collective bargaining for such public employees possible, and the public through its legislative representatives is in a mood to be adamant on the issue.

The rhetoric of Local 1352's president, Erwin Kelly, indicates some forces in this union are finally interested in moving in this unified, political direction:

> Most importantly, the union has achieved a tentative resolution of that basic issue that has from time immemorial plagued all fledgling trade unions (and been especially severe with teacher's unions)—which is more important: to be a "trade union" or a political organization? . . . Are we to put "bread and butter" or "social uplift" at the top of our priority list? At this moment the answer seems clear—without a union, without collective bargaining, political action can be made impossible by a repressive administration. The issue is no longer political action as trade unionism, but it has become the achievement of trade unionism in order to continue political action. Local 1352 will always be political—its membership will make certain of that; but also it must try to become the voice of the majority of the faculty.

Whether the union's membership can overcome its own liberal-radical commitments and past history so as to achieve majority faculty support is questionable.

The strike at San Francisco State was critical in the strategy to press for one organization committed to collective bargaining, and it could be crucial in the eventual outcome to unite and, if united, to achieve bargaining rights. Competing organizations for activist faculty loyalties had become a luxury faculty could not afford. San Francisco's strike convinced faculty leadership that the political forces in the state would never bend to the pressures of a divided faculty, especially a unilateral, minority action at one campus. And so the drive to become united was accelerated.

But while the AFT strike revealed the adamancy and power of the Establishment to faculty, it also disenchanted many middle-ground faculty with militant tactics, especially when they seemed to be controlled by groups who had varied motives and interests. This disenchantment could well handicap the movement to merge for self-protection, a movement that more and more faculty were inclined to support prior to the student disruptions and the AFT strike at State. The public hostility toward faculty militancy that was nourished by events at San Francisco—and pronouncements by Governor Reagan and President Hayakawa—might prove the death blow to this movement for collective bargaining.

If the San Francisco State experience is any barometer, the fact to be learned is that college faculty have little stomach for the travail of striking and collective bargaining negotiations. When these appeared the only alternative to impotency in traumatic, violent circumstances, they were chosen and pursued with dedication and self-sacrifice by a considerable number. But when circumstances became more routine, the union lapsed into a rear-guard protest to which few on the faculty responded with any real sense of commitment. Unless rampant repressions are ventured by those in power, this apathy and withdrawal could well become the faculty posture. However, those in authority seem quite capable of fomenting a full-scale rebellion even among such torpid troops. The urge for reprisals and decimation of faculty power looms large in the hearts of many now in a position to take such actions.

For nine years the trustees of the California State Colleges had made uneasy compromises with the historical, nationwide movement for faculty power. Democracy in government appealed only slightly to this combine of lawyers and business executives, but it seemed the direction the tides were moving. Concessions were made grudgingly, yet some resulted in a major sharing of power. Most lay governing boards desire to at least inflict their philosophy upon a college by taking a dominant role in the choice of the college president. In the California State College system, faculty presidential selection committees had achieved rare advise-and-consent prerogatives. San Francisco State's Academic Senate operated with a constitution approved formally by former President Paul Dodd, and tacitly by succeeding presidents, whereby the Senate had delegated to it by the president his wide powers for policy formation. But this authority was rarely tested, and throughout the system the sharing of powers had more shadow than substance to it. At times the statewide Academic Senate had considered pressing for private status and support, so disillusioned had it become with the trappings but not the reality of meaningful involvement in decision-making.

With the election of Reagan and the development of a public opinion deeply interested in higher education and hostile to faculty and students, an opportunity and a commitment developed to reverse this dilution of managerial power. The first stage in the plan consisted of the appointment of trustees more responsive to the governor and his point of view. Within two years the balance of power was reversed and the governor had a clear majority willing and able to place faculty in their proper subordinate status.

Dumke, who in times past took credit for the democratization of his college but more often blunted these thrusts in a bumbling fashion, now saw the chance to assume his natural prerogatives and impose his, the trustees', and the public imprint on the eighteen colleges. The fact that his job hung in the balance as a result of a concatenation of inept administrative decisions made him a willing instrument of this drive to ensure that decisions would be made at higher levels and passed down in an orderly and responsible way: from Governor Reagan to the trustees to the chancellor to the presidents to the deans to the department chairmen to the faculty.

San Francisco State under the administration of Acting President Hayakawa offered an excellent example for the testing of the new regime. Its faculty was the most obstreperous. Its condition could justify extreme measures. Its president had the inclination to operate in a managerial fashion, and public backing made resistance to his decrees difficult. And, finally, the student and faculty opposition was in complete disarray, polarized, demoralized, and impotent. The decline of faculty and student power and the ascendancy of Hayakawa and a highly managerial system of control became the dominant reality at San Francisco State College in the aftermath period. President Hayakawa moved his own Faculty Renaissance team into key administrative slots with scarcely a murmur from the Academic Senate about consultation. In the critical issue of disciplinary procedures for students accused by the administration of unlawful student behavior, the president refused to delegate his final authority to any other group. Decisions reached by the convoluted faculty grievance and disciplinary process had no impact on Hayakawa unless he desired to go along with the verdicts. In the fall he invoked a new version of these procedures on an interim basis with no Senate dissent. His purge of the Associated Students through a freezing of funds and his formal discontinuation of the *Gater* were achieved without faculty opposition. Although the Senate resolved to demand a new student body election in the fall to supersede the two disputed elections that endorsed differing slates of officers, the court order supporting the Hayakawa administrative election process went unchallenged.

When the Academic Senate demanded to know if President Hayakawa would recognize its constitutional legislative powers, he bluntly told the body these were powers he did not choose to delegate. The Senate continued to operate under what was now an illegal constitution. The president's aides played a key role in the conservative takeover of the Senate and its Executive Committee in the spring semester elections. From then on the Senate refused to engage in the customary faculty-administration jockeying for power. The culmination of this trustee-Hayakawa diminution of previously accepted faculty rights came when the trustees totally disregarded prior agreements with the faculty on the presidential selection process and appointed Hayakawa permanent president of San Francisco State College despite unanimous opposition to the choice by the faculty committee. The faculty committee made this action easier when it cavalierly recommended only three individuals to the trustees, all black, and two of whom had few accepted qualifications and had assumed frequent adversarial stances vis-à-vis the trustees. If L. von Sacher-Masoch had been directing their activities, the faculty could not have been more successful.

In the fall semester, 1969, President Hayakawa began to temporize with some agreements in the student settlement document that he had reluctantly allowed the faculty committee representing him to sign in March. Again, there was no outburst from the faculty. Even those who had gone on strike to ensure a settlement of the ethnic student grievances acceptable to the TWLF were able to mount no effective opposition. When one of the AFT's own strikers, Morgan Pinney, had been denied rehiring by the School of Business because he came back a day late, the union protested but to no avail. Much union energy was consumed in the reinstatement process before the State Personnel Board, and here President Hayakawa, Chancellor Dumke, and the trustees hesitantly supported the faculty strike settlement. All faculty who had not left the college or were not being terminated were reinstated with full benefits. But even here the delay had lost for several faculty strikers their sabbatical leaves for the following year.

In the contest between the black studies department and the administration in the fall semester, President Hayakawa assumed full authority for challenging the infringements on academic freedom, professional ethics, and curricular objectivity. The faculty became spectators quite willingly.

The ultimate shift from a regularized democratic administration to final managerial controls in the hands of the president was reflected in President Hayakawa's action to deny reappointment and tenure to a large number of AFT members. Some were given terminal appointments with a right of further investigation by the administration; others were not rehired by administrative action within the schools. This mass action had no precedent in recent years at the college. Both the statewide Academic Senate and the local Senate had taken positions opposing termination of services due to strike activities. The statewide body had even resolved to assume the leadership in a one-day walkout should faculty be fired for striking. Although no clear-cut proof could be offered that the administrative refusal to rehire had been motivated by a desire to threaten union activities, the evidence had circumstantial cogency. As of March 1970 no faculty movement to challenge this action was discernible except within AFT ranks. The Senate did investigate the procedures and finally referred the issue to a newly formed Academic Freedom Committee. By these actions and in these ways, President Hayakawa acted for himself and the governor, the trustees, and the chancellor in taking firm control of a college previously noted for its sharing of power between faculty and administrators. By simply asserting his powers, Hayakawa left it to the faculty to counter his actions. The faculty discovered that it had no power, unity, or inclination for renewing the struggle. Hayakawa had defeated the militant faction during the strike when it appeared at times that he had virtually no support within the college and almost no college in operation. To the victor belonged the spoils. He took them with zest.

President Hayakawa was aided in this takeover by his shrewd

continuation of a style that concentrated not on internal administrative details but rather on mass appeal through oversimplified, vivid, self-righteous depiction of the issues on television, in the headlines, and in speeches. His speaking fee went up to $1,500 and $2,500. The demand for his services never declined. Legislators vied with each other to have him keynote their preelection testimonial dinners. Everywhere he went outside of the campus he was recognized and acclaimed. Political rumor shifted from emphasizing his possible candidancy for the U. S. Senate to implying that he might well replace Dumke as chancellor.

In this context faculty opposition was unrealistic, and even the activists recognized this and immersed themselves in their teaching or other causes. For in the last analysis, what could they do? If the president cared to press on any issue, the only fundamental recourse was collective withdrawal of services or some variant harassment. Few had any desire for a rerun of such disruptions. Rather than drift into such a possibility, the faculty surrendered without even a series of *whereases* and a rhetorical *resolve*. At no point did they attempt to assume their prior role of equality in decision-making. The Academic Senate took on the more traditional posture of a debating society. President Hayakawa, unlike his predecessors, did not deign to accord it recognition even by his presence. Many of the Senate's achievements in the past had been illusory. When finally challenged by presidential power, the Senate discovered that it had no effective machinery for creating viable alternative policies and no capacity to enlist the full support of a disenchanted faculty.

The demolition of the vestiges of faculty power moved from the campus to the trustees and the Legislature in the aftermath of the San Francisco strike. The trustees took under consideration the possibility of taking back final authority for appointment and tenure decisions, as the regents at the University of California had actually done. They also seriously contemplated a revised salary system that, under the cover of "merit evaluations," would give the administration the power every year to impose economic sanctions on the recalcitrant professors. Faculty presidential selection committees were diluted by the addition of lay members, or bypassed by the arbitrary selection of acting president, or completely disregarded.

As of February 1970, the system was searching for replacements for presidents who had resigned at four colleges: Long Beach, Sacramnto, Fresno, and Sonoma. Administrators were told to create a new decision-making process that would clearly place authority and responsibility back in the administrative chain of command. By chancellor fiat, it was declared unprofessional for faculty to dismiss classes for the Vietnam moratoriums and presidents were told they must take disciplinary action against such faculty. Chancellor Dumke reflected this stern new mood in a speech he delivered to the elite Commonwealth Club in San Francisco on December 12, 1969:

> The traditional forms of academic governance simply don't work well under present conditions. When structured violence erupts, there is no time to call a committee and debate the issue. When human life and property are assaulted or endangered, somebody must be held responsible, clearly and promptly, and that person's authority must be commensurate with his responsibility. . . . As you can see, I am going against McGeorge Bundy and David Riesman and the dozens of other analysts of academe who inevitably return to the same old solution—all our questions will be answered if we put more power in the hands of the faculty. I say they won't. Nor will we answer our problems by putting more power into the hands of students. Further diffusion of responsibility is no answer, I assure you.

Besides casting his vote for managerial controls, Dumke struck powerfully against the politicization of the university under the banner of relevancy:

> The campus has ceased to be objective. It has joined in the fray. It has become institutionally partisan about the Vietnam war and our foreign policy, about urban problems, about poverty, about racial issues. Some of these causes may well be noble and worthy, but no matter how virtuous the cause, the scholar cannot afford to take sides. If he does, he ceases to be a scholar. . . . If the campus enters politics, no force under heaven can keep politics from entering the campus. . . . The institution, the college or the university, must remain pure and unsullied and above the battle.

Between Dumke's goal of remaining "pure and unsullied" and the black student objective "to strive to build a socialist society," a chasm of considerable proportions existed.

Although President Hayakawa's style of leadership gave his fellow administrators surcease from faculty pressures, it also burdened them with a wide range of messy problems. Many of these problems had their roots in a system attempting to educate a burgeoning mass of students while at the same time refusing to fund the system with money and facilities. The politicization of the system, the difficulties of lay control, and the confused leadership in the Chancellor's Office added to the problem. But for all of these extramural handicaps, President Hayakawa compounded the difficulties with his unique approach to college administration. Essentially he was attempting to rule without the support of his basic faculty constituency. A few faculty rallied to his banner in an attempt to preserve his values, reverse the previous "ultraliberal" tendencies of the college and place orderly procedures and the accepted academic goals of higher education back at the center of the institution. Most, however, sat back to watch the struggle between Hayakawa and the militant minority who vigorously opposed him. Few would enlist in any administrative move to solve the college's larger problems. Under any circumstances such noninvolvement threatened healthy institutional development. Given the pressing college dilemmas of more students desiring admission than could be accommodated, underfinancing, a permissive new general education program, a backlog of construction priorities, aggressive and complicated ethnic studies and Educational Opportunity Programs, and sticky issues of student behavior and professional faculty ethics, it is doubtful that the administration in its splendid isolation will be able to lead the necesary institutional changes.

Within the administrative echelons the new style has presented complications. Many department chairmen and deans of schools still reflect a philosophy that emphasizes primary loyalty to their faculty colleagues not to administrative authority. A shift in this orientation is difficult given the deep hostility toward Hayakawa of many of the faculty with whom the chairman and the deans must work. It is also complicated by the inexperience of the upper echelon and the sense of transiency that it radiates. A general mood of distrust permeates the operation, a mood that seems to say, "Protect your own area, who knows who will be in charge tomorrow." President Hayakawa's lack of concern with the college's fundamental administrative operations and frequent absences from the campus add to the uneasiness. Conditions in the system and the college have created a basically negative attitude: the central administration and the deans seem to have little enthusiasm for President Hayakawa, each other, the AFT, the Academic Senate, the faculty, the BSU, the students, the chancellor, the trustees or the governor. It is hardly a milieu for complicated problem solving.

A new administrative mood has developed at the college since Hayakawa renounced his political ambitions by stating that he was not a candidate for either the U.S. Senate or the superintendent of public instruction. Until this point, vice-presidents, deans, chairmen, and the Academic Senate generally treated him as a passing phenomenon—probably more transient than even the run of previous presidents. You coped with him, but you did not significantly modify policies or working relationships.

But now that President Hayakawa has begun to focus his energies and personality upon the college that he is supposed to lead, new vibrations pulse through the institution. The president has displayed some real concern with basic policies and institutional operations. If these policies or the administrators supposedly responsible for developing and implementing them are not producing—or do not reflect the president's emerging administrative philosophy—questions are being asked. This is a relatively new phenomenon at San Francisco State College. Way back to the presidency of Dumke in 1961 no central administrative force has radiated through the college. Whenever Hayakawa has not been pleased with the answers to his questions, he has begun to take steps to bring in new top-level personnel. One of his problems in this administrative reshuffling is that only faculty of a particular persuasion have been willing to consider working for him. This skews the orientation of the administration and denies it much faculty support. In many ways Hayakawa is beginning to employ an administrative style reminiscent of that of J. Paul Leonard, the benevolent paternalist whose managerial instincts produced the ground swell for faculty government.

One would think that the thirteen-year tradition of faculty power, augmented by a new faculty of greater distinction and encompassing younger elements committed to democratic forms, would cause a powerful reaction against this swing back to managerial controls. But it might well be that the shock of the Year of the Strike and the fundamental faculty urge to be unconcerned with much more than their private academic lives will mute a rebellion. Increasing numbers of faculty seem to sense that Hayakawa's hard line has temporarily given them a relatively peaceful, rational campus on which to pursue their careers, and they tacitly have been acquiescing in his tough line and tight control as a price to be paid in pursuit of tranquility and a job. Such relationships might endure for a while if no new powerful challenges to the institutional operation are mounted, forcing a new, fundamental moral reassessment. It is difficult to imagine such a climate fostering the educational innovation and cooperation necessary to give the college distinction in the current troubled society.

Now that the need to ride roughshod over student and faculty protests has receded for a period, President Hayakawa has also begun to display a flexibility in responding to certain differing points of view that few would have imagined him capable of a year ago. He is obviously more confident and secure in his role, and his ingrained needs to appear progressive, reasonable, and appreciated have reasserted themselves. In this he is not unlike Reagan, who, when not using the media to promote his political philosophy, has displayed a surprising fluidity. Both, of course, are impressionable only within clear parameters.

One of the most pervasive and destructive strike phenomena was the bitterness and alienation between striking and nonstriking faculty. Many lifelong friends refused to speak to each other. The estrangement colored departmental business as well as social intercourse. As issues came up in departmental meetings, all too often the faculty would split into two camps: strikers versus nonstrikers. Self-righteousness and recriminations were the order of the day. Many strikers were convinced their colleagues were being punitive. Several departments such as psychology, economics, sociology, and interdisciplinary studies in education were so evenly split that essential decisions strained resources. Caucuses would form and party-line votes were common. Selection to the all important hiring, retention, tenure, and promotion committees became pivotal: personnel decisions, faculty careers hung in the balance. Chairmen got caught in the middle between the two factions. Casual rules of operation turned into bitterly contested parliamentary challenges. Rules could shift back and forth depending on who happened to be absent or present at a particular meeting. Appeals were made to the upper echelons. Unwittingly this led to the withering of certain faculty prerogatives that neither faction desired—but preferred if it meant defeating the "enemy" in a certain instance. Other departments—philosophy, speech, English—had heavy majorities of strikers; others, such as biology, history, political science, music, business, physical education, and chemistry, had heavy majorities of nonstrikers. In such instances the minority opposition felt highly threatened as the majority might totally disregard their rights.

This climate of conflict, mistrust, hostility pervaded much of the college's operation during the spring semester. The customary summer hegira healed many wounds, but the scars remained. Interpersonal tension remained the dominant reality. The fragility of the fabric of trust that envelops most academic operations and relationships became apparent once it had been rent by the violence and hostility that accompanied the confrontations and the strike. By contrast the new grievance and disciplinary panel attempted to process fifty-seven separate requests for grievance hearings and disciplinary action in the spring semester, 1969. So overburdened were its members as they served on two, three, four cases, often simultaneously, that the panel had to be enlarged twice. Many challenges were bitter and highly adversarial. Use of the maximum number of peremptory challenges to prospective jurors became such a common practice that the panel became, by practice, split into three camps: those thought sympathetic to the AFT and hostile to Hayakawa, those deemed administrative fellow-travelers, and those few both sides thought impartial. Many litigants decided to request open hearings so their sympathizers among faculty and students could witness the repressive nature of the administration. All types of flaws in the process developed. In many cases the AFT litigant retained as his lawyer Victor Van Bourg, who it also turned out was simultaneously representing AFT members on the faculty jury he was addressing in their crucial hearing before the State Personnel Board for reinstatement of tenure and other prerogatives. These jurists had no minor conflict of interests. The panels had little experience with the quasi-legal nature of hearings that challenged the professional conduct of colleagues and consequently were often poorly administered. Unlimited energy was expended in these official recriminations and defenses with little personal or institutional profit. It could happen only in the aftermath of the unique conflagration that engulfed San Francisco State College.

The liberal student movement that had dominated student government at San Francisco State for the previous five years had as a major goal a change in the customary paternalistic, authoritarian attitude of faculty and administrators toward students. One of the basic contributions of the Experimental College had been to convince some students that they could direct their own education with profit without faculty domination and, where faculty were employed, that a new relationship of equality could develop that was mutually profitable. This trend was consonant with the national tendency for the younger generation to take control of their own lives.

Then the campus went on strike. Faculty and students marched together in the rain in rough clothes as they challenged the common enemy. There were no status differentiations on the line; no "Dr. McGuckin, would you please . . ." rang out from the endless pickets. In the coordinate planning of strategy and tactics for the strike, faculty participated often as no more than equals—and frequently as amateurs bowing to the shrewd proposals of the experienced student militants. This new relationship proved to be invigorating for some faculty, a catastrophe for others. It was only natural, then, when the strike was terminated and these liberated students returned to their classes that they would challenge the reimposition of the hallowed, paternalistic interaction of the "one who knew" and the "one who came to learn."

This movement for rethinking the relative status of student and faculty member was given momentum by another side effect of the strike. To some of the more perceptive student strikers the attempt to mobilize a heterogeneous mass of 3,000 to 5,000 students had inherent limitations. Loyalties did not rest with such inchoate groups; no sense of community existed; no opportunity was available for face-to-face interaction and involvement. But within departments many of these liabilities disappeared. Students did identify with their discipline and fellow majors; they did know each other and could communicate in this relationship. So why not organize into departmental caucuses? In an irregular fashion this departmental organization had been attempted in a number of cases in the past few years as a power base to attempt to make the curriculum, the teaching, and the personnel decisions more relevant to the clientele. For those in the forefront of this movement, this was a priority goal, for it was within the departments that critical power that could affect a student's life resided. If a commitment to student power could be achieved at this level, it could be a major victory for the strike.

Another concomitant of the strike had been the establishment of classes in faculty homes. Under these circumstances customary faculty attitudes disappeared and a spirit of informality and equality developed. Both students and faculty often found this attractive and discovered it was difficult and unrewarding to lapse into previous attitudes and relationships once classes were meeting back on campus.

This surge for more democratic student-faculty relationships was considered with sympathy by many faculty strikers. For some, such relationships were indigenous to their personal and academic styles already. Others found going back behind the podium adorned with coat and tie and expanding upon the esoteric erudition of their disciplines to obedient students a basic contradiction after the life of the strike. They joined their more liberal colleagues in pressing for departmental reforms. The most confused group consisted of those faculty who were political liberals or radicals but educational conservatives or reactionaries (not a small group in academe), whose minds caught the egalitarian message and rationale but whose emotional and professional fulfillment demanded the customary authoritarian relationship, or at least benevolent paternalism. And then there were those faculty for whom there was no confusion: faculty know, instruct, and demand; students are informed, listen, and obey.

Led by those students who could not return to even a benevolent paternalism in the classroom after the heady egalitarianism of the strike, and reinforced by sympathetic faculty, a poststrike movement burgeoned to enfranchise students in classes and in the departments. The philosophy department symbolically took its chairman's office and turned it into a student lounge. The almost unanimously prostrike speech department faculty engaged in extensive dialogue in mass democratic settings with their majors and emerged with an entirely new constitution for the department. At first this constitution vested final policy control in mass one-man, one-vote meetings of the few faculty and the many students, gave students a crucial role in faculty personnel decisions, and evolved a grading policy in which students could give themselves their own grades in all classes. Eventually it was brought to the attention of the department that these constitutional rules were in conflict with several college policies and so changes had to be made, but the speech department remains an important experiment in faculty-student equality and cooperation.

Since the large, powerful English department represented one of the strike bastions, with over 80 per cent of the faculty on strike or sympathetic, it was only natural that its English Student Union caucus would press for more student power. But the English department also has its full complement of faculty whose sense of role and academic standards dictate that faculty give the word, students listen—even if accompanied by libations in the faculty member's living room. Thus, the student-faculty English department poststrike confrontations found faculty members who weeks before had denounced administrative authority now making pleas for the natural prerogatives of the professor. At first the radical English majors pressed for participatory democracy procedures for all policy formulation. Eventually, however, they discovered that the subtle, long-acquired skill of the department's power structure in handling incipient revolts was able to contain their challenge. By the time student-faculty workshops and committees had pondered the possibilities and allowed a ventilation of dissatisfactions, a new power structure was created that at best gave students only a token voice in key decisions. This the students accepted and went on their individualistic paths.

In ways less obvious than a radical transformation of the balance of power, this movement in the English department for a curriculum and teaching procedures reflecting student wishes and needs had an impact. Requirements for majors changed, new courses oriented toward experimentation and relevant literature were created, and styles of teacher-student interaction were modified. Whether the insistent, voracious growth of faculty vested interests will obliterate this transient jungle clearing in ensuing years remains problematical. And equally questionable is the longevity of student urges to accept both the responsibility and freedom for their own education.

Departments in the School of Humanities were not the only areas affected by these democratic poststrike urges. In the social sciences and creative arts fields students formed guilds for their own advancement and protection. But the area to witness the largest reevaluation of its decision-making process was the entire School of Education. If the school and its faculty had reflected in operation only a portion of St. John Dewey's philosophy, one wonders why such a restructuring had been so long coming. This inclination for democracy in action had been bubbling in the school for some time prior to the strike. A faculty weekend workshop had earlier responded to the demands of a minority student delegation with a commitment to restructuring the school operation so as to involve students in policy formulation. The strike delayed implementation of this commitment, but in May 1969, a constitutional convention of equal numbers of faculty and students labored intermittently for two weeks to create a formal structure of decision-making that would reflect these values. The faculty endorsed the product of this convention. Beginning in the academic year 1969–70 an assembly of equal numbers of faculty and students had full power within the school to create policy in all areas except faculty personnel.

Within departments all committtees and meetings are required to allow student members in the ratio of one student for each two faculty members. Early reports on this operation indicate that considerable student and faculty apathy, now that people are no longer at the barricades, accompanied by the inevitable problem of student transiency, has slowed down the new order. As with many of these organizational attempts to share power with students, time and experimentation are needed to determine whether this is a passing panacea built upon guilt feelings and strike relationships or whether it represents indeed a viable system for restructuring higher education in a way that gives dignity and responsibility to students, and that will provide a learning environment that will elicit the greatest possible student growth. Since politics and power go everywhere entwined, the nature of student politics in this new setting, and student-faculty politics, could change the future of the School of Education.

Probably more important than official structural changes across the college will be the subtle modifications of the classroom climate as the individual professors redefine themselves and their mode of interacting with students and their disciplines in response to their insights from the strike and its causes. If this occurs on a large scale, it could outweigh many of the other consequences of the strike and transform San Francisco State in ways demanded by the nation's plight. The progress in this direction by the ethnic studies departments might well set the pace for other areas, or it might also create a backlash that will sweep aside other momentary advances.

A postscript to this aftermath phenomenon of experimentation in student-faculty democratization can be found in recent trustee and legislative debates. Those in both groups who have long seen self-indulgent faculty tendencies as the major roadblocks in improving the quality of education and in reducing the cost seem to be toying with channeled student power as a force that could constrain faculty finally to operate in the interests of students and their education. At the same time, these same representatives of California's power structure do not seem committed to democratic decision-making per se and are obviously worried that student power turned against faculty today could be student power turned against the Establishment and its vested interests tonight or tomorrow.

The challenge to the faculty and the academic administration in this poststrike period has been to channel and protect the creative insights and energy of these new educational thrusts while sorting out the transient, the shallow, the dross. Faculty apathy and hostility toward the administration and each other, and the declining credibility of the authority structure in the college, make this enhancement and this containment a dubious enterprise.

For most of the 1969–1970 academic year an Academic Senate committee probed alleged abuses and variations in grading standards as well as new faculty desires in this basic area of academic policy. Grading policy is also a fundamental concern of the liberated student. This probe was catalyzed by a terse letter from the regional accreditation team that had the misfortune to assess the campus during the strike period. With faculty grading reports held in escrow for a few weeks at the end of the fall semester, widespread and liberal use of the pass–no report option, grades allegedly being used in some instances to reward or punish a student for his strike allegiance rather than for his academic performance, and one-third of students responding to a poll indicating they received credit for from three to seven units for "little or no work," the committee had good reason to question the academic credibility of the college at this time. In consequence, the accreditation commission gave the college a minimal two-year accreditation. Coming on the heels of the loss of accreditation for the relatively new Master of Social Welfare degree, this shook the entire community.

President Hayakawa blamed the faculty, although steady rumors gave credence to the comment that the team also raised serious questions about the caliber of the college administration under the new president. The full details of the accreditation report have been kept secret. Most recently, Vice-President of Academic Affairs Donald Garrity persuaded the commission to disregard this poorly timed assessment and to initiate a new evaluation in 1970–71.

Many of the problems raised by the accrediting team and the college's own grading investigation are certain corollaries of the intense campus strife. Now that faculty have resolutely immersed themselves in their teaching and scholarly pursuits to the neglect of almost all extrainstitutional obligations, traditional standards should emerge. Whether the hopes of the liberated caucuses and the permissive, recently adopted general education pattern can be realized in this climate remains to be tested. Although much of that which characterized the cutting edge of San Francisco State disappeared during the turmoil, a basic, immutable reality at the college is that students are still going to classes and faculty are still teaching. But the bookstore reported almost a 50 per cent reduction in business during the spring semester, 1969.

These changes in administrative power, faculty government and interpersonal relations, union activism, student government, black and ethnic programs, white student dissent, and academic style and status represent the major consequences of the two years of confrontation and the Year of the Strike. Other residues contribute more to a mood than to categorization. Critical to this mood is a restless, disenchanted, aggressive student majority that currently bides its time pursuing idiosyncratic interests, but which has the power and the hostility to explode given the proper provocation. Little respect is apparent on the campus for authority or the amenities. Plastic knives and forks and paper plates and cups have given the Student Commons the atmosphere of a hole-in-the-wall restaurant. On the lawn in front of the Commons the grass is cluttered with used eating utensils, papers, leaflets. Packs of dogs snatch at one's lunch or race into classrooms. A Huey Newton speech blares from the BSU huts while a rock group's strident cacophony reverberates from building to building. By two o'clock the campus inhabitants begin to drift away to where the San Francisco action is. The mod, hip, frontier-style language, dress, and customs can no longer be treated as a passing aberration. One senses a life style deeply at odds with the institution, the curriculum, the over-thirty faculty. Somewhere, sometime, something is going to have to give.

These values seem catalyzed by the burgeoning influence of the large group of black and brown students. As affairs stand after the strike, institutional mores appear to be adapting to black culture rather than the black students' becoming acculturated by the customary bastion of middle-class America. Emerging values of State's special slice of the California student population are in tune with the spontaneity, activism, earthiness, emotions, and commitment of these new denizens of California higher education. Together, these dissenting, challenging white students and the aggressive, revolutionary black and brown brothers and sisters converge on an institutional structure that has been weakened by all the forces described in this case study. No longer does one observe much institutional resilience or personal commitment. Faculty teach and then leave. While there they lunch in their offices or are segregated at the AFT House or the Faculty Club. Should the students press in organized fashion, President Hayakawa could well be protecting the ramparts isolated from most of the faculty.

What is the prognosis? In the years ahead, San Francisco State will most likely witness revived confrontations as student-administration tolerance for each other is provoked by any of many threatening dissents or repressions, or it will become just another state college in what is becoming just another state college system. Such are the fruits of the cycle of events produced by widespread commitment to a self-righteous philosophy of "by any means necessary."

Appendix

Student-Faculty Opinion Survey

In May 1968, Kris McClusky, an administrative assistant later to become college registrar, sampled student and faculty opinion concerning the four-and-one-half-month campus crisis involving the student and faculty strikes. The student survey was administered to fifty out of 101 classes selected as a random sample from the total class schedule. The final sample of classes saw creative arts underrepresented by approximately 5 per cent and the sciences overrepresented about the same amount. The sample included 625 students, 3.8 per cent of the student body.

Surprisingly, composite class attendance on the days the student questionnaire was administered was only 54 per cent of students enrolled in the fifty classes. A similar questionnaire was mailed to a 20 per cent sample of voting faculty with a 42.7 per cent return. The School of Humanities was underrepresented (16.5 per cent of the faculty compared to 6.5 per cent of the survey); creative arts and science were overrepresented. The American Federation of Teachers, constituting 19.5 per cent of the voting faculty, was underrepresented with 14.5 per cent of those surveyed. The student and faculty samples overlapped in age; 10.8 per cent of students were twenty-nine years or older and 17.4 per cent of the faculty were in the twenty-five-to-thirty-two-year age group.

McClusky concludes that faculty and student perceptions were remarkably similar—for example, 57 per cent of students and 62 per cent of faculty strongly supported the fifteen strike demands or "supported most but not all" of the demands. Twenty-seven per cent of students and 34 per cent of faculty polled were "inclined to oppose" or "strongly opposed" the demands. Nineteen per cent of students and 21 per cent of faculty felt that the strike "was the only way to get a solution to the problem" of minority demands. At the other extreme, 21 per cent of the students and 19 per cent of the faculty believed "the strike was intended to destroy the institution rather than solve the problem." Thus, about one-fifth saw no alternative to the student strike and a contrasting fifth thought that striking groups intended to destroy the college.

If we add to the strong strike supporters those who thought the student strike "was a good idea but it went too far" (38.8 per cent of students and 28.0 per cent of faculty), opinion supporting the idea of a strike is 58 per cent among students and 49 per cent among faculty. Only 4 per cent of both students and faculty believed the student strike demands should have been non-negotiable, but another *37 per cent* of both students and faculty who responded believed making them non-negotiable was the only way student strikers could get the attention of the administration. The remaining three-fifths of students and faculty believed that the non-negotiability of the demands made workable solutions impossible, despite good faith on the administration's part (students 17 per cent, faculty 33 per cent); or the nature of the demands was calculated not to produce a solution (students 34 per cent, faculty 21 per cent); or 45 per cent of both believed no attempt should have been made to deal with demands which are non-negotiable. McClusky notes that estimates of the base of strike support range from Max Rafferty's "100 professional agitators and forty to fifty faculty members"[1] to Kingsley Widmer's "40 per cent of the 900 faculty and a probable plurality of the 18,000 students."[2] The latter figure appears much closer to the mark.

The sample shows that 6.8 per cent of students classed themselves as strikers, and another 15.8 per cent supported the strike with some action. Of the faculty responding, 29.2 per cent took active roles in strike support, of whom 14.6 per cent classed themselves as strikers. This figure is low because the AFT and the School of Humanities were underrepresented in the sample. As stated earlier, 57 per cent of students and 47 per cent of faculty who responded identified themselves as sympathetic to the idea of a strike by striking, engaging in strike support activities, or viewing the strike as "a good idea that went too far."

More than one-fourth of the students and one-fourth of the faculty accepted violence as a justifiable strike tactic. One in seven students and faculty believed "Black students and Third World students have special problems in dealing with the administration and have no other effective channel open to them" except violence. In short, combined with half again as many who selected a similar proposition stated differently, some 3,500 in the college community, responding six months after the student strike began, accepted violence as an aspect of a campus strike, if the survey findings can be generalized to the total population. Yet their college had weathered occasional bombings, arson, destruction of property and equipment, assault, firebombings of two faculty homes, and numerous police beatings over a period of four months.[3]

McClusky's study probably *understates* the militant views within the student body and the faculty. Like the faculty, students from the School of Humanities, more heavily represented in the strikes than some other schools, were underrepresented in the sample, and it is probable that the large number of absentees from the sampled classes

[1] "Can a Tough Policy Keep a School Open?" *U.S. News and World Report, 65,* December 1968, p. 11.

[2] Kingsley Widmer, "California, Why Colleges Blow Up," *The Nation, 208*:86, February 24, 1969, p. 240.

[3] *Fortune,* June 1969, "Report on Youth" notes that destruction of property as a tactic of protest is held to be justifiable "sometimes" by 14 per cent of white college youth and 45 per cent of black college youth. "Assaulting police" draws support of 18 per cent and 51 per cent respectively.

included a higher proportion of militant students than were among those in attendance. Among faculty, underrepresentation among AFT members in the sample and the exclusion of part-time faculty probably favored moderate and conservative views to some degree.

Three questions attempted to assess perceptions of the faculty strike as perceived by students and faculty and the import of the strikes on the college and the individual respondents.

Which statement most nearly reflects your feeling about the faculty strike?

	Students	*Faculty*
The faculty strike was a necessary and logical action on the part of concerned faculty in order to get a solution to the problem.	36.0	21.3
The strike was a disaster to the college.	11.4	28.0
The faculty were using the students only to further their own ends.	28.5	30.7
Faculty participation in the strike was a good idea since it helped cool the student violence.	12.6	13.3
Faculty should not have the right to strike.	4.9	2.6

What do you feel is the result of the strike?

	Students	*Faculty*
Repressive legislation	27.8	50.0
Made administration more responsive to the students	7.8	2.6
Made SFSC revolutionary model for American schools	12.3	5.3
Pointed out chronic deficiencies in the community and that there are social needs to be met	35.8	29.0
Made administration less responsive to students	8.9	5.3

What is the most significant outcome of the strike to you?

	Students	*Faculty*
Helped to push black studies	13.7	16.0
Polarized the academic community	18.5	28.0
Decrease of student power and loss of sympathy for their goals in the community	17.0	17.3

Reevaluated my personal commitment toward the left	21.8	20.0
Made me more conservative	19.5	17.3

The American Federation of Teachers and George Johns, Executive Secretary of the Central Labor Council, were convinced that a major gain of the faculty strike, which began five weeks after Hayakawa assumed office, was the ending of most violence on the campus. Among five possibilities, only about one in six faculty and students responded in that way, a number very close to the proportion of active strikers and strike supporters in the sample. More than twice as many felt "the faculty were using the students only to further their own ends."

The militants argued stridently from the Speakers Platform and during the convocations that the strike and the struggles surrounding it were establishing the San Francisco State College experience as a revolutionary model in education. Few students (12.3 per cent) and fewer faculty (5.3 per cent) captured this vision. Twice as many students and fully half of the faculty thought repressive legislation a more striking outcome.

The third question indicates the several ways in which individuals perceived strike-related polarization within the college. Fewer than one-fifth thought progress toward black studies the major outcome.[4] A shift of approximately one-fifth of the students and faculty to the left and another fifth to the right was reported as the major outcome of the strike for the individual. The report doubtless understates the movement away from the middle ground because it reports only on those for whom such shifts were the primary result among five choices. It foreshadows the stubborn polarization afflicting the campus during the fall of 1969.

Another question concerning how the strikes influenced student and faculty roles in college decision making disclosed that 53 per cent of students and 44 per cent of the faculty expected no change or less involvement in college decision making. Slightly more than half of the faculty and two-fifths of the students reported their intent to work more intensively at the departmental level and with their peers. A plausible inference is a double movement of significant proportions,

[4] The data were taken during a semester in which black studies had been deferred because of strike action and Nathan Hare, acting chairman of the black studies department, was being dismissed.

two-fifths of the students and faculty toward the ideological extremes, and a withdrawal of faculty and students from involvement at the all-college level. During the spring and fall of 1969, some version of the following statement was heard from students and faculty: "The trustees and the administration can have the college for now, let them try to run it. We'll take the departments."

The academic costs of campus disorder which disrupted all but six weeks of the 1968–69 fall semester are difficult to assess. The confusion in the instructional program by the end of the semester was so great that evaluation of student classwork and awarding of grades and course credit was ad hoc in many classes.[5] The responses to questions of the impact of the strike on classroom activities reflect this confusion. McClusky found great disparity in faculty and student responses in this area which she could not explain. Three specific issues were debated throughout the strike and after: Were professors meeting their classes? Many professors moved their classes off campus because of strike sympathy or because they believed classroom teaching and learning on campus impractical. If moved off campus, was significant classwork really possible? And were some students being penalized because of the strike and others over-rewarded for little or no academic performance? A more general question was: If the college were kept open at all costs, as the governor, the trustees, Chancellor Dumke, and President Hayakawa insisted, what really went on in an extended period of chronic disorder and tension? On campus, class attendance probably hovered between 20 and 30 per cent during December and January.

Four-fifths of the students reported that professors stopped meeting one or more of the classes for which they were registered. One-tenth reported that three or more classes were discontinued. Three-fourths of the students reported that one or more of their classes moved off campus during the strike; two-fifths reported three or more classes moved off campus. The greatest discrepancy between faculty and student reports in McClusky's data appears at this point. Three-fourths of faculty respondents report they "stopped meeting" no classes. Three-

[5] The general accreditation of the college was reduced from a possible ten to two years. The graduate program in Social Work was refused accreditation because of severe internal departmental struggles and the program was discontinued. The School of Education gained full accreditation by both national and state bodies—but was reduced to two-year accreditation because of the strictures on the total college.

fifths reported they moved no classes off campus. One-third reported they moved some or all classes off campus. Only about one-fourth of the students whose classes were moved off campus reported that off-campus classes were "worth it." Three of ten students reported that during off-campus classes the instructor "imposed his own bias on students." Conflict within classes and among faculty and students over their strike roles, as well as difficulties imposed on students in moving classes into the community with ad hoc arrangements, probably contributed to the above views.

Since most of the disorders on campus occurred between twelve noon and two-thirty, students were asked about class attendance on campus during the disturbances. About four-fifths had classes scheduled during those hours. Just over one-fourth of those students attended classes regularly. Two-thirds of the faculty with scheduled classes during those hours reported attending classes regularly. About one-fifth of the students felt intimidation or coercion, a third of those through fear of police action. Only 7 per cent of the faculty reported such feelings.

McClusky asked how the strike affected classes held on campus: When you attended classes on campus during the strike which statement most nearly expresses your feeling?

	Students	*Faculty*
Strike talk overshadowed course work because of professor's interest	38.5	4.0
Strike talk overshadowed course work because of students' interest	26.6	6.6
Strike talk overshadowed course work	16.5	22.6
Tried class as usual; unsuccessful	2.9	14.6
Class as usual; strike had no effect	4.6	34.6

Ninety-one per cent of the students thought strike talk in classes held on campus overshadowed the course work and another handful thought attempts to hold class as usual were unsuccessful. Yet thirty-five per cent of the faculty believed their classes went on as usual. This discrepancy in student and faculty perception is striking. If one teaches "as usual" there is no guarantee that students are learning "as usual." The conclusion must be that in the perception of students, little went on in classes either on campus or off that was not overshadowed by the strike and its issues. The established curriculum was in large measure suspended for some four months, even for those students who persisted in attending classes. The intensive learning experiences that resulted from the strikes and the counter-efforts to control the disorders and break the strikes were often not the learning experiences projected as established objectives of the curriculum.

The students and faculty were asked to select as most important to them one of five possible "proper functions of a college or university." The results are in striking contrast to assertions made about the student body in 1965 based on data collected during the early sixties.[6] At that time a strong majority of San Francisco State College students were reported to be basically interested in job preparation that would advance them socioeconomically. Only one in nine cited that as a first choice to this question: Which is the most important to you?

	Students	*Faculty*
Teaching students skills and knowledge with which they may improve the economic and social conditions of our society	32.8	32.0
Preparing citizens for effective participation in a democratic society	10.8	25.3
Providing the stimulus and means of free inquiry	24.7	18.6
Improving students' chances for economic success by granting degrees and providing job preparation	9.3	4.0
Providing students the opportunity for intellectual advancement for their personal satisfaction	19.7	14.6

Students were asked if as a result of the strike they received units of academic credit where they did "little or no work." Of 93.5 per cent responding, half said they received no gratis units; half said they did. A third of all students reported receiving three to seven semester units for little or no work. Six per cent received eight or more. Doubtless some students would so respond during a conventional semester. More than one-fourth (27 per cent) reported in May 1968 difficulties in getting all of their grades for the previous fall semester.

Students complain steadily about lack of relevancy to them in the established college curriculum. Responses to the following question

[6] David Riesman and Christopher Jencks, "The Viability of the American College," in Nevitt Sanford (Ed.), *The American College* (New York: Wiley, 1965), p. 187.

support the thrust of the experimental college, the community programs and projects within several of the schools which involved students in a variety of work-study arrangements: What type of activity could the college provide to make education most relevant?

	Students	*Faculty*
Class activity to include field investigations or participation	39.3	50.7
Interchange of teachers from other disciplines to lecture	12.6	8.0
Publishing of student/faculty works of merit which point out areas of social contradiction	8.8	2.6
Credit for work done in the community other than by the college	16.5	16.0
None of the above	14.2	17.3

The strike and its administrative aftermath moved the college and the trustees in the reverse direction as much tighter controls were placed on spending of student body funds, as funds were impounded by the attorney general, and the experimental college and the community programs withered. During the fall of 1969, numbers of students, independent of the college, have moved toward community organizing efforts among young adults and high school youth. As with the civil rights movement, the college is inclined to turn its back on significant areas of student concern.

Seventy-one per cent of students and 73 per cent of faculty believed violence should be used "rarely" or "never" as a means of promoting interests of an individual or a group. That leaves enough people in a college community of 20,000 to present major hazards during mass action. Twenty-four per cent of the students felt violence justifiable sometimes (21.2 per cent) or frequently (2.9 per cent), very close to the faculty's responses (20.0 per cent and 2.6 per cent). One-third of both faculty and students reported they were "most likely" to use as instruments of social change picketing, striking, and confrontation. The other two-thirds chose less militant alternatives including "peaceful persuasion through regular channels." Twenty per cent of the faculty but only 8 per cent of students stated willingness to get arrested if needed in achieving their ideals. "Sitting in" as a means of pursuing ideals was chosen by fewer than one per cent of respondents.

The study team was interested in the impact of the year of disorder on the personal goals of students and faculty. McClusky asked: Now that you have experienced confrontations and considered social issues, how has the last year affected your personal goals?

	Students	*Faculty*
Changed goals	8.0	37.0
Some ambivalence toward original objectives	17.3	22.6
Very little	28.8	12.0
Seriously disrupted	5.7	8.0
No change	36.3	17.3

The strikes appeared to have a stronger impact on the faculty than on students. Fewer than one-third of the faculty could report very little or no change in their goals contrasted with two-thirds of the students who could so choose; 46 per cent of the students and 62 per cent of the faculty believed the student government should be reformed and given more responsibility. Despite the disorder within the student government, its support of the strike and the impounding of its funds for alleged misappropriation, only one-tenth of the students and one-fifth of the faculty believed the best approach to student government was to make it function under the college president, in substance the policy adopted by the trustees following the strike. The state college system thus moved in a way contradictary to student and faculty views.

McClusky concludes she found no generation gap between students and faculty on the wide range of issues surveyed in her study. The patterns of student faculty groupings in response to issues were strikingly similar. If there was little evidence of a generation gap, there was much evidence of polarization within the academic community among both students and faculty about strike-related issues. "When the total responses of faculty and students were separated into groups according to roles in the strikes, each individual group shared similar attitudes toward the strikes." McClusky drew the above conclusion from a computer-assisted analysis of the groups who identified their varying roles in the strike. Each group was then described in relation to its pattern of responses to all other survey items.

Name Index

A

ALEXIS, JACK, BSU Central Committee member, 242, 309

ALIOTO, JOSEPH L., mayor of San Francisco: and the AFT, 236, 267, 268, 288; in the George Murray controversy, 122–126; *passim;* mediation during Summerskill administration, 62; during strike and closing of campus, 176, 179, 182, 184, 193, 227–228, 230; and striking students, 308, 314

ALLEN, ROBERT, founder, Afro–Americans for Survival, 156

ALLER, CURTIS, faculty, economics, 292, 309

ALVARADO, ROGER, Third World Student, 300

ANTON, ANATOLE, faculty, philosophy, 59

B

BARNHART, DONALD, faculty, social sciences, 307, 313

BARTELME, KEN, faculty, psychology, 21

BASS, RUSSELL, president, Associated Students, 44–45, 89, 91, 101, 108, 119–120, 252, 325–326

BEATTY, WALCOTT, chairman, Academic Senate, 57, 59

BECKER, ERNEST, dean and member of chancellor's staff, 51, 74–75, 76

BEDESEM, HELEN, financial aid officer, 152–153

BIDERMAN, BARRY, student, 59

GOODWIN, LEROY, BSU Central Committee member, 148, 155, 229, 304–306

GROSSMAN, JULES, Academic Senate, 306

H

HALLINAN, TERRENCE, lawyer for radical students, 50–51

HARE, NATHAN, faculty, sociology, black studies leader, 40–41, 88, 94, 130–132, 135, 141, 149–150, 156, 271–272, 291, 310, 315

HARKNESS, WILLIAM, faculty, physical education, 208, 327

HARMER, JOHN, state senator, 16

HARMON, HARRY, state architect, 104, 119, 120

HART, DONALD, chairman, board of trustees, 31

HART, GEORGE, trustee, 74

HARTFORD, BRUCE, student, 59

HAUGHTON, RONALD, mediator for Wayne State University, 236, 240, 304

HAWKINS, GARY, AFT president, 55, 139, 159–160, 183, 256–257, 277, 292–293

HAYAKAWA, S. I., acting president, San Francisco State College, 6, 74, 80, 271, 282; and Academic Senate, 230–231; administrative problems inherited by, 200n; and AFT, 233–246, 253–254, 255–272, 330–332, 337; events during administration of, 205–316; as folk-hero, 247–272; in poststrike period, 317–342; qualifications of, as seen by board of trustees, 208–210; relations of, with Dumke, 216–217; and Renaissance ad hoc group, 193–194, 206; seen as trustee puppet, 208, 210–212, 222, 291; student confrontations with, 171–172, 192, 196, 220–226; versus Third World leaders, 258–259

HEILBRON, LOUIS, member, board of trustees, 107, 119, 123, 237–238, 268, 269, 279, 280, 285–286, 287, 289–290; committee document compared with Johns memorandum of understanding, 294–299

HOOVER, ROBERT, administrative staff, College of San Mateo, 161

HURLEY, BISHOP MARK, 228, 308, 309, 311, 314

HUTCHINS, ROBERT MAYNARD, Center for the Study of Democratic Institutions, 32–33

J

JOHN, GEORGE, executive secretary, Labor Council, 110, 228, 236–237, 238, 240, 267, 268–269, 270, 274, 285, 286, 287, 294–299, 355

JONES, EARL, faculty, music, 208

JONES, LEROI, black militant writer, 14

JONES, LUCY, department chairman, undergraduate studies, 323–324

K

KAFFKE, ROBERT, instructor in Experimental College, 92

KARENGA, RON, black militant leader, 142

KEENE, MANSEL, vice chancellor, 69–70, 73, 108, 239–240

KELLER, TED, faculty, international relations, 21

KELLY, ERWIN, president, AFT executive committee, 332, 333

KENNEDY, JOSEPH, black municipal judge, 288

KINDER, RON, student politician, 14–15

KROEBER, TED, Academic Senate, 50, 306

L

LEAHY, MARGARET, student, 59

LEE, PETE, member, board of trustees, 79–80, 107n

LEMBKE, DARYL E., *Los Angeles Times* staff writer, 127

LEONARD, J. PAUL, ex-President, San Francisco State College, 3, 341

LEVIN, JOHN, SDS leader, 56, 59, 64, 80, 165, 329

LEWIS, DIANE, faculty, anthropology, 88

LINENTHAL, MARK, faculty, English, 62–63, 159–160

M

MCCLATCHY, LEO, chairman, Academic Senator, 72, 105, 214

W

WALDRON, HOWARD, faculty, industrial arts, 208
WEINGARTNER, RUDOLPH, faculty, philosophy, 39–40
WENTE, KARL, trustee, 237–238
WHITAKER, URBAN, dean, undergraduate studies, and member, Presidential Consultation Committee, 74, 80, 323, 324
WHITE, JOSEPH, black dean of undergraduate studies, 109–110, 130, 135, 141, 147, 156, 178
WIDMER, KINGSLEY, writer, *The Nation* article, 353
WILLIAMS, REVEREND CECIL, black community leader, 133–134, 226, 227
WILLIAMS, THOMAS, instructor, 322
WINDMILLER, MARSHALL, faculty, international relations, 20
WOLF, LEONARD, faculty, English, 21–22, 55

Y

YAMAZAKI, PAUL, Third World leader, 307–308
YORKE, HARVEY, college press officer, 115, 310
YU-HSU, KAI, faculty, world literature, 308

Subject Index